BERKSHIRE 宝库山
Essentials

THE INTERNET IN China

1980s–2000s

Cultural, Political, and Social Dimensions

网络在中国：从文化，政治和社会视角看中国互联网

Editors
Ashley Esarey
University of Alberta
Randolph Kluver
Texas A&M University

BERKSHIRE
A global point of reference

Digital editions
The Internet in China is available through most major ebook and database services (please check with them for pricing).

For information, contact:
Berkshire Publishing Group LLC
122 Castle Street
Great Barrington, Massachusetts 01230-1506 USA
www.berkshirepublishing.com
Tel + 1 413 528 0206
Fax + 1 413 541 0076
Printed in the United States of America

Library of Congress Cataloging-in-Publication Data

Internet in China / Ashley Esarey, Randolph Kluver, editors.
pages cm
Includes bibliographical references and index.
ISBN 978-1-933782-60-7 (hardcover : alkaline paper) – ISBN 978-1-61472-935-8 (paperback : alk. paper) – ISBN 978-1-933782-24-9 (ebook)
1. Internet–China. 2. Internet–Social aspects–China. 3. Social change–China. 4. China–Social conditions–1976-2000. 5. China–Social conditions–2000- I. Esarey, Ashley. II. Kluver, Randy.
TK5105.875.I57I55625 2013
384.30951–dc23
2013030328

Table of Contents

Part 4: Society and Social Welfare

Introduction

The Internet in China: Cultural, Political, and Social Dimensions

By 2010, more people from the People's Republic of China (PRC) were using the variety of technologies collectively referred to as the "Internet" than from any other nation. This was certainly a remarkable development, as the rise of the Internet corresponded with the "rise of China" to a remarkable degree. In the late 1980s, throughout China, few people had access to a computer, and access to the few that were available was tightly controlled. This was not all that remarkable. In the United States and Europe, few university students owned personal computers (PCs) at that time. In China, however, even telephones were rare; few Chinese people had access to them, let alone access to international data networks. That would all change.

The Internet became available in China in 1994–1995, first for scholarly use, then for popular use. At the time, there was little sense of how the technology would evolve, and how it might transform Chinese culture, society, economics, and politics. Within China, however, the expectations of the governmental ministries involved focused largely on the potential economic benefits of the new technology, associating the Internet with the next phase of modernization. A different set of expectations came to the fore in the West, as scholars, business strategists, and policy makers voiced expectations that the Internet would contribute to the ongoing "opening" initiatives within China, thereby transforming Chinese politics and markets, and removing social and cultural constraints.

At the time of this writing, the impact of the Internet on China, as well as the impact of China on the Internet, is far more complicated than it was in the early days. Contrary to the assumptions of many that the Chinese government would "resist the Internet" or limit its popularization, as was the case in such Communist Party–led countries as Cuba and North Korea, all aspects of the Internet have been thoroughly and completely embraced by every element of Chinese society. China is not only awash in PCs but in millions of other devices as well. In 2005, the Chinese corporation Lenovo bought out IBM's personal computer division—one of the giants in the industry—and practically overnight became the world's third-largest computer manufacturer. China is where many of the devices that are contributing to the increasingly rapid worldwide development of mobile computing devices, such as the iPhone and the iPad, are both designed and manufactured.

Not all of those devices are being shipped out for overseas consumption, as is the case with many Chinese products: as of 2013, China had well over half a billion Internet users and more than a billion mobile phone users, as well as the largest market in the world for iOS and Android activations. In addition, there are over a quarter of a billion users of Sina Weibo, China's most popular microblogging service, and Tencent QQ (instant-messaging software) has another 194 million monthly users. China's online population is now larger than the total population of every other individual country in the world except for India's.

Obviously, this rapid technological diffusion, and the accompanying social, economic, and cultural changes, has made understanding China's relationship with the Internet, and the reciprocal influence of the Internet on the nation, a very challenging task. Understanding those changes is critical, however, for scholars and academics researching the role of the Internet and associated technologies on society, as well as for businesses, entrepreneurs, and consultants, all of whom are concerned with determining market trends and making appropriate investments. Finally, understanding this relationship is critical for policy makers, both Chinese and foreign, who are attempting to strengthen the possibilities for the technologies to enhance economic growth and development. While these policy makers also aim to enrich China's political and cultural spheres through the spread of this technology, they are also concerned with political or social unrest, and with avoiding the potential negative social, emotional, and relational consequences of the new technology, such as Internet addiction and related maladies.

This project began in 2010 as an attempt to highlight some of the mileposts on the development of the Internet in China. But, as with all efforts to document the rapid development of such a transformative medium, there will inevitably be gaps in coverage and differences of perspective. Although a number of scholars have written detailed analyses elsewhere of many of the issues and events considered in this volume, *The Internet in China* covers a wider variety of important issues than any other book. It provides an essential framework to better understand the results of years of research on the origins, growth, development, and consequences of China's Internet. The volume's contributors, top scholars from around the globe, place at your fingertips the collective wisdom of two decades of research on the Internet in China.

Our editorial goals for this volume have been to provide a detailed overview of many of the key aspects of the development of, and the technological and social phenomenon associated with, the Internet in China, made relevant to a general audience. We have not sought to provide either a "snapshot" of the world in 2014, nor to write the "definitive" history and analysis of the Internet in China. (The latter would most certainly be an impossible task: it would be out of date as soon as the first word was written.) Rather, we have aimed to capture the key elements of the Internet's diffusion and impact in China. Of course, any observer will emphasize certain elements and de-emphasize others, and since this volume has been conceptualized and created by social scientists, it will become immediately clear that we have neglected the "technical" aspects of Internet diffusion to focus primarily on the social, educational, cultural, and political. Likewise, we have paid less attention to the economic and business uses of the Internet, although we have tried in this volume to capture at least some of the interaction between commerce, industrial practice, online activity, and economics.

A second key goal has been to include information that has "persistence," that is, information that is not immediately outdated but will continue to have relevance five, ten, and twenty years into the future—in other words, into a time frame in which we have no idea what the Internet will look like or how it will be used.

It is also appropriate to comment briefly on the boundaries of our coverage. We have deliberately excluded detailed accounts of technological developments, primarily because the technological development within China is largely shared with the rest of the world and has been considered in detail else where. Instead, we have focused on elements of Internet development, use, and impact that highlight the interaction of Chinese society with the country's technological development, with the aim of illuminating the impact of Internet technologies on the transformation of contemporary China.

Readers who are broadly familiar with the issues and events presented here will have much to gain, as will scholars, policy makers, and others who will find value in this volume's attempts to link the dynamic relationship between Chinese society and new media technologies.

Randolph KLUVER
Texas A&M University

Part 1
Business and Economics

Internet Service Providers (ISPs)

Hùliánwǎng fúwù gòngyìngshāng 互联网服务提供商

Summary: Internet Service Providers (ISPs) are companies or organizations that provide users with access to the Internet. There are two kinds of ISPs in China: commercial and non-commercial. Both types of ISP play an important role in governing and controlling the content that is accessible (or not) to Internet users in China.

Internet Service Providers (ISP), companies or organizations that provide users access to the Internet, have played an important role in Chinese "informatization" construction (i.e., the dispersal of information across the country) and Internet governance projects. In China, ISPs are regulated by the Ministry of Industry and Information Technology (MIIT). ISPs, however, also serve as regulatory tools for content regulation. This dual function has had a profound impact on China's Internet development.

The earliest network in China was the National Computing and Networking Facility of China (NCFC), funded by the World Bank in 1990 and devised to connect three major universities and research institutions in Beijing—Peking University, Tsinghua University, and the Chinese Academy of Science—to improve their scientific research capabilities. By the end of 1993 the three institutions had constructed their own sub-networks, and the NCFC managed to connect to the US Internet through an international channel in the following year. In 1996, the NCFC was renamed the Chinese Science and Technology Network (CSTNET) and was hosted by the Chinese Academy of Science. The other two components, owned by Peking University and Tsinghua University, were coordinated into a new network called the China Education and Research Network (CERNET), which linked many other universities together and was managed by the education authorities. As scientific research networks developed, commercial businesses also started to show an interest in the Internet. Two Internet nodes opened in Shanghai and Beijing and began to provide Internet access to the public in 1995. At the same time, a national business network called the ChinaNet was under construction by China Telecom. The telecommunication reforms of 1998 indicated a second stage of ISP development, in which telecom companies became legally independent from their political supervisors. According to a decision of the State Council, ChinaNet now belonged to the new China Telecom company.

In a subsequent reform in 2001, ChinaNet was split into two parts in order to promote competition among the existing telecom companies. The southern part remained in the hands of China Telecom and constituted the main body of the present China Telecom network. The northern part was merged with the competitive China Netcom's network, creating a new network, China169.net. Chinagb.net, another earlier core backbone (i.e., principal data route) network that belonged to the former Ministry of Electronics Industry, was also incorporated into China169.net. In addition, four newly established telecom companies—China Mobile, China Unicom, China Tietong, and China Satcom—all built their own commercial Internet backbones and provided access service to the public. Two new noncommercial networks have also been established since 2000, the China International Electronic Commerce Center and the Peoples' Liberation Army (PLA) Headquarters of the Central Staff.

In the telecommunication reform of 2008, in order to establish three big nationwide telecommunication networks and to issue three 3G licenses, the six commercial networks finally merged into three: China Netcom was united with China Unicom to form the new Unicom, the basic telecommunication business of China Satcom was incorporated into China Telecom, and China Mobile absorbed China Tietong. As a result, the ten backbones were reduced to seven, ending the stage of competition to a certain extent.

Legal Responsibility and Censorship

In China, ISPs have important responsibilities regarding Internet regulation. Both backbone and last-mile (i.e., the final leg of a network that connects to the customer) ISPs are responsible for online content blocking and filtering. At the national backbone level, the state asks its managing agents to apply blocking and filtering technologies to the international gateways to prevent domestic users from visiting certain foreign sites and foreign users from visiting certain domestic sites. Such actions are primarily taken in major cities such as Beijing, Shanghai, and Guangzhou, where most international gateways are located. The set of hardware and software used for blocking and filtering is (informally) known as "The Great Firewall" (GFW, *fánghuǒqiáng* 防火墙). The GFW is capable of scanning each data package passing through the international gateway, and preventing users from visiting politically sensitive sites or content using various measures, including IP blocking, Domain Name System (DNS) filtering and redirecting, URL filtering, packet filtering, and denial of service. A blacklist of sensitive words and phrases is decided on and revised based on the political needs of different central agencies. Renowned sites, especially social networking and user-generated content websites like Wikipedia, YouTube, and Facebook, are always on the blacklist and therefore inaccessible to the Chinese public, because they allegedly contain "harmful information" to the government that cannot be controlled. The operation of the GFW is confidential and complicated and "netizens" have no way of knowing for certain what sites they are allowed to visit and what information they can obtain. In practice, people are aware of the GFW and bothered by it, although some of them cannot distinguish government manipulation from pure technical mistakes. (For instance, a blocked website will not say, "Sorry, this site is blocked by the government"; it will simply appear that the link is broken.) More and more people, however, have the incentive to browse "across the wall." For these tech-savvy users, it is fairly easy to circumvent the GFW with free proxies (intermediary systems or applications) or software that is readily available on the Internet. Users with little political interest, however, can live quite well with business and entertainment content provided by domestic sites. (The Great Firewall is discussed at more length in this volume, in the article of that name.)

The Golden Shield Project

Many commentators confuse the GFW with China's Golden Shield Project (GSP), and it is helpful to clarify that these are two entirely different projects. While the GFW refers to a set of hardware and software equipped at the international gateways and managed mainly by telecommunication authorities, the GSP is one of the e-government and information highway projects launched in 1993.

The GSP was initiated in 1998 by the Ministry of Public Security (MPS) as part of its informatization project to spread information more uniformly across the country; it was approved by the State Council in 2001. In September of 2003, the GSP was officially recommended across the country; three years later the GSP was put into use nationwide. Its primary goal is to establish a nationwide communication system for the central and local agencies of public security, facilitating their cooperation and sharing of security information. The GSP is built on a set of complicated networks and information systems for the daily operation of the police, such as a special communication system, a population management database, a criminal information center, and more. The establishment of the GSP significantly improves the state's capacity in fighting crime, managing public services, and conducting surveillance.

Local Level

Even if a Chinese netizen gets around the GFW, it is unlikely he or she will spread blacklisted information domestically on a large scale due to the inspection of last-mile ISPs at the local level. While the GFW is directly managed by the central government, domestic practices of Internet censorship lie with local government. Several laws have ruled that ISPs will be held responsible for the information security within their own networks, including keeping the original records of user behaviors and reporting illegal activities to the police, the same obligations websites have. These obligations have elevated the level of self-censorship by ISPs. As in the case of the GFW, local last-mile ISPs apply a blacklist of keywords and websites prescribed by local governments to routers or main nodes covering one or more administrative jurisdictions. Since local blacklists can vary substantially, the self-censorship regime causes a split-up of the Internet among towns, cities, and provinces. In case of an emergency, provincial governments can order communication networks linked with other provinces to be cut off. Backbone ISPs such as China Telecom also launched an optional "Green Surfing" service, claiming to block certain harmful contents and ports for the protection of minor users.

Content control on the Internet has been a major concern of the Chinese Communist Party (CCP) since the inception of backbone networks. In 1995, there was a debate among the central leaders about whether to build commercial networks and increase the number of users at the expense of information security and social stability. The consensus then was that effective Internet regulations should be promptly established, and that the Internet should be developed at a slower pace. The state subsequently enacted three major regulations, requiring the existing network users (mainly research organizations and companies) to be recorded at local police stations and obliging ISPs to impose self-censorship. Thus, the increase in the number of Internet users was backed up by stricter regulations.

In addition to the state laws and regulations, backbone networks are subjected to different governance structures based on their respective natures. Noncommercial networks (i.e., public service networks) are governed by regulatory authorities (such as the Ministry of Education and the Chinese Academy of Science) that also act as the main content regulators. Due to the relatively small number of users (primarily teachers, researchers, students, and military personnel), it is relatively easy to exert control. By contrast, commercial networks are operated by telecommunication companies and supervised by the telecom agencies of local governments, while the information flowing over the Internet is governed by other special content agencies.

The two distinct patterns of network governance correspond to the government structure of *tiao-kuai* (vertical-horizontal) system in China. On one hand, the *tiao* (vertical) governance of noncommercial networks by the regulatory authorities ensures the exclusive control over their proprietary networks (primarily in the education sector), including content regulation and technical maintenance. For example, the Ministry of Education can control any information flow among users of CERNET, and purge any information deemed harmful or illegal at its sole discretion. On the other hand, the *kuai* (horizontal) governance of commercial networks by local telecom agencies demands self-censorship on the part of the ISPs and cooperation regarding content regulation among local agencies of several authorities. While backbone ISPs' subsidiaries and numerous last-mile ISPs impose self-censorship over Internet content on a daily basis, local telecom agencies coordinate "comprehensive strikes" against unlawful Internet content among several regulatory authorities on a periodic basis (a distinctive nature of *kuai* governance). In these official comprehensive strikes, the government heavily relies on ISPs to implement the clearing of harmful information, spam, viruses, and malicious software. For example, the MIIT will first send a notice to backbone carriers, requiring them to deal with the unlawful content within each network. The self-censorship or internal examination by ISPs is achieved through technologies such as keyword filtering, IP filtering of harmful sites and spam senders, closing illegal sites at the request of other government sectors, or certifying user's information and trusted servers. Finally, the ISPs will be assessed according to their behaviors after the campaign.

Conclusion

Telecommunications carriers have never been neutral: their daily operations are both technical and political. Such characteristics require being deeply embedded in the present political and Internet governance regime. They need to cooperate and coordinate with other special content regulators consistently, which obviously goes beyond pure business. Due to the monopolistic and state-owned nature of the telecommunications industry in China, however, it is quite natural for them to act this way. The future—toward a more open Internet—might depend on a more competitive market and stronger protection of free expression and innovation from the judicial branch.

Henry L. HU
Shanghai University of Finance and Economics

See also Internet Content Filtering; Internet Governance; Internet Regulation; Telecommunications Industry; The Great Firewall

Further Reading

Deibert, Ronald, et al. (Eds.). (2008). *Access denied: The practice and policy of global Internet filtering.* Cambridge, MA: MIT Press.

Harwit, Eric. (2008). *China's telecommunications revolution.* Oxford, UK: Oxford University Press.

Hu, Henry L. (2011). The political economy of governing ISPs in China: Perspectives of net neutrality and vertical integration. *China Quarterly, 207,* 523–540. doi: 10.1017/S0305741011000634

Solum, Lawrence B., & Chung, Minn. (2004). The layers principle: Internet architecture and the law. University of San Diego Public Law Research Paper No. 55. Retrieved April 25, 2013, from http://ssrn.com/abstract=416263

Wu, Irene S. (2009). From iron fist to invisible hand: The uneven path of telecommunications reform in China. Stanford, CA: Stanford University Press.

Xu Yan, & Pitt, Douglas. (2002). *Chinese telecommunications policy.* London: Artech House.

Internet and Economic Development

Hùliánwǎng yǔ jīngjì fāzhǎn 互联网与经济发展

Summary: Since its reentry into the global market economy in the 1980s, China has invested heavily in modern communication infrastructures, including the Internet, in a dual effort to support its export-dependent economic base and to move beyond this crisis-ridden growth model. This process and the high stakes involved open up several new and important areas of discussion regarding economic liberalization, national economic strategies, and class-based social relations.

Political economic research in the Anglo-American context has striven to understand communication in conjunction with the expansion and evolution of global capitalism. In the process of corporate growth, which has intensified ever since the 1970s, communications have played an underpinning role not limited to disseminating commercial messages and organizing transnational production networks. Media ownership, commodification of information, and globalization of media corporations are, therefore, among the outstanding themes to help understand the structural and historical relationships between communication and the dynamic capitalist system.

While the Western-led global expansion of corporate power had been used as the framework for understanding international communication, there has been an increasing awareness among political economists to understand the expansion of informationized (i.e., the process by which information technologies are applied in social and economic activities) capitalism on the global level as much as how it is "modulated by social forces" within emerging markets (Zhao and Schiller 2001, 140). In a changed global context where China has deepened entanglement with the global economy, it is even more important to understand how China takes up information and communication to address its own developmental problems.

Economic Liberalization and Internet Development

Since its re-entry into the global market economy in the late 1980s, China has become a major growth outlet. As China is keen to claim a share of the growing information economy, the country has not only built up a world-class information and communications technology (ICT) hardware manufacturing cluster in its coastal regions, but has invested heavily in modern communication infrastructures, including the Internet. One prominent group of empirical studies is guided by the dualism of the state and the Internet and presupposes that the Internet, as an instrument, could empower the civic society and materialize the liberal values of individualism, pluralism, and democracy (Zhang 2002; Yang 2003; Tan 2006; Zhou 2006; Zheng 2007; Tsui 2008; Jiang 2010; MacKinnon 2008). Along this lineal line of thinking, why or why not China's Internet fulfills its potential of liberation and empowerment is the leading research question.

Meanwhile, another prominent group of mainstream research reflects the business hype surrounding the "digital revolution" and is underpinned by the neoliberal ICT-for-development logic. Much has been written, therefore, about business-related topics of infrastructure development and digital economy (Mueller and Tan 1997; Qiang 2007; Carmel, Gao, and Zhang 2010; Yu and Li-Hua 2010), supplemented by market research on the correlations among consumer demographic, attitudes, and technology adoption (Leung 1998; Wei 2006). Although it is unclear whether these two directions of mainstream research are in conversation with one another, they converge on assuming the Internet is the harbinger of "revolutionary change commercially and politically" (Kluver and Yang 2007) and, therefore, focally explore what state policies and institutional arrangements have accounted for, impeded, and limited China's Internet development.

Political economic research, in contrast, explicates how the market economy with Chinese characteristics shapes the Internet as an institution. The commercialization of telecommunications set the stage for China's Internet development. Despite the neoliberal trends of privatization and deregulation that proceeded across the globe in the 1980s and 1990s (Schiller and Fregoso 1991), the Chinese state partially liberalized telecommunications through divesture. As a consequence, China's telecommunications are still dominated by a handful of state-owned enterprises. In 2008, the government rolled out its third restructuring plan of the industry. China Telecom acquired Railcom and Unicom's mobile network. Unicom merged with China Netcom. China Mobile would remain the third operator. Not only do these state-owned telecom carriers sit on an expanding mixture of fixed-line, wireless, and data networks, they have led the commercialization of information networks (Wong and Ling 2001, 32).

In the state-initiated, controlled commercialization process of telecommunications, the scope of foreign operation has nevertheless expanded incrementally. Not only did state-owned telecom operators deliberately go public via global stock markets, they also sought to sell corporate shares to "foreign strategic partners" (Zhao and Schiller 2001, 146). In the case of its public listing in 2002, China Telecom sought to leverage shares listed on foreign stock exchanges to justify some of its corporate decisions and to avoid bureaucratic interventions (Wu 2009, 75). As a condition to join the World Trade Organization

(WTO), China has opened up its telecom service markets, including the shares in Internet service providers, to foreign operators. Up to 49 percent ownership in China's Internet service–providing companies has opened up to foreign investors gradually since 2001 (Harwit 2008, 104).

Regardless of the origin of capital, China's telecommunications has undergone a substantial process of capitalization and marketization, and, as a result, telecom operators have internalized market logics. Likewise, the nature of China's Internet has shifted from a noncommercial network devoted to academia to a commercialized network. Since 1995 when China Telecom decided to construct a public national network for commercial purposes, the political directive of occupying commanding heights, the internalized accumulation logic, and the fierce competition among state-owned telecom operators have triggered large amounts of investment in the Internet (Qiang 2007, 52). To name a few, Jitong, backed by the Ministry of Electronics Industry in 1993, started the Golden Bridge Network, which provides value-added data services to state-owned enterprises; Netcom, backed by the State Administration of Radio, Film, and Television (SARFT), built Internet protocol (IP) backbone ready for Internet service providers (ISPs) to lease (Wu 2009, 54); and Unicom also runs the IP network UNINET (Wong and Ling 2001, 38).

While unleashing market forces, the state also rolled back its commitment of resources to achieving universal service. In the 1990s, the "telephones to every village" campaign was renewed. Since market reform, however, telecom operators have self-financed their own network development, as opposed to using a universal service fund. As a result, tensions between the carriers and the provincial branches that shoulder the "telephone to every village" assignment naturally arose. While transnational capital concentrated in coastal regions has generated a compelling demand for network systems and services (Zhao and Schiller 2001, 145), in interior regions, carriers' local branches have suspended rural access tasks, disconnected already existing telephone services, or refused to share network infrastructures due to the lack of commercial incentives (Xia and Lu 2008). The Internet, as a more luxurious form of communication than fixed-line telephone service, has displayed an even more serious situation of regional concentration and regional disparity. Growth-oriented telecom operators have prioritized coastal regions, which promise quicker returns on investment (Zhao 2000, 46). China Internet Network Information Center (CNNIC) has reported that, until 2007, 47.9 percent of China's Internet users were concentrated in the eastern coastal provinces; by January 2009, 71.6 percent of Internet users lived in cities and towns, and Internet users in the countryside only accounted for 28.4 percent (Sun 2010, 140, 143).

In 2005, while the proposed universal service fund failed to materialize, the Ministry of Industry and Information Technology distributed the remaining village access task among the country's telecommunication carriers on their basis of their revenues, profits, and the geographical locations of their networks (Zhao 2000, 115). In recent years, under the state's mandate, China Mobile has taken the largest share of responsibility in the "telephones to every village" campaign. The company reportedly has guided handset vendors to sell low-end handsets in rural areas as a way of creating demand (Harwit 2008, 180). Indeed, as wireless communication and data network access in urban and developed areas have reached market saturation, it is in telecom operators' long-term interest to turn rural regions and inland areas into a new growth outlet. How to win new customers without sacrificing profit margins, however, has remained an uncompromised priority for publicly listed companies. On the other hand, although new technologies, such as wireless and satellite communications, have been expected to help bridge the digital divide, telecom operators, along with equipment vendors with global ambitions, are more interested in occupying technologically driven new markets than spreading basic services to loss-making regions (Harwit 2008, 179). In recent years, China's telecom operators, along with foreign and domestic equipment providers, have single-mindedly pushed for 3G-network construction as a new market growth outlet despite the unfulfilled "telephones to every village" target originally set for the Ninth Five-Year-Plan period of 1996–2000 (Zhao 2008, 153).

Internet and National Economic Strategies

Political economic research of communication, as an academic tradition, has also been interested in social change and historical transformation. As for the Internet, how the Chinese state and corporate players harness industrial policy and technological change to the national advantage is a matter relevant to the global structure of capitalism. On the one hand, Internet development has accompanied China's rise as a production powerhouse. On the other hand, it has become, in recent years, a focal arena where national economic strategies are implemented with the purpose of improving the country's economic quality and upgrading its profile.

China has expected to achieve a "front-runner" status in the latest ICT technological applications (Tai 2006, 90). Technological adaptation, however, does not grant the country independent and sustainable design and innovation capacities. In fact, China's expanding networks have offered foreign vendors a huge market and created a new round of technological dependence. From the outset of the market reform, China has joined the International Monetary Fund and the World Bank to get loans to jumpstart its imports of advanced telecom technologies (Sun 2010, 132). Apart from loans, in order to jumpstart China's information technology–related industries, the state has liberalized foreign direct investment and, as result, has turned China into a world-class processing cluster of finished consumer electronics (Hong 2008). As Asian studies scholar Eric Harwit documented, in the fixed-line switching equipment market, China's domestic latecomers, including ZTE Corporation and Huawei, succeeded to some degree in grappling market shares away from transnational corporations in the 1990s. The prospect for China's industrial upgrading and corporate expansion, however, is not foreordained. When leading domestic equipment vendors entered the production of wireless and data communication equipment around the turn of the twenty-first century, transnational corporations had collectively and tactically claimed a controlling share of their joint ventures with Chinese partners in order to localize new technologies (Harwit 2008, 131). To what extent, under what circumstances, and with what industrial policies China's domestic industries would achieve upgrading and move ahead will be a relevant question for future research.

Indeed, while academic and policy discourses concerned with the Internet have narrowly focused on high-tech information technology (IT) applications, the separation between the Internet as a user-oriented medium and China's role in the global IT-related production chains has obscured some important trends in China. In the Chinese context, manufacturing has been the biggest segment of the ICT sector. No doubt, the share of the software industry grew from 6.3 percent of China's ICT in 2001 to 11.2 percent in 2005. Yet even by the end of 2007, while employment in above-scale ICT enterprises reached 7.77 million, as many as 6.75 million were hired in manufacturing enterprises whereas only 1.02 million were in software enterprises (Hong 2011). Given the disproportionate distribution of hardware and software capacities, China has faced the challenge of translating its sheer industrial size into some form of industrial leadership and of diversifying its economic portfolio to include some competitive service industries. In recent years the state has consciously mobilized domestic resources to set next-generation technical standards. Indeed, China's past attempts at standard development were mostly unsuccessful for a couple of reasons. The scholars Heejin Lee, Shirley Chan, and Sungjo Oh (2009) observed that in the case of China's own wireless security protocol, WAPI (Wireless Local Area Network Authentication and Privacy Infrastructure), the commercialization plan backfired largely because China failed to leverage the biggest chip maker, Intel, to customize chips compatible with WAPI. In other cases, the conflicted interests among various branches of the state and inter-capitalist rivalries among domestic corporate players also curtailed the techno-nationalist ambitions (Qiu 2010; Zhao 2010a). More recently, in the process of developing and commercializing China's own 3G telecom standard, the state took a number of policy instruments to enforce it, including creating an industrial alliance, setting up a Time Division Synchronous Code Division Multiple Access (TD-SCDMA) research-and-development and industrialization funding budget worth US$85.4 million, and assigning favorable frequencies to the standard (Yu and Li-Hua 2010, 76–79). Although China Mobile has adopted the TD standard and has started commercial services, it is uncertain to what extent the 3G-based development scheme will succeed in the long term.

Meanwhile, the broadband network, which can offer a combination of voice, data, and video services, has been identified as a nodal point for business development and industrial upgrading. In 2010, after a decade of contest, the state renewed the process of "triple network convergence," which will entail an ever-larger scale of creative deconstruction of existing physical networks. Importantly, the broadband network is expected to proliferate new ICT applications and content services (Qiang 2007). The "Instruction Opinions on Developing the News and Publication Industry" issued in 2009 called for the development of mobile phone publication and digital publication. Not accidentally, in 2009, the state kicked off the process of corporate transformation of news and publication institutions. Certainly, Internet-related economic activities have long been recognized as vital for China's economic development. Corporations started to seek online business opportunities, including web solutions, online advertising services, and Internet content provision (Tai 2006, 139–140). Meanwhile, the state has also expected the Internet to upgrade China's business and trade environment through online transactions. While China's IT and software industry grew at an annual rate of 30 percent during the 1990s, its software service outsourcing industry is growing (Carmel et al. 2010, 38).

Internet and Social Class

With the political economic interest in social change and historical transformation, it is logical to ask how the Internet contributes to the reconstitution of class power and state-society relationships in the broader context of China's market reform. Given that China's market reform has created some fundamental tensions between the bureaucratic capitalist system and the burgeoning disenfranchised groups of workers and peasants, how has the Internet been harnessed to silence social dissents and contain grassroots activism? And to what extent has the Internet been instrumental to grassroots initiatives?

Scholars have analyzed the multiple-layered control mechanisms over the Internet. On the physical infrastructure level, major telecom operators own and control all the major networks. The major networks (i.e., ChinaNet, CERNET, GBNet, CSTNet, UNINET, and CNCNET) have collectively formed China's Internet backbone and accounted for nearly 80 percent of all Internet businesses (Wong and Ling 2001, 34). ChinaNet, owned by China Telecom, includes eight regional network centers that cover thirty-one provinces and cities (Wong and Ling 2001, 32). Along with these main Internet service providers, in the late 1990s, the state approved more than three hundred ISPs. All ISPs along their computer networks have to connect with the Internet via China Telecom's national infrastructure, and all international Internet traffic must go through the few government-owned networks (Wong and Ling 2001, 51). The state exerts its licensing control to demand ISPs to follow state guidelines on which services are permitted and which are not (Zhou 2006, 143). Finally, on the content level, the state regulation stipulates that only the websites of central and provincial news organizations have the permission to report and collect news, and the vast majority of websites can only reformat and relay state news (Zhou 2006, 143). Meanwhile, the Xinhua News Agency, *People's Daily*, and China Central Television (CCTV) have launched their online outlets (Zhou 2006, 147). Indeed, in view of the skyrocketing expansion rates of Internet usage, the most prominent theme is about the potential, yet handicapped, democratizing influence of the Internet (Yang 2003; Tai 2006; Zhou 2006).

How Internet development contributes to class formation nevertheless is a relatively weak area of research. Yuezhi Zhao, a leading critical scholar on Chinese communications, has started to blaze the path by examining the correlations between "the unequal distribution of control over systems of communications and wider patterns of inequality in the distribution of wealth and power" (Zhao 2008, 7). The Chinese party-state has been the captain of media commercialization without unleashing a massive wave of privatization; in this unique path of media liberalization with Chinese characteristics, Zhao (2008, 79) argues, the state-monopolized commercialized media have developed a vested interest in the existing political economic order, and, therefore, Chinese media, including telecom carriers and Internet service providers, have been politically compliant and developed bias born of class with a few exceptions. Meanwhile, recognizing the asymmetric access to Internet resources, when China's economic reform has created a huge army of rural proletariats and urban underclasses, what does access to ICTs mean to these disenfranchised and underemployed people? Working-class connectivity through ICTs, as the journalism and communication professor Jack Linchuan Qiu has shown, is pervasive in contemporary China. High-end market saturation, intercorporate competition, and the development of a domestic equipment industry have accidentally created a working-class "have-less" network society. Clearly, the have-less strata, including migrant workers, laid-off workers, pensioners, and micro-entrepreneurs, have used a variety of communication devices to form their communities and cultures (Qiu 2009).

The unfinished history of class formation and class reconstitution will be relevant to future research on the broadly defined China Internet study. As ICT-related sectors have become a major growth outlet in the global and domestic market economy, China's efforts to move away from its export-dependent manufacturing economy have pivoted on ICT sectors. Clearly, pouring educational resources into developing high-tech ICT is a strategic step toward industrial restructuring and economic upgrading. Developing a high-tech ICT sector—according to China's Eleventh Five-Year Plan (2006–2010) and the National Long-term Guideline for Science and Technical Development of 2006–2020—rests upon the idea of prioritizing human capital formation in software, microelectronics, animation, and information service industries. By 2015, vocational schools and technical colleges are expected to train 1.2 million practitioners and generate 1 million new graduates for the software and information service outsourcing industry (Hong 2010).

Yu HONG
University of Southern California

See also Internet Governance; Internet Regulation; Social and Political Impact; Telecommunications Industry

Further Reading

Carmel, Erran; Gao Guodong; & Zhang Ning. (2010). The maturing Chinese offshore IT service industry: It takes ten years to sharpen a sword. In Mary C. Lacity, Leslie P. Willcocks & Zheng Yingqin (Eds.), *China's emerging outsourcing capacities: The services challenges* (pp. 37–56). New York: Palgrave Macmillan.

Harwit, Eric. (2008). *China's telecommunications revolution*. New York: Oxford University Press.

Hong Yu. (2008). Distinctive characteristics of China's path of ICT development—A critical analysis of Chinese developmental strategies in light of the eastern Asian model. *International Journal of Communication*, 2, 456–471.

Hong Yu. (2010). The politics of a socialist harmonious society in the aftermath of China's neoliberal development. *Chinese Journal of Communication*, *11*(1), 311–328.

Hong Yu. (2011). Labor, class formation, and China's informationized policy of economic development. Lanham, MD: Lexington Books.

Jiang Min. (2010). Authoritarian deliberation on Chinese Internet. *Electronic Journal of Communication, 20*. Retrieved May 1, 2014, from http://papers.ssrn.com/sol3/papers.cfm?abstract_id=1439354

Kluver, Randolph, & Yang Chen. (2007). The Internet in China: A meta-review of research. *The Information Society, 21*(4), 301–308.

Lee, Heejin; Chan, Shirley; & Oh, Sangjo. (2009). China's ICT standards policy after the WTO accession: Techno-national versus techno-globalism. *Info: The Journal of Policy, Regulation and Strategy for Telecommunications, Information and Media, 3*(2), 9–18.

Leung, Louis. (1998). Lifestyles and the use of new media technology in urban china. *Telecommunications Policy 1998, 22*, 781.

MacKinnon, Rebecca. (2008, June 18). Chinese Internet Research Conference: Getting beyond "Iron Curtain 2.0." *RConversation*. Retrieved May 1, 2014, from http://rconversation.blogs.com/rconversation/2008/06/chinese-inter-1.html

McChesney, W. Robert. (1999). *Rich media, poor democracy: Communication politics in dubious times*. Urbana: University of Illinois Press.

Mueller, Milton & Tan Zixiang. (1997). *China in the information age: Telecommunications and the dilemmas of reform*. Westport, CT: Praeger Publishers.

Qiang, Christine Zhen-Wei. (2007). *China's information revolution: Managing the economic and social transformation*. Washington, DC: The World Bank.

Qiu, Jack Linchuan. (2009). *Working class network society: Communication technology and the information have-less in urban China*. Cambridge, MA: MIT Press.

Qiu, Jack Linchuan. (2010). Chinese techno-nationalism and global WiFi policy. In Michael Curtin & Hemant Shah (Eds.), *Reorienting global communication: Indian and Chinese media beyond borders* (pp. 284–303), Urbana: University of Illinois Press.

Schiller, Daniel. (2000). *Digital capitalism: Networking the global market system*. Cambridge, MA: MIT Press.

Schiller, Daniel, & Fregoso, RosaLinda. (1991). A private view of the digital world. *Telecommunications Policy, 15*, 195–208.

Sun, Helen. (2010). *Internet policy in China: A field study of Internet cafes*. Lanham, MD: Lexington Books.

Tan, Z. (2006). *The Internet in China: Cyberspace and civil society*. New York and London: Routledge.

Tai Zixue. (2006). *The Internet in China: Cyberspace and civil society*. New York: Routledge.

Tsui, Lokman. (2008, June 13–14). The Great Firewall as Iron Curtain 2.0: The Implications of China's Internet most dominant metaphor for US foreign policy. Paper presented at the Sixth Annual Chinese Internet Research Conference. Hong Kong University.

Wei Ran. (2006). Lifestyles and new media: Adoption and use of wireless communication technologies in china. *New Media & Society, 8*, 991–1008.

Wong, John, & Seok Ling, Nah. (2001). *China's emerging new economy: The Internet and e-commerce*. Singapore: Singapore University Press.

Wu, S. Irene. (2009). *From iron fist to invisible hand: The uneven path of telecommunications reform in China*. Stanford, CA: Stanford University Press.

Xia, Jun; & Lu, Ting-Jie. (2008). Bridging the digital divide for rural communities: The case of China. *Telecommunications Policy, 32*, 686–696.

Yang, Guobin. (2003). The co-evolution of the Internet and civil society in China. *Asian Survey*, 43(3), 405–422.

Yu, Jiang, & Li-Hua, Richard. (2010). *China's highway of information and communication technology*. Basingstoke, UK: Palgrave Macmillan.

Zhang Junhua. (2002). Will the government "serve the people"?: The development of Chinese e-government. *New Media Society, 4*, 163.

Zhao Yuezhi. (2000). Caught in the web: The public Internet and the battle for control of China's information superhighway. *Info: The Journal of Policy, Regulation and Strategy for Telecommunications, Information and Media, 2*(1), 41–66.

Zhao Yuezhi. (2008). *Communication in China: Political economy, power, and conflict*. Lanham, MD: Rowman & Littlefield.

Zhao Yuezhi. (2010a). China's pursuits of indigenous innovations in information technology developments: Hopes, follies and uncertainties. *Chinese Journal of Communication, 3*(3), 266–289.

Zhao Yuezhi. (2010b). Rethinking Chinese media studies: History, political economy and culture. In D. Thussu (Ed.), *Internationalizing Media Studies* (pp. 175–195). London: Routledge.

Zhao Yuezhi, & Schiller, Dan. (2001). Dances with wolves? China's integration into digital capitalism. *Info: The Journal of Policy, Regulation and Strategy for Telecommunications, Information and Media*, 3(2), 137–151.

Zheng Yongnian. (2007). *Technological empowerment: The Internet, state, and society in China*. Stanford, CA: Stanford University Press.

Zhou Yongming. (2006). *Historicizing online politics: Telegraphy, the Internet and political participation in China*. Stanford, CA: Stanford University Press.

Advertising Online

Wǎngluò guǎnggào 网络广告

Summary: Online advertising is growing rapidly in China, giving advertisers one more channel to reach consumers. Deceptive and misleading advertising on the Internet, however, is a cause for concern among consumers and regulators. Lack of adequate legislation at the national level has forced regulators to rely on outdated advertising laws to police online advertising. Regulatory enforcement is problematic due to the multiple government agencies involved for different industries and at different levels of the process.

The role of advertising in a consumer society cannot be overemphasized. It not only keeps consumers informed of innovative products and services but also helps sustain the modern media industry. As free content has almost become a norm on the web, advertising has proved to be one of the more viable business models on which digital media companies can survive. In China, as elsewhere, online advertising has been growing fast.

Online Advertising Business in China

Like its growing economy, the development of China's Internet industry can be described as explosive. Within just two years, the Chinese Internet user population jumped from 457 million at the end of 2010 to over half a billion at the end of 2012, the largest in the world (CNNIC 2013). As in other countries, Chinese Internet users not only gather news and communicate with each other on the web, very frequently via their mobile phones, but also shop, socialize, and seek entertainment content. As a critical source of information and entertainment, the Internet has captured the imagination of marketers and advertisers who want to make online advertising part of their integrated marketing strategy.

Online advertising takes multiple forms and can be classified into four categories: search advertising, display advertising, classified listings, and email-based advertising (Evans 2008). The rise of social media for advertising purposes in recent years could be considered a fifth category. Online advertising resembles traditional advertising in a variety of ways. For instance, its use of text and graphics resembles print advertising, while its application of audiovisual effects is analogous to television advertising. Yet online advertising is different from traditional advertising in certain important ways. For example, as suggested in research by Wang Chingning and his colleagues (2002), online advertising is more interactive, can better target consumers, and may translate into a commercial transaction more easily than traditional advertising.

According to the journalism and electronic media scholars Barbara Kaye and Norman Medoff (2001), 1994 marked the beginning of online advertising when *Wired* magazine put banner advertisements on its website in the United States. In China, online advertising did not start until 1997, when the first paid online advertisement appeared on ChinaByte's website. Since then, the continued increase in Internet penetration and the expansion of online activities have fueled the growth of China's online advertising market, and the industry has grown in market size, revenue, and share in the overall advertising market.

In China, most online advertising spending is allocated to large local portals, such as Sina.com and Sohu.com, as well as China's top search engine, Baidu. The rise of Chinese social media such as social networking sites (e.g., www.kaixin001.com) and video sharing sites (e.g., Tudou and Youku) has given online advertisers one more channel to reach out to consumers. Research shows that in 2009, about 20 percent of Chinese Internet users visited video sharing sites, where advertisers spent 590 million yuan (US$90 million), representing an increase of 73.5 percent over the previous year (Data Center of China Internet 2010).

Regulating Online Advertisement

With the growth of online advertising has come misleading, deceptive, false, and fraudulent advertising that harms consumers' interests and hurts consumer confidence in online marketers. For this reason, governments worldwide have taken legislative and enforcement steps to regulate Internet advertising. The United States and the European Union, as well as their established Internet industries, for instance, have taken steps to not only regulate but also self-regulate Internet marketing practices since the 1990s (Venturelli 2002). China's online advertising industry is plagued by similar issues of mistrust found in developed countries. For instance, from 27 November 2007 to 7 February 2008, China's State Administration for Industry and Commerce (SAIC) detected violations in 41,360 Internet advertisements on 10,320 websites in its campaign to crack down on illegal online advertisements of sex-related products and treatments of venereal diseases by advertisers not certified to offer safe products and services of that category.

Although its online advertising industry is similar to those in developed countries in terms of format and business models, China's regulatory mechanism is characterized by two predicaments. First, advertising laws in China have failed to keep pace with new Internet technologies. In the face of fraudulent and misleading advertisements online, there has not been a legislative mandate at the national level to specifically address those challenges in the online environment. Second, the hierarchical structure of online advertising regulation has so many government agencies involved as to demand coordination among competing interest groups.

Laws and Regulations

On the legislative front, the Chinese government has relied on a number of laws and administrative rules established in the 1980s and 1990s to govern online advertising. The most important piece is the Advertising Law of the People's Republic of China, promulgated by the National People's Congress (China's highest legislative authority) in 1994, which lays the legal foundation for regulating advertising in general. Other national administrative rules include the Code of Ethics for Advertising Practice, and the Provisional Rules Concerning Language and Characters in Advertising. These general laws and rules have established the fundamental principles for China's advertising regulation; these rules apply to Internet advertising as well, such as truthfulness and conformity to socialist ethics. Moreover, those overarching principles set up the technical framework for government agencies and their local branches to promulgate and enforce specific administrative rules (Gao 2007).

Absent national legislation governing online advertising, some local governments have filled the gap with their own rules that target different aspects of online advertising. For instance, the Beijing municipal government issued provisional measures in 2001, which banned online advertising for tobacco and sex aids as well as requiring Internet service providers to check the content of online advertisements.

Regulatory and Enforcement Entities

The Chinese government adopts a parallel structure for its online advertising regulation and enforcement, with ministries and commissions at the same or comparable administrative rank participating from their sector-specific perspectives. In essence, with no agency outranking others, it is sometimes difficult for things to get done.

The SAIC acts as the primary government agency to regulate advertising, including Internet advertising, as part of its broad authority over industrial and commercial activities. The major approach it adopts to enforce China's advertising laws and regulations is to launch campaigns, sometimes called "key inspections" (*zhōngdián jiǎnchá* 重点检查) or "special crack-downs" (*zhuānxiàng zhěngzhì* 专项整治) (Gao 2007). Usually when complaints against a certain category of advertising rise dramatically, or the violations on an advertising medium exceed a threshold, the SAIC, with the assistance of its local offices, initiates a campaign to redress the situation. Since a national campaign to crack down on false and deceptive advertisements was launched in 2006, violations decreased substantially from 61,867 in 2006 to 51,599 cases in 2009. To punish violators, the SAIC and its local agencies levy penalties including cease-and-desist orders, fines, mandatory closure, and revocation of business licenses (National People's Congress 1994).

In addition to the SAIC, agencies such as the Internet Affairs Bureau of the State Council Information Office, the Ministry of Public Security, the General Administration of Press and Publication, the Ministry of

Culture, the Ministry of Health, and the State Drug Administration also participate in online advertising regulation and enforcement. Each of these bodies has the authority to issue advertising rules regarding specific media or products under their jurisdictions, and each has the authority to enforce rules and regulations on a specific category of advertising through mandatory certification and censorship systems (Gao 2007).

Local governments, authorized to issue local rules and measures regarding advertising, are directly responsible for enforcing national laws and regulations. Local campaigns to crack down on fraudulent and deceptive online advertising or marketing practices are often joint efforts of local government agencies, including local administrations for industry and commerce, health departments, and food and drug administrations. Their involvement complicates regulatory enforcement, however. Typical of the Chinese language, advertising laws and rules are couched in broad, vague, and rigid terms of political ideology and upheld by subjective enforcement (Corne 2002). As a result, the interpretation and enforcement of advertising laws and rules in the online environment can be inconsistent, and vary from region to region. Involvement by local governments may therefore give rise to local protectionism.

The Outlook for Online Advertising

In China, the government plays a central role in policy choices like online advertising regulation. That leaves little room for industrial players like the China Advertising Association or the China Commercial Advertising Association, which are not authorized by SAIC, to monitor compliance and handle complaints, or to step in and initiate self-regulation in their own interests. Without a strong self-regulatory system such as is well-established in developed countries, government agencies are left to struggle with the rising tide of deceptive, fraudulent, and unfair advertisements on the Internet. In order for China's online advertising industry to enjoy better growth opportunities, self-regulation by industrial players as a supplement to government regulation is critical.

Compared with that of the United States, China's online advertising market is much smaller in size, yet it has a greater potential for accelerated growth due to China's much larger population. Internet access will likely become more affordable to a greater percentage of the Chinese population as a result of innovations in technology and growth in disposable income, and advertisers will explore business opportunities in those new user populations and on new technological platforms. With transformations in technology, business development, and, potentially, legislation, online advertising will play a bigger role in China's advertising industry in the near future.

Liuning ZHOU
University of Southern California

Hongwei YANG
Appalachian State University

See also Consumers Online; Email; Internet and Economic Development; Internet Regulation; Shopping Online

Further Reading

Chan, Kara K. W., & McNeal, James U. (2004). *Advertising to children in China*. Hong Kong: The Chinese University Press.

China Internet Network Information Center (CNNIC). (2013, January). Statistical report on Internet development in China. Retrieved on April, 15, 2013, from http://www1.cnnic.cn/IDR/ReportDownloads/201302/P020130312536825920279.pdf

Corne, Peter Howard. (2002). Creation and application of law in the PRC. *The American Journal of Comparative Law, 50*, 369–443.

Data Center of China Internet. (2010). Twenty percent of Chinese people visit video sharing sites. Retrieved April, 25, 2013, from http://www.dcci.com.cn/publish/view/cid/3/id/416.html

Evans, David S. (2008). The economics of the online advertising industry. *Review of Network Economics*, 7(3), 359–391.

Gao Zhihong. (2005). Harmonious regional advertising regulation? *Journal of Advertising, 34*(3), 75–87.

Gao Zhihong. (2007). An in-depth examination of China's advertising regulation system. *Asia Pacific Journal of Marketing and Logistics, 19*(3), 307–323.

Ha, Louisa. (2008). Online advertising research in advertising journals: A review. *Journal of Current Issues and Research in Advertising, 30*(1), 31–48.

Huang, Y. and Xie, D. (2006). Present, future and development of online advertising in China. *Journalism Academy*, 2, 15–19. [in Chinese]

iResearch (2011). *Airui zixun: 2010 nian Zhongguo wangluo guanggao niandu shuju fabu* [iResearch: Release of 2010 China online advertising statistics]. Retrieved August, 14, 2013, from http://a.iresearch.cn/29/20110128/132400.shtml

Kaye, Barbara K., & Medoff, Norman J. (2001). *Just a click away: Advertising on the Internet*. Columbus, OH: Allyn and Bacon.

Venturelli, Shalini. (2002). Inventing e-regulation in the US, EU and East Asia: Conflicting social visions of the Information Society. *Telematics & Informatics, 19*(2), 69–90.

Wang Chingning; Zhang Ping; Choi Risook; & D'Eredita, Michael. (2002). Understanding consumers' attitude toward advertising. *Proceedings of the Eighth Americas Conference on Information Systems*, 1143–1148.

Wang Ying; Sun Shaojing; Lei Weizhen; & Toncar, Mark. (2009). Examining beliefs and attitudes toward online advertising among Chinese consumers. *Direct Marketing: An International Journal*, 3(1), 52–66.

Shopping Online

Wǎngshàng gòuwù 网上购物

Summary: Online shopping emerged in the early 1990s when consumers began to purchase goods and services in Internet marketspaces as well as traditional marketplaces. The Chinese are the world's largest community of Internet and mobile phone users, and thus an attractive market for online businesses. Online shopping in China has become increasingly popular, but its development has been constrained and shaped by the country's distinctive sociocultural, economic, and political environment. People in China tend to enjoy the social aspects of shopping, and the lack of universally enforced rules for commerce further hampers online business prospects.

Online shopping occurs when a buyer uses digital technology (such as the Internet or a mobile phone) to connect with a seller and purchases goods or services in a marketspace. Online shopping is an increasingly popular alternative to traditional shopping, which involves physically going to a marketplace. Online shopping began in the early 1990s as retailers in the United States gave buyers the option of making purchases from their home or office rather than visiting a store. Soon afterward, businesses such as Amazon were established to offer online-only shopping, thus saving on the time and expense of setting up a physical store.

Online shopping commonly involves a digital device, such as a computer with Internet access or a mobile phone, as well as either an account or a card from a financial institution that provides the buyer with credit or debit.

The People's Republic of China (PRC) has more mobile phone owners and more people with Internet access than any other country. The use of the Internet in China is also significantly above the global average. This makes China a very attractive market for online shopping. In order to explain the progress and prospects for online shopping in China, it is necessary to consider the fundamental process and the prevailing environmental conditions.

Processes of Online Shopping

Buyers commonly find the goods or service that they are interested in by searching the Internet or visiting the website of a specific retailer directly. They then add the item to an online shopping cart, which is similar to filling a shopping basket in a physical store. The analogy to a physical store continues with a checkout procedure, where the buyer pays for the purchase and, if necessary, provides delivery information. Confirmation of the purchase is commonly sent to the buyer via a text message or an email. Digital products such as music, videos, and software may be downloaded, while physical products are shipped to a convenient pick-up point or directly to the buyer.

In order to understand the challenges for online shopping in China, it is helpful to compare conditions in China with those found in the Western world. The business environment in the West encourages online shopping. Consumers have convenient, reliable, and inexpensive access to the Internet and telecommunication services. They can search for and compare products offered by many different online vendors and purchase their choice by using easily available and widely accepted credit and debit cards. Meanwhile, online security systems effectively verify identities, authenticate transactions, and protect privacy. Information goods can be downloaded immediately while physical goods are delivered rapidly using modern transportation networks and logistics services. Dissatisfied buyers can usually get a refund or credit toward another purchase. In the worst case, legal recourse is available because a comprehensive set of rules governs commercial activities and agreements. Online shopping in the West is not only convenient and cost-efficient but also fairly safe, since information is widely available, contracts are enforceable, and the underlying regulatory system is trustworthy.

Personal Relationships and Fragmented Markets

The growing affordability and reliability of digital technologies, telecommunication services, and remote payment systems have also encouraged online shopping in China. Its development, however, has been constrained and shaped by the distinctive sociocultural and economic environment.

A longstanding inability to rely on universally enforced rules and impartial courts has forced the Chinese people to depend greatly on personal connections, called *guānxì* 关系. Consequently, people in China tend to do business with those whom they know and trust personally, such as family, friends, and classmates. Key information tends to be shared selectively and exchanged informally.

Consumers in China prefer to interact personally with prospective sellers, inspecting products physically before purchasing them. Chinese consumers make more shopping trips and visit more stores per trip than their American counterparts, but they buy significantly less. They enjoy the social aspects of shopping, including the ability to haggle on prices and to ask for special deals. Online shopping lacks the social richness that is highly valued in the Chinese culture.

The prevalence of relationship-based business in China has also restricted the scale and scope of its markets. Consumer markets and supply chains remain fragmented and poorly coordinated. Retailers in the United States have greatly improved their competitiveness by expanding their scale and scope, modernizing their core business processes, and outsourcing peripheral activities. Walmart and Amazon are good examples of traditional and online retailers that effectively serve several hundred million consumers by selling a wide range of products at attractive yet profitable prices.

No retailer in China combines the geographic scope, product range, competitive prices, and customer service levels of either Walmart or Amazon. Retailers in China tend to operate on a small scale and collaborate informally with a few product and service suppliers whom they know and trust personally. They have been hesitant to extend credit primarily because the scarcity of reliable public information makes it difficult to evaluate creditworthiness.

The highly fragmented markets and localized nature of business in China have hindered the development of modern financial systems, transportation networks, and logistics services. The underdeveloped business infrastructure in China has in turn made it comparatively more difficult and expensive to operate an online shop. Meanwhile, the prevailing norms of the traditional Chinese culture have hindered the adoption of online shopping.

Power, Privilege, and Poverty

Many government officials in China are unenthusiastic about online shopping because it endangers their privileged status. State bureaus and government officials can benefit from their discretionary power to authorize, support, and restrict traditional retailing ventures. Retailers in China often have government patrons that facilitate their access to state-controlled resources and protect them from bureaucratic interference.

The transparency of the Internet reduces the discretionary power of regulators and other political actors. Digital databases and audit trails make it more difficult to give out preferential treatment. For example, a China-wide web database now can detect foreign exchange fraud that relies on forged customs declaration forms.

Online shopping also makes it more difficult for state officials to restrict arbitrarily the business activities of "untrustworthy" people (based upon their social origin or status) or to manipulate government records. The Chinese National Statistics Bureau is using the Internet to collect data directly from companies in order to reduce distortion by local governments.

The central government has reduced its direct control of China's economy, but different ministries and public agencies continue to shape the development of retailing. Online ventures seeking to achieve profitable economies of scale must typically satisfy regulators in numerous provincial and municipal jurisdictions across the country.

Problems of Online Shopping

Even with the steadily improving infrastructure in China, consumers have remained concerned about security issues, such as the reliability of encryption technologies, and legal issues, such as the enforcement of online commitments. General concerns about counterfeit goods increase when retailing goes online because sellers can remain anonymous or provide a false identify, and goods cannot be inspected physically.

Online retail sales in China during the first few years of the twenty-first century were remarkably low compared to those in the United States and most other major economies, even after adjusting for the lower disposable incomes of Chinese consumers. Based on purchasing power parity, online sales penetration rates in China between 2000 and 2005 were about one third of those in the United States and about half of those in Western Europe.

The comparatively slow transition in China from physical marketplaces to digital marketspaces can be explained by the importance of personal relationships in the Chinese culture, together with the comparatively poor quality and limited choice of products that have been offered by online vendors. The development of online shopping in China has been further inhibited by the relative underdevelopment of both the infrastructure that supports commerce and government institutions that regulate it. This underdevelopment has raised significant concerns among Chinese consumers about the credibility of online vendors, the security of online payments, and the timely delivery of physical products that are purchased online.

Progress of Online Shopping

Online shopping in China has grown rapidly in recent years, with double-digit percentage increases annually. Online shopping in China first exceeded 5 percent of the country's consumer purchases in 2009. It is expected to exceed 2 trillion yuan (US$300 billion) by 2016.

The most popular items purchased online in China are books, clothing, electronic goods, wardrobe accessories (such as jewelry), and footwear. Online purchases of both music and computer software are less popular in China than in Western countries because intellectual piracy has reduced the demand for legitimate copies of information goods. Young adults (aged nineteen to thirty-nine) and more educated consumers with higher family incomes make up a disproportionately high share of online purchases in China.

Many online vendors from the United States, including eBay and Yahoo, have faltered in China. Local online book sellers (such as Dangdang and Joyo) and name-your-price websites (such as Lalasho) initially emulated Amazon and Priceline, respectively, but they subsequently diversified and/or radically modified their business models to the circumstances in China. A common factor in their success was the development of relationships in order to overcome three key challenges: the scarcity of business services; the difficulty of achieving a profitable scale or scope of operations; and the opposition from privileged interests (or restrictions imposed by them).

The biggest beneficiary of China's online shopping growth has been Taobao, an online auction and shopping website operated by the Alibaba Group. Taobao has become the dominant online shopping site in China. Its business success can be explained primarily by its ability to adapt global standards and business models to local environmental conditions and consumer preferences. For example, Taobao implemented a proprietary chat program, named WangWang, that allows potential buyers to communicate directly with sellers. The development of the personal trust facilitated by WangWang, together with a reliable escrow-based online payment platform, called AliPay, have contributed to the national success of Taobao.

Potential and Prospects for Online Shopping

China is a rapidly developing country with 1.3 billion people and a strict birth control policy (although the government announced some easing of restrictions in November 2013). A would-be online retailer may thus envision attracting hundreds of millions of Chinese parents, each with a treasured single child. China, however, is a comparatively poor country. This relative poverty, together with the economic disparity across China, creates additional difficulties.

China may be divided conceptually into two parts that represent an oversimplified but useful dichotomy between its have and have-not regions. The southern and eastern coastal regions are heavily urbanized, industrialized (or post-industrialized), and comparatively wealthy. The transportation and telecommunication networks within and between these major centers are among the most advanced in the entire world.

Less than half of China's citizens, however, live in urban areas, compared to over two-thirds in both the United States and Japan. Most Chinese still work in agriculture or other primary industries. The Chinese countryside and even its western cities typically lack the infrastructure and services needed to support online shopping. Weak transportation networks create delivery concerns beyond major cities and the coastal provinces.

The infrastructure for moving physical goods across China is improving, partly because some online vendors are developing their own distribution networks. It continues to be impeded, however, by the regulation of postal services and inefficiencies in transport services that cross provincial boundaries.

The online share of total retail sales in the PRC remains lower than in the United States. Most people in China have never made an online purchase. Consequently, there are still significant opportunities to initiate and increase online sales to Chinese consumers. Social networking and word of mouth will play important roles in promoting specific vendors and their products to online shoppers throughout the country.

Online retail competition in China is becoming more intense as many traditional retailers launch websites, while others set up entire online shopping malls. Examples of the latter are Beijing Ule E-Commerce, a joint venture between China Post and Hong Kong's Tom Group, and Lekutian, meaning "Happy Cool Day," set up by Baidu, the leading search engine in China, and Rakuten, a leading online business in Japan.

As the credibility of suppliers increases, the market is consolidated, and transactions become more secure and better regulated, Chinese consumers will become more confident to shop online. This confidence together with the overall economic development of China will undoubtedly further the growth of online shopping in China for decades to come.

Maris Gunars MARTINSONS
City University of Hong Kong

See also Consumers Online; Digital Divides; Internet and Economic Development; Internet in Everyday Life

Further Reading

Burrows, Glen R.; Drummond, Damon L.; & Martinsons, Maris G. (2005). Knowledge management in China. *Communications of the ACM, 48*(4), 73–76.

China Internet Network Information Center (CNNIC). (2013, January). Statistical report on Internet development in China. Retrieved on April, 15, 2013, from http://www1.cnnic.cn/IDR/ReportDownloads/201302/P020130312536825920279.pdf

Liu Xia; He Mengqiao; Gao Fang; & Xie Peihong. (2008). An empirical study of online shopping customer satisfaction in China: A holistic perspective. *International Journal of Retail & Distribution Management, 36*(11), 919–940.

Martinsons, Maris G. (2002). Electronic commerce in China: Emerging success stories. *Information & Management, 39*(7), 571–579.

Martinsons, Maris G. (2008). Relationship-based e-commerce: Theory and evidence from China. *Information Systems Journal, 18*(4), 331–356.

Ou, Carol Xiaojuan, & Davison, Robert M. (2009). Why eBay lost to TaoBao in China: The Glocal advantage. *Communications of the ACM, 52*(1), 145–148.

Ou, Carol Xiaojuan; Sia, Choon Ling; & Banerjiee, Prober. (2007). What is hampering online shopping in China? *Journal of Information Technology Management, 18*(1), 16–32.

Shih Chuan Fong; Dedrick, Jason; & Kraemar, Kenneth. (2005). Rule of law and the international diffusion of e-commerce. *Communications of the ACM, 48*(11), 57–62.

Zhu, Jonathan J. H., & Wang Enhai. (2005). Diffusion, use and effect of the Internet in China. *Communications of the ACM, 48*(4), 49–53.

Consumers Online

Wǎngshàng xiāofèizhě 网上消费者

Summary: The Internet is increasingly shaping and changing Chinese consumers' decision-making and consumption patterns. Understanding the online impulses of Chinese consumers—over half a billion Chinese people were Internet users as of 2012—has become a crucial prerequisite for companies developing effective marketing strategies in China. Many Chinese consumers are worried about online financial safety. A lack of regulation combined with government censorship adds to their worries.

Over the past few years, the world has witnessed the quickly rising purchasing power of Chinese consumers. Besides the upsurge in domestic demands, Chinese tourists reportedly often spend a large amount of money on purchasing name-brand products abroad, surprising even well-off Westerners. Such media coverage is not coming out of the blue. The fact is that in 2010 China surpassed Japan as the second largest economy in the world (after the United States), and the country has enjoyed continuous economic growth even in the midst of global recession. Indeed, no company or business aiming for a global reach can afford to ignore the vigorous Chinese market. As such, understanding Chinese consumers has become a priority for many global businesses.

In the meantime, the world is becoming "flat" due to the advances of new technologies. (The word *flat* here refers to the journalist Thomas Friedman's meaning of the globalized world's more "level" economic playing field, as discussed in his 2005 book *The World Is Flat: A Brief History of the Twenty-First Century.*) The Internet has rapidly penetrated the Chinese market and has a profound impact on the life of Chinese people, from how they spend their leisure time and how they communicate with others to how they spend their money. According to statistics by the China Internet Network Information Center (CNNIC), by June 2010, Chinese "netizens" reached 420 million; that number had reached 538 million by June 2012 and continues to grow at an astonishing speed (CNNIC 2010; CNNIC 2013). Chinese netizens are using various Internet applications (e.g., emails, blogs, instant messaging, and social media) to satisfy their diverse needs.

Along with the dazzling growth of Internet usage, the body of Chinese online consumers is expanding quickly as well. The number of online shoppers reached 242 million by June 2012, up from 142 million in June 2010 (CNNIC 2010; CNNIC 2013). From information search, price comparison, and deal hunting to final purchase, the Internet is increasingly shaping and changing Chinese consumers' decision-making and consumption patterns. As this trend gains momentum, global marketers are now compelled to gain insights into these digital consumers in order to reach and engage them. Understanding the online impulses of Chinese consumers has become a crucial prerequisite for companies developing effective marketing strategies.

Profiles of Chinese Online Consumers

The Internet is global. Consumer behaviors, however, are greatly influenced by local cultures and constrained by stages of economic development and legal environment. Understanding the similarities and differences among consumers in different markets bears equal importance for online and traditional international marketing. Over the years, Chinese online consumers have demonstrated certain unique characteristics.

First, particular demographic or socioeconomic groups comprise a large share of the body of online consumers. Chinese online consumers, on average, have a higher socioeconomic status and education. The researchers Lynda Wee Keng Neo and Ramesh Ramachandra (2012), for example, found that Chinese cyber buyers tend to be young, well-educated, and technology savvy. Such a profile is consistent with the general characteristics of Chinese Internet users. As of 2012, about three-quarters of Chinese Internet users were between the ages of ten and thirty-nine (CNNIC 2013).

Second, Chinese online consumers seem to show considerable differences across geographical regions. A majority of online consumers reside in urban and coastal areas (the vast majority of Chinese people live in the eastern third of the country, mainly due to the availability of water). Online consumption takes place most frequently in developed cities like Beijing and Shanghai. The Internet penetration gap across regions has become less pronounced in China in recent years, ranging from a low penetration rate of 28.5 percent for Jiangxi Province (in southeastern China) to a high of 72.2 percent in Beijing; the penetration rate for all of China 2012 was 42.1 percent, a 3.8 percent rise over the year before, according to the 2013 CNNIC report. Even in rural regions or hinterlands, there is a relatively high Internet penetration and adoption rate. There is variance across regions, however, in terms of Internet policies, access convenience, and consumer preferences. For example, in less-developed areas such as Xinjiang Autonomous Region (north of Tibet and west of Mongolia), Internet access and surfing is strictly monitored and controlled, particularly after the 5 July unrest in 2009 (Wong 2009). The unrest resulted from rising ethnic tension between Muslim Uygurs and Han Chinese, and later descended into killings between riot police and ordinary citizens. Some supposedly "treacherous and anti-government" human rights advocates were reported to have organized the disturbance via the Internet. To prevent the riot from going viral, the government tightened its control over the Internet and mobile phones in the region. As a result, local people faced more barriers to accessing some websites compared with people in other regions of China. Furthermore, large cities are more likely to attract those having received higher education who are more likely to make a good income. All these factors could speak to the difference of online consumption patterns across regions in China.

The third reason that Chinese online consumers are unique is that they are more likely than others to engage in extensive information-seeking before making online purchases or decisions. According to research by Yuval Atsmon and colleagues (2010), about 25 percent of Internet users will not make a purchase without researching relevant product information online. Besides traditional word-of-mouth information, various new technology platforms have been serving important alternative communication channels where consumers seek product information. Channels include online forums, product web pages, and social network sites, among others. In recent years, social media have gained importance in affecting the decision-making process of Chinese online consumers. Although the popular Western social media, such as YouTube, Facebook, and Twitter, are blocked by the Chinese government, equivalent Chinese versions of such social media (e.g., Youku, Renren, Weibo) have attracted a large number of Chinese Internet users. Through these social media, consumers discuss, exchange, and recommend products, form virtual communities, and interact with brands and companies. The influence of the Internet word-of-mouth is more pronounced when the time comes for purchasing big-ticket items due to the fact that those items bear higher financial risks. Consumers are usually more cautious when making such decisions. One exemplar is the fast-growing automobile market in China. When considering buying a car, people often go online to seek information about their favorite models, and review others' comments and advice. The 2010 study by Atsmon and colleagues also revealed that retailer or company websites were the primary destinations where consumers searched for information. Other frequently-used channels were third-party reviewer websites (e.g., www.pc.com) and user-generated content (e.g., Bulletin Board System (BBS), forums). These platforms help consumers gather useful information as well as advise automakers in China on how to reach their targeted consumers.

Factors Impacting Online Consumption

People in China turn to online shopping for various reasons. According to one 2010 study, convenience and selection were the top two factors that drew consumers to online shopping. The reported conveniences included easy delivery, time savings, and freedom from the restricted opening hours of physical brick-and-mortar stores. The consumers reported enjoying a wider assortment of products that were customized to their needs, and unique or not available in stores. Other reasons included cheaper prices and the opinions that buying is a natural decision following online information search, and online shopping is a fashion trend that is here to stay (Atsmon et al. 2010).

The researchers Joseph Richards and Shen Dong (2006) reported that three main factors—fun, brand consciousness, and low perceived risk—contributed significantly to Chinese consumers' online activities. For the younger generation of consumers, however, the spectrum of online products of interest is wide, ranging from clothes and books to electronic devices. A Chinese consumer who comes across a book in a physical bookstore often does not make the purchase right away. Instead, he or she may put down the title, compare prices online, and then get the best deal.

Despite the above-mentioned diverse advantages of online shopping, a large number of Chinese people keep online purchasing at an arm's length. A 2010 survey revealed that consumers' primary concerns were product quality and after-service support, such as the convenience of returning products. A majority of people preferred to try the products out before purchasing (Chinese E-commerce Research Center 2010). Moreover, the survey indicated that more females than males shopped online. Nearly 90 percent of females, as compared to around 60 percent of males, had experience with online shopping at the time of the survey. Interestingly, female online consumers, on average, held higher concerns or worries about online shopping than did males. (Females make up roughly 44 percent of total Internet users in China, according to the 2013 CNNIC report.)

The online payment system is developing rapidly. About half of online transactions are carried out via third-party platforms such as Alipay and Tenpay, two well-known platforms affording virtual accounts and safeguards against fraud. Another option is cash-on-delivery, which is more popular in large cities. Despite the wide spectrum of payment options, the social system and policies pertaining to online business still lag behind. For example, online deception and credit card fraud are prevalent. Many people, therefore, hold a number of misgivings about the safety and fairness of online shopping. The researchers Chuan Pang, David Yen, and Michael Tarn (2007) found that the level of "e-trust" greatly influenced Chinese consumers' online purchasing. Those who held high trust toward online shopping were more likely to shop online than those with low trust.

Some would say that the collapse of social values and morality has posed severe challenges to the whole of Chinese society. Over the past several years, Chinese people have enjoyed the great benefits of economic development. People's preoccupation with money and other material goods, however, often has meant that social morality has taken a backseat to the ability to make a profit. The loss of social trust in dealing with what can be perceived as a faceless retailer also distances many people from online shopping.

Differences across Regions

It is also necessary to take into account the differences of economy across regions. For instance, Hong Kong, an international city returned to the sovereignty of the Chinese government in 1997, distinguishes itself in e-commerce from other Chinese cities. The researchers Niki Hynes and Ping Suewin (2007) studied online consumers in Hong Kong and found that males there were more likely to shop online than females, bucking the trend of the rest of China. Interestingly, Hynes and Suewin also reported that the people of Hong Kong were more likely to go online for entertainment tickets, banking, and for travel and vacation websites; however, they were less likely to buy furniture, electronics, and household appliances online.

The marketing expert Liu Xia and colleagues (2008) examined Chinese consumer's satisfaction with online shopping and found that delivery and customer service were the most important factors. Specifically, on-time delivery and immediate responses to customer concerns could greatly influence customer satisfaction. A major reason for Chinese consumers' online shopping is its convenience and fastness.

As Liu and colleagues stressed, the information service on the web warrants more attention. Particularly, the web design of some business websites often is not appealing or user friendly. Inexperienced online consumers are likely to encounter difficulty in making their purchases. Providing more valuable and comprehensive information should be on the agenda to best serve Chinese consumers.

Past research shows that both perceived risks and convenience were significant predictors of online consumption (Kolsaker, Lee-Kelley, and Choy 2004). Traditional Chinese culture has encouraged people to live a quiet and secure life. During periods of rapid (and, to many, disorienting) social transition, as China has seen in recent years, a majority of Chinese consumers are worried and anxious about financial safety and societal steadiness. The challenge of building up Chinese consumers' confidence about online shopping safety will be an ongoing task.

Future Trends

The number of online consumers in China will continue to grow at a fast rate. With advances in Internet technologies and the rapid growth of China's economy, there are some obvious directions of future Chinese online consumption.

First, the population of online consumers will be more heterogeneous, and online consumption will extend (more than it does today) to older, less-educated people. This trend will evolve with the further expansion of Internet user population in China. As more people go online, more businesses will invest larger and larger amounts of money in e-commerce. Consequently, the barriers (perceived or otherwise) for online shopping will become lower. Convenience will attract more consumers to online transactions. Because the average education level of Chinese population is increasing, there will likely be an easier adoption of new technologies.

Second, Chinese online consumers will increasingly access the Internet through mobile devices. Besides having the world's largest population of netizens, China also houses the largest body of mobile phone users. Smartphones, such as the Apple iPhone, have gained popularity among Chinese users. As of late 2012, around 422 million mobile users had access to the Internet via their phones (CNNIC 2013). The mobile characteristic of Chinese online consumers has significant implications for the development of e-commerce. For example, it would behoove companies to ensure that their website contents may be correctly displayed in multiple platforms, including those of mobile devices. Linking financial accounts to mobile phones adds another option to the current repertoire of paying for online transactions.

Third, Chinese consumers' online consumption behavior will become more complicated and is likely to take place with other online activities simultaneously. The 2009 survey conducted by CNNIC indicated that Chinese netizens used the Internet primarily for information seeking, entertainment, and email. Nonetheless, online purchases could have occurred while Chinese netizens were involved in these online activities. For example, consumers may have encountered products they were interested in buying while listening to their favorite music on the Internet.

Fourth, after-service support and product quality will become more important factors to keep veteran online consumers and to attract new consumers. With the steadily growing economy, more well-off Chinese consumers will shop online. Chinese consumers' online shopping frequency and patterns will vary greatly across different categories of products, however.

A fifth possible future trend is that Chinese online consumers will be more active in exchanging online information but more cautious of assessing information credibility. The Internet policy in China is quite different from that in Western countries. The Internet is closely monitored by the Chinese government, but, on the other hand, some Internet websites lack any type of regulation. Some people are hired by companies or businesses to post information online so as to influence or shape public opinions; thus, the line between advertising and reality becomes blurred. These people, named "online fighters," are rewarded for each online post as designated by particular organizations or businesses. The vigorousness and virility of online opinions could reduce the overall credibility of online information and add difficulty to online consumers' decision making.

Lastly, Chinese online consumers will do shopping not only on domestic Chinese websites but also on overseas English-language websites. The average English language competency of the younger generation is getting stronger. Meanwhile, more Chinese who receive their education overseas are returning home for job opportunities. This group of English-competent elites is more likely to make good use of both English-language and Chinese e-commerce sites. For products not available on Chinese websites, they could turn to English-language ones. For example, well-educated people in China are cognizant of Amazon.com in the United States and purchase some products from that site directly.

Globalization and e-commerce are the two most important trends of today's global market. In the coming years, China will play a more significant role in the world economy. With the fast penetration of the Internet and mobile phones in China, the market for e-commerce is expanding at full speed. To survive and succeed in the Chinese market, managers and entrepreneurs need to learn more about Chinese online consumers. It is imperative to gain insights on the background, beliefs, values, and behaviors of this particular population. To that end, more empirical research on Chinese online consumers is both warranted and expected. Furthermore, a partnership between academia and the marketing profession would help enhance the understanding of Chinese online shoppers.

Ying WANG
Youngstown State University

Shaojing SUN
Fudan University

See also Digital Divides; Internet in Everyday Life; Internet Governance; Shopping Online

Further Reading

Atsmon, Yuval; Dixit, Vinay; Magnim, Max; Narasimhan, Laxman; & Wu, Cathy. (2010). Digital nation on the rise: Profiting from China's Internet revolution. McKinsey & Company. Retrieved February 28, 2011, from http://csi.mckinsey.com/Home/Knowledge_by_region/Asia/China/Digital_Nation_on_the_Rise.aspx

Barboza, David. (2010, August 15). China passes Japan as second-largest economy. *New York Times.*

China Internet Network Information Center (CNNIC). (2010, July). Statistical report on Internet development in China. Retrieved January 18, 2011, from http://www.cnnic.net.cn/en/index/index.htm

China Internet Network Information Center (CNNIC). (2013, January). Statistical report on Internet development in China. Retrieved on July, 15, 2013, from http://www1.cnnic.cn/IDR/Report-Downloads/201302/P020130312536825920279.pdf

Chinese E-commerce Research Center. (July 2010). An analysis of online shopping. Retrieved January 2, 2011, from http://china.toocle.com/cbna/item/2010-07-22/5289328.html

Friedman, Thomas L. (2005). *The world is flat: A brief history of the twenty-first century.* New York: Farrar, Straus and Giroux.

Hynes, Niki, & Suewin, Ping. (2007). Online shopping adoption within Hong Kong—An empirical study. *Singapore Management Review, 31*(2), 1–19.

Kolsaker, Ailsa; Lee-Kelley, Liz; & Choy, Pui Ching, (2004). The reluctant Hong Kong consumer: Purchasing travel online. *International Journal of Consumer Studies, 28*(3), 295–304.

Liu Xia; He Mengqiao; Gao Fang; & Xie Peihong, (2008). An empirical study of online shopping customer satisfaction in China: A holistic perspective. *International Journal of Retail & Distribution Management, 36*(11), 919–940.

Pang, Chuan; Yen, David; & Tarn, Michael. (2007). Exploring online shoppers' e-trust in China. *Human Systems Management, 26*, 193–198.

Richards, Joseph, & Shen Dong. (2006). E-commerce adoption among Chinese consumers: An exploratory study. *Journal of International Consumer Marketing, 18*(3), 33–55.

Wee Keng Neo, Lynda, & Ramachandra, Ramesh. (2012). Cyberbuying in China, Hong Kong & Singapore: Tracking the profile of on-line buyers. Retrieved July 15, 2013 from http://ntutrump.wikispaces.com/file/view/Cyberbuying+in+China,+HK,+Singapore.pdf

Wong, Edward. (2009, July 5). Riots in western China amid ethnic tension. *The New York Times.*

Telecommunications Industry

Diànxìn gōngyè 电信工业

Summary: Telecommunications systems in China developed slowly during the Imperial, Republican, and Mao-era Communist regimes. From the 1980s, government investment policies focused on expanding the network. The arrival of foreign equipment manufacturers, and domestic state-owned corporate competition, led to improved quality and new services. Today, China leads the world in the number of mobile-phone and Internet users, but there continues to be a rural/urban telecommunications divide.

As a late-developing country, China was slow to introduce telecommunications services on a wide scale. As recently as the 1970s, telephone availability for average citizens was rare. Economic reform policies beginning in the 1980s put an emphasis on developing communications technologies, and the past three decades have seen remarkable growth in the sector.

Early Development: 1860s–1970s

China's first telecommunications systems arrived in the 1860s in the form of telegraph lines. Foreign colonial powers constructed these first electronic communications pathways in several coastal cities. By the early 1870s, telegrams had become a common means of communication. The 1880s saw major telegraph lines connecting Beijing, Shanghai, Tianjin, and the island of Taiwan. The Qing dynasty's (1644–1911/12) Imperial Telegraph Administration took monopoly control over the in dustry.

Telephones first appeared in 1900, in the city of Nanjing. By 1910, the nation hosted more than seven thousand telephone users (Wang 1977). The collapse of the Qing regime in 1912 led to civil war and a nation divided by regional warlords. The communications network suffered from battle damage, and China's central government lost its leading role in building and maintaining the network.

In the late 1920s and early 1930s, a new Nationalist government began rebuilding some of the telecommunications infrastructure. Most of this effort was focused in the coastal provinces under its control. The Japanese invasion of 1937 ended the Chinese efforts, but the occupying military continued to expand the network to consolidate control. Long-distance phone lines increased from 47,000 kilometers in 1936 to 59,000 kilometers in 1945 (*Zhongguo jindai youdian shi* 1984). By the end of China's civil war (1946–1949), won by the Communist forces, China had about 218,000 telephone users (mainly urban), and 310,000 phone lines nationwide. The majority of rural areas lacked any kind of communications infrastructure (*Statistical Yearbook* 1982).

The new Communist regime set out to expand the network, using a combination of investment and political exhortation. Regulation and operation of the sector came under control of the government's Ministry of Posts and Telecommunications. Total fixed assets of the telecommunications sector grew at an annual rate of 9.1 percent during the 1950s, and the number of telephone subscriber rose to about 1.6 million by the turn of the decade (Zhang 1989). The late 1950s' Great Leap Forward (a movement to industrialize China) inspired the rapid development of the telecommunications sector, although it also resulted in many improperly installed communications lines that later had to be replaced. China's Cultural Revolution (1966–1976) led to a slowdown in telecommunications growth, with investment funds reduced for the sector. By the middle of the 1970s, the number of telephone subscribers totaled only about two million.

Overall, though communications took some priority in the early years of the communist regime, the political turmoil of much of the first few decades slowed the network's progress. The lack of market forces in the form of commercial interests or private demand put the industry at a relatively low priority level, and it was not until economic reforms began in the late 1970s that the sector started a period of rapid growth.

Reform Era: 1980s–2010

As China's economy opened to domestic market forces and international investment, telecommunications tools came to be seen as vital to efficient growth. Newly mobile Chinese workers, competitive though mainly state-owned businesses, and foreign firms all sought an increase in the availability of telephones and, as newer technologies developed, mobile and data communications devices.

The Chinese government continued to play a leading role in developing the telecommunications sector, and new leadership under Deng Xiaoping, the successor of People's Republic of China (PRC) founder Mao Zedong, placed higher priority on building the network. Telecommunications was listed as a preferential construction item and seen as strategically vital. Funding matched this political rhetoric, and investment in the sector increased at an annual rate of 55 percent from 1985 to 1994 (*Zhongguo jiaotong nianjian* and *Zhongguo tongji nianjian*, various years); this was about triple the pace of China's gross domestic product (GDP) growth over the same period. By the mid-1990s, telephone subscriber numbers grew from about three million to more than forty million.

The Chinese leadership realized rapid deployment of a network would rely on technology available only from foreign corporations. It therefore opened the country's market to equipment imports from Japan, the United States, and other nations. Large coastal cities, such as Shanghai, Fuzhou, and others, were the initial beneficiaries of this policy, as modern switching and transmission technologies facilitated economic growth.

As the cost of equipment imports began to mount and drain the country's scarce foreign exchange reserves, the Chinese government moved to a different model, one designed to foster domestic telecommunications technologies through the use of joint venture corporations. Early foreign investing partners included the ITT Corporation (later acquired by France's Alcatel), which created Shanghai Bell, and Germany's Siemens, which founded a venture in Beijing. Both companies grew in the 1980s and 1990s, and by the year 2000 joint venture companies held 60 percent of China's market for switching systems, while imports of this equipment had ended. The availability of telephones grew along with equipment manufacturing, and at the end of the 1990s subscriber numbers topped two hundred million.

Joint venture manufacturing proved to be just a stepping-stone to China's long-term goal of encouraging primarily domestic, Chinese-owned manufacturers for its communications network needs. Two domestic companies became leading suppliers of the PRC's equipment. Privately owned Huawei Technologies and state-owned ZTE Corporation appealed first to rural markets sometimes ignored by foreign producers. The domestic companies used manufacturing cost advantages and a relatively high level of technology to expand sales both within China and, gradually, to mainly developing nations abroad. By 2009, Huawei had a global revenue of some 150 billion yuan (about US$22 billion) and a profit of about 21 billion yuan (US$3.1 billion) (Huawei 2014). The joint venture equipment companies in China, meanwhile, faced a further challenge of government programs promoting purchases of domestic companies' products. The foreign-invested companies thereby lost market share to these new Chinese rivals.

With the rapid expansion of telecommunications infrastructure, China began to join the ranks of developed nations in terms of communications penetration. In the year 2000, China had a teledensity (the number of telephone subscribers per 100 people) of 22.5. The 2005 teledensity of 57 put the nation at levels seen in Japan and Australia in the early 1990s, and by the middle of 2010, the teledensity of fixed and mobile phones had reached 85, with 1.1 billion phones for a population of 1.3 billion people.

Government funding and practical policies were key to the growth of the telecommunications sector, but market forces also played an important role in spreading and improving telephone services in the PRC. As China's reform era progressed, the nation's leaders realized that state-owned monopolies could lead to stagnated industries. Competition, even within the state sector, came to be a useful force for improving efficiency and inspiring innovation.

Market Competition and the Growth of Telephone Companies

To maintain political control over the means of communication, the government's cardinal rule was that foreign companies would not be allowed to actually operate or have a controlling ownership of a telephone services company. Such a foreign role could threaten the country's security or, in times of political uncertainty, its social stability. Nokia, Samsung, Siemens, Alcatel, and others could make or sell equipment in China, but AT&T, Deutsche Telecom, or Sprint would be barred from running a network within the country's borders. For similar reasons, Chinese private firms were also prevented from building large-scale telecommunications service operations.

Competition therefore came not in the form of foreign competition or even private Chinese companies, but of domestic state-owned companies working against each other for market share. The 1980s breakup of AT&T's near monopoly in the United States influenced Chinese policy makers to take similar steps to end monopoly control by the Ministry of Posts and Telecommunications (MPT), which had governed the sector since the founding of the PRC.

Early rivals to the ministry came from other government departments that had partially overlapping interests. In the early 1990s, the Ministries of Electronics Industry, Railways, and Electric Power promoted the creation of a new telecommunications corporation, one that could use their various technologies and physical communications pathways (such as railway or power line routes) to create a new network. Though the MPT opposed the action of these bureaucratic competitors, in 1993 the State Council approved the creation of a new telecommunications carrier, China Unicom. Central leaders saw this scheme as a way to bring corporate competition and resulting benefits to consumers.

China Unicom began operating in 1994, just as the MPT's telecommunications company was being rebranded as China Telecom. The MPT, however, continued to be China's national communications regulating authority, and China Unicom complained early on that the MPT naturally favored its own offspring company, China Telecom.

Though China Unicom initially envisioned itself as providing fixed-line phone services, new mobile phone technologies were emerging at the time of the company's birth. The central government saw China Unicom as a tool to spread this new technology, and to potentially offer services at lower cost than that of China Telecom. From 1995 to 1996, prices for a mobile phone connection in large cities such as Beijing and Guangzhou fell from 21,000 yuan (about US$2,300) to about 10,000 yuan (US$1,200) (BDAssociates 1996). China Unicom targeted other major urban areas and soon served thirteen cities with 100,000 customers (*USITO China IT Issue Report* 1997). Nationally, the number of mobile phone users rose, with China Unicom and China Telecom together hosting some four million subscribers by the middle of the 1990s.

Despite China Telecom's lead and other advantages, the MPT took steps to limit China Unicom's progress. The fledgling company's customers, for example, had a difficult time connecting their calls to subscribers of the rival carrier's services. China Telecom was also allowed to keep a monopoly on lucrative international services.

To combat the MPT's tactics, China Unicom sought to use a gray area in telecommunications regulations to invite in foreign capital and technical expertise for support. It did so by constructing arm's-length joint ventures that came to be known as "Chinese-Chinese-Foreign," or "CCF," agreements. The first *C* in the scheme was China Unicom, and the second was another Chinese company that had shareholding interests in China Unicom—typically electronic or power company-related entities. These two Chinese companies would form an enterprise that would then establish a joint venture with a foreign telecommunications company, such as France Telecom or Bell Canada. Since the foreign company was not partnering directly with China Unicom, nor was it operating telecommunications services itself, this seemed to be permissible under the PRC's rules on limiting foreign involvement in telecommunications. From 1995 to 1998, China Unicom set up more than forty CCF ventures with companies that invested nearly US$1.5 billion (*South China Morning Post* 2000a). These funds were a valuable tool to sustain China Unicom in its competition with China Telecom.

Despite the influx of funds, China Unicom continued struggling to gain market share, and by 1998 the company held only a 6 percent market share of China's 25.3 million mobile phone users. That year, the MPT and the Ministry of Electronics Industry were combined to form a new Ministry of Information Industry (MII), with former MPT minister Wu Jichuan at the helm. The combination essentially ended the interministerial rivalry, though it did not halt the competition between China Unicom and China Telecom for mobile phone customers. While the MII did end its discrimination against China Unicom, since it was now essentially under the ministry's purview, the leadership of the two companies continued to vie for subscribers, often using price competition as incentives. By the year 2000, when the mobile services of China Telecom were split to form the company China Mobile, China Unicom had a 15 percent market share of some ninety-five million subscribers. Throughout most of the next decade, China Unicom held about a third of the mobile phone market, with China Mobile taking the rest.

Under the new MII regulatory leadership, the government took steps to end the CCF agreements. The MII had opposed the agreements initially. As China Unicom planned an overseas stock listing to raise capital, breaking ties with the foreign companies would clarify the company's financial obligations. When the foreign CCF partner companies were notified of contract cancellations, many were displeased but eventually reached settlements with China Unicom. The June 2000 initial public offering was a success and raised US$4.91 billion for China Unicom (*South China Morning Post* 2000b).

Despite the loss of foreign support and technology, China Unicom used the new capital to expand its network and capitalize, along with China Mobile, on a tidal wave of Chinese demand for mobile phones. New technologies had led to a rapid fall in the costs of mobile handsets and transmission equipment. With China's strong economy, consumers enjoyed growing incomes, and the proliferation of new businesses, along with greater worker mobility, increased the need for mobile communications. In 2007, the total mobile market in China numbered nearly 550 million, with China Unicom taking 31 percent and China Mobile the remainder. As of June 2010, the total subscriber number stood at 785 million mobile phones, ranking China first in the world.

Telecommunications Trends in the New Millennium

In addition to the spread of communications manufacturing and the proliferation of mobile phones in the PRC, new technologies and services contributed to other consumer benefits in the telecommunications arena. Voice over Internet protocol (VoIP), which allowed consumers to slash costs on long-distance calls by using data links (i.e, Internet connections), was put into full service in China in 1999. Customers typically bought prepaid cards to access the network, and China Unicom, China Telecom, and the Internet company Jitong were the first to offer the service. As with mobile phone competition, the companies slashed prices to attract customers, with a new competitor, China Netcom, cutting rates in half in 2001. The other companies moved to match these rates, and discounts as high as 65 percent off the official long-distance rate persisted through 2010.

Another new technology that essentially provided mobile phone services at local phone rates appeared in the late 1990s. Xiaolingtong mobile phones were typically limited to roaming in local municipalities, and connection quality was lower than that of fixed-line service, but unlike traditional mobile phone service, customers could receive calls without any charges. The fixed-line phone companies, China Telecom and later China Netcom, were the main suppliers of this service, as they lacked government licenses to offer full nationwide mobile phone service. By 2005, there were more than seventy million customers for Xiaolingtong (*Xinhua Financial News Network* 2005). This number, however, accounted for only about a fifth of the total 350 million traditional mobile phone users, and Xiaolingtong's growth slowed and its numbers eventually declined as customers began to abandon local phone service in the latter part of the decade. With a reorganization of China's phone companies that provided more mobile phone licenses in 2009, the government ordered phone companies to end the service within a year.

The number of major telecommunications companies, as well as their purposes, changed throughout the first decade of the new millennium. First, in 2002, the fixed-line phone provider China Telecom split in two, with a new company, China Netcom, taking control of the network in ten northern provinces, and China Telecom retaining control of twenty-one southern and northwestern provinces. Despite the division, the companies began to compete for customers in each other's areas of control. Another major shift came in early 2009, when China Unicom took over the assets of China Netcom, and China Telecom received a license to offer mobile phone service. With this change, the PRC had three major telecommunications providers: China Unicom, China Telecom, and China Mobile, all with the ability to offer mobile phone services.

These three mobile phone companies took advantage of yet another new technology, the "third generation," or "3G," system for more rapid transmission of data through mobile phones. China was somewhat slow to choose a standard transmission mode for its 3G network, as it wanted to resist paying royalties to foreign companies for using their technologies. In the late 1990s, Chinese technology companies had begun work on their own standard, known as Time Division Synchronous Code Division Multiple Access (TD-SCDMA) The goal was to use this format rather than the more globally adopted Wideband Code Division Multiple Access (W-CDMA) or CDMA-2000 standards. The country continued to resist committing to the foreign technology even as it became apparent that its own standard was less reliable and efficient than the foreign variants. Despite fears that the government would force its telecommunications companies to adopt the indigenous technology, which was first given approval in 2006, political leaders allowed the other two foreign standards to be deployed in the following year. Chinese "netizens" were then quick to adapt to the new method of data access, with 24 percent using a mobile device for access in 2007, a figure that rose to some 75 percent by the end of 2012 (CNNIC 2013).

Rural Telecommunications

Most of the Chinese government's attention in the early years of economic reform focused on the nation's coastal and urban areas. In the mid-1990s, as telephone services became more common in the urban areas, political leaders turned their attention to the rural inland parts of the nation. Regions that had only rudimentary communication tools became targets for connection to the national network. Early goals included making sure each of China's several hundred thousand villages had at least one telephone.

The new policy had some success early on, as 60 percent of villages had one or more phones by 1998 (*South China Morning Post* 1998). To further facilitate the spread of the network, the government reduced the fee for connecting a new phone line. In 1999, the cost fell from 2,000 yuan (US$240) to between 500 and 1,500 yuan (US$60 to US$180), and was totally eliminated in 2001 (*Xinhua Economic News Service* 2001). By early 2003, about 85 percent of villages had telephones (*Financial Times Information* 2003). The goal of connecting all villages was essentially achieved three years later, with a connection rate of about 99 percent. Some villages remained unconnected, however, as their remoteness in mountain or desert regions complicated the connection process. These areas had to depend on more expensive satellite links.

Mobile phones also began to penetrate rural regions, though they lagged the rapid growth of the coastal and urban areas. By 2005, overall penetration rates for mobile phones had reached 50–100 per 100 people, but the rate was only about 15–25 per 100 rural residents. As prices for mobile handsets began to fall, reaching 400 yuan (about US$50) or less in 2006, the technology became more accessible to those with lower incomes. Saturation in the urban mobile phone market began to make rural inland markets a new frontier for the national mobile phone companies, and the rural share of mobile subscribers stood to rise in the second decade of the new millennium.

China's telecommunications growth from the 1980s to 2010 was one of the fastest in global history. Government policy makers played a vital role in formulating policies and orchestrating mainly state-owned corporations to lead the effort. After some three decades, the PRC had created an enormous network of connected citizens, as well as the capability to be a world-class competitor for building network infrastructure. China continued, and will likely continue in the future, to adopt and utilize the world's most advanced technologies and to deploy them to reinforce the nation's overall economic development.

Eric HARWIT
University of Hawaii at Manoa

See also Digital Divide; Internet and Economic Development; Internet Service Providers; Text Messaging

Further Reading

BDAssociates, Ltd. (1996, April). *China Telecom update*. Hong Kong.

China Internet Network Information Center (CNNIC). (2013, January). Statistical report on Internet development in China. Retrieved April, 15, 2013, from http://www1.cnnic.cn/IDR/ReportDownloads/201302/P020130312536825920279.pdf

Fan Xing. (1996). *China telecommunications: Constituencies and challenges*. Cambridge, MA: Program on Information Resources Policy, Center for Information Policy, Harvard University.

Financial Times Information, February 13, 2003 report.

Harwit, Eric. (2008). *China's telecommunications revolution*. London: Oxford University Press.

Huawei Technologies. (2014). Homepage. Retrieved April 21, 2014, from http://www.huawei.com/en/

Lu Ding, & Wong Chee Kong. (2003). *China's telecommunications market: Entering a competitive age*. Cheltenham, UK: Edward Elgar.

Lynch, Daniel C. (1999). After the propaganda state: Media, politics, and "thought work" in reformed China. Stanford, CA: Stanford University Press.

Mueller, Milton, & Tan, Zixiang. (1997). *China in the information age*. Westport, CT: Praeger Publishers.

Qiang, Christine Zhen-Wei. (2007). China's information revolution: Managing the economic and social transformation. Washington, DC: World Bank Publications.

Shen Xiaobai. (1999). *The Chinese road to high technology*. New York: St. Martin's Press.

South China Morning Post (1998, June 11), Business Review, p. 1.

South China Morning Post (2000a, January 11). Business Post, p. 1.

South China Morning Post (2000b, June 17). Business Post, p. 1.

Statistical Yearbook of China, 1981 (English ed.). (1982). Hong Kong: Economic Information & Agency.

Ure, John (Ed.). (2008). *Telecommunications development in Asia*. Hong Kong: Hong Kong University Press.

USITO China IT Issue Report, 1. (1997, July).

Wang Shu-hwai. (1977). China's modernization in communications. In Hou Chi-ming & Yu Tzong-shian (Eds.), *Modern Chinese economic history*. Taipei, Taiwan: Institute of Economics, Academia Sinica.

Wu, Irene. (2008). From iron fist to invisible hand: The uneven path of telecommunications reform in China. Stanford, CA: Stanford University Press.

Xinhua Financial News Network. (2005). July 12, 2005 report.

Xinhua Economic News Service. (2001, July 6).

Yan Xu, & Pitt, Douglas. (2002). *Chinese telecommunications policy*. Boston: Artech House.

Youdian shi bianjishi [Office of compilation of the history of posts and telecommunications]. (1984). *Zhongguo jindai youdian shi* [Modern history of China's posts and telecommunications]. Beijing: Renmin youdian chubanshe.

Yu, Frederick T. C. (1963). Communications and politics in Communist China. In Lucian Pye (Ed.), *Communications and political development*. Princeton, NJ: Princeton University Press.

Zhang Duanquan. (1989). Development and modernization of telecommunications in new China. *China Telecommunications Construction 1*(4), 4–14.

Zhongguo jiaotong nianjian [China communications yearbook]. (Various years). Beijing: Zhongguo jiaotong nianjian she.

Zhongguo tongji nianjian [China statistical yearbook]. (Various years). Beijing: Zhongguo tongji chubanshe.

User-Generated Content

Yònghùshēng chéng nèiróng 用戶生成內容

Summary: User-generated content (UGC) is expected to have positive economic, political, and cultural impacts by creating more active and participatory (online) societies. To serve the increasing demand by Chinese Internet users for consuming, producing, and sharing content, various global and Chinese domestic online platforms have been developed. Some political and economic factors still constrain UGC's full potential in diversifying voices, encouraging civic engagement, and increasing market competition.

User-generated content (UGC), or user-created content (UCC), contributed by Chinese-language users has not only contributed to "the rise of a transnational Chinese cultural sphere" (Yang 2003) but has also influenced online activities and purchasing decisions of Internet users in mainland China (Netpop Research 2007). During the first half of 2010, the content produced by amateur Chinese Internet users surpassed that produced by professional websites, according to a statistical report by the Data Center of China Internet (Qiang 2010). Three years later, around 66.1 percent of Internet users used blogs or personal spaces, 54.7 percent used microblogging (a Twitter-like service), and 48.8 percent used social networking websites (CNNIC 2013). One US market report found that 47 percent of Chinese broadband users contributed to some form of UGC, including online review sites, online forums, and blogs, and that UGC influenced 58 percent of purchase decisions in China—much higher numbers than their counterparts in the United States (Netpop Research 2007). While both global and Chinese websites, commercial or otherwise, aim to maximize the full potential of UGC contributed by Chinese Internet users, several challenges regarding content regulation, copyright agreement, and fair market competition remain.

Definition and Potential Benefits

Driven by the growth of broadband usage in households, ICT-skilled young users, and lower costs of content creation, UGC has attracted attention from global and Chinese policy makers and market players (OECD 2007). The Organisation for Economic Co-operation and Development (OECD) describes UGC as one of the main features of the "participative web," where users rate, collaborate, create, and distribute Internet content, and sometimes also build customized applications. The OECD also proposes three central characteristics to define UGC: it is published online in certain public or social contexts, made with some level of creative effort, and produced "outside of professional routines and practices" (OECD 2007, 8). The OECD's definition thus distinguishes UGC from content created by professional and established institutions and commercial markets, and also from daily messaging practices such as instant messages and email.

An empirical research based on a sample of Hong Kong student users suggested that online content generation enhances psychological empowerment (Leung 2009). Practices of user-generated content were also believed to have the potentials in improving civic engagement and participation in the public sphere (Benkler 2006; Shirky 2010). In addition to these psychological and civic benefits, according to a United Nations Educational, Scientific and Cultural Organization (UNESCO) world report on cultural diversity and intercultural dialogue, user-friendly software, and user-created content can "empower individuals and groups that were previously marginalized" by helping them to find a voice (UNESCO 2009, 150). It also has the potential for "diversifying voices, thereby creating new opportunities for interactive exchanges among participants from different cultural backgrounds" (UNESCO 2009, 137). Several benefits of UGC become visible across Chinese societies, including mainland China.

Commercial Cases

Several Chinese online commercial successes depend on UGC. As part of what has been described as the "domestication of the Chinese Internet" (Yang 2012), these Chinese commercial cases are subject to Beijing's censorship inside mainland China while other competitors outside mainland China, commercial or not, are often blocked, as exemplified by the Baidu vs. Google competition in search and Baidu Baike vs. Chinese Wikipedia in user-generated encyclopedias (Liao 2014).

For example, microblogging services such as Sina Weibo and Tencent Weibo have contributed to the growth of online advertising markets (CNNIC 2013; iResearch 2013). The OECD report also notices the popularity of UGC video-sharing platforms in China, with examples including Tudou.com and Qyule.com (OECD 2007). China also has many online review websites that depend on reviews contributed by local users, including DianPing, a major online review website comparable to Yelp (but established earlier) (McKenzie 2012). These UGC platforms are often provided by major Internet companies in order to increase their web traffic and to secure online advertising revenue. Several other popular UGC websites in Hong Kong and Taiwan include major photo sharing / blog websites (e.g., wretch.cc, pixnet.net, xuite.net), restaurant review websites (e.g., openrice.com), and game and gadget review websites (e.g., mobile01.com, gamer.com.tw), which have constantly been among the top websites for the respective regions according to Alexa.com.

The growth of UGC in mainland China has also helped create the public opinion monitoring sector (*yúqíng jiāncè fúwù shìchǎng* 舆情监测服务市场). Managers (mostly from public sectors) buy up-to-date information services on the latest online public opinion in mainland China, which relies heavily on processing and mining UGC from microblogs, personal spaces, and online forums. The most successful case of the Public Opinion Monitoring and Measuring Unit of the People's Daily Online 人民网舆情监测室alone has an annual revenue near 200 million yuan (US$3,220,000) (Luo and Li 2010; Tan 2012).

As will be discussed in the section below, the for-profit user-generated knowledge website Hudong.com has been monetizing its own Chinese Wikipedia (that attracts major investment from the United States), distinguishing itself from the global nonprofit Wikipedia project (Englehardt 2009; Fannin 2011). Nonetheless, its competitor Baidu Baike, also a UGC encyclopedia website that is hosted by the top search engine company Baidu.com in mainland China, presents a major threat to Hudong's viability. Hudong reported to the Chinese authorities for an anti-monopoly investigation to Baidu on the ground that Baidu alters its search result pages in such a way users are unable to find Hudong's website (Faure and Zhang 2013; Yang 2011). Research on search engine results showed that Baidu's results consistently favoured its own UGC websites, much more so than other search engines such as Google and Yahoo, raising concerns on the issue of fair market competition (Liao 2013). The same study also shows that in addition to major user-generated encyclopedias such as Baidu Baike, Hudong Baike, and Chinese Wikipedia, specialized user-generated content, for example MBAlib.com focusing on business management, has a higher online visibility.

Nonprofit Cases

Some Chinese online nonprofit successes that depend on the UGC model include Yeeyan and various Chinese versions of Wikipedia. Yeeyan started as a group of volunteer translators who collectively translated news articles from English to Chinese. They attracted attention from English news sources and Chinese authorities, due to the implications of fostering a more participatory culture (Zhang and Mao 2013). The leader of Associated Press' Overview Project, Jonathan Stray, believes that Yeeyan is a pioneer in tackling the major global problem of "the ghettoization of information by language" with cost-effective solutions (Stray 2010). Yeeyan has been discussed as one of the major innovative "crowdsourcing websites" in China that face various revenue and copyright issues (Chen and Liu 2011; Yang 2010). Yeeyan successfully translated earthquake-related manuals when China was hit by the 2008 Sichuan earthquake (Ning 2008). With over 120,000 registered users, Yeeyan also built formal collaboration efforts with foreign media such as the *Guardian*, but was eventually blocked and shut down by Chinese authorities for a few months (Chen and Liu 2011; China closes Yeeyan 2009; Yang 2010). *Global Times*, an English-language Chinese tabloid newspaper under the *People's Daily*, reported that while Yeeyan's cofounder Zhao Jiamin did not know which article triggered the shutdown, "Yeeyan still isn't allowed to publish political content". In the report, Zhao admitted that Yeeyan had keyword filters like any other mainland Chinese websites and relied on users' judgment not to cross the government's red line (Xuyang 2012).

UGC and Online Encyclopedias

All three major Chinese-language online encyclopedias—Chinese Wikipedia, Baidu Baike, and Hudong—have adopted the user-generated model for content creation. This model was first popularized by Wikipedia, a system where "anyone can edit." As the term *wiki* refers to a general web technology that supports collaborative authoring, any online encyclopedia that uses wiki-like technologies may claim to be a "*wéijī bǎikē*" 维基百科, literally meaning "Wiki encyclopedia." Thus, although the Chinese term and concept of *weiji baike* has dominated Chinese online encyclopedias with its user-generated model, it does not always refer to the Chinese Wikipedia or the Chinese version of Wikipedia.

Global Wikipedia Movement and Chinese Wikipedia

Wikipedia, a global encyclopedia project hosted and operated by the nonprofit Wikimedia Foundation, is often cited as the most successful case of user-generated content websites that harness voluntary user contribution online (Benkler 2006; Lih 2009). The participation of Chinese users from around the world has produced several language versions of Wikipedia, including Chinese (zh, for *Zhōngwén* 中文), Classical Literary Chinese (zh-classical), Cantonese (yue), Wuu (wuu), Min Nan (zh-min-nan), Hakka (hak), Gan (gan), and Min Dong (cdo). Based on the quantity of content and registered editors, the (Mandarin) Chinese version has been the biggest among them. The growth in Cantonese and Wuu (which includes the Shanghainese dialect) versions has benefited from increasing digital linguistic support and user base (Nigh and Liao 2011).

Competition and Censorship

Along with other versions of Wikipedia, Chinese Wikipedia faced censorship in mainland China as early as 2004, and then suffered constant blocks from October 2005 to July 2008, during which the Chinese Internet penetration rate experienced an unprecedented rapid growth from 8.52 percent to 22.6 percent overall, and from around 27 percent to 60 percent for cities such as Beijing and Shanghai (Liao 2013). The blocks by China also have negative impacts on user participation outside mainland China (Zhang and Zhu 2011). In terms of the number of articles and registered users, both Baidu Baike and Hudong had grown quickly to overtake Chinese Wikipedia, including copying content from Chinese Wikipedia while exercising censorship (Farrar 2009; Nystedt 2007; Woo 2007). Nonetheless, Chinese Wikipedia is ranked by *China Internet Weekly* (2009) as the close third after Baidu and Hudong on its influence and user experience in mainland China. Founded in 2005, Hudong is called by some "China's Wikipedia" (Zhao and Song 2012). Although the Chinese term for Wikipedia, *weiji baike*, was first decided by a vote casted among thirteen contributors of the Chinese Wikipedia community in 2003 (zhWP 2008b), it was registered by Hudong in 2007 as its trademark and later donated to the Wikimedia Foundation in 2009 (Hudong.com 2009).

Founded in 2006, Baidu relies on salaried reviewers to filter user contributions, and Baidu Baike does not filter marketing, self-promotion, and copyright infringement content as aggressively as Chinese Wikipedia (Liao 2013).

Some argue that the blocks of Chinese Wikipedia in mainland China indicate a clear favoritism by Chinese authorities toward censored efforts made by Baidu Baike and Hudong (Farrar 2009a; Woo 2007), whereas some argue that Baidu Baike is more compatible with Chinese society because its business model and user reward incentives work better than the charity-operated and volunteer-minded Wikipedia (Suo 2007). Based on user testimony and webometrics data (i.e., data collected through the study of the quantitative aspects of the construction and usage of the Internet), some research confirms the quantity versus quality contrast that has been described as the main difference between Baidu Baike and Chinese Wikipedia (Liao 2013).

Geographical, Linguistic, and Political Aspects

As Chinese Wikipedia is hosted outside mainland China and accommodates traditional Chinese content, it has continued contribution from Chinese-speaking regions outside mainland China, including Hong Kong, Macao, and Taiwan (Liao 2013). Baidu Baike and Hudong claim to provide better "Chinese" "homegrown" technologies and services (Webster 2008), which may account for the fact that they are less bothered by government censorship. Nonetheless, various reports and research on the geographic and linguistic profiles of the editors, readers, and online citations have indicated that Chinese Wikipedia is also dominated by Chinese-language users, content, and sources, including those from Hong Kong, Macao, and Taiwan, outside mainland China's filtering and censorship regime (Graham 2010; Liao 2008, 2014; Zhao and Song 2012; zhWP 2008b).

The tensions in Chinese Wikipedia are sometimes intensified because of the cultural and political differences among users from different regions and/or with different political viewpoints. This was exemplified in a series of recall elections on whether a mainland user had abused his administrator power on specific articles, which upset some users, especially from Hong Kong (Mingpao 2010a, 2010b, 2010c).

Financial Viability

Both Hudong and Baidu aim for online advertising revenue from Chinese market (Zhao and Song 2012), whereas Chinese Wikipedia, without online advertisement, depends on the global fund-raising of the nonprofit Wikimedia movement.

As one of the several platforms and services provided by Baidu, whose central business is online search, Baidu Baike depends on the financial viability of Baidu as a whole. Similarly, as part of the movement, Chinese Wikipedia's financial viability depends on that of the Wikimedia Foundation. As the host of Chinese Wikipedia, the foundation has been hiring more staff and supporting local chapters with their annual fund-raising events.

It is difficult to judge, without specific and publicly available data, whether the nonprofit model of Chinese Wikipedia is more viable than the advertisement model of Baidu Baike and Hudong. Either way, both models need users to contribute content and traffic to stay relevant. Like other user-generated content websites, the success of the online encyclopedias depends on whether they can recruit and retain new contributors from the pool of growing Chinese-language Internet users while attracting enough visitors' traffic.

It remains to be seen whether Baidu or Hudong will provide space for languages other than Mandarin Chinese. Before that happens, Wikipedia's southern Chinese language versions, such as Cantonese and Wuu, are expected to grow without competition. For Mandarin Chinese, Baidu Baike's dominance and popularity is likely to persist if Baidu continues to dominate the search engine market in mainland China. On the other hand, Chinese Wikipedia's popularity in Hong Kong, Taiwan, and other Chinese-speaking regions is probably secured partly because Baidu has not yet entered these markets or prepared to offer formal traditional Chinese support. Hence, the competition among these online encyclopedias represents not only different models for running a Chinese-language user-generated website, but also different notion of "Chineseness" regarding its users and content.

Future Developments

Some of the UGC potential for "diversifying voices, thereby creating new opportunities for interactive exchanges among participants from different cultural backgrounds"(UNESCO 2009, 137) is realized in China; the records of China's blocking of Chinese Wikipedia, Yeeyan, and other user-generated websites (particularly those hosted outside mainland China), however, reflect the Chinese authorities' political and cultural concerns about UGC (Liao 2014). While certain nonprofit UGC cases show some promise in enhancing civic engagement in Chinese societies, their impact on political participation remains uncertain (Liao 2014; Zhang and Mao 2013).

As UGC presents several "opportunities and challenges for users, business and policy" (OECD 2007, 40), the practices across Chinese societies, especially in mainland China with its growing number of Internet users and intensity of use, are expected to be the focus of attention of domestic and global players in both public and private sectors. For example, while extensive political filtering and censorship activities continue, it remains to be seen whether and how the "UGC Principle and Fingerprinting Filtering," first proposed and implemented by mostly US-based corporations to stop the so-called copyright-infringing "user-uploaded content" will evolve and interact with the Chinese regulations (Song 2011). Also, as the volume of Chinese UGC and related data amount to the so-called big data development, it is expected that collecting, analyzing, and interpreting UGC will continue to be an essential and major component of the growing advertising and "online public opinion monitoring" industry in mainland China, raising issues about representation, manipulation, and commercialization of Chinese web data (Liao, et al. 2013). Since the legitimacy of online public opinion is acknowledged, at least on the surface by the official 2010 white paper on "The Internet in China," the growing power of Internet is thus responded by "the strategic importance the growing penetration of political and commercial interests into the civic cyber sphere" (Yang 2009), of which user-generated content and platforms are central. Whether and how UGC's potential in diversifying voices, encouraging civic engagement, and increasing market competition reflects the overall political economic and cultural development of the Chinese Internet remains to be seen.

Han-Teng LIAO
University of Oxford, Oxford Internet Institute

See also Blogging; Chinese Language and Computing; Communities Online; Internet Monitoring; Microblogging

Further Reading

Benkler, Yochai. (2006). *The wealth of networks: How social production transforms markets and freedom*. New Haven, CT: Yale University Press. Retrieved April 25, 2014, from http://www.congo-education.net/wealth-of-networks/

Chen Zhongxiao, & Liu Xingnan. (2011, November 24). 众包翻译在中国 [Crowdsourcing translation in China]. *Southern Weekend*. Retrieved April 25, 2014, from http://tech.qq.com/a/20111125/000316.htm

China closes Yeeyan website that translated Guardian stories. (2009, December 3). *Guardian*. Retrieved April 26, 2014, from http://www.guardian.co.uk/world/2009/dec/03/yeeyan-china-guardian-media-mandarin

China Internet Network Information Center (CNNIC). (January 2013). Statistical report on Internet development in China. Retrieved April, 28, 2014, from http://www1.cnnic.cn/IDR/ReportDownloads/201302/P020130312536825920279.pdf

China Internet Week. (2009). 百科全书类网站综合排行榜TOP10—本土创新之路[Top 10 Online Encyclopedia Websites—The path for Indigenous Innovation]. *China Internet Week, Big Country Style of National Brands* (18), 76.

Englehardt, Lucas. (2009, November 24). How Hudong thumped Wikipedia in China. The Next Web. Retrieved April 25, 2014, from http://thenextweb.com/asia/2009/11/24/hudong-thumped-wikipedia-china/

Fang Qianqian. (2006). 文泉驿: 先驱 之旅 [Journey of a pioneer]. *Software World, 19*, 72–74.

Fannin, Rebecca. (2011, August 23). Why Draper funded China's Wikipedia. Retrieved April 25, 2014, from http://www.forbes.com/sites/rebeccafannin/2011/08/23/why-draper-funded-chinas-wikipedia/

Farrar, L. (2009, October 15). It's tricky for wikis and online encyclopedias in China. *CNN.com/technology*. Retrieved 25 October 2009, from http://edition.cnn.com/2009/TECH/10/14/wiki.china/

Faure, M., & Zhang, X. (2013). *The Chinese Anti-Monopoly Law*. Cheltenham, UK: Edward Elgar Publishing.

Fu, K.; Chan, C.; & Chau, M. (2013). Assessing censorship on microblogs in China: Discriminatory keyword analysis and impact evaluation of the "real name registration" policy. *IEEE Internet Computing, 17*(3), 42–50.

Graham, M. (2010, May 30). The Geographies of Wikipedia in China. *floatingsheep*. Retrieved 26 October 2010, from http://www.floatingsheep.org/2010/05/geographies-of-wikipedia-in-china.html

iResearch. (2013). Sina's Weibo new advertising model marks monetization of the long-tail marketing strategy (press release). iResearch Consulting Group. Retrieved April 26, 2014, from http://www.iresearchchina.com/views/4809.html

King, Gary; Pan, Jennifer; & Roberts, Molly. (2012). How censorship in China allows government criticism but silences collective expression (paper, American Political Science Association Annual Meeting). Retrieved April 26, 2014, from http://papers.ssrn.com/sol3/papers.cfm?abstract_id=2104894

Leung, Louis. (2009). User-generated content on the Internet: An examination of gratifications, civic engagement and psychological empowerment. *New Media & Society, 11*(8), 1327–1347. doi:10.1177/1461444809341264

Liao, Han-Teng; Fu Kingwa; Jiang Ming; & Wang Ning. (2013, June 15). *Chinese Web Data: Definition, Uses, and Scholarship*. To be presented at the 11th Annual Chinese Internet Research Conference (CIRC 2013), Oxford, UK.

Liao, Han-Teng. (2008). A webometric comparison of Chinese Wikipedia and Baidu Baike and its implications for understanding the Chinese-speaking Internet. In *9th annual Internet Research Conference: Rethinking Community, Rethinking Place*. Copenhagen.

Liao, Han-Teng. (2009). Conflict and Consensus in the Chinese version of Wikipedia. *IEEE Technology and Society Magazine, 28*(2), 49–56. doi:10.1109/ MTS.2009.932799

Liao, Han-Teng. (2013). How does Chinese localization influence online visibility? A study on Chinese-language search engine result pages (SERPs). (Accepted). To be presented at the 11th Annual Chinese Internet Research Conference (CIRC 2013), Oxford, UK.

Liao, Han-Teng. (2014). The cultural politics of user-generated encyclopedias: Comparing Chinese Wikipedia and Baidu. (Doctoral dissertation). University of Oxford, Oxford, UK.

Lih, A. (2009). The Wikipedia Revolution: How a Bunch of Nobodies Created the World's Greatest Encyclopedia. Hyperion.

Luo Ting, & Li Cheng. (2010). How to develop public opinion monitoring products? The modes of operation of the Public Opinion Monitoring Unit, People's Net [如何开发舆情监测产品?—人民网舆情监测室的运作模式]. *Chinese Journalist*, 6. doi:10.3969/ j.issn.1003-1146.2010.06.028

MacKinnon, Rebecca. (2008). Flatter world and thicker walls? Blogs, censorship and civic discourse in China. *Public Choice, 134*(1), 31–46. doi:10.1007/s11127-007-9199-0

MacKinnon, Rebecca. (2009). China's censorship 2.0: How companies censor bloggers. *First Monday, 14*(2). Retrieved April 26, 2014, from http://firstmonday.org/htbin/cgiwrap/bin/ojs/index.php/fm/article/view/2378/2089

McKenzie, H. (2012, August 6). Why China's Yelp is more than just online reviews. PandoDaily. Retrieved May 13, 2013, from http://pandodaily.com/2012/08/ 06/why-chinas-yelp-is-more-than-just-online-reviews/

Mingpao 明報. (2010a, April 22). 工程師寫上癮變全職維基人[Addicted to writing Chinese Wikipedia, An enginneer become fulltime Wikipedian]. Retrieved from http://dailynews. sina.com/bg/chn/chnpolitics/mingpao/20100422/15521377592.html

Mingpao 明報. (2010b, April 23). 维基用户罢免争议管理员失败政治审查过滤「六四」「席扬」 [Chinese Wikipedia's Administrator Recall Election failed. Disputes over political censorship over 'June Fourth' and 'Xi Yang' articles]. Retrieved from http://life.mingpao.com/cfm/dailynews3b.cfm? File=20100423/nalgh/gha1h.txt

Mingpao 明報. (2010c, April 25). 遭罷免維基管理員：我非五毛 編輯方針不變[Narrowly escaped from recall election, Shizhao: I am not '50 Cent Party', editorial policies unchanged]. Retrieved from http://life.mingpao.com/cfm/dailynews3b.cfm? File=20100425/nalgh/ghc1.txt

Netpop Research. (2007). Chinese surpass Americans in web 2.0 use. Retrieved April 26, 2014, from http://www.marketingcharts.com/wp/ interactive/chinese-surpass-americans-in-web-20-use-2257/

Nigh, A., & Liao, Han-Teng. (2011). Linguistic networked readiness index for selected languages in China (paper, 9th Chinese Internet Research Conference [CIRC 2011]), Washington, DC: Institute for the Study of Diplomacy, Georgetown University.

Ning, X. X. (2008). 译言：传播和分享集体的智慧[Yeeyan: The dissemination and sharing of collective wisdom]. *Programmer, 10*, 36–37.

Nystedt, D. (2007, August 6). Baidu May Be Worst Wikipedia Copyright Violator. *IDG News Service*. Retrieved from http://www.pcworld.com/ article/id,135550-page,1/article.html

Organisation for Economic Co-operation and Development (OECD). (2007). *Participative web and user-created content: Web 2.0, wikis and social networking*. Paris: OECD. Retrieved April 26, 2014, from http://www.oecd-ilibrary.org/content/book/9789264037472-en

Qiang, Xiaoji. (2010, July 23). User-generated content online now 50.7% of total. *China Daily*. Retrieved April 26, 2014, from http://www.chinadaily.com.cn/business/2010-07/23/content_11042851.htm

Shirky, C. (2010). Cognitive surplus: Creativity and generosity in a connected age. New York: Penguin.

Song, S. H. (2011). New Challenges of Chinese Copyright Law in the Digital Age: A Comparative Copyright Analysis of Isp Liability, Fair Use and Sports Telecasts. Netherlands: Kluwer Law International.

Stray, J. (2010, June 25). The Wikipedia of news translation: Yeeyan.org's volunteer community. Nieman Journalism Lab. Retrieved April 26, 2014, from http://www.niemanlab.org/2010/06/the-wikipedia-of-news-translation-yeeyan-orgs-volunteer-community/

Suo, H. (2007, November 7). 中国维基网站发展原因之初探[The development of Wiki sites in China: An exploratory study]. *Academic.mediachina.net*. Retrieved 21 December 2009, from http://academic.mediachina.net/article.php?id=5476

Tan, Y. F. (2012, January 29). 探照网络舆情监测[Online public opinion monitoring: an exploratory report]. 财经*CAIJING Magazine*, 312. Retrieved April 26, 2014, from http://magazine.caijing.com.cn/2012-01-29/111641737.html

United Nations Educational, Scientific and Cultural Organization (UNESCO). (2009). *UNESCO world report 2: Investing in cultural diversity and intercultural dialogue*. UNESCO.

Woo, E. (2007, November 13). Baidu's Censored Answer to Wikipedia. *BusinessWeek*. Retrieved from http://www.businessweek.com/globalbiz/content/nov2007/gb20071113_725400.htm

Xuyang, J. (2012, November 11). Gained in translation. *Global Times*. Beijing, China. Retrieved from http://www.globaltimes.cn/content/743599.shtml

Yang, Guobin. (2003). The Internet and the rise of a transnational Chinese cultural sphere. *Media, Culture & Society*, *25*(4), 469–490.

Yang, G. (2009). The Power of the Internet in China: Citizen Activism Online. New York: Columbia University Press.

Yang, Guobin. (2012). A Chinese Internet? History, practice, and globalization. *Chinese Journal of Communication*, 5(1), 49–54. doi:10.1080/17544750.2011.647744

Yang, X. (2010). 译言 离开39 天[Yeeyan: 39 days when gone]. 南方人物周刊[*Southern People Weekly*], *4*, 68–69.

Yang, Y. (2011, February 25). China's "Wikipedia" submits complaint about Baidu. *Economic Observer News*, *508*, 28.

Webster, G. (2008, April 22). Baidu's William Chang: 'No reason for China to use Wikipedia'. *CNET News.com*, *Tech news blog*. Retrieved from http://news.cnet.com/8301-10784_3-9926474-7.html

Zhang, W., & Mao, C. (2013). Fan activism sustained and challenged: participatory culture in Chinese online translation communities. *Chinese Journal of Communication*, *6*(1), 45–61. doi:10.1080/17544750.2013.753499

Zhang, X. (Michael), & Zhu, F. (2011). Group Size and Incentives to Contribute: A Natural Experiment at Chinese Wikipedia. *American Economic Review*, *101*(4), 1601–1615. doi:10.1257/aer.101.4.1601

Zhu, T.; Phipps, D.; Pridgen, A.; Crandall, J. R.; & Wallach, D. S. (2013). The velocity of censorship: High-fidelity detection of microblog post deletions. *arXiv:1303.0597*. Retrieved April 26, 2014, from http://arxiv.org/abs/1303.0597

zhWP. (2008a). Wikipedia: 2005 年維基媒體國際大會[Wikipedia: Wikimania 2005 Frankfurt]. Retrieved from http://zh.wikipedia.org/w/index.php?title=Wikipedia:2005%E5%B9%B4%E7%B6%AD%E5%9F%BA%E5%AA%92%E9%AB%94%E5%9C%8B%E9%9A%9B%E5%A4%A7%E6%9C%83&variant=zh-tw

zhWP. (2008b). 中文維基百科[Chinese Wikipedia]. Retrieved from http://zh.wikipedia.org/wiki/%E4%B8%AD%E6%96%87%E7%BB%B4%E5%9F%BA%E7%99%BE%E7%A7%91

Zhao Dawei 赵大伟, & Song Xiaowei, 宋小伟. (2012, September 14). 信息烟尘里的中文路径:国内百科类网站十年小史[Chinese pathways from Data Smog: A ten year mini chronicle of encyclopedia websites] *Nanfang dushi bao* 南方都市报. Retrieved from http://gcontent.oeeee.com/6/15/615a16142503acac/Blog/747/c2bce9.html

Part 2
Governance, Law, and Politics

E-Government

Diànzǐ zhèngwù 电子政务

Summary: The original goal of e-government initiatives in China was to enhance the nation's information technology infrastructure so as to facilitate greater economic expansion. This early thrust later gave way to broader goals, including improving the transparency of governmental processes, improving the quality of governmental data for fiscal and other purposes, and facilitating citizen input to and transactions with the government, all the while maintaining firm political control.

The term *e-government* refers to a variety of efforts by governmental units (including local, county, provincial or statewide, and national) to use technology to improve governmental services such as information provision, data collection, citizen transactions, and data mining, with the goal of improving government efficiency and citizen satisfaction. E-government (alternatively, e-gov) initiatives globally have followed the widespread dissemination of information technologies, and in much of the developed world, these initiatives have been focused on improving citizen access to governmental services. By way of contrast, e-gov initiatives in China have concentrated less on citizen services and focused more on improving the quality of governmental data and decision making, while still enabling a limited amount of citizen input for governmental policies. In addition, e-government in China aims to improve the transparency of governmental processes and decisions, and to enhance government accountability to citizen populations, while still maintaining tight political control. Globally, e-governance has largely been seen to have a transformative potential for the processes of governance because of the ability to enable citizen input and attention to problems and projects. The range of available services is often categorized by a number of informal shorthand indicators of the type of services offered, such as G2G (government to government), G2C (government to citizen), G2B (government to business), and C2C (citizen to citizen).

China's government, at multiple levels, has spent considerable effort and money on developing e-government programs that would significantly enhance governmental function. In addition, China's investment in e-government counters the common view that China's government opposes the rapid spread and use of information technologies, especially the Internet.

The *United Nations E-Government Survey 2010* delineates several key aspects of e-government (UNDESA 2010). These include the delivery of governmental services online, capacity for citizen input, scrutiny of public funds, online bidding for government contracts (G2B), and e-participation (the ability of citizens to participate in governmental decision making).

China's efforts at e-governance differ somewhat from the UN definition in that the latter specifically states that e-government initiatives should be "citizen-centric," giving primary importance to the services provided to citizens. Efforts that do not have a citizen-centric focus are therefore discounted, which is why China was not listed highly on the UN's "e-government readiness index" in 2010. Because China's e-government initiatives have focused primarily on improving governance through increasing information accuracy and efficiency rather than citizen services, China ranks only seventy-second in the world by these rankings. A 2008 survey of global e-government initiatives ranked China at number sixty-seven, based on various aspects dealing with information availability, service delivery, and public access (West 2008).

Origins of China's E-Government

In the early 1990s the Chinese government embarked on an ambitious plan to not only broadly implement information technology (IT) but also to become a global leader in the industry. This initiative has included a number of separate processes, such as telecommunications reform, regulatory reform, and the complete reorganization of relevant governmental bodies.

By the late 1990s the government was focused on enhancing the IT infrastructure so as to prepare the way for greater economic expansion. For example, in 1999 the government began a large-scale Government Online project, primarily focused on creating informational websites for information dissemination. This later evolved into more ambitious and interactive forms of e-governance. In 2002 the State Council Document No. 17 was released, outlining the infrastructure for China's e-government procedures. Subsequent plans to harness the Internet for economic development emphasized a series of "golden projects" to modernize the IT infrastructure and support the IT industry.

Early e-government initiatives sought to develop the network infrastructures necessary to enhance economic integration and development. In February 2003 the Chinese government issued its first formal guidelines for e-government in a document entitled "Guidance on E-government Issued by the State Informatization Leading Group." Although this document was not the only guide on e-government practices, it summarized the key principles for e-government in China.

The guidance document stated that the nation's e-government initiatives would first and foremost be guided by political considerations, notably the ideological teachings of Deng Xiaoping theory and the Three Represents theory. The document further stated that the purpose of the Golden Projects was to "help to transform the function of government, enhance its working efficiency and supervision effectiveness, and provide better services to citizens so as to adapt to the changes brought about by reform and open-up and meet up with the newly-emerged requirements of modernization" (SCILG 2003). This document clearly indicated that the goal of the e-government initiatives was to improve government work to be more "scientific, harmonious and democratic." E-government was clearly directed toward furthering economic development, as improved efficiency would enhance economic and social stability. The document laid out several key principles for e-government in China:

- To unify and strengthen leadership.
- To be demand-oriented and focused on strengthening governmental goals and economic and social benefits.
- To integrate information and resources so as to further develop information industries.
- To establish uniform standards and ensure network security.

After the release of this document, the government identified several major tasks to be undertaken during the Tenth Five-Year Plan (2001–2005), including the introduction of a number of comprehensive "golden projects" to improve public services, develop adequate network security, standardize system functionality to ensure coordination between systems, raise the standards for governmental officials responsible for e-government, and develop a more comprehensive set of laws and regulations for e-governance. Subsequent developments of e-government in China have largely followed these principles.

In June 2010 the Information Office of the State Council announced that by the end of 2009 there were more than forty-five thousand government Internet portals, although the report does not identify all of them. The report indicates that the seventy-five central and state organs, thirty-two provincial governments (although China has only twenty-two provinces—twenty-three if Taiwan is included), 333 prefectural governments, and more than 80 percent of county-level governments had established websites.

China's "Twelve Golden Projects"

The first large-scale e-government efforts involved the ambitious "Twelve Golden Projects," which were expected to significantly increase economic and technological development. (There are actually more than twelve projects, but this moniker is traditionally used to refer to the overall set of e-government initiatives.) These have been variously identified by a number of authors, who sometimes disagree as to what should be included. These projects, however, do demonstrate an expectation that e-government initiatives would significantly enhance governmental procedures and transparency, and provide the basis for further economic development. The initial twelve projects included the following:

Core systems designed to strengthen supervision and enhance efficiency (i.e., the Administrative Resources System and the Golden Macro Project).

Projects designed to safeguard government revenue and rationalize government spending (i.e., the Golden Tax Project, the Golden Customs Project, the Golden Audit

Project, the Golden Finance Project, and the Golden Card Project).

Systems designed to ensure basic order in the national economy and social development (i.e., Golden Shield, Golden Quality, Golden Agriculture, Golden Water Conservancy, and Golden Social Security).

Another explanatory scheme set forth by Peter Lovelock and his colleagues identified several tiers of golden projects as a way to differentiate their focus (see table 1). The first tier comprises projects designed to strengthen the central government's ability to collect better data for policy-making purposes. The Golden Bridge project was designed to provide basic information about the ongoing economic activities to central and local governments for the purposes of planning and coordination, to foster the sharing of information resources in the economy, and to facilitate macro-level control, in the sense of enabling central authorities to exercise more control over local or provincial officials. The Golden Sea project, aimed at creating an information system linking top governmental leaders, provides them direct access to all institutions, organizations, and offices under the direct control of the Central Committee. Similarly, the second tier of projects focuses on harnessing IT to accelerate economic growth and reform.

The most controversial of the second-tier projects, the Golden Shield, is geared to establish Internet surveillance and content monitoring, and to allow the government to actively control the content available to Internet users. This project, which was heavily criticized in the West and by free-speech activists, deploys technologies that would allow police and other officials to monitor or redirect web traffic that might undermine the authority of the Chinese Communist Party (CCP). Western activists especially criticized Western firms that produced technology to facilitate the Golden Shield project, notably Nortel and Cisco. Outside of China, this project became informally known as the "Great Firewall of China."

Finally, the third-tier projects provided infrastructure for more specialized governmental functions, including health information, agriculture, and trade.

Table 1: Summary of Golden Project Tiers and Names

Table 1 provides an overview of the three tiers of golden projects

Tiers and Project Names	**Goals**
Tier One	**National-level data gathering and dissemination in critical areas of governance**
Golden Sea (also called Golden Macro) 金海工程 *Jīnhǎi gōngchéng*	To provide an integrated data and information system for the Central Economic and Financial Leading Group for macro control over economic activities.

Golden Bridge 金桥工程 *Jīnqiáo gōngchéng*	The first national public economic information network aimed to link government agencies with state-owned enterprises and the public.
Golden Customs 金关工程 *Jīnguān gōngchéng*	To network foreign trade and economic statistics; to shift toward online transmission of forms and documents; and to create an integrated data communications system connecting foreign trade companies, banks, and the customs and tax authorities so as to strengthen the authorities' macro-level adjustments and surveillance.
Golden Card 金卡工程 *Jīnkǎ gōngchéng*	Focused on issuance of credit cards and the creation of a unified payment clearance system. Also sought to establish a national banking exchange system to improve financial regulation.
Golden Intelligence 金智工程 *Jīnzhì gōngchéng*	To realize resource sharing, research exchange, and scientific and technological cooperation worldwide.
Golden Tax 金税工程 *Jīnshuì gōngchéng*	To enable the governing bodies to access, analyze, and supervise information about value-added tax payers and their use of value-added tax receipts, to prevent tax evasion.
Tier Two	**To harness IT to accelerate economic growth and reform.**
Golden Shield 金盾工程 *Jīndùn gōngchéng*	To integrate information technology within the public security system and the national crime databases, and to provide information support to the public security structure within five years.
Tier Three	**Sector-specific applications of e-governance**
Golden Health 金卫工程 *Jīnwèi gōngchéng*	To optimize medical care services nationwide, and to set up a national Internet- and intranet-based medical information transmission network.
Golden Agriculture 金农工程 *Jīnnóng gōngchéng*	To accelerate the informatization progress in rural areas and in the agricultural industry, and to set up a comprehensive information system to improve convenience and efficiency in agricultural management and services.
Golden Audit 金审工程	To track financial information and electronic data in financing, banking, tariff, and customs administrations; to supervise the reli-

Jīnshěn gōngchéng	ability and legitimacy of fiscal income and expenditures; to standardize management; and to disclose corruption and to fight against criminal activities.
Golden Enterprises 金企工程 *Jīnqǐ gōngchéng*	To inform the country's commodity circulation system.
Golden Tourism 金旅工程 *Jīnlǚ gōngchéng*	To inform the tourism industry and to develop e-commerce within the industry.
Golden Water Conservancy 金水工程 *Jīnshuǐ gōngchéng*	To build a database to incorporate information resources into the water conservancy system.
Golden Finance 金财工程 *Jīncái gōngchéng*	A national finance management information system aimed to enhance the rationalization and standardization of finance distribution, and to improve the efficiency in financial management and in utilization of fiscal incomes, thus realizing better management of the national revenue.
Golden Trade Project 金贸工程 *Jīnmào gōngchéng*	To promote e-commerce by establishing a regulatory framework for e-business development and an intellectual property system.

Source: Kluver (2005).

E-Government and Governmental Transparency

One aspect of China's e-government initiatives that has been markedly different from those of other nations, both developed and developing, is the emphasis on increasing governmental transparency and accountability while still maintaining firm political control. China's initiatives have often included mechanisms for citizen complaints and reporting of governmental corruption, although complaints about government abuse have not totally eliminated the problem. To this end, the central discipline inspection and supervision authorities, the Supreme People's Court, the Supreme People's Procuratorate, and other relevant bodies established informant websites on which citizens can report suspected corruption. Other sites established for this purpose include those maintained by the CCP Central Commission for Discipline Inspection and the Ministry of Supervision and by the National Bureau of Corruption Prevention (NBCP).

The battle against corruption in China is not a new one. In April 2008 the CCP Political Bureau adopted a five-year (2008–2012) anticorruption plan in which, along with punitive measures, the CCP highlighted the potential supervisory role of the Internet as a mechanism to expose corruption. In late 2007 the NBCP established a website for reporting of corruption; in its first several days of operation, overwhelming interest in the site caused it to crash.

Based on these examples, it is clear that the advent of e-governance has made China's government more accountable, if not more democratic. The Chinese government certainly believes that the e-government initiatives are creating a more responsive and transparent government.

Outlook

China's e-government initiatives have been ambitious and far-reaching, although the focus has been on two primary goals: providing information from the government to citizens, and data collection for use by the government. These initiatives have been citizen-centric only to the extent that they allow citizen complaints and facilitate some services. To date, the e-government initiatives have not been as transformative as many early e-government experts had hoped, in the sense of giving citizens a much greater sense of control in transactions and exchanges with the government. China's e-government initiatives are still largely government-centric, designed to strengthen governmental control, enhance the ability of the government to respond quickly to citizens, and to further enhance the legitimacy of the government. In that sense, the e-government initiatives have strengthened central control but in some ways have diminished the power of local governments in terms of data collection and control.

Nevertheless, these e-government initiatives have also broadened citizen expectations for governmental responsiveness, and to some extent, the golden projects have contributed to better governance by providing better information and allowing governmental bodies access to more accurate information and to public sentiment. To the extent that China's e-government programs seek to improve governance, regardless of democratic intent, they will continue to enhance the lives of Chinese citizens.

Randolph KLUVER
Texas A&M University

See also Communities Online; The Great Firewall; Internet Regulation; Social and Political Impact; Telecommunications Industry

Further Reading

Chen Yang, & Kluver, Randolph. (2006). Information society and privacy in the People's Republic of China. *Journal of E-Government*, 2(4), 83–103.

State Council Informatization Leading Group (SCILG). (2003). 国家信息化领导小组关于我国电子政务建设的指导意见 [Guidance on e-government given by the State Informatization Leading Group]. Beijing: China Internet Information Center.

Guo Liang. (2006). Under the "Golden Shine": China's efforts to bridge government and citizens. Retrieved June 10, 2010, from http://www.apdip.net/projects/e-government/capblg/casestudies/China-Guo.pdf

Holliday, Ian & Yep, Ray. (2005). E-government in China. *Public Administration and Development*, 25(3), 239–249.

Kluver, Randolph. (2005). The architecture of control: A Chinese strategy for e-governance. *Journal of Public Policy, 25*(1), 75–97.

Kluver, Randolph. (2009). Communism online: E-governance and Chinese political culture in the 16th Party Congress. *China and Sinology, 8*, 141–174.

Lau, Tuen-yu; Fung, Anthony; & Ji, Michael. (2006). E-government in China: Keeping up with the Joneses? *Journal of E-Government, 2*(4), 15–38.

Ma, Liajie; Chung, Jongpil; & Thorson, Stuart. (2005). E-government in China: Bringing economic development through administrative reform. *Government Information Quarterly, 22*(1), 20–37.

McNally, Christopher. (2006). Global capitalism vs. Leninist controls: "Informatization" and e-government in the People's Republic of China. *Journal of E-Government, 2*(4), 3–15.

United Nations Department of Economic and Social Affairs (UNDESA). (2010). *United Nations e-government survey 2010: Leveraging e-government at a time of financial and economic crisis*. Retrieved June 21, 2010, from http://unpan1.un.org/intradoc/groups/public/documents/un/unpan038851.pdf

West, D. M. (2008). Improving technology utilization in electronic government around the world, 2008. Washington, DC: Brookings Institution. Retrieved May 22, 2014, from http://www.brookings.edu/~/media/research/files/reports/2008/8/17%20egovernment%20west/0817_egovernment_west.pdf

Zhang, Junhua. (2002). Will the government serve the people? The development of China's e-government. *New Media & Society, 4*(2), 163–184.

Zhang, Junhua. (2006). Good governance through e-governance? Assessing China's e-government strategy. *Journal of E-Government, 2*(4), 39–72.

Zhou, Xiang. (2004). E-government in China: A content analysis of national and provincial web sites. *Journal of Computer Mediated Communication, 9*(4), 4–19.

The Great Firewall

Fánghuŏqiáng 防火墙

Summary: In its embrace of the Internet era, the Chinese government has developed what is generally believed to be the world's most sophisticated online surveillance mechanism: the "Great Firewall of China." A variety of content is targeted for filtering, but the primary candidates are sites connected with the "Three Ts"—Tiananmen Square, Tibet, and Taiwan. The censoring has led to never-ending efforts to bypass the official mechanisms of information censoring by various technical means. Much to the authorities' consternation, the Chinese language is also uniquely suited to creating rich wordplays in order to disseminate subversive ideas.

China is reputed to have developed and deployed the world's largest and most sophisticated online surveillance system in the Internet age. The crown of this information censorship system is the "Great Firewall of China," the nickname of China's information filtering system, officially known as the National Public Network Surveillance System. The Firewall is often pejoratively referred to as GFW by Chinese "netizens" in popular forums and online discussions. "To GFW" has also become a verb to symbolize official actions of blocking certain online content. A common phrase among online threads on China's Internet, for example, is "the message was GFWed," meaning it was blocked by the official surveillance system. Interestingly, searches using "Great Firewall" on Baidu.com, China's most popular search engine, are "partially filtered in accordance with relevant [Chinese] laws, statutes and policies," the results show.

The National Public Network Surveillance System is a critical component of the Golden Shield Project (discussed in the section of that name below) that was started in the late 1990s and went into full effect in 2003. The first reference to Internet restrictions as the "Great Firewall" was traced by Zixue Tai to an *Asiaweek* article titled "'Great Firewall of China?' Beijing Slaps Restrictions on Internet Access," by Tim Healy and David Hsieh, published on 18 October 1996. This reference was quickly picked up by others in the ensuing years in various discussions of intensifying official regulations of online communication in China, both in the Western academic literature and in popular literature. At about the same time, triggered by the explosive development of the Internet in China, network security experts (who were echoed by propaganda bureaucrats) repeatedly expressed concerns over a variety of potential security breaches and the possible influx of subversive and unhealthy information from overseas. The security experts avidly searched for technical and regulatory measures to protect China's networked space from vicious attacks and informational threats from both within and outside of the country. As the Great Wall was originally built to defend the ancient Chinese Empire from nomadic barbarians, the metaphor is a natural extension of this historic endeavor to a contemporary network fortification of China's fast-growing Internet. Since then, the term *Great Firewall* has referred to the dynamic, constantly updated online information control apparatus in China.

The Great Firewall in essence functions as a megafilter that blocks access to websites containing what the government classifies as objectionable (e.g., politically sensitive or pornographic) information within Chinese online space. All online traffic connecting China and the global Internet (including inbound traffic to China's Internet and outbound traffic originating from within China) has to be rerouted through the national backbones (i.e., principal data routes) administered by state-appointed censors, who are trained by and take orders directly from the Central Propaganda Department of the Chinese Communist Party. Additionally, at major provincial and metropolitan network hubs, similar filtering systems enabled by both software and hardware installations are in place to "cleanse" online traffic within their scope.

Technological Implementation

The technological implementation of China's Internet surveillance system relies on a combination of software and hardware configurations to pinpoint proscribed content. While software applications have been developed and are constantly being refined by Chinese engineers, many of whom are believed to come from military backgrounds, the Great Firewall hardware technology has benefited enormously from participation by high-tech companies in countries such as the United States, the United Kingdom, and Israel. In particular, US-based Cisco has designed and supplied about 80 percent of the "mirror routers" that are currently in use in China to eavesdrop on Internet transmissions (Israel 2009; Santoro 2009). (Mirror routers allow a domain to be stored on two different servers; they enable people in different parts of the world to access a single domain.) In recent years, however, a number of Chinese tech firms such as Huawei, TP-LINK, and Tenda have made significant breakthroughs in their router product development to cater to the needs of both Chinese domestic and overseas markets. As another example, Novell, which is headquartered in Waltham, Massachusetts (a suburb of Boston), has been engaged in multiple collaborative projects with Chinese partners to develop biochemical, artificial intelligence, and automatic recognition surveillance technologies to be used in the Great Firewall.

One ingenious and effective strategy to reign in online content across China's Internet is to exercise intensified control at the few international gateways interconnecting China and the rest of the world. This is in stark contrast to the original design of APARNET (Advanced Research Projects Agency Network) in the United States, which was to allow each packet of information to find the most optimal route based on the particular traffic conditions of the network at any given moment. Switching services that connect China's Internet space and the outside world are provided by a small number of state-sanctioned Internet bandwidth gateways, which diligently apply a variety of control mechanisms to cleanse online content that goes into and out of Chinese cyberspace. Global Internet connectivity in China is effectually controlled in a duopolistic arrangement, with China Telecom and China Unicom maintaining control of the vast majority of the Internet bandwidth at the border points of exit/entry.

The "Physical" Wall

The physical connectivity that links China and the rest of the world is accomplished by a small number of heavily monitored fiber optic cables at three points along China's cyber borders: the Beijing–Tianjin–Qingdao connection (servicing northern China), via undersea cables from Japan; the Shanghai connection (servicing the central coastal area), also through undersea cables from Japan; and the Guangzhou connection (servicing southern China) with cables from Hong Kong. Although there exist a few lines connecting China with Central Asia and Russia, the volume of traffic is minimal along these routes.

Because all Internet traffic connecting China and the rest of the world is essentially aggregated to a limited number of national gateways, content filtering is mainly achieved through the installation of network "sniffers" via customized hardware and hardware configurations at these gateways. The sniffers operate on an autopilot mode, and constantly monitor and analyze online traffic. By making a copy of the network data without redirecting or altering the original through the process called mirroring, mentioned earlier, the sniffers eavesdrop on real-time Internet traffic by "peeping" into the content of the copy and then decide if the original packet should be stopped or let through.

Four Methods of Blockage

In general, there are four ways that the Great Firewall acts to block content. First, a Domain Name System (DNS) block renders a number of websites using certain textual hostnames permanently inaccessible to Chinese web surfers. DNS is the alphabetical address associated with a particular site that human beings type in order to access the site. The Internet, however, is really based on IP (Internet Protocol) addresses—numeric values separated by dots—to uniquely identify each interconnected computer across the gigantic network. For example, www.epochtimes.com is the global Internet presence of the Falun Dafa (or Falun Gong), a religion movement that has been banned in China and whose members are targets of official persecution; the website is linked to the IP address of 72.52.81.107. The same IP address is also associated with www.dajiyuan.com. Under normal circumstances, once a user submits the alphabetical address, or URL, of a site through the browser on a computer hooked up to the Internet, the DNS server will automatically translate the URL into the corresponding IP address and then retrieve the site by connecting to the remote hosting server. DNS block (also known as DNS poisoning or DNS spoofing), however, is the technique that prevents users from accessing the entire targeted site based on its particular domain names, by instructing the DNS server to return no valid IP addresses for these blacklisted sites. Instead, a user's request by typing in the URLs will get a "Site not found" or other error message display on the browser.

The second system of content filtering is "packet dropping" (also known as IP blocking), in which all traffic to specific IP addresses is discarded by the routers, thus making the content hosted there inaccessible. Because this has become a standard component of today's firewall and routing technologies, packet dropping is rather inexpensive and easy to deploy. The drawbacks are mainly twofold: it requires that the list of blocked IP addresses must be up to date in order to be effective, and it may suffer from "overblocking" (i.e., blocking more sites than is necessary) due to the popular practice of the one IP address hosting multiple websites.

The third method of content blocking, called "connection reset," is similar to the above in that it targets websites based on their corresponding IP addresses. The difference is that, instead of dropping packets en route to the requesting computer as found in packet dropping for websites whose IP addresses are on the blacklist, connection reset simply interrupts the communication between the requesting computer and the remote site by sending an Internet "Reset" (i.e., an RST packet) command to both, thus halting the traffic between the requesting computer and the requested site temporarily (for at least ten seconds) (OpenNet Initiative 2009). While reset is a routine client-server function in the network world to repair unsynchronized connections, its adaptation in the Great Firewall goes in the opposite direction of forcefully disrupting attempted communication between users in China and blacklisted IP addresses.

The fourth system is the most sophisticated and also the most powerful surveillance function of the Great Firewall. It has a variety of technical names, such as "packet drop attack," "blackhole attack," "TCP connection cut-off," "TCP reset attack," or "Intrusion Detection System," and it can potentially block single pages or single images while letting other information pass through. In this case, the scanner inspects the actual content of data packets in transit from the requested site to the individual user and decides whether it should stop the packet by comparing the contents of the packet against a list of forbidden terms or taboo keywords. When the surveillance system finds suspicious content, it will immediately turn on the TCP (Transmission Control Protocol) reset flag and shut down the offending connection. While the aforementioned IP is responsible for handling addressing and routing information for networked computers, the TCP provides the service of data exchanges between two networked hosts (e.g., a web surfer and a remote site). Interfering with the TCP, therefore, is powerful in identifying and blocking targeted content. As a result of this system, for example, it is possible for the Chinese authorities to block particular offending pages of the *New York Times* or CNN—a story about the Falun Gong, for example—while allowing the rest of the content hosted on the servers to get through the Firewall.

It is worth mentioning that the above systems are not just relevant to web-based traffic but are equally applicable for email as well. In particular, the last method is especially effective in singling out individual email messages for blocking or selecting certain messages for further scrutiny.

Golden Shield Project

To call China's online surveillance apparatus a Great Firewall, however, is not without controversy. There are two main problems with the nomenclature (Tai 2010): first, traditional firewall technologies have been primarily developed for protecting computer networks from a wide range of malicious attacks for various purposes, while the central purpose of the so-called Great Firewall of China is to spy on users and to censor online information; second, to reduce China's sophisticated Internet surveillance system to a simple filter (albeit a "megafilter) is misleading, as it fails to capture the multidimensionality and full scope of this gigantic undertaking.

The archetype of China's online surveillance system, the Golden Shield Project, is a central component among large national "golden" projects. Other projects range from the Golden Bridge (a national public information and communication network interconnecting all provinces and major cities throughout the nation) and the Golden Gate (a digitized national customs-processing network under the auspices of the General Administration of Customs) to the Golden Card (a national network infrastructure for monetary transactions servicing the national banking industry) and the Golden Tax (a national computerized taxation system for the State Administration of Taxation and its regional offices). (There are other golden things besides large projects: people in China also celebrate Golden Week holidays.) These projects were initiated by different government ministries beginning in the early 1990s, as part of the national efforts led and coordinated by the State Council to mobilize technical talent for the development of state-of-the-art network applications adapted to the needs of their respective administrative responsibilities.

There are six overarching goals for the Golden Shield Project, according to Li Runsen (2002), one of the chief scientists behind the design and development of the project:

First, it lays in place a national network information infrastructure interconnecting public security (i.e., Chinese police) forces via land-based and mobile- as well as satellite-delivered multimedia communications.

Second, it creates a database-oriented information-sharing application system, of which a critical component is the China Crime Information Center (CCIC), which serves the information needs of Chinese police in relation to different domains of their functionality.

Third, it promotes a national technology and terminology standard that makes interagency information-sharing possible across the country.

Fourth, it enhances network safety and data integrity through development of its own information security systems; critical components here include LAN (Local Area Network), WAN (Wide Area Network), and Internet security issues, as well as encryption and data security matters.

Fifth, it is a network management platform that facilitates the day-to-day performance of China's computer networks. Toward that end, it is entrusted with the task of training and certifying network professionals within China.

Finally, and most importantly, it is a public network information surveillance system that monitors real-time traffic and keeps unwanted content out of China's Internet space.

It is only this last goal of the Golden Shield that has received so much attention in international media reports about the Internet in China. Unfortunately, it is not uncommon for Western pundits and media analysts to unequivocally equate the Golden Shield Project with the Great Firewall, although the latter is merely a part of the former.

The Relevant Bureaucracies

The Ministry of Public Security (MPS) is the official bureaucracy directly overseeing the daily operations of the Golden Shield. The predecessor of the Golden Shield was the China Crime Information Center, fully operational by 1994. The decision to start the brand-new Golden Shield Project was made by the MPS in September 1998—just at the time when China's central government made information technology (IT) a national priority in order to encourage the embrace of the Internet throughout Chinese society (a goal that is rapidly being realized). The project won the approval from the State Council in November 1998, and was formally enlisted as one of the key informatization initiatives by the State Planning Commission (now the National Development and Reform Commission) in January 2001. From 1998 to 2002, a total of RMB¥5.4 billion (approximately US$790 million) was invested in the Golden Shield Project across China, with the State Planning Commission injecting another RMB¥3 billion (about US$439 million) into the next phase of the project in 2003 (Tai 2006).

The Ministry of Industry and Information Technology (MIIT), which was founded in 2008 as part of the government institutional reform plan to streamline bureaucracy functions in the new millennium, has overall regulatory responsibility over the telecommunications sector. Its main mission is to make strategic planning and informatization policies, develop national standards, and promote innovation and competitiveness in China's telecommunications industry; it also coordinates multiple interministerial agencies in the protection of information securities (State Council 2008).

In addition to the MIIT and MPS, other ministries that play major roles in managing particular areas of online content include the Ministry of Culture, the National Copyright Administration of China (NCAC), the Ministry of State Security (MSS), the Ministry of Education, and the State Administration of Radio, Film and Television (SARFT). Supervising all of these state bureaucracies from above is the Central

Propaganda Department of the Chinese Communist Party (CCP), which issues overarching orientations for all ideological control and information purification in China.

Golden Shield Development

The development of the Golden Shield has gone through three key benchmarking stages thus far: initialization (1998–2001), nationalization (2001–2005), and expansion (since 2006). The initialization stage witnessed the conceptualization and initial infrastructural completion of the project. Noticeably, the Golden Shield was incubated—both financially and technically—as a single-ministry (e.g., MPS) undertaking during this time. The project received a significant boost from being designated as a project of national priority by the State Planning Commission in 2001, because this recognition provided much-needed additional financial support and expanded the scope of participation to the supraministerial (national) level. The focus during the nationalization stage was on connecting all provincial cities and major metropolises throughout China to the national network via fiber optics and creating an encrypted, shared virtual private network (VPN) for law-enforcement and public security forces. The expansion stage, which started in 2006, extends connectivity to all county-level police and enhances surveillance capabilities by incorporating multimedia, electronic-eye, and mobile monitoring technologies (Tai 2010).

In order to strengthen the surveillance functions of the Golden Shield and to streamline technological development and implementation, a mega bureau called the MPS Information Center 公安部情报信息中心 was set up in March 2004 to be exclusively in charge of network surveillance. The Information Center was granted the status of a public institution with the following core mission: routine maintenance of the network backbones; development of key software and hardware applications; staff training and professional certification; access authorization and data protection for the MPS intranet; and data security and surveillance across all computer networks within China. (Institutions in China have been traditionally classified in three ways: government agencies, public institutions, and enterprise units. Government agencies fulfill official administrative responsibilities, and enterprise units engage in profit-making endeavors and therefore pay taxes to the central and local governments. Public institutions, on the other hand, are mostly nonprofit organizations that provide service to society in designated areas with no tax obligations.) As a public institution, the Information Center has more leeway in hiring technical talent within specialized areas and as managers, as most of the employees are not professional police. The MPS, however, exercises oversight over most of the center's daily operations. This dual arrangement (oversight but no staffing obligation by the MSP) is thought to best suit the administrative needs of the center as it allows the center to hire civilian personnel to work for public security-related tasks.

The Information Center certifies surveillance workers in China through administering the Information Network Security Professional Certification (INSPC) test to network managers. Another test that network managers have to pass is the Network Management Skills Examination (NMSE) administered by the Information Security Coordination Bureau 信息安全协调司 under MIIT, which focuses mostly on networking knowledge and skills. The MPS and MIIT work in tandem to keep an eye on the tens of thousands of network managers (*wǎngguǎn* 网管) dispersed in hubs of network centers throughout China. These *wangguan* are hired by respective websites and online content providers, but they regularly receive instructions and directives from public security officials and government offices about what content (or sites) must be blocked. At the center of the chain of command is the Network Technology Center of the Central Propaganda Department 中宣部网络技术中心 and its delegates in the local governments.

Content Targeted for Blocking

Three broad categories of websites are the targets of blocking. First, websites, numbering in the hundreds, if not thousands, published by exiled Chinese dissidents or "international hostile forces" such as Amnesty International, Human Rights Watch, Reporters Without Borders, Falun Gong, and other blacklisted organizations, are permanently banned from Chinese cyberspace. Wikipedia and many other Wiki publications are blocked in China for entries related to politically sensitive subjects and officially denounced information. The most comprehensive definition of prohibited content on the Internet is offered in the Computer Information Network and Internet Security Protection and Management Regulations, approved by the State Council and promulgated by the MPS, with an effective date of 30 December 1997. This directive criminalizes the production, circulation, and accessing of nine categories of content over the Internet ranging from subversion, defamation (to individuals or government institutions), sabotage of national unity, and disruption of social order; to superstitious, pornographic, and rumor-mongering information. Additionally, it prohibits any type of information or behavior that may endanger national security or damage "national, social, and collective interests." This directive has undergone several updates and revisions since its original promulgation (Tai 2006, 2010).

In particular, primary candidates for blacklisting are sites with connections to the "Three Ts"—namely, Tiananmen Square (the massacre of 1989), Tibet (its independence or freedom), and Taiwan (independence or separatism). It is worth noting that, although the Chinese authorities typically cite online pornography as a driving reason for government regulation of the Internet in their public rhetoric, the regime in practice pays much more attention to politically sensitive and subversive materials in information cleansing and control.

Next, websites run by international media organizations such as the BBC, CNN, or the *New York Times* may be blocked at sensitive times, such as around the anniversaries of the Tiananmen Square crackdown (4 June 1989) or whenever objectionable stories are published. This category also extends to non-news sites, among them Flickr, Blogspot, Twitter, Facebook, YouTube, and Technorati, that garner many visits from Chinese Internet users. The fact that they are popular among Chinese "netizens" makes them targets for blocking when forbidden content appears in their domains.

Finally, there are those forever-changing lists of individual sites that are associated with certain types of prohibited content. These sites, or offending pages within these sites, may sporadically become inaccessible to Chinese web surfers from time to time. Control is especially tight and surveillance is elevated during sensitive times or on occasions of high political significance, such as every anniversary of the Tiananmen massacre, or on the ninetieth anniversary of the founding of the Chinese Communist Party (in 2011), or during the annual sessions of the National People's Congress. The surveillance apparatus is on full alert during breaking news stories that have significant sociopolitical implications, as manifested in the bloody Lhasa riot of March 2008 and the deadly Xinjiang ethnic violence in July 2009. Notably, global attention to Internet censorship reached a new height prior to the 2008 Beijing Olympics. The Chinese authorities eventually made the conciliatory move of giving the order to loosen most of the blocks of the Great Firewall to Internet connection points at the Olympic media center and in major hotels where foreign visitors resided during the games, while leaving the filtering in place for Chinese users.

Internet censorship is supported by a large number of laws and administrative statutes that hold Internet Content Providers (ICPs) and Internet Service Providers (ISPs) responsible for any "illegal" content published in the web space under their respective jurisdiction, regardless of the originating source. Violators (in these cases, the ICPs and ISPs, as well as individual perpetrators who published the content) may face hefty fines and other punishments, including the possible suspension and revoking of their licenses. As a result, in order to preemptively keep state censors at bay, major Internet content and service providers have developed their own internal systems to monitor content on their sites. One of their greatest concerns is keeping track of user-generated content. The need to police real-time online content has led to the rise of one profession in China, the aforementioned network (or website) managers, whose job is to filter user-submitted content to their web pages. As the first line of blocking in the Great Firewall surveillance mechanism, user-generated content through online forums, blog publishing sites, or online text chatting containing any banned keywords are automatically blocked for processing, and users either have to modify the content or give up trying with the proscribed content. Material that successfully goes through this software-enabled automatic check will then be manually (i.e., by a human) cleared for publication. A similar program has now been adopted for mobile content distribution platforms such as "moblogs" (also known as mobile blogs), microblogs (the Chinese equivalent of Twitter-like applications), and text messaging.

As a way to encourage public participation in the state-orchestrated surveillance network, the Internet Information Service Commission (affiliated with the semiofficial Internet Society of China) founded the China Internet Illegal Information Reporting Center (CIIRC) on 10 June 2004 (hosted at net.china.com.cn) under the auspices of the State Council Information Office. Local centers have also been set up in provincial capitals and major metropolises across the nation. CIIRC solicits information from individuals on tips concerning a wide range of "harmful" content via email, phone, or online postings, and offers cash rewards to anyone providing valid incriminating evidence. Since its debut, the center has processed millions of tips, which has led to the deletion and/or removal of millions of pages, links, and graphical images.

Outlook: Climbing over the Great Firewall

People have built ladders to scale walls since time immemorial. The Great Firewall, likewise, is neither airtight nor crack-free. An ever-expanding base of activists, tech nerds, software gurus, and, above all, average users across the globe has developed and distributed a variety of applications and technologies to circumvent the Chinese surveillance system. Two commonplace and easy-to-use methods to get around the Great Firewall are the proxy server and the virtual private network, or VPN.

A proxy server acts as an intermediary and allows users in China to connect to it first (as long as it is not on the state censors' blacklist) before establishing points of contact to websites hosted by third-party servers. Essentially, a proxy server functions like a go-between by taking requests from Chinese users, then finding what the users want and delivering the information back to the users. Because there is no direct contact between the Chinese users making the request and the third-party target sites, this communication process is hard for the Great Firewall to detect. The most effective way to stop traffic is to shut down the proxy server altogether, which has proven to be a major challenge for censors. There is an ever-changing list of popular proxy server services available to Chinese users, and most of them are free and require no installation of software.

VPN is a technology that allows a user to connect to a remote private network through an easily available public network (typically the Internet). As a common business practice, a VPN enables an individual user to create an encrypted channel of communication with an Internet server located elsewhere and to browse the Internet free from the prying eyes of Chinese censors; people around the world use VPN for telecommuting purposes. Because of the enormous presence of international business communities within China (most of which depend on VPNs to conduct daily business operations), it is virtually impossible to ban the use of VPNs. For individual users who don't have access to proprietary VPNs, there are a number of alternatives for web-surfing purposes. Two of the most popular applications freely available on China's Internet are WiTopia and HotSpot Shield.

Additionally, Chinese netizens have become remarkably savvy and ingenious in constantly inventing ways to trick auto filters and bypass official censors in communicating sensitive information. The Chinese language, for that matter, is uniquely suited to creating rich wordplays to disseminate subversive ideas and discontent. Heavy-handed official suppression of the Chinese Internet space has, therefore, not totally stifled dissent, nor has it homogenized online discourse, and it does not seem feasible that state-centric Internet surveillance in China will be able to achieve this goal in the future.

Zixue TAI
University of Kentucky

See also Internet Content Filtering; Internet in Everyday Life; Internet Governance; Internet Monitoring; Internet Regulation; Internet Service Providers (ISPs); Social and Political Impact

Further Reading

China Digital Times. (2010). Great Firewall. Retrieved November 1, 2010, from http://chinadigitaltimes.net/china/great-firewall/

Clayton, Richard; Murdoch, Steven J.; & Watson, Robert N. M. (2006). Ignoring the Great Firewall of China. Retrieved November 5, 2010, from http://www.cl.cam.ac.uk/~rnc1/ignoring.pdf

Deibert, Ronald J. (2002). Dark guests and Great Firewalls: The Internet and Chinese security policy. *Journal of Social Issues, 58*(1), 143–159.

Deibert, Ronald J.; Palfrey, John G.; Rohozinski, Rafal; & Zittrain, Jonathan (Eds.). (2008). *Access denied: The practice and policy of global Internet filtering.* Cambridge, MA: The MIT Press.

Fallow, James. (2008, March). The connection has been reset. *Atlantic Magazine.* Retrieved November 22, 2010, from http://www.theatlantic.com/magazine/archive/2008/03/-ldquo-the-connection-has-been-reset-rdquo/6650/

Israel, Brian R. (2009). "Make money without doing evil?": Caught between authoritarian regulations in emerging markets and a global law of human rights, US ICTs face a twofold quandary. *Berkeley Technology Law Journal, 24*(1), 617–655.

Li Runsen. (2002). Strengthening police work through science and technology: An outline of the National *Public Security Work Informatization Project (Golden Shield) Project. Public Security Studies,* 4(90), 4–12. [in Chinese]

Liang Bin &Lu Hong. (2010). Internet development, censorship, and cyber crimes in China. Journal of Contemporary Criminal Justice, 26(10), 103–120.

Liu Rufang & Huang Shuhua. (2001). The Golden Shield Project and its safety: An interview with the Science and Technology Commissioner of the Ministry of Public Security. *Net Security Technologies and Application,* May Issue, 6–7.

Open Net Initiative. (2009). Internet filtering in China. Retrieved November 10, 2010, from http://opennet.net/sites/opennet.net/files/ONI_China_2009.pdf

Thornton, Patricia M. (2010). Censorship and surveillance in Chinese cyberspace: Beyond the Great Firewall. In Peter H. Gries & Stanley Rosen (Eds.), *Chinese politics: State, society and the market* (pp. 179–198). London: Routledge.

Santoro, Michael A. (2009). China 2020: How Western business can—and should—influence social and political change in the coming decade. Ithaca, NY: Cornell University Press.

State Council. (2008). Circular on the main charge, institutional and personnel establishment of the Ministry of Industry and Information Technology. Retrieved May 15, 2012, from http://www.miit.gov.cn/n11293472/n11459606/11606790.html

Tai Zixue. (2006). The Internet in China: Cyberspace and civil society. London: Routledege.

Tai Zixue. (2010). Casting the ubiquitous net of information control: Internet surveillance in China from Golden Shield to Green Dam. *International Journal of Advanced Pervasive and Ubiquitous Computing (IJAPUC),* 2(1), 53–70.

Wang Tong & Liu Yuying. (2009). CIIRC follows over a million leads in prosecuting unhealthy content. Retrieved May 10, 2012, from http://tech.qq.com/a/20090610/000402.htm

Internet Content Filtering

Hùliánwǎng nèiróng guòlǜ 互联网内容过滤

Summary: The screening of Internet content by the Chinese government is common and far-reaching, overseen by thousands of private and public monitors that filter content sent through websites, blogs, forums, and email. A majority of Chinese Internet users have said in surveys that they prefer that the Internet be controlled.

The Chinese government's control over the Internet, including Internet content, is well documented and hardly a surprise to anyone. All media in the country is tightly controlled, which, to most people in the West, amounts to unacceptable censorship. The actual scope of Internet content filtering is difficult to determine because the monitors continually shift their attention to certain sites and topics they deem undesirable.

Technical Mechanisms

Technical filtering mechanisms can be found at all levels of the Internet, from the basic architecture to personal computers (PCs) located in hotels and Internet cafés. Although Internet Service Providers (ISPs), Internet cafés, search engines, and other network services can and do operate their own filtering systems, all network traffic is subject to a uniform system of filtering, known collectively as the "Great Firewall," at three major international gateways in Beijing, Shanghai, and Guangzhou. (More information on the Great Firewall is available in the article of that name in this volume.) Filtering is centralized and largely consistent across each of the international gateways. This gateway level of filtering is an unavoidable last line of defense. Research by the OpenNet Initiative (ONI), a joint project that monitors and reports on Internet filtering and surveillance practices by governments, has uncovered three forms of filtering at these international gateways: Domain Name System (DNS) tampering, keyword filtering, and Internet Protocol (IP) blocking.

DNS tampering works by interfering with the system that cross-references domain names with the numerical address associated with them. Users are directed to an invalid IP as if the site they requested did not exist. By contrast, IP blocking targets the numerical address. This type of blocking can cause major collateral filtering of unrelated content because different domain names can share the same IP address host.

Keyword filtering targets the URL path—and, increasingly, the webpages—searching for banned terms. When one is found, the routers send what are known as RST packets, which terminate the connection between sending and receiving computers, effectively preventing that computer from making requests to the same server for an indefinite period. Because the system works both ways (for requests exiting and entering China), it can be tested by searching for banned keywords like *Falun Gong* or *Tibet* on search engines hosted in China. In each case, users requesting banned information receive an error message on their web browsers, making it appear as if the information is not available or that there is something wrong with their Internet connection. Users trying to access banned content do not receive a block page informing them that the content is officially filtered, as is the case in some other countries that censor the Internet.

During the Tibetan protests in 2008, another sophisticated form of blocking appeared: the use of distributed denial of service (DDOS) attacks. There have been persistent and increasing charges that DDOS attacks against servers in the United States, the United Kingdom, Canada, and elsewhere have their origins in mainland China. Such attacks were prominent during and following the demonstrations in Tibet, with the servers of many Tibetan and Chinese human rights organizations systematically targeted. It is difficult to pinpoint the source of these more aggressive methods of denying access to information, which effectively target and disable the sources of information themselves rather than passively blocking requests for information, as the filtering systems do.

Technical means of filtering are complemented by an extensive set of social and legal or regulatory measures. Legal or regulatory measures tend to be vague and broad; they offer a wide scope for application and enforcement as well as uncertainty among users. Most have the effect of holding end users and services—such as café operators, ISPs, blog-hosting services, and media—responsible for censoring the content they post and host. Since enforcement can be arbitrary, users and operators of services tend to err on the side of caution, preferring to prevent or remove offending material rather than risk censure.

Social measures are even more general and thus harder to define, but they include operating norms, principles, and rules that are propagated through media and official channels and are combined with extensive techniques of surveillance, which together affect behavior in both formal and informal ways. These include self-discipline pacts signed by Chinese Internet service companies pledging to uphold public values and self-censorship by Internet users. The first thing many users see when logging on are two cute cartoon police officer characters, Jingjing and Chacha, that pop up and warn users not to visit banned sites or post harmful information.

Content

Content targeted for blocking is wide-ranging and covers social, cultural, security, and political topics considered a threat to Communist Party control and social or political stability. Among the topics most frequently blocked are Tibetan and Taiwanese independence (the People's Republic of China considers Taiwan, or the Republic of China, to be a province of China), Falun Gong, the Dalai Lama, the Tiananmen Square incident, and opposition political parties. Tibet, Taiwan, and Tiananmen Square are collectively known as the "Three Ts."

ONI investigations revealed that China's filtering tends to focus disproportionately on content in local Chinese languages. Users searching for the equivalent English language terms, for example, will often get a higher proportion of results than they would for the same terms searched for in Chinese.

During the 2003 SARS (severe acute respiratory syndrome) epidemic, the government tried to restrict news about the outbreaks in the early days of the crisis while officials and experts tried to work out a course of action. But groups inside and outside China used the Internet, along with mobile phones and satellite broadcasts, to ensure that information about the disease was widely distributed.

In January 2009 the Internet Affairs Bureau under the State Council Information Office launched a campaign against pornography and vulgar content online. The campaign led to the shutdown of 1,250 websites and the arrest of forty-one people. Similar actions have been taken against online gaming sites that may be too violent or too political. Websites and services that help people evade government censorship are also regularly filtered.

Although the filtering system appears consistent and relatively stable from day to day, the Chinese government has also demonstrated a propensity to use what ONI calls just-in-time blocking in response to special situations as they emerge. For example, during the demonstrations in Tibet in 2008, the government implemented blocks against YouTube.com and other video-streaming services that were circulating images of protests. The blocks were later lifted.

Monitoring the Monitors

Reports of China's Internet filtering come from the activities of bloggers, academics, nongovernmental organizations, and watchdog groups such as ONI, both within and outside the country, that monitor China's filtering system and compare and discuss its characteristics on email lists, blogs, and other public forums.

In a 2005 report, ONI described China as operating "the most extensive, technologically sophisticated, and broad-reaching system of Internet filtering in the world." China's filtering program employs a combination of technical, legal, and social measures applied at a variety of access points and overseen by thousands of private and public monitors who filter content sent through a range of communication methods, such as websites, blogs, forums, and email. Together, these measures create a matrix of soft and hard controls and induce a widespread climate of self-censorship.

Government Response

Official acknowledgment of censorship of Internet content has been inconsistent. Officials deny or do not discuss details of content-filtering practices. On the rare occasions when public officials do raise the subject, they compare it to similar practices in the West and justify it as a way to protect public safety, core social values, and stability. When Google.cn was established and agreed to abide by government rules, there was an international outcry over censorship. But searches on Google.cn on controversial topics brought up many sites that were critical of the government. The full scope of China's censorship regime, however, is never spelled out in official circles or public government documents.

Generally speaking, Chinese Internet users accept government intervention much more readily than users in Western countries would. In surveys conducted in 2003, 2005, and 2007, more than 80 percent of respondents in China said that the Internet should be controlled and that the government should be the controlling agent, a role that the government intends to maintain. It will be interesting to note if this trend holds true in the future.

Ronald J. DEIBERT
The Canada Centre for Global Security Studies

See also The Great Firewall; Internet Events; Internet Monitoring; Internet Service Providers (ISPs)

Further Reading

Deibert, Ronald. (2008, June 18). Testimony to the US-China Economic & Security Review Commission. Retrieved February 6, 2009, from http://deibert.citizenlab.org/deibertcongresstestimony.pdf

Deibert, Ronald; Palfrey, J.; Rohozinski, R.; & Zittrain, J. (Eds.). (2008). *Access denied: The practice and policy of global Internet filtering*. Cambridge, MA: MIT Press.

Tai Zixue. (2010). Casting the ubiquitous net of information control: Internet surveillance in China from Golden Shield to Green Dam. *International Journal of Advanced Pervasive and Ubiquitous Computing (IJAPUC)*, 2(1), 53–70.

Thornton, Patricia M. (2010). Censorship and surveillance in Chinese cyberspace: Beyond the Great Firewall. In Peter H. Gries & Stanley Rosen (Eds.), *Chinese politics: State, society and the market* (pp. 179–198). London: Routledge.

Internet Monitoring

Wǎngluò jiānkòng 网络监控

Summary: Internet monitoring in China is pervasive, powerful, and sophisticated. Users' activities on the Internet in China are often subject to monitoring without the users' knowledge or consent. The monitoring is achieved by surveillance of the users' computers, the entire Chinese web space, and the data flow between China and the Internet overseas. Many users take advantage of anti-censorship tools to evade monitoring.

Internet monitoring is pervasive in China. Almost every form of communication is monitored, including emails, regular webpages, online forums, instant messages, blogs, and tweets.

Scope of Internet Monitoring

Topics being monitored are wide-ranging. Information concerning the Tiananmen Square protests in 1989, the persecution of Falun Gong in 1999, and freedom in Tibet are most closely and perpetually monitored. Government or Communist Party scandals are also classified as "sensitive," therefore many common terms have made their way into the censor's watch list, such as *milk powder* (referring to the 2008 scandal when contaminated milk powder caused the death of several infants and injured many thousands more) and *earthquake* (referring to the aftermath of the 2008 earthquake that struck Sichuan Province). Finally, as traditional media is owned and controlled by the government with set guidelines and agendas of propaganda, online dissemination and discussion of current affairs by ordinary web surfers are also closely watched to ensure they do not deviate from the official tone.

Though the scope of the monitoring is far-reaching and constantly expanding, the process is not completely transparent. A regular Internet user is often not able to fathom exactly where the boundary is. When posting a blog entry, for example, a user does not know beforehand if the entry will be published or deleted. And even if the blog entry is deleted, the user is usually not given a specific reason—all that is offered is a brief message saying "your entry has been deleted."

How the Internet Is Monitored

Internet monitoring in China is a multidimensional operation. It strategically covers three critical areas of the cyberspace: end-user computers, the Chinese web space, and the international gateways.

A Chinese user's computer is often infested with a variety of monitoring software. Popular applications, such as the Chinese version of Skype (TOM-Skype), may covertly record users' online chat-messages and scan them for sensitive keywords, as revealed by overseas researchers (Villeneuve 2008). The Chinese government even sponsored the development of the powerful monitoring software, Green Dam Youth Escort software, and attempted to mandate the installation on all computers sold in China in 2009. Green Dam was designed to categorically monitor texts typed, images viewed, programs launched, and websites visited by the user, presumably to protect younger users from adult content and politically sensitive material. After heavy national and international protests, the government eventually withdrew the project. Finally, antivirus software produced by Chinese companies often intentionally classifies monitoring-evasion tools such as Freegate and Ultrasurf as a virus, or disables these tools outright.

The Chinese web space as a whole is also closely monitored. This is a labor-intensive operation, performed by tens of thousands of professional web censors. They regularly monitor personal websites, which are subject to deletion, heavy fines, or temporary shutdown if contents deemed "subversive are published there. Big commercial websites exercise strong self-discipline (i.e., self-censorship), employing their own army of webmasters to inspect online postings by users, and to weed those "inappropriate" messages out before anyone sees them.

Search engines operating in China have to consciously filter search results. In addition, Internet companies are subject to demands to surrender their user information in order for the authorities to track down dissidents. Shi Tao, a journalist sentenced to ten years in prison in 2004 and finally released in late 2013, was arrested after the authorities pressed Yahoo! for his personal details and email communications.

A unique feature of Chinese Internet censorship is the proactive manipulation of public opinions on the web by thousands of paid, anonymous "web commentators." The authorities deploy these commentators to forums, especially the popular ones, to pose as ordinary web users and publish comments along the official lines to "guide" their fellow users, or to suppress, distract, and attack unorthodox thoughts or opinions. This operation has also expanded to overseas websites, where their presence could be seen in the readers' comments of major online news articles concerning China, especially those critical of the Chinese government on issues such as human rights, freedom of religion, and freedom of speech.

Finally, the massive Internet traffic flowing in and out of China is meticulously checked at several (inter)national gateways. These gateways serve as an Internet firewall along the virtual Chinese borders in cyberspace, and every second, hundreds of gigabytes of data are examined in real time by extremely sophisticated and powerful Internet monitoring machinery. This so-called Great Firewall of China ensures the monitoring of the information flow between Chinese Internet users and the Internet overseas, and the disruption of it as soon as sensitive keywords are detected in the data streams. To achieve this, the Great Firewall looks deep into each data packet passing through these gateways, and compares it against precompiled blacklists of sensitive keywords, Internet Protocol (IP) addresses, and domain names of websites. It blocks, misdirects, or disrupts a user's connection instantly if a match is detected in a data packet. The censors work industriously to keep these blacklists up to date. The keywords that blacklists contain are not only human language terms deemed sensitive but also binary data fragments serving to identify traffic patterns, particularly those used by popular anticensorship software tools.

These three areas of Internet monitoring complement one another to form a tightly watched and controlled cyberspace for Chinese Internet users.

Efforts to Defeat Internet Monitoring

Many Internet users in China have been trying to elude or defeat the monitoring of their Internet activities. This need is particularly acute when they try to visit overseas websites, many of which are blocked or subjected to filtering by the measures described above.

During the first few years of the twenty-first century, tens of thousands of overseas websites deemed "offensive" by the government were simply blocked by a blacklist. Any direct connection from a user's computer to any of these sites was silently dropped. Many users in China would circumvent such blocking by finding open proxy servers outside China, and by setting up their web browsers to use these proxy servers as a spring board to access the blocked sites.

But soon the Chinese government started to track down and block these proxy servers. In addition, it perfected its network inspection capacity at its national gateways, in order to look deep into the data streams flowing through the Great Firewall in real time, and to cut off the connection as soon as any of the predefined keywords was detected. This is a much more powerful monitoring mechanism. In response, many overseas organizations developed various anticensorship tools, specialized software applications designed to defeat the monitoring. Typically, after a user in China installs and launches such a tool, it will establish an encrypted connection to one of the many overseas computers either maintained by volunteers or by the tool providers. These computers act as intelligent proxy servers and work either under the censor's radar or with rapidly changing IP addresses to avoid being tracked. Since the traffic is encrypted, it can evade the detection of the keywords by the Great Firewall.

The widespread use of these tools in recent years, however, spurred the Chinese government to develop countermeasures. It has studied the inner workings of the leading tools and implemented specialized monitoring systems to detect and disable the communication originating from such tools. Not to be outdone, many of the tool developers actively modify and improve their software in order to stay ahead. Examples of such large-scale anticensorship tools in China are Freegate and Ultrasurf, serving tens of millions of users every month.

This back-and-forth battle between Chinese Internet monitors and anticensorship developers will likely ensue for a long time. For determined Internet users in China, however, the smart anticensorship tools have made Internet monitoring more symbolic than real. In addition, as the dimension of the Chinese Internet has grown explosively, the world's largest and most motivated online population has found many creative ways to communicate with each other and the outside world. Online video sharing, mobile applications, and social networks have made it increasingly hard for the censors to keep full control of information flow and maintain propaganda hegemony, as they had been doing until the beginning of this century.

David TIAN
Global Internet Freedom Consortium

See also Chinese Language and Computing; The Great Firewall; Internet Content Filtering; Internet Events; Internet Service Providers (ISPs)

Further Reading

August, Oliver. (2007 October). The Great Firewall: China's misguided—and futile—attempt to control what happens online. *Wired*, Issue 15.11.

Beiser, Vince. (2010 November). Digital weapons help dissidents punch holes in China's Great Firewall. *Wired*. Retrieved April 14, 2013, from http://www.wired.com/2010/11/ff_firewallfighters/?

Fallows, James. (2008, March). The connection has been reset. *Atlantic*. Retrieved April 14, 2014, from http://www.theatlantic.com/magazine/archive/2008/03/-the-connection-has-been-reset/306650/

Global Internet Freedom Consortium (2007). New technologies battle and defeat Internet censorship. Retrieved February 8, 2011, from http://www.internetfreedom.org/archive/Defeat_Internet_Censorship_White_Paper.pdf

Hughes, Christopher R., & Wacker, Gudrun (Eds.). (2003). *China and the Internet: Politics of the digital leap forward*. New York: Psychology Press.

Mr. Tao. (2007). China: Journey to the heart of Internet censorship. Retrieved February 8, 2011, from www.rsf.org/IMG/pdf/Voyage_au_coeur_de_la_censure_GB.pdf

Villeneuve, Nart. (2008). Breaching trust: An analysis of surveillance and security practices on China's TOM-Skype platform. Retrieved February 8, 2011, from http://www.nartv.org/mirror/breachingtrust.pdf

Wolchok, Scott; Yao, Randy; & Halderman, J. Alex. (2009). Analysis of the Green Dam censorware system. Retrieved February 8, 2011, from http://www.cse.umich.edu/~jhalderm/pub/gd/

Zittrain, Jonathan, & Edelman, Benjamin. (2003). Empirical analysis of Internet filtering in China. Retrieved February 8, 2011, from http://cyber.law.harvard.edu/filtering/china/

Internet Governance

Hùliánwǎng zhìlǐ 互联网治理

Summary: China has invested in its hard and soft infrastructure to support the world's largest number of Internet users, but its Internet governance model is still traditional and "top down," which leads to regulatory deadlocks and lack of competition. Many online companies find that they need to deal with multiple government agencies—of culture, education, food and drugs, and broadcasting, to name a few—in order to operate.

China has seen a phenomenal growth of the Internet. By the end of 2012, the number of Internet users in China totaled more than 564 million people, up from 457 million in 2010, according to the China Internet Network Information Center's (CCNIC) 2013 report. The expansion and diffusion of the Internet to some extent demonstrates the success of China's Internet governance policy.

Significance of Internet Governance

China has the largest Internet population, and how it approaches Internet governance has gained great interest in the global community. Internet governance has been defined by the United Nations Working Group on Internet Governance as "the development and application by governments, the private sector, and civil society, in their respective roles, of shared principles, norms, rules, decision making procedures and programmes, that shape the evolution and utilization of the Internet" (United Nations Working Group 2005, 4). This is a very broad definition of Internet governance, encompassing not only the rules that govern the use of the Internet, but also the administrative processes to follow the rules.

Governance of the Internet has always loomed large in China, even as the country invested heavily in the information infrastructure and reformed the telecommunication sector. It has also encouraged and enabled public access to e-government services and to e-commerce. Such development of the economic and social aspects of the Internet have been coupled with strong concerns over stability and security, and, hence, government presence (Chen and Ang 2011).

Infrastructure Investment

The Chinese economy has been playing catch-up since China opened up to the rest of the world in 1978. The first computer networks in China, the China Academic Network (CANet) and the Institute of High Energy Physics (IHEP) network, were built in 1987. In 1990, the China Research Network (CRNet) was established. In 1996, under the auspices of the Chinese Academy of Science, the CANet, IHEP network, and CRNet were combined to form the Chinese Science and Technology Network (CSTNet). In 1993, the Ministry of Education began to build the China Education and Research Network (CERNET), with the goal of connecting all the universities, middle schools, and primary schools in China. That same year, the Ministry of Posts and Telecommunications (MPT) began to build its own data transmission network, ChinaNet, and the Ministry of Electronic Industry (MEI) built China Golden Bridge Net (ChinaGBN) under the Golden Project to build a Chinese information highway. (China's Golden Projects are discussed below in the "Government Use of the Internet" section.) In 1997, CERNET, ChinaNet, CSTNet, and ChinaGBN were interconnected. Later on, China Unicom's Uninet, China Mobiles CMnet, the military-controlled telecommunication company China Great Wall's CGWnet, and the Ministry of Foreign Trade and Economic Cooperation's CIETnet appeared (Loo 2004).

Besides building major networks, China has also invested heavily in telecommunications and has restructured the telecommunication sector to make it competitive. To break up the monopoly in basic telecommunication services held by China Telecom, the State Council in 1993 approved the establishment of the second telecom operator—China Unicom—albeit still a state-owned enterprise (SOE). In 1999, China Telecom was restructured as China Telecom, which held the fixed line business, and China Mobile, which focused on the mobile phone business. In 2000, two other SOEs, China Network Communications Corporation (China Netcom) and China Railway Telecommunications Corporation (China Railcom), obtained licenses to supply basic telecommunication but not mobile services. In 2001, the China Telecommunications Broadcast Satellite Corporation (ChinaSat) was founded as a Chinese satellite communications services provider. Also in 2001, China Telecom was further divided into northern and southern parts. The northern part was merged into China Netcom to form a new company called China Network Communications Group Corporation (China Netcom Group). The southern part set up a company called China Telecommunications Group Corporation, now known as China Telecom (Loo 2004).

Thus, six companies dominate the domestic telecom market. Of these, ChinaSat provides only satellite communications services. Four companies have licenses for the local fixed-line services, although China Unicom's license is restricted to Tianjin, Chongqing, and Chengdu, and China Railcom provides services only to China's railway system. Five companies—China Telecom, China Netcom, China Unicom, China Mobile, and China Railcom—have licenses for long distance telephone services. All five can also provide Internet Protocol (IP) telephony services, which are services such as phone and fax delivered over online connections rather than via land lines. Only China Mobile and China Unicom have licenses for the burgeoning mobile telephone services. Not surprisingly, these two are the strongest players. (It should be mentioned that the Chinese approach has been to allow controlled competition in the telecommunications market.)

To increase market competition, the Ministry of Industry and Information Technology (MII), the National Development and Reform Commission (NDRC), and the Ministry of Finance (MOF) restructured the industry in 2008. Under this plan, China Telecom would purchase China Unicom's CDMA ("code division multiple access") network, China Unicom would be merged with China Netcom, the fundamental telecom service of China Satcom would be merged into the business of China Telecom, and China Railcom would be merged into China Mobile. By 2009, the restructure was completed, and three major operators—China Unicom, China Mobile, and China Telecom—remained in the market. An assessment of the 2008 restructuring suggests that while market mechanisms did play a significant role, ultimately, it was high-level politics that was the determining factor in shaping the industry (Fu and Mou 2010).

Government Use of the Internet

While investing in hardware, the Chinese government was also aware of the need to work on software. In 1993, the government initiated several "Golden Projects" to establish the backbone of the information economy in China. The first Golden Projects were Golden Bridge, Golden Card, and Golden Customs. Golden Bridge built the infrastructural software backbone for information services, such as email, electronic data interchange, and database services. Golden Card created a countrywide banking and credit card system. Golden Customs automated customs checks to speed up international trade. The success of the first three Golden Projects led to subsequent Golden Projects, ranging from agriculture, education, health care, government macroeconomic management, and taxation, among others. The State Council Document No. 17 of 2002 listed a total of nine other Golden Projects (OECD 2005).

Parallel to the implementation of these projects, a "government online" project was initiated in 1999 to make government work more efficient and transparent. By 2008, the central government, ministerial departments, and provincial governments all established their official websites, and 99 percent of governments at the prefecture level and 92 percent of the country's county-level governments had their own websites. To encourage governments at all levels to use information technology to better their work, an annual evaluation of the government websites has been conducted since 2002 to examine the government's openness of public records, the ability of online services, and the involvement of public participation. In 2007, China's Regulations on Open Government Information listed the Internet as a major channel for the government at all levels to disclose information.

Contrary to assertions in literature from the West, the Chinese use of the Internet suggests that it is possible to offer services to citizens without necessarily empowering them; control can still reside in the hands of government. The Chinese approach to e-government services suggests that they are mainly a means to supervise lower level officials, thereby increasing transparency, reducing corruption, and minimizing dissatisfaction with the central government (Seifert and Chung 2009).

Business Use of the Internet

Because the Internet went public only around the mid-1990s, China's e-commerce was understandably slow off the mark compared with the United States. China's first e-commerce website, China Chemical Network (chinachemnet.com), was launched in 1997. This company developed a business-to-business (B2B) sales model in the chemical industry. To encourage and regulate the development of e-commerce, the government launched the "enterprise online" project in 2000. In 2005, the General Office of the State Council issued "Some Advice on Promoting the Development of E-commerce." In this document, the government stated that e-commerce was vital to the development of the national economy and society, and it promised to improve online trust, certification, payment systems, and the legal environment of e-commerce. Several laws enabling digital certificates (in 2005), digital signature (in 2005), and e-banking (in 2001) were passed. Some apparently were passed hurriedly. For example, the Interim Measures on the Administration of Internet Banking was passed in 2001 and superseded by the Measures for the Administration of Electronic Banking in 2006 (Ng 2009).

It should be noted that many of the large US online companies are either blocked in China or the rules disadvantage them; YouTube, Facebook, and Twitter are blocked, but there are Chinese equivalents such as Youku, Renren, and Sina Weibo (run by the large online company Sina), respectively. In 2010, Google closed its search engine for China, citing censorship as one cause. It has been argued that the superiority of Chinese companies over companies that are companies that are ordinarily ahead of their competitors in most other markets points to censorship as a trade barrier (Fiveash 2010). Chinese companies have to comply by the laws of the land; the editors of video site Youku, for example, view (and censor if necessary) every uploaded video. At the search engine Baidu, sites that are blocked by the government are not displayed in the search results. Chinese officials therefore point to the fact that these companies continue to thrive in the Chinese regulatory environment as evidence that the laws are not so punitive as to stifle business. (The article "The Great Firewall" elsewhere in this volume has more information on Internet censorship.)

The Regulatory Environment

To be sure, China has passed many laws that impact the computer and Internet industries. Even from the onset, the Chinese government has been aware of the need to update its laws on computer crime. The 1997 Criminal Law has three provisions—articles 285, 286, and 287—that address computer-related crimes, and violators can be sentenced to prison for five years. Article 285 deals with unauthorized access of computer systems of state affairs, national defense, and top scientific and technological institutions; article 286 criminalizes the tampering with computer information systems; and article 287 criminalizes the use of a computer for financial fraud, theft, corruption, misappropriation of public funds, stealing state secrets, or other crimes.

Many of the subsequent rules also address computer crime. The 2000 "Decision of the Standing Committee of the National People's Congress on Maintaining Internet

Security" criminalizes, among other computer crimes, the production and dissemination of computer viruses and unauthorized hacking. The 2000 Decision was significant in that it stated that criminal activities committed using the Internet were analogous to those in the respective provisions of criminal law; that is, the penalties that applied to offline criminal offences also applied to crimes committed using the Internet as a means of commission.

Because cybercrimes, such as gambling and fraud, are likely to be transnational, China has coordinated with international agencies and other countries to fight online cross-border criminal activities. For example, China has established mutual-legal assistance with thirty countries and an annual meeting cooperative mechanism with the Asia Pacific region on cybercrimes. China also participates in the Cybercrime Technology Information Network System (CTINS) with fourteen Asian countries to exchange information and share technologies.

More controversial, and a subject that is commonly associated with the Chinese Internet, is prohibited online content. The highest legislative body, the National People's Congress, consolidated in December 2000 all governmental programs and measures to define prohibited online content in one decree titled "Decisions on Protecting Internet Security." That long list spelled out what was allowable online content and what was prohibited (Chen and Ang 2011).

The definition of Internet governance includes the participation of civil society and the private sector in policy formation. The Chinese mode of governance, however, has yet to embrace this multistakeholder (referring to forms of governance where many different groups and individuals have a voice) model.

The Chinese government has been the sole regulator in Internet governance, effectively displacing, for the most part, the multistakeholder process. Internet governance in the Chinese government, however, is not monolithic. There are many government agencies that exercise some authority over the Internet.

One reason is that the Internet is a general-purpose platform, available for use by different industries. For example, the Ministry of Information Industry (MII) takes charge of the large-scale developments of China's information and telecommunication industry; the Ministry of Public Security has jurisdiction over cybercrime, illegal and harmful online information, and the safety of the Internet; and the Ministry of Culture is in charge of Internet games, Internet cafés, and so on. The General Administration of Press and Publication supervises such issues as Internet publication, intellectual property; and the State Administration of Radio, Film, and Television (SARFT) has a say in the audiovisual aspects of the Internet. In addition, because offline laws are treated as applicable to the online world, the Ministry of Health, the Ministry of Education, the State Food and Drug Administration, the State Administration for Industry and Commerce, and the People's Bank are all involved in Internet-related issues that mirror the offline world (Chen and Ang 2009).

Many online companies, therefore, will find that they need to deal with multiple government agencies in their daily operations. For example, Internet service providers are required to obtain permits to conduct business. If their business is not confined to one category, they need to apply for a range of permits for each category of the service from different authorities. For example, in 2013, thirteen permits, or "license plates" as they are known in China, were displayed at the bottom of the front page of Sina (www.sina.com.cn), one of China's largest web portals. These licenses, up from twelve in 2010 but down from fourteen in 2011, are obtained separately from the authorities of culture, education, food and drugs, broadcasting, and press and publication.

Generally, each state agency is in charge of Internet-related issues in their specific jurisdiction. Their jurisdiction, however, is not clear-cut and sometimes overlaps with another. Without a single overseeing unit to coordinate the policies and strategies, state agencies actively participate in profit-seeking activities and engage in turf wars of Internet regulation.

With so many entities involved, inevitably, there are conflicts and missed enforcements. For example, the central government had proposed a convergent overseeing telecommunications, cable television networks, and Internet as early as 1998 that would involve the Ministry of Information Industry and the State Administration for Radio, Film, and Television (Kalathil and Boas 2003). Technically speaking, the networks regulated by MII and SARFT have the capacity to provide multimedia communications including VoIP (voice over Internet Protocol), IPTV (Internet Protocol television), etc. It was therefore only logical that it was proposed that these two networks be integrated and services shared. Both MII and SARFT, however, wanted to enter the field, but neither was willing to give up its monopoly. As MII had the authority on telecommunication and SARFT had the final say on broadcasting, both ministries restricted the other's expansion by employing the trump card of licensing; that is to say, TV broadcasting organizations are not allowed to operate telecommunication services and telecommunications operators cannot be involved in broadcasting audio-visual programs. Both telecommunications and broadcasting sectors are therefore not competitive; operators are reluctant to invest in the respective sectors. The turf war between MII and SARFT means that the proposal for a convergent regulator remains a plan on paper after more than ten years.

The fallout from the conflicts is well illustrated by the development of IPTV and VoIP services in China. IPTV delivers television programming using Internet protocols. In 2005, China Telecom experimented with an IPTV service in Quanzhou, Fujian Province. SARFT quickly declared the experiment illegal and stopped the IPTV service. TV manufacturers, however, were adding modules and Internet set-top units to enable users to receive TV signals via the Internet. In January 2010, the State Council settled the turf war by issuing a "guidance" to award SARFT the oversight of IPTV.

The situation of VoIP development is similar. VoIP has the potential to offer local and long-distance telephone services that are cheaper than conventional phone calls, thus exerting a competitive pressure on telecommunication services monopolized by the MII. In 2005, the MII declared that only China Telecom and China Netcom could provide VoIP service in China. Both state-owned enterprises, however, were not interested in offering VoIP, as they feared cannibalization of their own services. In September 2005, the MII agreed that China

Telecom should pilot two VoIP trials (in Shenzhen, Guangdong Province, and Shangrao, Jiangxi Province); and China Netcom should pilot two trials in Changchun, Jilin Province, and Tai'an, Shangdong Province. Years elapsed, and in 2011 the pilots in these four cities were still experimental, and the two companies had no intention of expanding VoIP service to other cities. With strong market demand for VoIP service, many operators went underground by offering the service without a license. These underground operators risk being shut down at any time. Indeed, in 2009, the VoIP service provided by Hanzhou Youheng Internet Technology Co. Limited was forced to shut down.

Implications

In May 2011, the Chinese government announced that it had created a central agency to oversee the Internet. Western observers immediately saw this as political intervention (Wines 2011), although, as pointed out above, it could also be argued that this central agency was aimed at avoiding turf battles.

A year earlier, in June 2010, the Chinese government published a white paper on the Internet where it said it would "unswervingly stick to its opening-up policy, open the Chinese Internet market in accordance with the law" (Information Office 2010). The six-part white paper outlined the regulatory plans to promote greater use of the Internet, protect Internet security, promote international cooperation, and guarantee freedom of speech on the Internet. At first sight, the document is in line with the sense that Chinese citizens are feeling increasingly em powered. On closer examination, however, many of the statements in the white paper are heavily qualified. Probably the best way to view the document is to see it as an outline of the aspirations of the Chinese government.

Conclusion

It would appear that the multistakeholder model of Internet governance has much to offer China. The large government investments in both the hard and soft infrastructure of the Internet means that China is well on its way to being the country with both the largest number of Internet users as well as the largest Internet economy. China's laws are considered controversial by many in the area of content control. As with much of China, the prohibitions on content are passed with little consultation by the private sector or civil society. Consultation would make the laws not only more palatable and enforceable but also would enhance their legitimacy.

The multistakeholder model would also minimize turf wars because the regulatory system for the Internet is currently fragmented and chaotic. At the very least, the multistakeholder model will compel all parties involved to arrive at a decision rather than leave matters in limbo.

China's path to progress is to encourage information flow but also to have state control; it is a cautious approach. It appears to be in line with the Chinese culture of "crossing the river by feeling the stones"—slowly, small steps a time, moving only when one is stable, and avoiding being swept away by any current (Zhang 2006).

Peng Hwa ANG
Nanyang Technological University

Xiaoyan CHEN
Xiamen University

See also E-Government; Internet Regulation; The Great Firewall; Telecommunications Industry

Further Reading

Authorities in Fujian ban SMG and China Telecom's IPTV business. (2006). C114. Retrieved January 6, 2006, from http://www.cn-c114.net/576/a286400.html

Chen Xiaoyan, & Ang, Peng Hwa. (2011). Internet police in China: Scope, regulation and myth. In David Herold & Peter Wolfgang Marolt (Eds.), *Online society in China: Creating, celebrating, and instrumentalising the online carnival.* London: Routledge.

China e-Business Research Center. (2010). *Report on China's e-commerce market.* Retrieved April 26, 2013, from http://b2b.toocle.com/zt/upload_data/down/2010dsjc.doc

China Internet Network Information Center (CNNIC). (2011). *The 27th survey report.* Retrieved April 26, 2013, from http://www.cnnic.cn/research/bgxz/tjbg/201101/P020110221534255749405.pdf

China Internet Network Information Center (CNNIC). (2013). *Statistical report on Internet development in China.* Retrieved April 15, 2013, from http://www1.cnnic.cn/IDR/ReportDownloads/201302/P020130312536825920279.pdf

Fiveash, Kelly. (2010, September 9). "Internet censorship is trade barrier," says Google exec. *The Register.* Retrieved April 26, 2013, from http://www.theregister.co.uk/2010/09/09/google_pressure_on_censorship/

Fu Hanlong, & Mou Yi. (2010). An assessment of the 2008 telecommunications restructuring in China. *Telecommunications Policy,* 34(10), 649–658.

Government websites established, service ability needs improvement. (2009 April 17). *China News.* Retrieved April 26, 2013, from http://www.chinanews.com.cn/it/itxw/news/2009/04-17/1650420.shtml [in Chinese]

Herold, David Kurt, & Marolt, Peter. (Eds.). (2011). Online society in China: Creating, celebrating, and instrumentalising the online carnival. London and New York: Routledge.

Information Office of the State Council of the People's Republic of China. (2010, June 8). White paper on the Internet in China. Retrieved April 26, 2013, from http://china.org.cn/government/whitepaper/node_7093508.htm

Kalathil, Shanti, & Boas, Taylor C. (2003). Open networks, closed regimes: The impact of the Internet on authoritarian rule. *First Monday, 8*(1). Retrieved September 6, 2013, from http://firstmonday.org/htbin/cgiwrap/bin/ojs/index.php/fm/article/view/1028/949

Loo, B. P. Y. (2004). Telecommunications reforms in China: Towards an analytical framework. *Telecommunications Policy, 28,* 697–714.

Lovelock, Peter; Clark, Theodore; & Petrazzini, Ben. (1996). The "Golden Projects": China's national networking Initiative. *Information Infrastructure & Policy, 5*(4), 265.

Ng, J. (2009, June). Barriers to e-commerce policy in logistics: An exploratory study of the Pearl River Delta, China. *International Journal of Logistics: Research & Applications, 12*(3), 195–212.

SARFT takes control of IPTV in China. (2010, June 10). C114. Retrieved April 26, 2013, from http://www.cn-c114.net/583/a515211.html

Seifert, Jeffrey W., & Chung Jongpil. (2009). Using e-government to reinforce government-citizen relationships comparing government reform in the United States and China. *Social Science Computer Review, 27*(1).

United Nations Working Group on Internet Governance. (2005, June). *Final report of the Working Group on Internet Governance.* Geneva: United Nations.

Wines, Michael. (2011, May 4). China creates new agency for patrolling the Internet. *New York Times.* Retrieved April 26, 2013, from http://www.nytimes.com/2011/05/05/world/asia/05china.html?_r=1&ref=world&wh=0E1EBE6D60C0202FAE0871ADC9BB471D

Zhang, Lena L. (2006, August). Behind the "Great Firewall": Decoding China's Internet media policies from the inside. *Convergence: The Journal of Research into New Media Technologies, 12* (3), 271–291.

Internet Regulation

Wǎngluò guǎnzhì gàishù 网络管治概述

Summary: The content that is allowed on the Internet in China has always been strictly regulated; unsuitable content is organized under twelve general categories. As a result, guerrilla-style digital warfare is waged between the Chinese government and high-tech libertarians. The goal of Internet regulation for the authorities is to provide a "healthy" environment for both political and economic development.

By December 2012, the number of Internet users in China had reached 564 million, representing a drastic jump from just 620,000 users in 1997, when the China Internet Network Information Society (CNNIC) carried out its first survey (CNNIC 2013). It is not only "netizens" in China that have embraced the information revolution but also the Chinese authorities. Yet what the Chinese Communist Party (CCP) desires is economic growth and prosperity, and increasing investment opportunities; it does not desire unfettered discussion that may disrupt social stability or threaten state security.

Content Regulation

Although freedom of expression is guaranteed under China's constitution, the CCP has been extremely cautious with any form of politically sensitive information, which is often defined vaguely and broadly. The state authorities are armed with numerous pieces of legal regulation, backed by an elaborate system of control. Direct regulation by the state goes hand in hand with indirect methods of co-regulation with the Internet industry, which include detailed legal duties and liabilities on Internet service providers (ISPs) to filter illegal (or unwanted) information, monitor online activities, retain data, and report to the authorities.

The Great Firewall of China

The primary way of Internet control adopted by the Chinese government is through restricting access to cyberspace by marking a division between "global cyberspace" and "domestic cyberspace" using a virtual firewall, a massive filter, and a block system that are collectively known as the "Great Firewall." At the national level, only ten government-approved agencies are permitted to establish interconnecting Internet networks and to license the operation of ISPs. No individual or single unit is allowed to establish a direct international connection, as the primary entry and access points to China are under strict control. This structure arguably provides the basis for an "intranet," an internal network that can be shut off from the outside world, and for the creation of a firewall, which is a system of Internet blocks and filters to regulate access to politically undesirable and objectionable materials.

At various points in time, and depending on the region in China, sites blocked include Economist.com, Cable News Network (CNN), and the *New York Times*. YouTube, Facebook, and Twitter are also usually inaccessible in China, although this blockage is certainly not foolproof. Anti-blocking technologies (i.e., blocking the blockers) have been developed and used by netizens in China to bypass the censored system. A guerrilla-style digital warfare is constantly waged between the Chinese government and high-tech libertarians. The majority of average netizens in China, however, are living behind the so-called Great Firewall.

The Legal Rules Governing Unlawful Content

The content that is allowed on the Internet has always been strictly regulated in China. Under the Regulations on Internet Information Services of 2000, the production, duplication, release, and dissemination of content in nine categories are absolutely forbidden. These include information that

1. Opposes the basic principles laid down in the Constitution.
2. Endangers national security, discloses state secret, subverts the ruling regime, or undermines national unity.
3. Is detrimental to the honor and interests of the state.
4. Instigates ethnic hatred or ethnic discrimination, or undermines ethnic unity.
5. Undermines the state's policy toward religions, or preaches the teachings of evil cults or that promotes feudalistic and superstitious beliefs.
6. Disseminates rumors, disturbs social order, or undermines social stability.
7. Spreads pornography or other salacious materials; promotes gambling, violence, homicide, or terrorism; or instigates crimes.
8. Insults or slanders other people, or infringes upon other people's legitimate rights and interests.
9. Contains other information prohibited by the law or administrative regulations.

In 2002, the Interim Provisions on the Administration of Internet Publication added one more forbidden area: that of "compromising public morality or the refined indigenous culture and traditions." Furthermore in 2005, the Provisions of the Administration of Internet News Information Services added two additional forbidden categories of information. They were "information inciting illegal assemblies, association, demonstrations, protest, and gatherings that disturb social order" and "information concerning activities of illegal civic associations." In total, therefore, under Chinese regulations there are twelve forbidden areas that should not be published or discussed on the Internet.

In addition, the scope of the above mentioned categories may expand. In 2013, the Supreme People's Court and the Supreme People's Procuratorate issued the joint Interpretation Concerning Several Issues of the Application of Law in Handling Criminal Cases in the Use of Information Networks Governing Criminal Defamation and other Crimes (hereinafter referred as Joint Judicial Interpretation). Information networks are defined to include the Internet, television broadcasting, fixed-line telephones systems, and mobile devices information systems. Under the Joint Judicial Interpretation, criminal defamation under article 246 of the Criminal Law will now include the "intentional fabrication" and dissemination through information networks of false information that "seriously endangers social order and national interest." Under the Criminal Law, fabrication of false information about others under "grave circumstances" may lead to a maximum of three years imprisonment, criminal detention, surveillance, or loss of political rights. According to the 2013 Joint Judicial Interpretation, "grave circumstances" refers to information that has been visited more than five thousand times or reposted by others for more than five hundred times; information that has led to the injured party or his close relatives suffering from mental disorder, committing self-harm or suicide, or any other serious consequence; or a defaming party that has already been subject to administrative punishment for defamation in the preceding two years. Another critical provision in the Criminal Law provides that criminal defamation may be brought on by aggrieved parties, and by agents of the state in cases "where serious harm is done to public order or to the interests of the state." According to the Joint Judicial Interpretation, the latter includes defamation in the information networks that cause (1) a mass incident, (2) public chaos, (3) ethnic or religious conflicts, (4) defamation of multiple persons that creates a repugnant social impact, (5) harms the national image or seriously endanger national interest, (6) causes a repugnant international impact, or (7) other situations that may gravely endanger social order and national interests. Hence, the offences under the Joint Judicial Interpretation are vaguely defined in both their conceptual definitions, scope, and punishment. It has been criticized for its chilling effect on Internet free speech (Lubman 2013).

In fact, netizens in China always have to navigate carefully through the legal minefield. A notorious example of one who failed to do so is Liu Xiaobo, the 2010 Nobel Peace Prize winner. In 2009, he was sentenced by the Chinese authorities to eleven years in prison for "inciting to overthrow state power" for co-drafting and posting a manifesto, Charter 08, on the Internet. The manifesto called for political reforms, the end of corruption, and respect for human rights.

As is discussed in the following section, state agencies are not only required to carry out direct regulation on Internet content through various means, but the Internet industry is also given the duty of co-regulation.

Direct Regulation

Under the law, every individual, organization, and company in China is held criminally liable for sending harmful content as defined by law. Other than legal measures, the government has also attempted to control and "purify" Internet content through technological means. For example, in 2009, the government attempted to require the installation of Green Dam Youth Escort software to restrict access to "unhealthy" websites for all computers sold in China. This was done in the name of screening out pornographic materials and to protect the youth. Eventually, the project was abandoned due to a large public outcry from netizens in China, and from the international business community.

In addition to using legal means and technological advances to control the Internet, it is believed that in 2004, the CCP already had a special task force of more than thirty thousand cyber police to patrol the Internet, to block foreign news sites, and to terminate domestic sites with politically sensitive information (Watts 2005). Also starting in 2004, different provinces in China recruited members of the so-called *50 Cent Party*: undercover Internet commentators who actively contribute pro-government statements on the Internet in chat rooms and on forums. (The term *50 Cent Party* reflects the amount that an undercover commentator would be paid for each posting—which is actually about eight US cents.) In this way, public opinion is being shaped by the authorities.

Co-regulation

Other than imposing direct control on users, the Chinese authorities have built a co-regulatory regime, imposing various duties and liabilities of filtering, monitoring, and reporting on the Internet industry.

Internet service and content providers are regulated directly under the Regulation on Internet Information Services of 2000. The general rule is that all Internet service providers are required to provide online users with quality services and to ensure the legality of the information. ISPs that offer news coverage and Bulletin Board Systems (BBSs) are required to keep a sixty-day record of the information that they distribute, when it is distributed, and the web address where the information is located. Other ISPs are similarly required to keep records of the time of use, accounts of Internet addresses or domain names, and dial-in telephone numbers of online users for sixty days. The measures are considered the prime model for the strict control of Internet administration. In addition, the Law on Guarding State Secrets amended in 2010 imposes a duty on ISPs to keep records on the disclosure of information involving state secrets, and to report to state organs.

Electronic bulletin service providers, including those that disseminate information through online interactive forums, electronic bulletin boards, electronic white boards, Internet forums, online chat rooms, and message boards, are governed under the Electronic Bulletin Services Provisions of 2000. They are also required to keep a record of users, monitor their activities, and report any violations to the authorities. Similar duties of data retention and reporting to the authorities extend to Internet email service providers under the Measures for the Administration of Internet Email Services of 2006. In addition to the duties of keeping record, monitoring, and reporting, Internet news information service providers, including websites, are required to reproduce content from official news organizations under the Provisions for the Administration of Internet News Information Services (2005).

Draconian as it may sound, regulation, co-regulation, and self-regulation became the prevailing style of rule after 2000. Other than keeping records and reporting unlawful content or behaviors, Internet cafés, Internet bars, computer lounges, and other places that provide Internet access to the public are required to install tracking software, institute surveillance and monitoring measures, and report to the relevant authorities if a user employs the Internet for illegal activities (article 19 of the Regulations on the Administration of Business Sites of Internet Access 2002). In addition to this structure, Internet publishers, web portals, and web managers are also required to shoulder monitoring duties under the Interim Provisions on the Administration of Internet Publication of 2002. In March 2005, the Registration Administration Measures for Non-Commercial Internet Information Services stipulates that all owners of personal websites and webmasters of bulletin boards and blogs must register with the government, with violators risking a heavy fine or closure of their webpages.

The same standard also applies to providers of Internet cultural products, which are defined under article 2 of the Interim Provisions on the Administration of Internet Culture (issued in 2003, amended in 2011) to be Internet entities that produce, disseminate, or circulate audio and video products or game products; or show plays, works of art, cartoons, or other cultural products.

ISPs and other intermediaries are part of the co-regulatory team of Internet control in China. In early 2011, *Time* reported that Sina Weibo (a large microblogging service) employed up to seven hundred censors to track and block content (Ramzy 2011). Companies (including Microsoft's MSN and Yahoo!) have generated their "blocklists" based on educated guesswork, which easily results in overblocking of content (MacKinnon 2009).

The role of the ISP is illustrated in the 2004 Shi Tao case, when Yahoo! turned over information about the Chinese journalist Shi Tao to the Chinese authorities. Little did Shi know that the anonymous email he sent to a human rights organization in the United States through his Yahoo! account would get him a ten-year prison sentence. He was convicted for illegally providing state secrets outside the country.

In the foreseeable future, ISPs are likely to assume an increasingly active and compliant role in reporting any suspects under the real name registration system. This system requires everyone who uses information services (including Internet and phones) to register with their real names and identity numbers starting in September 2013 under the Provisions on the Registration of Real Identity of Telephone Users by the Ministry of Industry and Information Technology, and the Decision Concerning Strengthening Network Information Protection by the State Council.

Intellectual Property Rights

Rapid development of information technology poses serious challenges to the traditional legal regime for intellectual property rights. China has been able to quickly come up with legislation for intellectual property protection in this information era. Important developments have taken place in two major areas: protection of computer software and domain name disputes.

Protection of Computer Software

The first regulation relating to the protection of computer software was made in 1991. A dual-track system was created for domestic and foreign software: there is no registration requirement for foreign software, and the protection period is fifty years, while registration is required for domestic software, and the protection period is twenty-five years, with the possibility of extension for another twenty-five years. Such discriminatory practice did not last long. In 1993, the Supreme People's Court abolished the requirement of registration, but the different protection periods still existed.

The situation changed completely when the new Regulations on the Protection of Computer Software was enacted in 2001 by the State Council. Registration is not compulsory under the newer regulation, but the registration certificate can serve as preliminary proof of ownership.

Software is normally owned by the author (i.e., creator) who develops it. When it comes to joint authorship, the ownership is determined by the written agreement among the authors. The software copyright owners enjoy the rights of publication, authorship, revision, duplication, lease, and translation. Economic rights are protected for the lifespan plus fifty years if the copyright owner is an individual, or fifty years after first publication for corporations who own copyrights.

The user is not allowed to reproduce, publish, or distribute the software without the consent of the owner. Copyright infringements include situations where the user intentionally avoids or breaches the technical measures adopted by the owner to protect the software copyright, or intentionally deletes or alters the electronic information of software right management.

Domain Name Disputes

The CNNIC was set up as a nonprofit organization in 1997. One major function of the CNNIC is to serve as a domain name (.cn) registry and manager. In view of the rapid development of domain name dispute resolution around the world, the CNNIC adopted the Chinese Domain Name Dispute Resolution Measures in 2000, which was revised in 2002, 2006 and 2012.

The Chinese Domain Name Dispute Resolution Measures intends to use an alternative dispute resolution procedure to resolve domain name disputes in a quick, cheap, and fair manner. To win the case, the complainant needs to prove the following three elements: (1) the disputed domain name is identical or confusingly similar to the name or mark in which the complainant has civil rights and interests; (2) the disputed domain name holder has no lawful rights or interests in respect to the domain name or the major part of the domain name; and (3) the disputed domain name holder has registered or has used the domain name in bad faith.

Emerging Problems

In addition to minding the political and economic dimensions of Internet governance, the authorities have to tackle the problem of privacy violations when netizens use the Internet as a "human flesh search engine" (*rénròu sōusuǒ* 人肉搜索), a somewhat alarming-sounding name for collaboration by many people who use the

Internet to expose the personal information and privacy of wrongdoers as a form of social punishment. (The term *human flesh* refers to the fact that these online searches lead to real people, and thus have real consequences.) Though some may applaud this as an alternative means to check against officials' abuse of power, the result can be devastating to ordinary citizens. Victims face various forms of harassment, people lose their jobs, and at least one has lost her life. In 2010, the new Tort Law became effective, with provisions to protect citizens' right of privacy, name, and reputation. Yet the phenomenon of *human-flesh search hunting* has not stopped. An effective and comprehensive piece of legislation on personal information protection is yet to be enacted, which is essential for e-banking, electronic medical records, and other aspects of privacy protection on the Internet frontier.

Anne S. Y. CHEUNG and ZHAO Yun
The University of Hong Kong

See also The Great Firewall; Internet Content Filtering; Internet Governance; Internet Monitoring; Internet Service Providers (ISPs)

Further Reading

Bandurski, David. (2008, July-August). China's guerrilla war for the web. *Far Eastern Economic Review, 171*(6), 41–44.

Cheung, Anne S. Y. (2006). The business of governance: China's legislation on content regulation in cyberspace. *New York University Journal of International Law and Politics*, 38(1–2), 1–37.

China Internet Network Information Centre (CCNIC). (2011). The statistical reports of Internet development in China. Retrieved September 22, 2013, from http://www1.cnnic.cn/en/index/0O/index.htm

Deibert, Ronald; Palfrey, John; Rohozinski; Rafal; & Zittrain, Jonathan. (2008). *Access denied*. Cambridge, MA: MIT Press.

Gao Fuping. (2004). The e-commerce legal environment in China: Status quo and issues. *Temple International & Comparative Law Journal, 18*, 51–75.

Global Internet Freedom Consortium. (2007). Defeat Internet censorship: Overview of advanced technologies and products. Retrieved September 22, 2013, from http://www.internetfreedom.org/archive/Defeat_Internet_Censorship_White_Paper.pdf, 1-22.

Lubman, Stanley. (2013, September 18). The "Legalization" of China's Internet crackdown. *Wall Street Journal Blog*. Retrieved September 22, 2013, from http://blogs.wsj.com/chinarealtime/2013/09/18/the-legalization-of-chinas-internet-crackdown/

MacKinnon, Rebecca. (2009). China's censorship 2.0: How companies censor bloggers. *First Monday, 14*(2). Retrieved September 22, 2013, from http://firstmonday.org/htbin/cgiwrap/bin/ojs/index.php/fm/article/view/2378/2089.

Miao, Felix. (2007–2008). Protection of intellectual property rights in software products and how to accomplish a technology transfer transaction in China. *Fordham Intellectual Property, Media & Entertainment Law Journal, 18*, 61–115.

Ramzy, Austin. (2011 February 21). Wired up. *Time*. Retrieved September 22, 2013, 2011, from http://www.time.com

Watts, Jonathan. (2005, June 14). China's secret Internet police target critics with web of propaganda. *Guardian*. Retrieved September 22, 2013, from http://www.theguardian.com/technology/2005/jun/14/newmedia.china

Zhang Chu; & Lei Lingfei. (2005). The Chinese approach to electronic transactions legislation. *Computer Law Review & Technology Journal, 9*, 333–354.

Zhang Mo. (2002). Governance of Internet domain names against cybersquatters in China: A framework and legal perspective. *Hastings International & Comparative Law Review, 26*, 51–81.

Zhao Yun. (2009). Reflection on the finality of panel's decisions in domain name dispute resolution process, with reference to China's practice. *John Marshall Journal of Computer & Information Law, 26*, 395-413.

Zheng Yongnian. (2008). Technological empowerment: The Internet, state, and society in China. Stanford, CA: Stanford University Press.

Zittran, Jonathan, & Edelman, Benjamin. (2003, March 20). Empirical analysis of Internet filtering in China. Retrieved September 22, 2013, from http://cyber.law.harvard.edu/filtering/china/

Part 3
Entertainment and Education

Blogging

Bókè 博客

Summary: Blogging has gained tremendous popularity and has become a daily communication tool for hundreds of millions of people in China, which went from having virtually no bloggers in 2000 to having a third of a billion bloggers by 2012. Despite issues of censorship and surveillance, blogging remains an extremely popular activity and has contributed much to the development of online journalism and public discourse of conflicts and problems in Chinese society. Many bloggers hope to be able to bring more transparency to China's political sphere.

As webpages that are frequently updated with posts centered around one topic and arranged in reverse chronological order, blogs are characterized by self-generated content, volunteer commenting, and connected networks of discourse through features such as links, cross-postings (posting identical material on multiple pages), track backs (records of the pages that link to a specific page), and tags (metadata that assist in sorting and finding articles on a particular topic). Blogs, and the networked community encompassing them (the blogosphere), has been documented to have deliberative potential by advancing discussion on social problems, enhancing civic involvement, and contributing to a global public sphere that is "more open to participation by more kinds of people than in the pre-Internet era" (MacKinnon 2008, 254). Accordingly, the huge volume of blog use in China has invited discussion about whether it represents a new media form that could eventually break through China's restricted media environment and nurture a transparent and fair communication system that, it is hoped, might lead to improvements in China's policy making.

History of Development

As with any form of communication that depends on technology, blogging has seen a remarkable number of changes in its short life span. China went from having no bloggers in 2000 to a third of a billion bloggers by 2012. Blogging has developed in various stages.

EARLY STAGE: 2002–2006

Born in the 1990s in the United States, blogs were introduced to China in 2002. In that year, the Internet critics and analysts Fang Xingdong and Wang Junxiu coined the Chinese name *bókè* 博客 for blog, contending that blogging would bring "a revolution" in China (Fang and Wang 2003). In August 2002, Fang and Wang founded blogchina.com, further promoting the practice of blogging. Many Blog Service Provider (BSP) systems appeared afterward, including blogcn.com, Blogbus.com, and Blogdriver.com. At that time, however, blog users were limited to a handful of people in the areas of information technology, economics, and science. Blogging in China received its first big boost in June 2003, when the magazine writer Mu Zimei's sexual diary on blogcn.com (now bokee.com) created tremendous traffic, peaking at 160,000 page views in November, and made the word *blog* a popular Internet search keyword (Sina News 2003). Chinese "netizens" started to witness the enormous influence of blogs from that point on. From the second half of 2003 through the first half of 2004, China saw the beginning of the commercialization of blogging. On the one hand, the emergence of professional BSPs such as Blogchina, Blogcn, and Blogdriver provided services for users to set up and maintain a blog. On the other hand, leading Internet portals also joined to launch blog services and to compete with BSPs in aggregating blog users. In September 2005, the largest Chinese portal, sina.com, launched its blog service, blog.sina.com.cn. Shortly afterward, the other two commercial portals, Sohu and Netease, also launched blog services.

The nationwide popularization of blogging had to wait until 2005 to take off, however; at that time, hundreds of celebrity blogs started to aggregate on blog.sina.com and soon attracted enormous numbers of visits. A blog on Sina by Xu Jinglei, a Chinese movie star, claimed the number-one spot on Technorati 100 in 2006. According to Technorati's statistics, there were 45,700 inbound links to Xu's blog from 28,151 websites, a number much higher than that of websites linking to the second-ranked *Boing Boing* blog. These were just linking websites to Xu's blog homepage, not including the ones linking to any single post. Therefore, even ranked as number one, the total of inbound linking websites to Xu's blog was still seriously underestimated by the Technorati's statistics. The best-selling author Han Han became another popular celebrity blogger after criticizing established personalities, including literary critics, writers, directors, and musicians, for what he saw as their pretentiousness and capriciousness in Chinese cultural criticism.

Celebrity blogs on other BSPs also aggregated big traffic. Wang Xiaofeng, a Chinese magazine writer who is well known for sarcastic comments on problematic social and culture phenomena in his blog, had millions of blog readers, and was named by *Time* magazine as one of the fifteen "citizens of the new digital democracy" in the year 2006.

Blogs run by average citizens also started to rise sharply at this time. Most citizen blogs focused on personal reflections of daily life, such as records of life and work routine, as well as information about private hobbies. Blogs devoted to discussions of sociopolitical issues were comparatively fewer in number at this stage.

With the flush of venture capital to the blog business, blogging technologies and services continue to expand and develop. The practice of blogging has evolved due to the increasing use of multimedia such as video, music, and podcasts on blogs; these serve personal as well as organizational purposes for fields such as education and marketing.

Rapid Development Stage: 2007–Present

The year 2007 saw the emerging success of leading Internet portals over professional BSPs, since portals typically include search engines and large directories of websites that are categorized by topic, such as news, technology, and entertainment, which tend to attract a larger number of users and financial resources. Portals such as Sina, Sohu, and QQ further strengthened and promoted their blog services by advertising on the portal page, as well as at the bottom of the posts in existing celebrity blogs. These strategies accelerated the process for portal users and blog readers to set up their own blogs on the portals. Professional BSPs such as Blogbus that focus only on blogging, however, have less of an advantage than these portals do in respect to users and financial resources.

Another noticeable trend in this stage is the convergence of blogs and social network service (SNS) websites. Starting in the middle of 2008, SNS became one of the most popular Internet applications. Rising SNS websites such as kaixin001.com and xiaonei.com (now renren.com) provided various plug-ins to integrate social networking functions, among which built-in blog features helped to drive a large number of web users to become active bloggers. When opening a SNS website account, one simultaneously sets up a blog that is hosted by this website. In other words, blogs become an enclosed feature of social network service. The affiliation thus helps to increase cross-links among bloggers who may have been interacting with each other as community members in the social network.

In 2006 the number of bloggers more than doubled from the previous year; in 2009, this number had increased by five times again. By the end of 2012, there were 372 million bloggers—about 66 percent of the overall number of netizens (CNNIC 2013). Bloggers' enthusiasm in expression has been substantially increasing, and the number of active blogs has seen explosive growth (CNNIC 2009).

Blog Service Providers

The uniqueness of blogging in China, as compared with its Western counterparts, lies in the fact that a majority of blogs do not exist independently but are hosted by BSPs. There are two major types of BSPs: one type is associated with portals, such as blog.sina.com.cn and blog.sohu.com. The other type, professional BSPs such as bokee.com and blogbus.com, focuses only on blog services.

In general, BSPs have both a negative and positive effect on blog communication. Without an autonomous domain, blogs hosted by BSPs are constrained in terms of space capacity, diversity of webpage design, and control of content. For example, BSPs can censor a blog or a post if it is considered politically sensitive. At the same time, however, blogs also benefit from depending on BSPs, which often have greater economic resources (e.g., financial support and advertisement source) and social leverage (e.g., support from state) than independent blogs. In 2007, for example, the largest BSP, blog.sina.com.cn, was ranked by Technorati as the most popular blog (having the most incoming links) in the world. With such a high ranking, the BSP may help to direct attention to a blog through mechanisms such as first page recommendation.

Bloggers and Blog Readers

According to the 2008–2009 Survey Report on Chinese Blog Market and Blogging Behavior released by the China Internet Network Information Center (CNNIC), bloggers had the following demographic characteristics at that time. The proportion of female bloggers (55 percent) was about 10 percent higher than male bloggers (45 percent). Students with no income were the major bloggers, accounting for more than half of the number, and white-collar workers with monthly income above 3,000 yuan (approximately US$441) were the second largest group. Bloggers tend to be young, with 86 percent under the age of thirty. Bloggers who spent two hours or more online every day accounted for 67 percent.

Blogging behavior also varies among bloggers. Regarding the motivation to blog, the report shows that 64 percent blogged to record daily mood and feelings; 40 percent to back up photos, text, and other information; and 37 percent to share resources with others or to express point of views. Other motivations include making friends, commenting on current sociopolitical issues, and assisting learning, working, or other activities. About half of bloggers surveyed updated blogs at least once a week, indicating a considerably high level of activity. More than half of bloggers tended to express their views on "social phenomena," showing a high level of engagement in public issues.

Studies found that blogging has provided many people in China with a medium for making sophisticated critiques of the regime without encountering harsh repression. Blogs have also initiated vehement arguments on social unfairness, corruption among government officials, suppression of freedom of speech, and other topics. Scholars, therefore, have concluded that "blogs with a 'bottom-up' pattern [i.e., not from the authorities] can serve as alternative sources for sensitive issues, set the agenda of the Chinese government on occasion, and force changes in the upper echelons of the world of politics" (Zhou 2009, 1007).

As the blogging phenomenon develops fast, blog reading also has become popular in China. Most readers access blogs through links in other blogs, search engines, or by recommendation from BSPs and friends. When asked about preferences, three-quarters of the respondents to the survey tended to visit friends' and colleagues' blogs, indicating a close link between reading behavior and the real world.

Among the type of content that blog readers visit most often, about half is entertainment content. Other popular content includes lifestyle, culture, art and history, social issues, sports, and alumni and other forms of networking. This shows that, in general, blog-reading behavior is entertainment oriented. In recent years, however, content related to social issues is getting more and more attention among readers as netizens become more active in public events.

Less than half of blog readers in the survey believed what they read in others' blog posts; another half of readers reported difficulty in distinguishing between credible and unreliable information in the blogosphere.

Censorship and Surveillance

Blogging is under the censorship and surveillance of the Chinese government. Various control strategies are employed to ensure that blogging activity does not sow dissent and threaten the stability and safety of the Chinese Communist Party's (CCP) rule. These strategies include removing posts from a service system, stopping visits, or removing entire blogs. The Internet Society of China released the Public Pledge of Self-Regulation on Blog Service in 2007, signed by more than ten leading BSPs, including people.com, sina.com, sohu.com, netease.com, QQ.com, and MSN China. The obligation was for the BSPs to ensure politically acceptable and morally appropriate content through constraining the behavior of individual bloggers on these BSPs. The pledge requires that the bloggers agree to abide by China's laws and regulations, and not disseminate pornography, rumors, or sensitive information. Bloggers are also required to agree to monitor and manage postings and comments, and to delete those that are illegal or objectionable. If a blogger does not adhere to the terms, the service provider has a right to delete undesirable information, or terminate the blogger's service. Under such surveillance, scholars have argued that political discussion in the blogosphere is often "the result of a compromise between what bloggers want to express and what the regime allows them to write" (Esarey and Xiao 2008, 756).

In recent years, the control has even gone beyond the hands of party regime to the commercial companies. Rebecca MacKinnon, a former CNN journalist and expert on Chinese Internet censorship, conducted a systemic testing of Chinese BSPs in 2009 and found that blogs suffer from commercial BSPs' wide variation of censorship, ranging from being prevented from posting at all, to being "held for moderation" or partial visibility to the public, and to being fully deleted after publication (MacKinnon 2009). The multiple strategies of content filtering thus constitute a technical barrier for bloggers to get their opinion distributed—they have to be able to know when not to cross the line in order to increase the likelihood of survival of politically sensitive information.

Foreign corporations providing blog service in China are also subject to the local laws of censorship. Microsoft's MSN Spaces, for example, censors its Chinese language blogs, and in 2005 it took down the popular blog written by Michael Anti, one of China's edgiest journalistic bloggers, to show its determination to comply with the Chinese regulation on Internet speech.

Blogging versus Journalism

Studies have documented the link between the popularity of political blogging and public suspicions of traditional journalistic values, as well as blogs' potential to improve the work of journalists (Glaser 2004; Lowrey 2006). In the context of China, such competition between bloggers and journalists is even more remarkable, since the media's dominant role as government mouthpiece is still assumed, and inadequate information and intractability of political problems and solutions is normal in news coverage.

Blogging has demonstrated advantages in distributing information more rapidly, and sometimes with more in-depth and eyewitness accounts. For example, on 18 February 2005, China's biggest online game operator, Shengda, purchased stocks of China's most influential portal, Sina. Because both are leading Chinese Internet companies, the change in ownership structure may affect the pattern of the entire Internet in China. Due to strict confidentiality, however, no media reported the news, and it was first revealed instead by a well-known information technology (IT) critic, Wang Jipeng, in his blog. Similarly, during the earthquake in Jiujiang, Jiangxi Province, on 26 November 2005, a blog reported the earthquake fifteen minutes earlier than mainstream media did.

In addition to the speed of information distribution, there are also examples in which a blog has also beaten traditional journalism regarding the exposure of politically unpleasant news. On 1 August 2008, a landslide occurred in an iron mine in Loufan, Shanxi Province, and the local government alleged that it was a natural disaster. The *Oriental Outlook* published Sun Chunlong's and Wang Xiao's reports that revealed cover-up and falsity in the official report of the accident. This article was cross-posted by Netease, Tencent, and Phoenix's news websites, but was deleted soon. On 14 September, Sun Chunlong posted "An Informant's Letter to the Premier of Shanxi Province" in his blog, trying to reveal the true story. Sun's blog soon had 631,231 visits, and the letter was cross-posted on various message platforms online by netizens who hailed Sun's courage. Then it was picked up by the central leaders. The State Council investigated the accident and confirmed that the local government had concealed the truth and changed the alleged "natural disaster" into a "major liability accident." In this case, although Sun, as a journalist, first published his article in traditional media, it was his blog post that invited extensive attention: once an article is removed from mainstream media, it disappears in the public's field of vision, but a blog post often has been reproduced everywhere by its readers or subscribers, even if it has been removed.

Implications

Despite the fact that the popularity of blogging in China was initially advanced by people's entertainment and social networking needs, rather than a passion for public discussion of sociopolitical issues, and that censorship and surveillance in the blogosphere often threatens free speech, Chinese blogging has demonstrated a profound impact on the creation of a freer media environment and a more democratic deliberation.

The fact that blogs have recently initiated heated public discussion on issues related to social unfairness and suppression of free speech has demonstrated blogging's function as a deliberative tool in conveying the public opinion and distributing speaking opportunities. In the well-known 2007 Xiamen PX chemical project case, for example, former journalist Lian Yue published a series of blog posts questioning and protesting the project, which may cause environmental pollution and threaten citizens' health. Lian's blog posts activated a twenty-thousand-strong citizen protest, and the municipal government eventually abandoned the project. In a more recent case, the popular writer and blogger Han Han posted an open letter to the CEO of Baidu, China's most popular search engine, accusing Baidu of copyright infringement (Baidu allowed literary works to become available online without the authors' prior approval) and its "disgraceful manner" in addressing the protest from a group of best-selling Chinese writers (Han 2011). Han's blog post was soon cross-posted on various message platforms and aroused public sympathy, which forced Baidu to remove unauthorized literary works from its free online literary database (Wénkù 文库) within three days.

In addition, regulations and intermittent restrictions do not eclipse the fact that there is still leeway for bloggers to evade regulation pressures. By installing certain blogging software or using euphemisms, for example, bloggers often successfully bypass controls from cyber police. Studies have found that blogging has provided people in China with a medium for making sophisticated critiques of the regime without encountering harsh repression. Although the critique usually takes the form of a compromise between what bloggers want to say and what the government allows them to say, it presents voices and opinions that would otherwise go unheard. In this sense, blogging, like the Internet in general, creates a virtual space for the Chinese people to practice democratic discussions on issues they care about. The more people begin to engage in public deliberation of problems and conflicts, the deeper the aspiration and sense of democracy in their minds. In this regard, blogging represents a rehearsal for democracy.

Jia DAI
Tsinghua University

See also Communities Online; Microblogging; Social and Political Impact; User-Generated Content

Further Reading

China Internet Network Information Center (CNNIC). (2009). 2008–2009 survey report on Chinese blog market and blogging behavior. Retrieved August 14, 2010, from www.cnnic.cn/uploadfiles/pdf/2009/10/10/105733.pdf

China Internet Network Information Center (CNNIC). (2011). The 27th statistical report on Internet development in China. Retrieved March 22, 2011, from http://www1.cnnic.cn/uploadfiles/pdf/2011/2/28/153752.pdf

China Internet Network Information Center (CNNIC). (2013, January). *Statistical report on Internet development in China.* Retrieved April, 15, 2013, from http://www1.cnnic.cn/IDR/ReportDownloads/201302/P020130312536825920279.pdf

Esarey, Ashley, & Xiao, Qiang. (2008). Political expression in the Chinese blogosphere: Below the radar. *Asian Survey, 48*(5), 752–772.

Fang Xingdong & Wang Junxiu. (2003). *Boke: E-shidai daohuo zhe* [*Prometheus in the E-era*]. Beijing: China Fangzheng Publishing House.

Glaser, Mark. (2004, February 11). "Watchblogs" put the political press under the microscope. *Online Journalism Review.* Retrieved July 3, 2009, from http://ojr.org/ojr/glaser/1076465317.php

Grossman, Lev. (2006, December 16). Wang Xiaofeng: Bart Simpson in Beijing. *Time.* Retrieved September 17, 2010, from http://www.time.com/time/magazine/article/0,9171,1570727,00.html

Han Han. (2011). 给李彦宏先生的一封信 [An open letter to Mr. Li Yanhong]. Retrieved April 29, 2013, from http://blog.sina.com.cn/s/blog_4701280b01017ijj.html

Internet Society of China. (2007). 博客服务自律公约 [Public pledge of self-regulation on blog service]. Retrieved April 29, 2013, from http://www.isc.org.cn/ShowArticle.php?id=7955

Lowrey, Wilson. (2006). Mapping the journalism-blogging relationship. *Journalism*, 7(4), 477–500.

MacKinnon, Rebecca. (2008). Blogs and China correspondence: Lessons about global information flows. *Chinese Journal of Communication*, *1*(2), 242–257.

MacKinnon, Rebecca. (2009). China's censorship 2.0: How companies censor bloggers. *First Monday*, *14*(2). Retrieved September 17, 2010, from http://www.uic.edu/htbin/cgiwrap/bin/ojs/index.php/fm/article/view/2378/2089

Sina. (2003, November 11). 女写手用身体写作 木子美性爱日记访问量激增 [Body writing: Visits to the sexual dairy by Mu zimei increase sharply]. Retrieved April 29, 2013, from http://news.sina.com.cn/s/2003-11-11/02312109068.shtml

Zhou Yuqiong, & Moy, Patricia. (2007). Parsing framing processes: The interplay between online public opinion and media coverage. *Journal of Communication*, *57*(1), 79–98.

Zhou Xiang. (2009). The political blogosphere in China: A content analysis of the blogs regarding the dismissal of Shanghai leader Chen Liangyu. *New Media & Society*, *11*(6), 1003–1022.

Chinese Language and Computing

Zhōngwén yǔyán yǔ jìsuànjī 中文语言与计算机

Summary: The development of computing reflects the diversity of dialects and languages that exist in China. For example, one of the words for "computer" in Chinese, *diànnǎo* 电脑, is a combination of "electric" (*diàn* 电) and "brain" (*nǎo* 脑); "malware" is literally translated as "evil intention code" or "malicious code" (*èyìdàimǎ* 恶意代码). Various technical tricks allow users to quickly and easily type Chinese characters and Romanized pinyin into keyboards and keypads.

One of the most daunting tasks for a new user in the computer world is to master the vocabulary, acronyms, and idioms of the field. When approaching the same problem in a foreign language, the difficulties are ameliorated by the standards of the computing world. While one might not know the vocabulary, "File / Open" is usually the first item on the first drop-down menu on the navigation bar. Navigating an Internet page offers additional positional cues to the meaning of various buttons, menus, and link options. In many Western languages, the major terms for web navigation and computers bear some semblance to one another, and the same is true of Chinese. Many of the terms are direct translations from one language into another. "Open" is *kāi* 开 in Chinese, and "file" is *wénjiàn* 文件; so "open file" is *kāi wénjiàn* 开文件. The difficulty arises when one consults a dictionary and finds that "to open" can also be *huō* 豁, *chēng* 撑, *chāi* 拆, or *bāi* 捭. Each of the terms is used in specific situations and may include the idea of spreading something open, opening a container, or opening space, but would never be used in the phrase "open file."

Characteristics of Chinese Languages

Chinese is a multilevel symbolic language. One might think of it as the ultimate encryption, as meaning is assigned to symbols in what may appear to be a haphazard manner, but which makes sense when one knows the derivations. Languages based on an alphabet are written for pronunciation; the letters symbolize the sounds, which in turn can be considered either arbitrary designators or traditional designators of some object or action. The sound "computer" derives from the language of the Romans, who never saw a computer, but who did count and used the word *computare* to talk about it. When we look at the collection of alpha-symbols, like the word "computer," we associate certain visual and experience-based ideas with it. We can also pronounce it. Most people wouldn't know either the Latin or the French derivation of the word and wouldn't care to. All language is symbolic. We are so accustomed to the phonetic form of language that we rarely consider it as symbolic since the letters have a purpose: pronunciation.

In Chinese, the written form of language is directly symbolic. Chinese is not a phonetic or alphabetical language. It uses unique symbols, some twenty thousand of them, to stand for ideas. For instance, the modern symbol for electricity, 电 (*diàn*), was part of the character 電 (*diàn*) and originally meant "lightning." The upper part of the character is the symbol for rain, 雨 (*yǔ*), and the lightning comes down from the rain. Lightning is related to electricity, so in the modern language, 電 (*diàn*) came to mean electric, electricity, and electrical in general. Lightning became known as *shǎndiàn* 閃電 (simplified: 闪电) to differentiate it from electricity.

Historically, Chinese was developed as a written language to communicate with people who spoke a multitude of languages and dialects. The symbols were pronounced in different ways, depending on the language of the speaker. Within ancient China, the written form allowed government, trade, and literature to cross language barriers. Cantonese speakers today (mainly found in south China) still use the same symbols but apply different pronunciations in their spoken language.

Almost all television programming produced in China is spoken in standard Mandarin (*pǔtōnghuà* 普通话) but includes subtitles in simplified characters so that speakers of other dialects can understand the programs. The central government uses television to promote Mandarin as the standard spoken language. The symbolic nature of the characters continues to connect the different dialects of China, just as it has for thousands of years.

Since the Chinese language is based on unique symbols, logically there could be no end to the additions. Rather than making up new symbols, early in history, writers grouped symbols to make new meanings. Sometimes these would become new characters, but more often two or more symbols would become an expression or word containing related ideas. Thus, "television" became *diànshì* 电视, a combination of "electric" and "vision," much as the English word *television* is a combination of "tele" and "vision," or "far vision." Anything that is run by electricity or transmits electricity can contain the character 电. One of the words for computer, *diànnǎo* 电脑, is a combination of "electric" (*diàn* 电) and "brain" (*nǎo* 脑). The second common term for computer, *jìsuànjī* 计算机, is a combination of "to plan" (*jì* 计), "calculate" (*suàn* 算), and "machine" (*jī* 机). Both terms combine previously known concepts to create a new idea.

Computer and Internet Language

Technical terms describing computer components and concepts use ordinary descriptive terms in new combinations, just as they do in English. Nontechnical terms can employ more whimsical or poetic words. Brand names are often chosen for the positive association of the characters or the pleasant way they sound. Another method is to borrow the sound from the original language of the term and find appropriate characters to represent it. Yet another method is to use direct translation from a foreign language, particularly when the original term is well known. For example, "Bluetooth" was literally translated to Chinese as *lányá* 蓝牙 and shares the same incongruity of the English term. The original Danish term had historical associations to convey meaning. The English term was chosen because it sounded like the Danish term and had the attractiveness of mild humor. The Chinese term shares the humor, and once known, simply becomes the term for wireless connectivity, just as it does in English.

To pronounce the characters, one just needs to memorize their sounds. There are phonetics embedded in certain characters to give a hint to their pronunciation, but for the most part, they simply need to be learned. Each of the characters has a single syllable for pronunciation: 电 = *diàn*; 计 = *jì*; 视 = *shì*; 是 = *shì*; 事 = *shì*; and 世 = *shì*. The number of sounds in Chinese is very limited, giving rise to a great number of homonyms. To distinguish concepts without elaborating the sounds, another layer of linguistic "coding" was added to the pronunciation. These are called the four tones; they change the inflection of the syllable. The syllable *shi* can be pronounced as follows: 诗 = *shī* = poem; 湿 = *shī* = wet; 时 = *shí* = time; 石 = *shí* = stone; 史 = *shǐ* = history; 始 = *shǐ* = begin; 是 = *shì* = to be; 事 = *shì* = thing; and 世 = *shì* = world. The context helps clarify which meaning is intended in speech, but exact meaning is most often achieved by combining characters and thus syllables. "World" (*shì* 世) becomes 世界 = *shìjiè*, distinguishing it from other forms of *shi*. It still has homophones, although reduced in number: 视界 = *shìjiè* = "field of vision," and 事界 = *shìjiè* = "event horizon." Since it is unlikely that these combinations would occur in the same context, the meaning is as clear as when an English speaker says "I read the red book."

The Roman characters used to write the pronunciation are a system called pinyin (or Hanyu [Chinese] pinyin) adopted by the People's Republic of China (PRC). There are several other pronunciation systems (notably Wade-Giles), but pinyin is now the standard. (As an example, the Wade-Giles names "Mao Tse-tung" and "Peking" that many Westerners will recognize are written as "Mao Zedong" and "Beijing," respectively, in pinyin.)

Computer language and Internet language enter the Chinese language in a number of ways. Many terms were developed independently by the PRC, Hong Kong, and by Taiwan (the Republic of China, or ROC), and even regional terms can also be found within mainland China. Regional variation in computer terms is usually limited to common items like USB flash drives—also known by a variety of names in English—as people make up nicknames, distributors use different terms to attract attention, and different parts of the industry adopt different translations. (See table 1.)

Another way that the Chinese language is altered is when manufacturers, service providers, and advertisers create language to translate terms from other languages into Chinese, either directly or by creating "concept strings" (i.e., a means for representing computer text that shows for each word both the part of speech and related concepts for that word). Finally, the Internet itself acts both as a filter and creator of computer terms and phrases. Within the Internet community there are a host of subgroups and subcultures coining terms and combinations of terms that can only be understood within the context of the group. Some of these will make it out of the subgroup to become a part of standard Chinese; most will die as a new generation creates their own shorthand and slang.

Table 1. Regional translations for "USB" (Universal Serial Bus)

Pinyin	**Characters**	Literal Translation
Tōngyòng chuànxíng zǒngxiàn	通用串行总线	Universal serial bus
diànzǐpán	电子盘	Electronic disc
shǎncúnpán	闪存盘	Flash disc
U pán	U盘	U disc
USB shǒuzhǐ	ＵＳＢ手指	USB finger
Yōupán	优盘	[The brand name of the first USB in China]

Regulating Internet Terminology

The official body that oversees terminology and translation is the China Computer Federation 中国计算机学会. This group established the Technical Committee of the China Computer Federation 中国计算机学会专业委员会 and gave it the official responsibility to suggest new terminology in the field. Change happens so quickly within both computer science and the computer industry that the Technical Committee acts more as a clearinghouse rather than an instigator of new terms or translations.

Other sources of terminology include the Institute of Computing Technology of the Chinese Academy of Science 中国科学院计算技术研究所. It has three journals that are central to the computer field: the *Chinese Journal of Computers* 计算机学报, the *Journal of Computer Research and Development* 计算机研究与发展, and the *Journal of Computer Science and Technology* 计算机科学技术学报; the last journal is written in English. The Ministry of Information Industry (MII) sets the standards for coding Chinese input, oversees the manufacture of electronic and information products, and supervises the communications and software industries. They are a regulatory agency and part of the State Council. Finally, the Standardization Administration of the People's Republic of China 国家标准化管理委员会 has broad responsibility to set and maintain national standards in many fields, including technology. The Standardization Administration has the official responsibility to coordinate at an international level with the International Organization for Standardization (ISO) and the International Electrotechnical Commission (IEC).

Translating Terminology

The computer industry itself generates terms for new concepts and coins translations of both hardware and software discovered in other languages. Translators work continuously to deliver the latest developments to the scientific and commercial communities. Most scientists and technicians read one or more foreign languages so they can keep abreast of change. Translations of terms fall into several categories. The standard is to combine characters whose concepts convey the meaning of the item, process, or action. For example, "malware" is literally translated as "evil intention code" or "malicious code": *èyìdàimǎ* 恶意代码.

A second method of translation is to make the term sound like the original language. Examples from English include the term *geek*, which is translated as *jíkè* 极客 and literally means "extreme customer or guest." The term probably originated in Hong Kong, where Cantonese is the dominant language, and then spread to Mandarin speakers in mainland China. The pronunciation in Cantonese is very close to the English word *geek*. Similarly, the term *hēikè* 极客 or "hacker" was coined to sound like its English equivalent, but it also combines appropriate concepts. The literal meaning is "black or sinister customer." The common terms for blog (*bókè* 博客) and blogger (*bókè xiěshǒu* 博客写手) use the syllable *bó* 博 as an English homophone, but *bó* 博 includes "gambling" and "playing games," as well as "broad," in its meaning.

Brand Names

Computer manufacturers and software companies are very careful with their translations of brand names. Some terms enter the language unchanged, for example IBM is IBM, and Windows is Windows. Both have official translations, but the English is more commonly used. Most companies attempt to use pronunciations that bear some relation to the original, and choose characters that will have a pleasing association. Compaq becomes *Kāngbǎi* 康柏, where *kāng* means "healthy, peaceful, abundant," and *bǎi* means "cypress." *Dài'ěr* 戴尔 literally means "support you" and was a perfect choice for Dell Computers. Sony chose Chinese characters that sound like Sony pronounced in English. The Japanese characters for Sony are ソニー while the Chinese characters are 索尼 (*Suǒní*). Sony features the Romanized characters "Sony" on its websites in both Japan and China. It markets the VAIO computer under that name on both Chinese and Japanese websites. A Chinese translation is available for VAIO (*Wǎyuē* 瓦约), although it is seldom seen. Toshiba is known in Japan as *Dōngzhī* 东芝 and uses the simplified form of the characters to market its products in China. Like Sony, Toshiba features the Romanized version of its name in all markets.

New Vocabulary

The entertainment world has added a whole new dimension to languages around the world. China is no different. China has blogs, social sites, microblog sites, online gaming, and the full host of encyclopedias, dictionaries, databases, and search engines. Baidu (*Bǎidù* 百度) is the dominant search engine and has developed corollary sites. There are social networking sites ranging from the college site Xiaonei (*Xiàonèi* 校内), founded by students at Tsinghua University and Tianjin University, to QQ Space (QQ *kōngjiān* QQ空间). In addition to Twitter, Sina (*Xīnlàng wēibó* 新浪微博) and Sohu (*Sōuhú wēibó* 搜狐微博) both have microblogging sites. Each type of website introduces new terminology to the Chinese web. The term for "microblogging" (*weibo* 微博 or *zhīwéibó* 织围脖) is the equivalent of "to twitter" and literally means "to knit a scarf." Most terminology isn't as colorful. The user interface requires that common terms be used to describe functions and links. "Add a friend" has to be clear to a new user to support the widespread use of an application. Terms like "search," "find," "download," and "next page" become universals. Ambiguity or techno-speak would defeat the purpose.

The picture is also interesting in the online gaming world. Vocabulary builds on several levels. Online games are homegrown and imported from South Korea, Japan, the United States, and other countries. Developers plan for a multinational market. The base vocabulary must allow a fast learning curve for both new users and for users attracted from other games. Specialized vocabulary is used to describe characters, scenes, and dangers. The names of the games are often translated directly from one language to another. *CrossFire* (*Chuānyuè Huǒxiàn* 穿越火线) means the same thing in both languages. *World of Warcraft* is readily recognizable as WOW in both languages, but the Chinese (*Móshòushìjiè* 魔兽世界) literally means "Devil Beast World." "Hellgate," from the same game, becomes "Gate of Darkness" (*Ànhēizhīmén* 暗黑之门). The Christian reference to hell is replaced by an appropriate cultural reference to mysterious, dark evil in Chinese.

Typing Chinese

The acronyms so popularly used in Western languages sometimes make their way into Chinese, but for the most part, the method of entering Chinese characters into the computer makes them unnecessary in Chinese. When typing Chinese, there are several methods possible, but the most popular way is to type the pinyin for the character and then choose characters from a list of choices. The standard QWERTY keyboard is used. When the phoneme "shi" is typed in, about eighty-seven characters will be returned by the program. Tone numbers can be added in better software; when "shī" (*shi* with the first tone) is typed in, the list of possible characters is narrowed to about nineteen choices. Chinese character encoding software programs have built-in "macros" to learn user preferences, and the most commonly used characters will appear first. (A macro is a coding shortcut that applies a series of commands to text, such as transforming regular text to HTML code or eliminating double spaces.) If a double- or triple-character word is desired, one simply continues typing, and chooses from a much shorter list of possible combinations. If the combination is not yet in the dictionary, the character encoder program learns the new combination and will present it as the first choice the next time that combination is entered. Further, good programs include macros that allow people to type in the first letters of syllables, rather than typing the entire phrase. Thus, if "zg" is typed in, the macro interprets it as *Zhongguo*, and the characters for China, 中国, appear in the choice list. The time-saving acronyms used in English, such as IMHO ("in my humble opinion"), are unnecessary because they occur as a part of character entry. Typing Chinese in text messages and within games is made quite efficient through the use of macros.

The development of terminology and slang is constrained in Chinese by the inability to create completely new characters, but the combination of characters and idiomatic references to shared experience, using the characteristics of the Chinese language, abound within the language of the Internet.

Marilyn SHEA
University of Maine at Farmington

Lin LIN
University of Southern Maine

See also Internet Events; Internet in Everyday Life; Parody; Text Messaging

Further Reading

Amnesty International. (2002). *People's Republic of China: State control of the Internet in China.* London: International Secretariat.

Chang, Raymond. (2001). Speaking of Chinese: A cultural history of the Chinese language. New York: W. W. Norton & Company.

Chase, Michael S., & Mulvenon, James C. (2002). *You've got dissent!: Chinese dissident use of the Internet and Beijing's counter-strategies.* Santa Monica, CA: Rand. Retrieved March 5, 2011, from http://www.rand.org/pubs/monograph_reports/MR1543.html

Chen, Matthew Y. (2000). *Tone Sandhi: Patterns across Chinese dialects* (Cambridge Studies in Linguistics 92). New York: Cambridge University Press.

Gao Liwei. (2007). Chinese Internet language: A study of identity constructions. Munich, Germany: LINCOM Europa.

Giles, Herbert Allen. (1902). The Chinese language. Lecture 1 of *China and the Chinese.* New York: Columbia University Press. Retrieved March 5, 2011, from http://www.gutenberg.org/ebooks/18021

Graham, Tony. (2000). *Unicode: A primer.* Foster City, CA: M&T Books.

Hughes, Christopher R., & Wacker, Gudrun. (Eds.). (2003). *China and the Internet: Politics of the digital leap forward* (Politics in Asia Series). London, New York: RoutledgeCurzon.

Korpella, Jukka K. (2006). *Unicode explained.* Sebastopol, CA: O'Reilly Media.

Shearer, Walter, & Sun Hongkai. (2002). *Speakers of the non-Han languages and dialects of China* (Chinese Studies, vol. 20). Lewiston, NY: Edwin Mellen Press.

Standardization Administration of the People's Republic of China (2010). Homepage. Retrieved March 5, 2011, from Chinese: http://new.sac.gov.cn/ English: http://new.sac.gov.cn/sac_en/

Sun, Helen. (2010). *Internet policy in China: A field study of Internet cafés* (Lexington Studies in Political Communication Series). Lanham, MD: Lexington Books.

Tai Zixue. (2005). *Internet in China.* New York: Routledge.

Unicode Consortium. (2010). About the Unicode standard. Retrieved March 5, 2011, from http://unicode.org/standard/standard.html

Xu Wu. (2007). Chinese cyber nationalism: Evolution, characteristics, and implications. Lanham, MD: Lexington Books.

Zhang Junhua, & Woesler, Martin. (Eds). (2002). China Science and Scholarship: Vol. 5. China's digital dream: The impact of the Internet on Chinese society. Bochum, Germany: European University Press.

Zhou Minglang, & Sun Hongkai. (Eds.). (2004). *Language policy in the People's Republic of China: Theory and practice since 1949.* Boston: Kluwer Academic Publishers.

Digital Divides

Shùzì hónggōu 数字鸿沟

Summary: The digital (use) divide, or the divide between those who use and those who do not use the Internet, is closely linked to several economic, geographic, and social factors in China, as it is elsewhere. Indicators of the divide include statistics about Internet usage (conveniently presented in the biannual reports from the China Internet Network Information Center), computer ownership, and Internet penetration rate (i.e., the percentage of people using the Internet).

Three trends need to be highlighted when trying to understand the digital divides (*shùzì hónggōu* 数字鸿沟) in China, all of which pertain to networking devices. First, personal computer ownership, or the ability to access the Internet at home, is a major contributor to the high Internet penetration rate in China today. There is still a wide rural-urban divide in computer ownership, however, which will be discussed later in the section titled "Rural/Urban Divide."

Second, Chinese citizens access the Internet using a variety of networking devices. Over the last few years there has been a decrease in the number of people using desktops and laptops to access the Internet, and an increase in users who access by cell phone or other mobile devices. Because of its flexibility and ease of use, mobile Internet use may one day level the gap in penetration rates.

Third, broadband Internet connections have become the dominant way to access the Internet. Even in rural areas, a large majority of the counties and villages have broadband connections in one form or another.

Digital Divides in China

Digital divides can be separated into multiple categories. Seven of these will be discussed in this section: age (generational), gender, education, income, occupation, geographical location, and the rural/urban divide.

Age (Generational) Divide

Although percentages vary slightly over the years, the general age structure of Chinese Internet users remains consistent. Almost two-thirds of the Chinese Internet population is under thirty years old, according to the latest 2013 statistics from the China Internet Network Information Center (CNNIC). Young adults from twenty to twenty-nine years old form the largest group of users, with 30.4 percent, followed by the thirty- to thirty-nine-year-old group (25.3 percent), forty- to forty-nine-year-olds (12.4 percent), fifty years old and up (6.4 percent), and ten years old and less (1.7 percent). While the number of elderly Internet users in China is growing, there is still a wide generational digital divide (CNNIC 2013).

The fastest growing group of Internet users in China is children under ten years old, a group that more than quadrupled its use from 2008 to 2012, from 0.4 percent to 1.7 percent. The basis for this growth is the availability of Internet access in primary schools in China and the development of online educational courseware in a nationwide project called "Networks between Schools."

Gender Divide

Males are significantly more likely than females in China to use the Internet; 55.8 percent and 44.2 percent in 2012, respectively (CNNIC 2013), although this gap has narrowed dramatically since the turn of the century, when there was a 3:1 male to female user ratio (CNNIC 2000). A gender divide also exists among mobile Internet users, in both rural and urban areas, and in the wetter, more populous eastern part of China and the dryer, less populated western parts of the country.

Educational Divide

Less-educated Chinese citizens are less likely to use the Internet than are more-educated citizens. According to the 2013 CNNIC report, penetration rates for those with a high school, middle school, and primary school education are 32.3 percent, 35.6 percent, and 10.9 percent, respectively. The fastest growing educational group is primary school students.

Income Divide

Income is strongly related to Internet use in China, as it is in most other countries. Those with upper middle-class incomes account for roughly two-thirds of Internet users, whereas those with lower incomes account for roughly one-third of Internet users. The latter percentage is inflated, however, because it includes students in grades K–12 who most often have no income, as well as students in college (CNNIC 2013).

Part of the rural/urban digital divide, discussed later, is attributable to differences in income in the two areas. Just a few years ago, in relatively prosperous urban areas of China such as Beijing, the computer ownership rate was forty-five computers per one hundred households, whereas in poverty-stricken areas such as Ningxia, Guizhou, and Inner Mongolia, there was less than one computer for every hundred families (National Bureau of Statistics of China 2009).

Occupational Divide

It is not surprising that professionals and students are the largest groups of Internet users, whereas migrant workers, farmers, and the retired make up the smallest groups. Professionals, including freelancers, the self-employed, white-collar workers, and government officials, accounted for 44 percent of the Internet population in China as of

2012, according to the 2013 CNNIC report. Students, the second largest group, accounted for around a quarter of the Internet population. Unemployed and laid-off workers together accounted for somewhat less than 10 percent of Internet users. Similarly, migrant workers and farmers accounted for less than 10 percent of users.

Geographic Divide

There is a physical regional digital divide in China that is strongly related to the economic regional divide. The relationship between per capita GDP (gross domestic product) and Internet penetration is as high as 0.92, meaning that areas with a higher GDP also have a higher Internet penetration rate. Internet penetration rates are much higher in the more wealthy eastern and northeastern parts of the country, and lower in the central and western portions of the country.

Internet use among the provinces of China parallels use among regions. For example, Beijing, in the northeast, and the province with the highest Internet use in all of China, had an Internet penetration rate of 72.2 percent in 2012, four times greater than Jiangxi, a southeastern province with the lowest penetration rate (28.5 percent). Interestingly, the provinces that lag behind in Internet penetration rates are the provinces with the highest Internet growth rate. For example, Guizhou, a province in the southwest whose Internet penetration rate is 28.6 percent, lower than the national and world average, has the highest Internet growth rate, 28.5 percent (CNNIC 2013), suggesting that these provinces are motivated to make their Internet penetration rates closer to those of the other provinces

Rural/Urban Divide

In 2012, the number of rural Internet users in China was 156 million, slightly more than a quarter of the total Internet population, whereas urban users accounted for slightly less than three-quarters of the population. The Internet penetration rate in rural areas was less than one-fourth of the population, whereas in urban areas it was about 60 percent (CNNIC 2013). At the beginning of 2011, the annual growth rate of rural Internet penetration in rural areas was, for the first time, slightly higher than in urban areas. These differences in growth rate may ultimately end the rural/urban digital divide.

Rural and urban Internet users also differ in the nature of their online activities. Entertainment, such as online music and games, is equally popular in the two areas, but online gaming is more frequent among rural Internet users than urban users (CNNIC 2010a). On the other hand, online video gaming in rural areas is lagging behind that of urban areas, probably because of the limited bandwidth and infrastructure in rural areas. E-commerce and network-based communication are also less frequent in rural areas than in urban areas, probably because there is less online information created specifically for rural Internet users.

Overall, three factors are believed to be responsible for the rural/urban digital divide in China, factors similar to those responsible for this divide in other countries. First, knowledge about technology appears to be the greatest barrier to Internet use in rural areas. A CNNIC report (2010b) indicated that among rural Internet nonusers, more than one-third said they did not use the Internet because of inadequate knowledge about the technology. Moreover, what knowledge they did have about the Internet may have discouraged Internet use, thanks in part to media coverage of the Internet's "dark side," such as Internet crime, pornography, and addiction. Such information discourages Internet use by rural citizens, who tend to be more conservative in their lifestyles and values than their urban counterparts.

Second, the costs of computers and Internet access is partly responsible for the lower rate of Internet use in rural compared to urban areas. About one-fifth of rural citizens said in 2010 that they did not use the Internet because they could not afford computers. Supporting their statements is the evidence that per capita GDP in rural areas is roughly one-third that in urban areas (CNNIC 2010b). According to a 2009 report, rural households owned a meager five computers per hundred households, whereas urban households had an average of sixty computers per hundred households (National Bureau of Statistics of China 2009).

Third, rural areas, especially the central western areas, suffer from an infrastructure that is inadequate for supporting Internet use. In the absence of substantial infrastructure changes, the Internet will remain inaccessible to many rural citizens, according to the CNNIC.

Other factors contributing to the rural/urban digital divide are differences in literacy and the type of information available online. The literacy divide is a significant and complex issue in China, as it is in other developing countries. Urban adolescents have greater literacy skills and use more Internet communication tools than their rural peers. This rural/urban gap in online communication activities holds true for adults as well.

Urban Internet users spend more time online because there are richer information services and resources of interest to them than to their rural peers. Additionally urban Internet users are generally better educated and have more of the knowledge and skills needed for online activities compared to their rural peers.

Closing the Digital Divides in China

Two of the big online challenges that China is facing at this point are how to close the digital divides described above, and how to provide Internet access evenly to the entire population.

Digital Infrastructure

The first step in closing the digital divides in China is to address inadequacies in infrastructure in rural areas. This responsibility falls squarely on the shoulders of the Chinese government. The government can facilitate Internet use by making computers and broadband Internet access more available and affordable not only for the average citizen but for poor citizens, especially those living in remote rural areas.

Investment in mobile and wireless technology will facilitate closing the digital divides in China. There are currently a number of national initiatives designed to address this issue. For example, the "Telephone for Every Village, Internet for Every County" project, which by 2010 had attracted more than 50 billion yuan (US$7 billion) in investments, succeeded in wiring 99.3 percent of the counties with Internet connections (98.6 percent of them with broadband connections) and 90 percent of the villages in China with broadband Internet access by 2010 (CNNIC 2010b). Additional investments are still needed to expand Internet access, however, especially in the distant central and western regions.

Information Services

Another possible government intervention tactic is to create more online materials to meet the needs and interests of China's large and highly diverse population. (Many existing international websites are already programmed to run in multiple languages, including Chinese because of China's large population.) There is a national project underway that endeavors to increase the quantity and quality of agriculture-related online information and to be responsive to the information needs of rural citizens. The project's goal is to establish at least "one information station for every county, one information service center for every village, one website for every county, and one online agricultural information center for every village" (CNNIC 2010b). Rather than waiting for these time-consuming goals to be accomplished, in the interest of expediency, China should begin now to make agriculture-related information available online and accessible via mobile phones, a popular communication device in rural China.

Information Literacy

China's massive and diverse population poses a particular challenge to increasing the literacy rate to 100 percent. Some efforts initiated by the central government could prompt an increase in literacy; however, especially in the outlying rural areas, illiteracy contributes significantly to the nonuse of technologies like the Internet. At the same time it is important to instill in Chinese citizens the importance of their own behavior and initiative in the creation and consumption of Internet content. Technology literacy, or what is referred to as technology fluency, can be part of the effort to produce general literacy among all of China's people. The process of developing technology literacy should begin early in life, during primary school, in order to close the information gap in China. The payoff for technology literacy will exceed the costs of developing it. For example, a rural famer in the distant countryside will see significant benefits to having his children attend school and develop the literacy needed to sustain the family farm into the twenty-first century and beyond. The urban citizen will perceive significant benefits to technology literacy by providing the option of continuing education for themselves and their children beyond high school, facilitated by Internet courses that prepare students of any age for the desirable and available jobs in a burgeoning information and communications technology workplace.

Educating the general public about the nature of the Internet is another task that falls squarely on the shoulders of the central government in China and other countries. With access to all regions of the country, the central government should make citizens more aware of the benefits of the Internet and less concerned about the "dark side" currently emphasized in the media (for example, the dangers of pornography). Citizens of China and around the world will only be attracted to technology if using it has more benefits than costs.

Linda A. JACKSON
Michigan State University

Wei QIU
Webster University

Alexander GAMES
Microsoft

Yong ZHAO
University of Oregon

See also Children Online; E-Government; Online Game Industry; Social and Political Impact; Telecommunications Industry

Further Reading

China Internet Network Information Center (CNNIC). (2000). 1999 statistical survey report on Internet development in China. Retrieved May 14, 2010, from http://www.cnnic.cn/download/manual/en-reports/5.pdf

China Internet Network Information Center (CNNIC). (2010a). 2009 statistical survey report on Internet development in China. Retrieved May 12, 2010, from http://www.cnnic.cn/uploadfiles/pdf/2010/3/15/142705,pdf

China Internet Network Information Center (CNNIC). (2010b). 2009 statistical survey report on Internet development in rural areas of China. Retrieved May 14, 2010, from http://research.cnnic.cn/img/h000h11/attach201004201316070.pdf

China Internet Network Information Center (CNNIC). (2010c). Research report on the 2009 online behavior of the Chinese adolescents and youth. Retrieved May 14, 2010, from http://research.cnnic.cn/img/h000h11/attach201004261314150.doc

China Internet Network Information Center (CNNIC). (2010d). Statistical survey report on internet development in the western regions of China. Retrieved May 14, 2010, from http://www.cnnic.cn/uploadfiles/pdf/2009/924/135812.pdf

China Internet Network Information Center (CNNIC). (2013, January). Statistical report on Internet development in China. Retrieved April 15, 2013, from http://www1.cnnic.cn/IDR/Report-Downloads/201302/P020130312536825920279.pdf

Jackson, Linda A., & Wang, Jin-Liang. (2013). Cultural differences in social networking site use: A comparative study of China and the United States. *Computers in Human Behavior, 29*(3), 910–921. doi:10.1016/j.chb.2012.11.024.

Jackson, Linda A.; Witt, Edward A.; & Games, Alexander Ivan. (2012). Information technology use and creativity: Findings from the Children and Technology Project. *Computers in Human Behavior, 28*, 370–376.

Jackson, Linda A. (2012). The upside of video game playing. *Games for Health Journal, 1*(6), 452–455. doi:10.1089/g4h.2012.0064

National Bureau of Statistics of China (2009). *China statistical yearbook*. Retrieved May 15, 2010, from http://www.stats.gov.cn/tjsj/ndsj/2009/indexch.htm

Distance Education

Yuǎnchéng jiàoyù 远程教育

Summary: In the past several decades, the increase of traditional "face-to-face" universities in China has not been able to keep up with the country's population growth and its subsequent increasing demand for education. Distance education, including online education, has been instrumental in creating learning opportunities for large numbers of learners who otherwise might be deprived of the right to learn and to prosper in society.

China faces problems of extending educational opportunities to ever-larger numbers of its population, especially disadvantaged, marginalized, and low-income groups. Distance education has been a powerful venue for providing equitable educational opportunities to these populations. The development of the Internet, including higher access rates in rural areas and easier access to the Internet for lower-income and education users, plays an important role in the recent developments of distance education programs.

Distance education in China has gone through three generations, much as it has in Western countries: (1) education via correspondence, (2) education via television and broadcast education, and (3) education via computer networks and multimedia. The last one is known as "modern distance education." With the recent launching of "open" universities in China, a new generation, coined "modern open distance education" is forming. (An open university may or may not have standard entry requirements, and may or may not be a correspondence institute.) As a new and emerging educational model, modern open distance education is rooted in the fast development of modern information technology, and is also hailed as a robust venue for lifelong learning in the new era of a knowledge-based economy, which has been a goal of the national government in recent years.

Media-use scholars have identified four additional stages of development in China's distance education: audiovisual media (1978–1994), multimedia (1995–1998), information and communication technology (ICT) (1999–2005), and ICT integration (2006 to present).

During the first stage, tools used in distance education mainly included film, television, audio recorders, and slide projectors. The second stage involved the common use of desktop computers and various kinds of computer-assisted teaching and learning tools. The ICT stage refers to the use of networked computers and the Internet. The ICT integration stage features learner-centered learning, where learners can choose one or more of the aforementioned media based on their particular learning needs.

Development of Distance Education

The China Central Radio and TV University (RTU) was established in 1979 and has branches in every province as well as the main cities, such as Beijing and Shanghai. These universities tend to have large numbers of students and have been the main force in educating adult learners who pursue a college degree or who seek continuing education. By the end of 2009, RTU had more than 3 million students around the nation, with more than 2.8 million of those in higher education, and the rest in secondary education.

Table 1 displays the timeline of the evolution of distance education in China, marked by the establishment of teaching and learning centers, the launching of large-scale distance education projects, and the publishing of national standards for distance education.

Table 1. Timeline of Distance Education in China

Year	Key Events
1978	Launch of China Central Audio-visual Center
1979	Launch of China Central Radio and TV University
1986	Launch of China Education Television (ETV)
1999	Modern Distance Education Project initiated by the Action Scheme for Invigorating Education towards the 21st Century
2001–2005	School to School Project
2003–2007	Modern Distance Education Project for the Rural Schools
2004	Launch of National Resource Center for Basic Education under the Ministry of Education
2004	Publishing of National Standards on K2–K12 Teachers' Competence of Educational Technology (trial)
2008	Class to Class and Lesson to Lesson Project
2009	Establishment of a Consortium of Universities for Educational Open Source
2010–2020	Release of China's 10-year National Plan for Medium and Long-term Education Reform and Development, where "open university" replaced "radio and TV university"

Recent Milestones

In 2010, *Distance Education in China,* a top journal in the field, collaborated with leading scholars and experts in education to identify ten milestone events of distance education in China:

1. In January 1999, the Modern Distance Education Project was initiated as part of the "Action Plan to Invigorate Education towards the 21st Century," issued by China's Department of State. The Modern Distance Education Project advocates more widespread use of information and communication technology in distance education.
2. In March 1999, the Ministry of Education approved four pilot colleges (associated with formal universities) for online education. By 2010, about 10 million online students had enrolled in these colleges and over 5 million had received their degrees or certificates.
3. In 2000, the Ministry of Education began to promote the creation of well-developed online courses and digital education resources. By 2009, 149 courses had been identified as nationwide exemplary open courses.
4. In June 2002, the Ministry of Education required students of online colleges to take the standardized national exams that are given to students from regular four-year universities; they must pass these exams to obtain a diploma. Online colleges now have an opportunity to show their capacity in cultivating high-caliber graduates.
5. In February 2003, a pilot model of public service system for modern distance education was launched. By 2010, one such service system, Open Edutainment, had established over 1,400 learning centers in off-campus communities.
6. In 2006, three influential projects all made major breakthroughs: China's Next Generation Internet established the Education and Research Network 2 (CERNET2), the Internet for Educational Research built ChinaGrid, and the Research and Application of Online Education identified the crucial technologies needed for its successful implementation.
7. In October 2007, the Chinese Communist Party's national congress report included a plan for "developing distance and continuing education." The importance of distance education was officially recognized at the national level.
8. In December 2007, the Ministry of Education endorsed the summing-up assessment of a pilot study on the paradigm shift from traditional distance and continuous education to open education in China. This laid the foundation for the evolution from Radio and TV universities to open universities.
9. From 2001 to 2009, the government invested about US$1.7 billion in the School to School Project. The goal of this project was to provide Internet access to over 90 percent of all primary and secondary schools nationwide.
10. In the early 2000s, several educational companies went public and led the trend of investing in online education and training. These companies can provide alternatives for users who have different learning needs.

Open Universities and Their Implications

Since 1999, the Ministry of Education has established nationwide test beds for modern distance education in higher education, which involves the use of up-to-date technologies (computers, Internet, and satellite) and new teaching and learning models (hybrid learning, interactive learning, and mobile learning). The phrase "Radio and TV" is still in the names of many distance universities, but changes are on the way: Shanghai Radio and TV University changed to Shanghai Open University in 2010. This move has been followed by RT universities in several other provinces.

Chinese scholars have commented that the name changes mark the starting of a new historical era in China's distance education. The changes have also stirred debates on the operation of these open universities, in aspects such as institutional structure, learning resource management, the use of technology, models for teaching and learning, and learner management. In October 2010, an Open-U Construction research team was formed in China Central TV and Radio University, and researchers have been conducting in-depth research on many of the crucial issues associated with this transition. For instance, which Open-U model to follow (the United Kingdom's or India's), what are the challenges unique to China, and what are the standards for administrative and instructional operations.

Modern Distance Education Project for Rural Schools in China

As a developing nation, China faces problems of extending educational opportunities to disadvantaged and low-income populations. Distance education, therefore, has been a powerful venue in providing equitable educational opportunities to these populations.

The Modern Distance Education Project for the Western Rural Middle and Elementary Schools (MDEPRS) in China, launched by China's Ministry of Education, represents one type of project that aims to develop education in rural China through modern distance education technologies such as computers and satellite-receiving stations. It originated from a project named "Preparing Tomorrow's Female Teachers," which had trained more than a thousand female teachers and established over a thousand distance-education receiving stations in six provinces in western China: Yunnan, Guizhou, Sichuan, Shanxi, Gansu, and Guangxi. Each receiving station was equipped with one computer and one set of satellite-receiving system (MOE 2000).

The original goal of MDEPRS was to provide free high-quality educational resources for teachers and students. From 2003 to 2007, the project created a wide educational information infrastructure for supporting over 80 million pupils in primary schools and over 30 million students in secondary schools in rural China. After 2007, the aim switched to providing training for teachers integrating ICT and educational resources into their everyday teaching (Chen 2010). According to one member of the Ministry of Education, during the project, over 45,000 computer-equipped classrooms; 279,000 satellite receiving stations; and 402,000 CD-based educational resource stations were put into use at rural primary and secondary schools (Chen 2008). Three instructional strategies were developed for teachers to operate these devices and resources. By April 2010, about 700,000 users had registered at the National Resource Network for Basic Education (www.cbern.gov.cn), from which over 7 million teaching materials and tools were downloaded.

As the Internet becomes more accessible and electronic devices, such as computers and telephones, are more readily available to people throughout China, the importance of a strong distance education system will grow as well. The initiatives and organizations discussed here are working toward that goal, and will continue doing so in the future.

Minjuan WANG
San Diego State University

Hai ZHANG
Northeast Normal University

See also Children Online; Internet in Everyday Life; Social and Political Impact; Telecommunications Industry

Further Reading

Bates, Tony. (1991). Third generation distance education: The challenge of new technology. *Research in Distance Education*, 3(2). Retrieved April 5, 2010, from http://www.eric.ed.gov/ERICDocs/data/ericdocs2sql/content_storage_01/0000019b/80/22/f5/5f.pdf

Chen Xiaoya. (2008). Speech at 2008 National Submit of ETC heads. Retrieved April 5, 2010, from http://www.hnczdj.com/news/djxw/2009/8/098191556568461_2.html

Chen Xiaoya. (2010). Speech at 2010 National Submit of ETC heads. Retrieved April 5, 2010, from http://www.zjedu.org/html/detial/info/201011/20101105144048 7178.html

China Education and Research Network. (2010). 2009年度中国现代远程教育十大新闻事件评选结果揭晓 [Results of the 2009 election of the ten milestones in modern Chinese distance education revealed]. Retrieved March 24, 2014, from http://www.edu.cn/yuan_cheng_jiao_yu_161/20100203/t20100203_447561.shtml

Gu Aihong. (2010). Strategies for student population change in modern open distance education—A case study of Shanghai TV University. *Open Education Research, 16*(4), 78–81.

Nipper, S. (1989). Third generation distance learning and computer conferencing. In Robin Mason, Anthony Kaye & Robert Mason (Eds.), *Mindweave: Communication, computers and distance education*. Oxford, UK: Pergamon.

Qin Nong. (2011). The inspiration from the university for industry in UK for the founding of open university in China. *Open Education Research, 17*(1), 103–107

Yu Shanyun, & Yao Wenjian. (2010). Research on the development of *open education in China. Open Education Research, 16*(4), 9–14.

Yu Shanyun. (2011). Rational thoughts on the passion for founding open universities in China. *Open Education Research, 17*(1), 51–55.

Email

Diànzǐ yóujiàn 电子邮件

Summary: The first email from China to other parts of the world was sent in 1987 to West Germany. By the end of 2012, the number of email users in China had surpassed 250 million (roughly half the number of people who went online), although email has taken a back seat to newer means of communication, like instant messaging, in recent years.

The term *email* is the abbreviation of "electronic mail," usually used to refer to a method to exchange digital information across computer networks among senders and receivers. Email is one of the most ubiquitous and pervasive Internet-based communication channels in our age. The Chinese term for email is *diànzǐ yóujiàn* 电子邮件, a direct translation of "electronic mail" in English. In daily settings in urban China, most Internet users also use the English word *email*.

Email is one of the oldest applications and services on the Internet; several points highlight its significance. First, although email is an old application, it is still among the most widely used of Internet services. In 2012, according to data from the China Internet Network Information Center (CNNIC), email was in the top ten most-used Internet services in Chinese cyberspace, with 44.5 percent of Chinese Internet users using email. Second, the number of email users is huge: by December 2012, the number of email users in China had reached 250 million, a 15.2 percent increase compared with 2010 (CNNIC 2013). Third, as a pervasive Internet application, email has become a fundamental component for e-business (*diànzǐ shāngwù* 电子商务), online banking (*zàixiàn yínháng* 在线银行), and other applications such as Google maps. An email address is generally the first step for people to enjoy more advanced Internet services, such as buying something online. To apply for an account on the alipay.com (Zhīfùbǎo 支付宝) platform, a Paypal-like online transaction platform of 300 million users, an email address is a prerequisite. For anyone who has interest in Internet use or the Internet market in China, email is therefore an essential entry point.

History of Email in China

The development of email in China can be divided into three periods: from the late 1980s to late 1990s, from 2000 to 2004, and after 2005. In the first period, email was the dominant Internet service; in the second period, email was the most important Internet service among many other services; in the third period, although still widely used, email is no longer the most-used Internet service in Chinese cyberspace.

Early History and Development

The history of email in China can be traced back to the late 1980s. The first email from China to other parts of the world was sent on 14 September 1987 from China to West Germany, between the Chinese Institute of Computer Applications and Karlsruhe University. The subject of the email, appropriately enough, was "First Electronic Mail from China to Germany"; the message was in German and English and begins, "Across the Great Wall we can reach every corner in the world" (Zorn 1988; Hauben 2010). This China–Germany email connection project was considered the first step toward connecting China with the Computer Science Network (CSNET), a US-based computer network developed in the early 1980s. The official approval of the extension of email service and the CSNET to China from the US National Science Foundation (NSF), the institution that funded CSNET, was granted in November 1987, less than two months after the first technological email connection between China and West Germany was established.

By 1992, some leading universities and academic institutions in Beijing, such as Peking University, had built their college-level network and gained the technological and physical capacity to establish email connections (CNNIC 2008a). In July 1995, the backbone network of the China Education and Research Network 中国教育和科研计算机网 was built and began to provide basic Internet service for universities and academic institutions in eight major cities, including Beijing, Shanghai, Guangzhou, and Xian (CNNIC 2008a). In August 1995, a nationwide governmental project to build the backbone network connecting twenty-four major provinces, named the Golden Bridge Network Project (Jīnqiáo wǎngluò gōngchéng 金桥网络工程), was completed. Internet and email access became available for individual users outside the universities and academic institutions in 1996. In September 1996, China Golden Bridge Network (Zhōngguó jīnqiáo wǎngluò 中国金桥网络) began to provide Internet connection service for commercial users and individual users. In February 1997, Ying Haiwei, the first private Internet service provider, began to offer Internet connections for commercial users and individual users in eight major Chinese cities (CNNIC 2008a).

Based on nationwide surveys since 1997, CNNIC has released the Statistical Report on Internet Development in China twice annually. These reports represent one of the only sources of data by which researchers can evaluate use of email in China over time. CNNIC reports show that email was the most-used and most important Internet service in the early stage of the Internet in China. In the fourth report, released in July 1999, email was the most used Internet service: 90 percent of the users chose email as their most-used Internet service, almost 25 percent more than the second most-used application, the search engine (*sōusuŏ yĭnqíng* 搜索引擎), at 65.5 percent (CNNIC 1999). CNNIC's January 2000 report provided more detailed information regarding email use in China during the late 1990s. The report showed that, by 1999, the number of email accounts in Chinese cyberspace had reached 35.6 million. Email was still the most-used Internet service for Chinese users. More than 71 percent of users indicated that email was their most frequently used Internet service. Spam had become a serious problem: 62.9 percent of the users reported receiving spam (CNNIC 2000).

Losing Ground: 2000–2004

From 2000 to 2004, email was one of the most-discussed topics among various issues regarding Internet use in China. In December 2004, CNNIC released a special report regarding email use and e-business. The January 2005 CNNIC report also provided in-depth analysis on email use. These two reports provide a good resource for understanding the use of email in China in the first five years in the new century.

The January 2005 report (the fifteenth) showed that, by 2004, email was still the most-used Internet service: 85.6 percent of the responders chose email as a frequently used service, more than 20 percent ahead of the second most-used Internet service, online news (*zàixiàn xīnwén* 在线新闻), at 62 percent. This report also compared 2004's data with the data from the previous four reports (tenth to fourteenth) from 2002 to 2004 (CNNIC 2005).

Table 1. Amount of Emails Received/Sent and Spam Messages Received per Week by Chinese Internet Users

CNNIC Report No.	Time	Mails Received per Week	Mails Sent per Week	Spam Received per Week
10th	July 2002	6.9	5.3	6.5
11th	January 2003	7.7	5.5	8.3
12th	July 2003	7.2	5.3	8.9
13th	January 2004	5.8	4.1	7.9
14th	July 2004	4.6	4.3	9.2
15th	January 2005	4.4	3.6	7.9

Source: China Internet Network Information Center (CNNIC), various years.

The data in table 1 show that the number of emails received/sent per week had been decreasing since 2003. At the same time, according to CNNIC's ninth through fifteenth reports, from 2002 to 2004, the number of Internet users had increased from 33.7 million to 94 million (CNNIC 2002a; CNNIC 2005). The number of emails received/sent per week, therefore, was not positively correlated with the number of Internet users. Researchers argued that the decrease of emails sent/received per week was partly the result of the diversification of online communication channels in Chinese cyberspace. The emergence of other communication channels such as instant messaging (IM) (*jíshí tōngxùn* 即时通讯), text messaging, and mobile phones had resulted in the decrease of the number of emails sent/received (CNNIC 2002b). Spam continued to be an irritant for email users. Data from these six reports showed that users received more spam than "real" emails, with data from the fourteenth report indicating that spam was twice as common as real email.

Free versus Paid Email Services

Another important topic concerning email use and the email market in this period was the competition between free email services and paid email services. Netease.com (Wǎngyì 网易) was the first free email service provider in China. In December 1997, Netease developed and launched the first free email service in China, named 163.com. From 1997 to 2001, leading portals in Chinese cyberspace, including sohu.com 搜狐, sina.com 新浪, and 263.com began to provide free email services. From 2001 to 2002, the email market experienced a debate regarding the most competitive business model. Some leading portals like sina.com and 263.com shifted to a paid email model. In August 2001, sina.com, which had more than 22 million users at the time, launched its paid email service. At the same time, it dramatically decreased the mailbox storage size of its free email accounts from 50 megabytes (MB) to 5 MB. A more complete shift was experienced by 263.com, which had 20 million email users at that time (Na 2009). In March 2002, 263.com launched its paid email service and began to close its free email accounts. Other free email service providers took a mixed model. For example, in December 2001, Netease launched its paid email service, with bigger mailbox sizes and better services, but continued providing free email service for its free mailbox users (netease.com 2010). The cost of a paid email account was around 180 yuan (US$25) per year. The response from the public and the users to the shift was generally negative. Sina.com and 263.com were seriously criticized by Chinese "netizens" for their new business model. After 263.com began to close its free email accounts, within three months, 263.com had lost almost 97 percent of its users (Na 2009). Since 2005, the debate regarding free email versus paid email has moved out of the focus of public attention. Paid email coexisted for a while with free email, but free email, as a business model targeting general users, eventually became the mainstream in China's email market. Although it is hard to say whether there is a causal relation, many people have connected the emergence of Google's email service Gmail with the success of the free email model in China (Jiang 2009; Na 2009). In April 2004, Chinese Internet users were allowed to apply for a 1 gigabyte (GB) free Gmail mailbox via invitations from other users. To compete with Gmail, on 28 October 2004, Sina.com upgraded its free email inbox storage space to 1 GB. In October of that year, Netease.com updated its free email box to 1.5 GB.

Statistical data from CNNIC's reports also show free email service providers have gradually expanded their market share among the competition with paid email service providers.

Table 2. Percentage of Free Email Accounts, 2000–2002

Time	Percentage of free (vs. paid) email accounts
January 2000	75 percent
July 2000	84.6 percent
January 2001	88.5 percent
July 2002	87.5 percent

Source: China Internet Network Information Center (CNNIC), Various years.

Table 2 shows that from 2000 to 2002 the percentage of free email accounts, relative to the total number of email accounts in Chinese cyberspace, gradually increased (CNNIC 2002b). Moreover, CNNIC's December 2004 special report on email and e-business showed that 96.5 percent of Internet users had free email accounts at that time, and only 8 percent had paid email accounts. Nearly 90 percent of users at that time said a free email account was their most used email account (CNNIC 2004a). These data showed that, from 2000 to 2005, free email service gradually expanded its market share and had become the mainstream business model, while paid email's market share gradually shrunk.

Steady Decline in Emailing: Since 2005

In the history of email use in China, 2005 was an important year; to some extent, it was a turning point. In CNNIC's January 2006 report, for the first time, email lost the number-one position to other Internet applications. At the same time, a new Internet communication channel, IM, had risen. This represented not only the change in the way people communicated online, but also a change in the communications market, with the emergence of new business models and new leading information technology (IT) giants.

In CNNIC's January 2006 report, the top four most-used Internet services/functions of 2005 were reading online news (68 percent), search engine (66 percent), email (65 percent), and IM (42 percent) (CNNIC 2006). Email lost its number-one position while IM became a new, frequently used Internet service. Since then, email has not returned to the number-one position, except (briefly) as reflected in the January 2007 report. In CNNIC's July report of that same year, among communication tools or services, email, the most important Internet service in the first two periods, gave way to IM: nearly 70 percent of the users used IM, more than 14 percent higher than email (55 percent) (CNNIC 2007). Since then, IM has been leading email in adoption rate in all of CNNIC's reports. (See table 3.)

Table 3. IM Adoption Rates vs. Email Adoption Rates, 2007–2013

Time	IM Adoption Rate	Email Adoption Rate
July 2007	69.8%	55.4%
January 2008	81.4%	56.5%
January 2009	75.3%	56.8%
January 2010	70.9%	56.8%
January 2012	80.9%	47.9%
January 2013	82.9%	44.5%

Source: China Internet Network Information Center (CNNIC), Various years.

Table 3 shows that by 2007, IM had replaced email as the most popular communication channel in Chinese cyberspace. Email was still a widely used Internet service, however, and the number of email users continued increasing. Also in this period, Tencent 腾讯, the company holding around an 80 percent market share in IM, replaced the Internet portals that got their big names partly by providing free email services (netease.com, for example). By 2009, the number of active Tencent IM accounts had reached nearly 523 million (Tencent 2010).

Many factors contributed to the relative decline of email and the rise of IM in Chinese cyberspace. Among them, two will be highlighted here. The first was the entertainment orientation of Chinese Internet users and the IM service providers' incorporation of new features. It is widely agreed that early Chinese users saw the Internet mainly as a source of entertainment and an attractive medium for social exchanges. IM service providers in China successfully incorporated new entertainment and socializing features into their IM applications and platforms. For example, Tencent incorporated games, music sharing, photo sharing, and social networking features into its IM application, Tencent QQ. Tencent developed its game platform, QQ Game (QQ 游戏), and its social networking platform, Qzone (QQ 空间). These new platforms all centered around its flagship application, Tencent QQ. These entertainment features and new platforms greatly contributed to the increase of IM's popularity in Chinese cyberspace. For example, by 2009, the active user accounts of Qzone had reached 387.8 million, and the peak simultaneous online user accounts of QQ Game had reached 6.2 million (Tencent 2010). The second factor that contributed to the rise of IM was the IM service providers' technological and business innovations. One example was the extension of IM communication to the mobile phone network. Around 2000, six years earlier than Twitter, Tencent began to extend its IM service to mobile phone networks. Tencent developed a new IM terminal for mobile phones, named Mobile QQ (移动 QQ). Through mobile QQ, IM users could communicate with their IM friends either on computers or on mobile phones. By 2012, nearly 83 percent of IM users sent instant messages via both computers and mobile phones (CNNIC 2013). At the same time, because mobile phone IM was a paid service, it became a business model that allowed IM service providers to profit from the huge wireless communication market.

Development and Future Research

Email, as the oldest and most fundamental Internet service, has undergone nearly a quarter century of development in China. Even though email is no longer the most popular Internet service in Chinese cyberspace, the increasing number of users and the fundamental role of email in many more advanced Internet services highlight its significance in Chinese cyberspace.

Future research on email in China may focus on two directions. First is the role of email in more advanced Internet services such as e-business and online banking. CNNIC's report showed that e-business such as online shopping (*zàixiàn gòuwù*

在线购物) has shown a rapid increase since 2010. By the end of 2012, the adoption rate of online shopping had reached 42.9 percent, and the number of online shoppers had reached 242 million (CNNIC 2013).

Second, wireless Internet and mobile access have had a large impact on the use of email. Mobile phones have become the new terminal for people to access the Internet. By January 2013, the number of users who accessed the Internet via their phone had reached 420 million (CNNIC 2013). How these new technologies will influence the use of email in China is another interesting question for future research.

Song SHI
McGill University

See also Blogging; Telecommunications Industry; Text Messaging; Internet in Everyday Life

Further Reading

China Internet Network Information Center (CNNIC). (1999). The 4th statistical report on Internet development in China. Retrieved September 24, 2010, from http://www.cnnic.net.cn/download/manual/en-reports/4.pdf

CNNIC. (2000). The 5th statistical report on Internet development in China. Retrieved September 24, 2010, from http://www.cnnic.net.cn/download/manual/en-reports/5.pdf

CNNIC. (2002a). The 9th statistical report on Internet development in China. Retrieved September 24, 2010, from http://www.cnnic.net.cn/download/manual/en-reports/9.pdf

CNNIC. (2002b). The 10th statistical report on Internet development in China. Retrieved September 24, 2010, from http://www.cnnic.net.cn/download/manual/en-reports/10.pdf

CNNIC. (2004a). Special report on hot topics regarding the Internet in China—email and e-business. Retrieved September 24, 2010, from http://www1.cnnic.cn/download/manual/2004111602.doc

CNNIC. (2004b). The 14th statistical report on Internet development in China. Retrieved September 24, 2010, from http://www.cnnic.net.cn/download/2004/2004072003.pdf

CNNIC. (2005). The 15th statistical report on Internet development in China. Retrieved September 24, 2010, from http://www.cnnic.net.cn/download/2005/2005012701.pdf

CNNIC. (2006). The 17th statistical report on Internet development in China. Retrieved September 24, 2010, from http://www.cnnic.net.cn/download/2006/17threport-en.pdf

CNNIC. (2007). The 20th statistical report on Internet development in China. Retrieved September 24, 2010, from http://www.cnnic.net.cn/download/2007/20thCNNICreport-en.pdf

CNNIC. (2008a). China's Internet development memorabilia (1987 to 2007). Retrieved July 04, 2010, from http://www.cnnic.net.cn/html/Dir/2003/10/22/1001.htm

CNNIC. (2008b). The 21st statistical report on Internet development in China. Retrieved September 24, 2010, from http://www.cnnic.net.cn/uploadfiles/pdf/2008/2/29/104126.pdf

CNNIC. (2008c). The 22nd statistical report on Internet development in China. Retrieved September 24, 2010, from http://www.cnnic.net.cn/download/2008/CNNIC22threport-en.pdf

CNNIC. (2009a). The 23rd statistical report on Internet development in China. Retrieved September 24, 2010, from http://www.cnnic.net.cn/uploadfiles/pdf/2009/3/23/153540.pdf

CNNIC. (2009b). The 24th statistical report on Internet development in China. Retrieved September 24, 2010, from http://www.cnnic.net.cn/uploadfiles/pdf/2009/10/12/114121.pdf

CNNIC. (2010a). The 25th statistical report on Internet development in China. Retrieved September 24, 2010, from http://www.cnnic.net.cn/uploadfiles/pdf/2010/3/15/142705.pdf

CNNIC. (2010b). The 26th statistical report on Internet development in China. Retrieved September 24, 2010, from http://www.cnnic.net.cn/uploadfiles/pdf/2010/8/24/93145.pdf

CNNIC. (2013, January). Statistical report on Internet development in China. Retrieved April, 15, 2013, from http://www1.cnnic.cn/IDR/ReportDownloads/201302/P020130312536825920279.pdf

Guo Zixiu; Tan, Felix B.; Turner, Tim; & Xu Huizhong. (2008). An exploratory investigation into instant messaging preferences in two distinct cultures. *IEEE Transactions on Professional Communication, 51*(4), 396-415.

Hauben, Jay. (2010). "Across the Great Wall": The China-Germany email connection 1987-1994. Retrieved October 22, 2010, from www.columbia.edu/~hauben/china-email.doc

Jiang Xiyushi. (2009). The big events in the history of free email. Retrieved June 09, 2010, from http://tieba.baidu.com/f?kz=634852179

Li Nai, & Kirkup, Gill. (2007). Gender and cultural differences in Internet use: A study of China and the UK. *Computers & Education, 48*(2), 301-317.

Na Ying. (2009). The history of email you did not know. Retrieved June 7, 2010, from http://news.iresearch.cn/0200/20090713/97154.shtml

Netease.com. (2010). Introduction of Netease.com. Retrieved June 20, 2010, from http://gb.corp.163.com/gb/about/overview.html

Tai Zixue. (2006). *The Internet in China: Cyberspace and civil society*. New York: Routledge.

Tencent. (2010). 2009 annual report. Retrieved February 4, 2011, from http://www.tencent.com/en-us/ir/reports.shtml

Wolff, Stephen S. (1987, November 8). David Farber and Ira Fuchs [Letter from the US National Science Foundation regarding the extension of BITNET and CSNET]. Retrieved July 07, 2010, from http://www.cnnic.cn/html/Dir/2007/05/25/4607.htm

Yang Guobin. (2009). *The power of the Internet in China: Citizen activism online*. New York: Columbia University.

Zhu, J. J. H., & Wang, E. (2005). Diffusion, use, and effect of the Internet in China. *Communications of the ACM, 48*(4), 49–53.

Zhu, Jonathan J. H., & He Zhou. (2002). Perceived characteristics, perceived needs, and perceived popularity: Adoption and use of the Internet in China. *Communication Research, 29*(4), 466-495.

Zorn, Werner. (1988). How China was connected to the international computer networks. Retrieved July 12, 2010, from www.ais.org/~jrh/acn/acn15-2.articles/zorn.pdf

Game Industry Online

Wǎngluò yóuxì 网络游戏

Summary: The Internet has become a major source of entertainment in China. Stringent government regulation and media censorship cultivate a nationalist form of Internet entertainment culture for content created online. The main form of Internet culture, however, still remains largely commercial due to competitive market forces and the rapid expansion of online users. Both political and economic factors have transformed Internet entertainment into an emerging media culture that makes room for grassroots expression through user-generated content in China.

China's "netizens" have a growing interest in online entertainment, which is reflected in their Internet usage. According to the China Internet Network Information Center (CNNIC), China's top six Internet applications in 2012 were instant messaging (IM) (82.9 percent), search engines (80 percent), online music (77.3 percent), blogs and personal space (66.1 percent), online videos (65.9 percent), and online games (59.5 percent) (CNNIC 2013). These statistics illustrate that Chinese netizens spend most of their time using Internet technology to engage in entertainment activities such as social chats, music downloads, information searches, and online game play.

Since the late 1980s / early 1990s, when China made its first connection to the global Internet network, years of development have transformed China into a wired nation with the largest Internet market in the world. The total number of online users grew from 23 million in 2000 to 538 million in 2012 (CNNIC 2013). By December 2012, the rate of Internet penetration in China had reached 41.1 percent. Compared to other countries, however, China still has a relatively low Internet penetration rate. For instance, in 2011 Internet penetration in the United States, Japan, and South Korea had reached between 78 and 80 percent. China remains an emerging online entertainment market, one that holds massive potential for growth.

China's rapid growth in Internet penetration nourishes a particular form of Internet entertainment culture. Media censorship of film and television cultivates an

Internet culture where Chinese netizens go online to look for entertainment (Barboza 2010). At the same time, the Internet culture also has grown nationalistic (Kshetri 2009). Most Internet users in China belong to younger generations and reside in metropolitan areas; in 2012, 56.1 percent of all users were below the age of thirty, while nearly 73 percent of them lived in urban centers (CNNIC 2013). The consumption power of these online users is most evident in the online gaming sector: in 2010 alone, China's online gaming market took in revenue of US$5 billion (PricewaterhouseCoopers 2010).

The Game Industry

Online games can be used as a model for the Internet entertainment industry in China. The producers of massively multiplayer online games (MMOGs) have created the most profitable media industry in China. By 2009, the country's online game industry served the largest online game market in the world, outbidding South Korea to occupy 56 percent of the Asian market (PricewaterhouseCoopers 2010). This was still a small part of the worldwide video game market, of which China occupied only 6 percent. In contrast to the United States, where most video game players use console games at home, China has looked to Internet cafés to provide the major infrastructure that gamers use, favoring the rapid growth of the country's online game market (Ernkvist and Strom 2008), although that trend is changing with the growth and diffusion of smartphones.

China's online game industry has earned its reputation largely in China's domestic market. Building on their success at home, however, some top-tier game companies have also begun to export their products to other Asian countries. Some of the spectacular successes of this industry can be attributed to China's overall political-economic structure. The state plays an active role in designing relevant policies to protect domestic online game producers. The results are clear: according to fieldwork and interviews with industry professionals in China, among a total of 115 approved applications for new online games licenses, the government approved 80 domestic games while approving only 35 foreign ones (Chung and Yuan 2009). Surely, this ratio reflects the impact of state protectionism on the industry's development. The total number of games under commercial operation has grown significantly in recent years, from 293 in 2008 to 361 in 2009. The same is true of market share and growth rate. (See table 1.) Revenue grew from US$210 million in 2002 to US$1.35 billion in 2007, a sixfold increase.

Table 1. The Online Game Market Growth from 2002 to 2007

	2002	2003	2004	2005	2006	2007
Market size (US$ million)	210	240	416	600	960	1,350
Growth rate	N/A	14%	73%	44%	60%	40%

Source: KMPG (2011).

An analysis of China's online game industry's structure reveals many factors responsible for the success of these games in the domestic market. From a political perspective, China's efficient system of government control and stringent regulation for the dissemination of information online has fostered rapid commercialization of Internet entertainment. Many believe that the Internet possesses the ability to facilitate decentralized information and horizontal (instead of top-down) communication that may in return challenge the Chinese Communist Party's one-party rule (Lum 2006). The regulatory dispute between Google and the Chinese government that took place in 2010, however, showed how difficult the crossover into China can be for foreign game companies. Claiming that it was forced to act in order to protect its data security from hackers inside China, Google redirected its Chinese-language website to the company's uncensored server in Hong Kong. In another instance, the government adopted a strong posture in the case of *World of Warcraft*. In 2009, the game's California-based game developer, Blizzard Entertainment, found itself unable to operate its service in China due to an internal political struggle between the Ministry of Culture (MOC) and the General Administration of Press and Publication (GAPP). While Blizzard switched its service from The9.com to a new local business partner and server, Netease.com, the company lacked any license to operate from June to November 2009.

From a regulatory perspective, Internet censorship provides the most effective kind of surveillance system to monitor social activities that might later become "political." The MOC created the most influential policy on online game control when it formed a monitoring central committee together with GAPP and the Ministry of Public Security and State Administration of Industry and Commerce, and charged it to work on legal tasks that "purify online game culture." The government shut down fifty-two game operators because they failed to meet the government's requirement that they follow its anti-addiction and anti-gambling regulations.

China's regulations include specific rules intended to control the following parties involved in the online game industry:

Foreign game companies. China monitors the corporate activities of foreign game companies according to a set of stringent rules. It also denies foreign companies direct entry into the Chinese market. Control was further tightened in 2009 when the GAPP issued a "Notification on Strengthening the Administration of Approval of Imported Internet Games" to limit the commercial activities of foreign game companies in China.

Non-state publishing companies. The Chinese government encourages local private companies to dominate the domestic game industry. In 2009, the GAPP issued "Guiding Opinions on Further Advancing the Reform of the Press and Publication System" to increase the collaboration between state-owned and private companies in the local publishing industry.

Internet cafés. The government uses Internet cafés to maintain its control over gamer activities. In 2007, the Ministry of Culture required Internet cafés to follow and support state anti-gambling and anti-addiction policies, and to cooperate with the government's campaigns to encourage healthy lifestyles among young gamers in China.

Individual online gamers. The Chinese government sets up online monitoring systems to prevent misconduct by online gamers. Individual gamers can file criminal reports with the Internet police through a website dedicated to online game portals. Regulations on Internet behavior include restricted parental control, the "Great Firewall," and anti-addiction monitoring systems.

From an economic perspective, local online game companies enhance competitiveness within a protectionist industry environment. Compared with the development strategies of game companies in South Korea, Japan, and the United States, Chinese game companies establish their industry specialty by offering lower-quality games manufactured cheaply and sold at a lower price. This strategy conforms with China's overall strategy since the 1970s to build a reputation as a low-cost outsourcing center for many information and communications technologies (ICT) industry sectors. As a result, the country has grown particularly strong in computer graphics and animations for media production, so much so that it now attracts international game companies like Ubisoft to set up production studios in China. As foreign investment grows, foreign game companies transfer knowledge, which benefits local game development, making local game companies the dominant player in China's domestic online game market. While this strategy has fostered growth, it has not necessarily fostered competition between foreign and local game companies.

The market has grown highly centralized, with three top-tier local game companies controlling almost 50 percent of the total market. The largest company, Tencent, controlled 21 percent of the market. Shanda and Netease followed as the second- and the third-largest companies, capturing 15 and 12 percent of the market, respectively. All these online game companies began as publishers that released foreign games from South Korea and the United States. Using their profits from game publishing, these companies then extended their commercial operation into the developing sector. For instance, Shanda became successful publishing South Korean games by owning the country's largest distribution network, integrating them through Internet cafés. Tencent gained its market advantage by serving the country's largest instant messaging population through its technology platform, QQ. Other companies, such as Netease, Sohu, Giant, Kuanyu Huaxia, Kingsoft, and Nineyou, all became strong players in China by starting with game publishing. *Perfect World is the only company to earn a profit mainly from developing and publishing its own game, Perfect World. In a world where most of the online games developed by Chinese companies succeed only in the domestic market, Perfect World* stands out as the exception to the rule, competing successfully in both the Chinese and international markets.

Global and Local Dimensions of Online Games

Some scholars have argued that China's connection to the global information network points its people in the direction of media reforms and toward an "open door" policy (Liang and Lu 2010). Such high hopes to improve Chinese democracy do not easily appear on the Internet, however, as many—but by no means all—Chinese netizens tend to use the medium for the purpose of entertainment rather than for civic engagement. While this relative lack of political discourse among Internet users in China may have contributed to the "delay" of democratic reform, it overlooks the potential of Internet entertainment to impact China's democratic development. In order to understand consumption of popular Chinese entertainment information on the Internet, it is important to look at this from both a global and a local perspective.

Global Dimension

Open access and ease of information flow have created a commercialized culture where China's integration into the web encourages the coalescence of global popular culture and local mass culture. Internet entertainment contains more foreign programs than other mainstream media channels such as film, radio, and television in China. Whereas piracy frustrates most global media companies, local Internet companies and users in China benefit from the easy digital downloads of foreign media available to them online.

The influence of global media content on the Internet in China can be seen most conspicuously in the Chinese Internet companies that universally replicate the business models of Western companies that demonstrate success in the global markets. Tudou.com, China's largest video-sharing website, imitates the commercial operation of YouTube and allows its users to upload user-generated content to its website. "Flexible" copyright regulation allows customers of Tudou.com to freely upload and download media content without adhering to copyright regulations. The company's website carries a wide variety of television dramas and movies that are produced in Taiwan, South Korea, Japan, and the United States. While a company like Tudou functions as a content aggregator, local Internet companies also use foreign media content to invent a unique business that remains free to access and is marketable by generating advertising revenue in the Chinese market.

In online gaming, global game content has exerted great influence on the determination of styles for game content in China. The early commercial success of South Korean games like *Lineages, Legend of Mir,* and *Moo Online* set a standard pattern for game production in the Chinese market. Chinese game companies rely on foreign games to offer an item-based model to collect revenue from gamers. Gamers play the game for free, and transactions only occur when gamers purchase virtual items within the game.

In all, foreign game content has played a key role in the rapid commercialization and national success of the online game market in China, but it can also lead to critical market failure. Evidence is clear in two cases, when Shanda benefitted from releasing the South Korean game *Legend of Mir,* and when The9.com lost its market share to the US-made game *World of Warcraft.* Shanda achieved dominance of the Chinese market due to its well-developed distribution system, while learning the skills of game production through releasing games from South Korea. The company produced its own local game, *The World of Legend,* similar to the South Korean game *Mir,* hoping to further localize its game publishing market. In 2004, Shanda made its first venture overseas by purchasing the South Korean game developer ActozSoft. Six years later, the company ranked as the second-largest game company in China (CNNIC 2010). In contrast, The9.com experienced a different fate. In 2007, when The9.com oversaw *World of Warcraft,* the company was ranked fourth among online game operators, occupying 10 percent of China's total market (Chung and Yuan 2009). Once the company lost its contract to continue releasing *World of Warcraft,* however, it quickly dropped from the list of top-ten game companies. In 2009, the9.com's revenue fell 94 percent after the loss of *World of Warcraft* (Elliot 2009). Market competition grew not only more diversified but also more aggressive, as local Chinese game companies appropriated high-quality foreign games to compete with each other in the Chinese market.

Local Dimension

Compared to global media content, local Internet content presents a much more complicated social struggle for the media entertainment industry in China. Local game companies make use of Chinese stories in order to comply with the government's nationalist game policy. At the same time, game companies at the corporate level localize foreign content in order to meet gamer tastes particular to China. At the gamer level, two-thirds of the more than 500 million online users in China play online games (Scarlatelli 2011). Due to the popularity of *wǔxià* 武侠(martial arts) novels and films, Chinese gamers also enjoy *kung fu games, such as Kung Fu Fighter and Kung Fu Grandma.* In 2009, Shanda established an affiliate development studio, Shanda Literature, to develop so-called literary games (i.e., games based on traditional novels and stories). The company adopted an online novel that was popular in 2007, *Ghost Blows Out the Candlelight,* to produce its first thriller-style MMOG.

Table 3 shows the top-ten most popular games in China in 2009. Even though *DNF, World of Warcraft,* and *CrossFire* came from the United States and South Korea, seven out of the ten games in the top ten in that year were produced domestically. These games included *Kaixin Online, Asktao, Moyu, Westward Journey Online, Jade Dynasty, Tianlong babu,* and *Zheng tu.* The narrative and visual design of these games clearly reflect Chinese culture. In the game *Jade Dynasty,* for example, gamers can take "taichi pills" to increase their level of gaming experience. *Zheng tu* players must understand Chinese philosophy and religion in order to play. They pray to Quan Yin, the female goddess in charge of delivering newborn babies, in the hope that she will bless their children, in keeping with Daoist religious beliefs.

Other Types of Internet Entertainment

Freedom of expression takes on a subculture form in Internet entertainment on the individual level. Online users are able to deconstruct and discuss serious themes in Chinese society that normally may be taboo, using the styles of "copycat" (*shānzhài*山寨) or parody (*ègǎo* 恶搞) in readjusting their user-generated content. User-generated content also allows Chinese Internet users an alternative space to create a world of cultural diversity that may not be possible in their physical world. Together, these examples show the potential that online entertainment creates for the development of public discourse on a grassroots level in China.

Table 3. China's Top 10 Online Games (2009)

Game	Developer	Country
1. *DNF*	Neople/Nexon	South Korea
2. *Kaixin Online*	TQ Digital Entertainment	China
3. *Asktao*	G-Gits Networks	China
4. *Moyu*	TQ Digital Entertainment	China
5. *World of Warcraft*	Blizzard Entertainment	USA
6. *Westward Journey Online II*	Netease	China
7. *Jade Dynasty*	Perfect World Co, Ltd.	China
8. *Tialong babu*	Changyou.com Ltd.	China
9. *Zheng tu*	Giant Interactive Group	China
10. *CrossFire*	Smile Gate	South Korea

Source: MMLC Group (2009). Retrieved May 26, 2014, from http://iamasiam.typepad.com/1001/2009/11/top-ten-online-games-in-china.html

China's most popular remixed culture, called *egao* ("evil work" or parody/spoofing), illustrates the opportunities that Chinese online culture offers people who wish to challenge forms of cultural authority and heritage in Chinese society, by transforming themselves into "prosumers" (a portmanteau word combining *producer* and *consumer*) of media texts. The *egao* community is part of an emerging form of Internet production whose content is characteristically humorous, satirical, and subversive.

Another form of subculture in China's Internet entertainment is *shanzhai*, or copycat. *Shanzhai* literally means "mountain village" in Chinese, but it has recently come to mean an illegitimate copy of a famous brand product or well-known genre. The *shanzhai* culture illustrates a form of cultural hybridization, as Chinese netizens use their creativity to invent new practices and redefine the social value of Internet entertainment in China (Jiang 2009. Take, for example, the *shanzhai* version of the *Spring Festival Gala. The government's televised version of the Spring Festival Gala has been a traditional part of the Chinese New Year celebration. In recent years, however, the Internet version of Spring Festival Gala* has grown so popular that, in 2010, the government agreed to recognize both the China Central Television (CCTV) and *shanzhai* versions of Spring Festival Gala on its Spring Festival Gala's website. This is one demonstration of the progressive value of online collectivism.

Conclusion

Internet entertainment has served Chinese netizens as an alternative space for public expression. Whereas Chinese netizens often hesitate to engage in outright political debate on Internet forums, a commercialized public space within the domain of Internet entertainment provides non-state actors, including both local private companies and Chinese netizens, to engage in a form of cultural production that is vernacular and hybrid. On the corporate side, local companies negotiate for maximum autonomy under the stringent rules of Internet censorship in China. At the same time, the state's protectionist policy—one that favors local game production—has had an influence (some would say positive, some negative) on the online game industry's success in China. From the perspective of the user, the content they themselves generate provides a clear example of how Chinese netizens are empowered by using the content production cycles of prosumers. The cultures of *egao* and *shangzhai* reveal the social space that Internet technology has created for Chinese citizens. Users who produce copycat and parody content online perform their own brand of individual autonomy, and demonstrate to us the social value of remixed culture in China's Internet entertainment.

Peichi CHUNG
The Chinese University of Hong Kong

See also Children Online; Internet Cafés; Internet in Everyday Life; Virtual Reality

Further Reading

Barboza, David. (2010, April 18). For Chinese, web is the way to entertainment. *The New York Times.* Retrieved October 15, 2011, from http://www.nytimes.com/2010/04/19/technology/19chinaweb.html

Chung Peichi, & Yuan Jiangping. (2009). Dynamics in the online game industry of China: A political economic analysis of its competitiveness. *Revista de Economía Política de las Tecnologías de la Información y Comunicación (EPTIC Online), 9*(2). Retrieved August 4, 2010, from http://www.eptic.com.br/arquivos/Revistas/vol.XI,n2,2009/11-PeichiChungJiangPingYuan.pdf

China Internet Network Information Center (CNNIC). (2010). The 26th statistical survey report on Internet development in China. Retrieved October 15, 2011, from http://www.cnnic.cn/upload-files/pdf/2010/8/24/93145.pdf

China Internet Network Information Center (CNNIC). (2013, January). Statistical report on Internet development in China. Retrieved April, 15, 2013, from http://www1.cnnic.cn/IDR/ReportDownloads/201302/P020130312536825920279.pdf

Elliot, Phil. (2009, November 27). The9 revenues fall 94% following loss of Warcraft. *Gameindustry.biz.* Retrieved August 4, 2010, from http://www.gamesindustry.biz/articles/the9-revenues-fall-94-percent-following-loss-of-warcraft

Ernkvist, Mirko, & Strom, Patrik. (2008). Enmeshed in games with the government: Governmental policies and the development of the Chinese online game industry. *Games and Culture, 3*(1): 98-126.

Internet World Statistics. (2011). Internet usage in Asia. Retrieved October 15, 2011, from http://www.internetworldstats.com/stats3.htm

Jiang, Fei. (2009). Game between "Quan" and "Shi": Communication strategy for "Shanzhai" subculture in China cyber space. Retrieved August 4, 2010, from http://www.scribd.com/doc/15919031/Fei-Jiang-Chinese-Shanzhai-Culture-Studies

KPMG (2007). The video game market in China: Moving online. Retrieved May 26, 2014, from http://trpc.biz/wp-content/uploads/2008-07_KPMG_VideoGamesInChinaMovingOnline_Report.pdf

Kshetri, Nir. (2009). The evolution of the Chinese online gaming industry. *Journal of Technology Management in China, 4*(2), 158-179.

Liang, Bin, & Lu, Hong. (2010). Internet development, censorship, and cyber crimes in China. *Journal of Contemporary Criminal Justice, 26*(1), 103-120.

Lin, Chun (2010). *China's fifteen years of Internet development: 1995–2009* [in Chinese]. Beijing: China CITIC Press.

Lum, Thomas. (2006). Congressional Research Service Report: Internet development and information control in the People's Republic of China. Retrieved July 26, 2010, from http://www.fas.org/sgp/crs/row/RL33167.pdf

PricewaterhouseCoopers. (2010). *Global entertainment & media outlook: 2010–2014*. New York: PricewaterhouseCoopers LLP.

Qing, Huang. (2006, November 22). Parody can help people ease work pressure. *China Daily*. Retrieved August 8, 2010, from http://www.chinadaily.com.cn/cndy/2006-07/22/content_646887.htm

Ren, Qun, & Hardwick, Phillip. (2009). Analysis of strategic alliance management—Lessons from the failure of Korean and Japanese licensed games in China. *International Journal of Chinese Culture and Management*, 2(1), 1-13.

Scarlatelli, Andrea. (2011). Top 10 most popular online gaming companies in China. EChinacities.com. Retrieved October 15, 2011, from http://www.echinacities.com/expat-corner/top-10-most-popular-online-gaming-companies-in-china.html

Wager, Skiff. (2007). Media and entertainment—Use of digital assets and digital management: Industry outlook 2006-2010. *Journal of Digital Asset Management*, *2007*(3), 5-9.

Microblogging

Wēibó 微博

Summary: Microblogs are a type of blog that lets users publish short text updates and photos. Because the world's best-known sites (Twitter and Facebook) have been blocked by the Chinese government since 2007, China is instead dominated by homegrown microblogging websites. In a relatively short time, China's microblogging platforms have given the netizens a relatively anonymous forum in which to speak to each other and to, and about, their leaders.

Microblogs (*wēibó* 微博) are online social media platforms through which users share short written messages, photos, and other media. In the West, microblogs are most commonly associated with Twitter, one of the most widely known global microblogging services. In China, where Twitter has been blocked by the government since 2007, homegrown microblogging websites are incredibly popular among Internet users and have rapidly become the dominant medium for online discourse. The two major players, Sina Weibo 新浪微博and Tencent Weibo 腾讯微博, each boasted more than 400 million registered users at the end of 2012. Microblogging platforms provide an important medium through which China's rapidly growing Internet population can interact with each other and, through galvanized public opinion, interact and influence the Chinese leadership.

The Rise of *Weibos*

The first Chinese microblog service was launched by FanFo.com in 2007. The obvious tension between the rapid and decentralized dissemination of content facilitated by microblogs and the Chinese government's desire to control information came to a head during the violent 2009 Uygur protests in Xinjiang Province. In July 2009, the Chinese government shut down all existing domestic *weibo* platforms and blocked access to international providers like Twitter and Facebook. Established online media players Sina Corp and Tencent wasted no time stepping into the vacuum created by government censorship and launched competing platforms by the end of 2009.

With the launch of Sina Weibo and Tencent Weibo, the number of Chinese microbloggers exploded. By the autumn of 2012, in just three years, both Sina Weibo and Tencent Weibo each boasted more than 400 million users, a conspicuous 70 percent of the nearly 570 million Internet users estimated by the China Internet Network Information Center (CNNIC) at the end of 2012 (CNNIC 2013). Registered users, however, reveal only part of the story. By virtually every other meaningful measure (hours spent on the platform, volume of posts, reposts, and message threads), Sina Weibo is the leading microblogging platform in China. Tencent Weibo ranks a close second and, as of early 2013, had gained market share in hours spent on its platform by leveraging users' preexisting connections with its ubiquitous instant messaging (IM) platform Tencent QQ (腾讯QQ).

Functionality

Chinese microblogging's core features are similar to those of Twitter, the US-based microblog giant that launched in 2006 and by 2012 boasted more than 500 million users. In China, microblog posts are limited to 140 Chinese characters, which is closer to 140 English words than Twitter's 140 Romanized characters, which therefore permits more content. Users of Twitter will also be familiar with the use of "@username" to reference or mention other users and the "#hashtag" function to link a post to a broader topic or theme. Chinese microblogging users can also repost other users' comments on their own timeline with or without comments.

While similar to Twitter in many regards, Chinese microblogs have also developed a number of localized features that have prompted users to aptly describe the platform as a hybrid between Facebook and Twitter. Most notably, users may incorporate various media seamlessly into their posts, including emoticons, pictures, video, and audio files.

There are several other key differences in the classification of content between Chinese microblogs and Twitter. For example, Sina Weibo allows users to comment directly on other users' posts. Unlike the Twitter "Reply" function, which just adds a "@username" to a separate tweet, the Sina Weibo comment feature organizes user responses and commentary in reverse chronological order under each original post. Responses posted on a comment thread can also be posted simultaneously to the user's own profile. In effect, this creates concentrated, temporary, content-based groups through which information is rapidly flagged and transmitted to the wider microblogging community. Due to these broader but more impersonal connections between users, microblogging can facilitate much faster dissemination of content than traditional social networking platforms, like Facebook, in which interactions occur between smaller groups of more personally connected users.

Case Study: Sina Weibo and Its Users

While there are other smaller microblogging services such as Renmin Weibo 人民微博and Xinhua Weibo 新华微博, the following discussion will focus primarily on Sina Weibo because of its status as the largest and best-known microblogging platform in China.

Sina Weibo is owned by Sina Corporation, a leading online media company in China. While Sina Corp still derives the lion's share of its revenues from its search and news portal, the company is rapidly working to monetize its enormous user base through advertising revenues.

In an October 2012 report detailing user demographics, Sina Weibo announced that registered users had reached 400 million, while daily active users reached 42.3 million, roughly 10 percent. Time spent per active user has remained constant at roughly one hour per day. The core demographic of Sina Weibo users is also strikingly young and highly educated, a powerful combination. According to Sina Weibo's latest report on user statistics, a massive 92 percent of its users were born after 1980, while nearly 60 percent of users reported at least a college level education. The heaviest concentration of users is in China's more developed and densely populated eastern provinces. No less significant is the fact that, according to Sina management, over 70 percent of the roughly 100 million posts per day are generated from mobile devices. These mobile posts contain a wide range of content: from advertisements for smartphones to videos of music concerts, photos of the physical indulgences of government officials, protests and demolitions, abuses of power, and random acts of kindness. They are all broadcast from handheld devices and disseminated with fury via Sina Weibo. User activity on Sina Weibo during key events is measured in posts per second rather than average posts per day, while active users are distinguished by hours spent generating and consuming content per *day* as opposed to quantity of blog posts per *month*.

Censorship and Control

In recent history, China's traditional media sector, such as newspapers, magazines, and TV and radio broadcasts, has been highly centralized and tightly controlled by the Chinese Communist Party (CCP). The less hierarchal, more democratic, and increasingly critical content produced on the Internet through blogs, instant messages, online communities with Bulletin Board Systems (BSS) and chat services, and microblogging platforms provide a popular alternative to this system.

As the ranks of China's microbloggers have swelled, online discourse has become increasingly obtrusive and critical of both the CCP and the broader Chinese society. As there is generally "greater security in voicing dissent that is analogous to criticism articulated by numerous other bloggers" (Esarey and Xiao 2008), the scale of microblogging provides a mode of security that allows users to push the envelope and more directly speak their minds.

While the grassroots exposure of corruption at the local level may be welcomed in many ways by the central government as the CCP fights to maintain legitimacy with the Chinese people, it remains to be seen whether or not government censors can successfully insulate central party leadership in Beijing from criticism on microblogs. As the scholar Jonathan Hassid concludes, "In some domains, the CCP seems comfortable allowing bloggers free reign to comment on, or even castigate, official actions. This applies to issues where the agenda is set by the mainstream media, such as coverage of corruption, energy issues, and the Diaoyu/Senkaku Islands dispute, or by the central government, such as environmental protection" (Hassid 2012, 225). Hassid goes on to argue, however, that when Chinese "netizens" push the envelope and address topics with which the central government is uncomfortable they are "likely to face increased censorship and state scrutiny" (Hassid 2012, 226).

Through the scale and speed of content dissemination on microblogs, for example, Sina Weibo has greatly reduced the government's ability to employ surgical and targeted censorship. After the wholesale suspension of all domestic and international microblogging sites in the wake of the July 2009 Xinjiang protests, the next serious suspension of such services occurred on 31 March 2012, when the Beijing police bureau announced a three-day suspension of all users' ability to post comments on Sina Weibo and Tencent Weibo in the wake of widespread rumors of a coup in Beijing.

Short of completely blocking access to microblogging sites, there remain a number of measures that the CCP can employ to control and influence the dialogue on microblogs and to skew the public forum in their favor. Most obviously, the government will continue to actively censor content. On 30 January 2013, for example, Lee Kai Fu 李开复, a businessman labeled 2012's most influential microblogging personality by Sina, posted an image of every *weibo* post deleted from his account by censors over the previous six months, a total of seventy-eight posts. The *China Digital Times*, a well-respected blog, commented that for Lee Kai Fu, who is by no means a political activist, to "broadcast such carefully documented evidence of censorship to his audience of over 27 million followers is to bring a 'fringe' concern to the mainstream" (Henochowicz 2013). Second, should the CCP desire, they have ample room to strengthen the enforcement of real name registration and thereby increase the pressure to self-censor microblogging posts for fear of reprisal.

Lastly, and perhaps most insidiously, the CCP appears poised to intensify state-directed participation on public microblogging platforms in an attempt to directly influence the direction and tone of online discourse. According to a *Beijing News* 新景报网report, later picked up by the Hong Kong–based *South China Morning Post*, the Beijing propaganda department held a meeting on 18 January 2013, in which those in attendance were told by Beijing propaganda chief and deputy mayor Lu Wei that all government agencies, media outlets, and administrative offices will be required to open microblogging accounts in order to guide online discourse in a "positive" direction.

The most significant measure taken by the CCP to control online content, other than the instances where censors have blocked access to entire platforms or restricted certain key functions, was the implementation of a mandatory real name registration policy. On 16 December 2011, four local government bureaus in Beijing jointly announced a policy of real name registration for all microblogging platforms based in Beijing. The announced framework for the policy stipulated that all users must register real names with microblog operators in order to post messages or comment on other users' posts. The government subsequently announced a 16 March 2012 deadline for the implementation of this policy. In the months directly following the announcement of the real name registration policy, however, widespread enforcement remained elusive and user behavior remained largely unchanged.

Whither *Weibo*?

Besides their obvious entertainment value and social networking function—much like Twitter and Facebook in the West—the ability of Chinese microblogging platforms to disrupt traditional media, shape social discourse, and ultimately impact the decisions of the Chinese leadership is no longer in doubt. At the end of 2012, the two largest microblogging platforms each boasted more than 400 million users (Sina Weibo even more than 500 million), and through a torrent of posts, photos, videos, and forwards, these users have successfully held government officials both at the local and central level accountable for transgressions both small and large.

The durability of the microblogging medium in its current form, however, remains in doubt, especially with new services such as WeChat fast gaining popularity among Chinese netizens. First, online user habits are fickle, and preferred venues for consuming and disseminating information are constantly evolving. The start-up graveyard is littered with formerly disruptive and popular but now defunct technologies and social networks. While Sina Weibo or Tencent Weibo may well be replaced by other mediums and technologies, however, it is difficult to imagine that Chinese Internet users, if left to their own devices, will revert to once again to passively consuming centrally crafted media.

The Chinese leadership has tolerated and even promoted public criticism of certain subjects like local corruption, environmental degradation, foreign affairs (particularly when expressing nationalism in the face of an external threat), and food inflation, among others. Allowing criticism of selective topics not only serves as an important social safety valve that contributes to social stability, but also helps the central leadership control powerful local actors that have historically been left unaccountable in a country as large and diverse as China.

As opposed to traditional media, social media is both more pervasive in terms of the large quantity of content delivered constantly in real time as well as more invasive in the sense that content is delivered ceaselessly and directly to individual mobile devices. The medium remains in its infancy and is evolving quickly. In a remarkably short period of time, China's microblogging platforms have given Chinese citizens a public forum in which to speak to each other and their leaders.

Andrew D. Goodwin
Independent Scholar

See also Blogging; Internet Content Filtering; Internet Governance; Social and Political Impact; User-Generated Content

Further Reading

Ansfield, J. (2012, December 4). How crash cover-up altered China's succession. *New York Times*. Retrieved April 23, 2014, from http://www.nytimes.com/2012/12/05/world/asia/how-crash-cover-up-altered-chinas-succession.html?pagewanted=all

China Internet Network Information Center (CNNIC). (2013). Statistical survey report on the Internet development in China. Retrieved May 23, 2014, from http://www1.cnnic.cn/IDR/ReportDownloads/201302/P020130221391269963814.pdf

China Media Project. (2012, August 13). Power progeny 官二代. Retrieved April 23, 2014, from http://cmp.hku.hk/2012/08/08/8833/

Esarey, Ashley, & Xiao Qiang. (2008). Political expression in the Chinese blogosphere: Below the radar. *Asian Survey, 48*(5), 752–772.

Hassid, Jonathan. (2012, April). Safety valve or pressure cooker? Blogs in Chinese political life. *Journal of Communication, 62*(2), 212–230.

Henochowicz, Anne. (2013, January 30). Kai-fu Lee: 78 innocent weibos hounded to death. *China Digital Times*. Retrieved April 23, 2014, from http://chinadigitaltimes.net/2013/01/kai-fu-lee-78-innocent-weibos-hounded-to-death/?utm_source=twitterfeed&utm_medium=twitter&utm_campaign=Feed%3A+chinadigitaltimes%2FbKzO+%28China+Digital+Times+%28CDT%29%29

Hu Yongqi. (2012, November 23). Chongqing official in sex video removed from post. *China Daily*. Retrieved April 28, 2014, from http://www.asianews.co/chongqing-official-in-sex-video-removed-from-post/

Johnson, I. (2012, September 3). China faces new scandal over crash of a Ferrari. *New York Times*. Retrieved April 27, 2014, from http://www.nytimes.com/2012/09/04/world/asia/after-ling-jihuas-demotion-news-of-sons-crash-in-ferrari.html

Kennedy, J. (2013, January 18). Beijing orders its 2.06 million "propaganda workers" to get microblogging. *South China Morning Post*. Retrieved April 27, 2014, from http://www.scmp.com/comment/blogs/article/1130801/beijing-orders-its-206-million-propaganda-workers-get-microblogging

Ong, J. (2012, August 13). With 393 million messages, Sina Weibo logs over twice as many Olympics posts as Twitter. Retrieved April 27, 2014, from http://thenextweb.com/asia/2012/08/13/chinese-netizens-preferred-sina-weibo-micro-blog-olympic-tweets/

Osnos, E. (2012, October 22). Boss rail. *The New Yorker*. Retrieved April 27, 2014, from http://www.newyorker.com/reporting/2012/10/22/121022fa_fact_osnos#ixzz2JZhRlzEH

Perry, E. (2007, January). Studying Chinese politics: Farewell to revolution? *China Journal, 57*, 10.

Sina Corporation. (2012, October). 2012 年新浪微博用户发展调查报告. Retrieved April 27, 2014, from http://doc.baidu.com/view/fa503a7e31b765ce0508144c.html

Wade, S. (2012, March 31). Weibo comments suspended in coup rumor aftermath (updated). *China Digital Times*. Retrieved April 27, 2014, from http://chinadigitaltimes.net/2012/03/weibo-comments-suspended-in-coup-rumour-aftermath/

Xinjing bao 新京报. (2013, January 18).百项文物修缮今年完成计划[Restoration of hundreds of cultural relics planned to be completed this year]. Retrieved April 27, 2014, from http://www.bjnews.com.cn/news/2013/01/18/244856.html

Yang Lina. (2011, December 16). Beijing requires real names in microblog registration. *Xinhua News Agency*. Retrieved April 27, 2014, from http://news.xinhuanet.com/english/china/2011-12/16/c_131310381.htm

Yao, A. (2011, July 5). A new chapter for Sina Weibo; upgrading to hold. Deutsche Bank Global Markets Research.

Parody

Ègǎo 恶搞

Summary: *Egao* is a form of online spoofing culture in China that is closely linked to digital technologies and digitally active youth. It is a mode of grassroots expression and a means for Chinese Internet users to engage in play, resistance, and the subversion of authority. Due to its perceived cynicism and irreverence, egao is frowned upon by the government, which has taken measures to control it.

Ègǎo 恶搞 combines the Chinese words for "evil" and "do" or "work" and has been variously defined as "reckless doings," "evil joking," and "spoofing." The term arose in the mid-2000s to denote a new type of amateur multimedia production that parodies an original work. In China, particularly since 2006, *egao* has become a popular form of new media "prosumption," a word that reflects the blurring of the traditional distinction between producers and consumers (Tapscott 1996). Such prosumption is enabled by the widespread diffusion of digital technologies and access to high-speed Internet access, not only in China, but around the globe. The term *egao* is used to denote a variety of practices meant to be humorous, such as digitally altering pictures, producing lip-synched music videos or parodies of famous movies, or imitating celebrities or other public figures. *Egao* is seen by many as a form of urban youth culture in China and is thus closely associated with the "post-eighties" and the "post-nineties" generations, or those youth born in the 1980s and 1990s, respectively. In China, *egao* has stirred up controversy for a number of reasons, including the way it disregards the "sacredness" of media texts, copyright and authorship norms, and typical modes of media production and distribution. It has thus generated much attention from scholars, journalists, and Chinese government officials. Understanding *egao* helps to shed light on how everyday Internet users (or "netizens") in China engage in play, voice discontent, subvert authority, form community, and resist a political environment that sets strict limits on certain types of personal expression.

The Rise of *Egao*

Reflecting the flow of cultural goods and practices within Asia, *egao* is rooted in the

Japanese *kuso* subculture that satirizes everything from poor-quality Internet games to anime and manga. As the term *kuso* evolved, it took on a broader meaning to denote anything humorous, in particular spoofs and practical jokes. Some have traced the spirit and attitude of *egao* back to the 1980s, when young authors such as Wang Shuo stirred up controversy through what came to be called "hooligan literature" (*liúmáng wénxué* 流氓文学) due to its crude language and cynicism. For most, however, *egao* is associated with new media technologies and digitally active youth, since all the examples of popular *egao* have circulated online via computers and mobile phones.

In its earliest online form, *egao* (though not necessarily called *egao* at this point) often consisted of digitally altered images, with the most famous being that of "Little Fatty" (*Xiǎo Páng* 小胖), a teenager from Shanghai whose face was ubiquitous in 2003, as it was superimposed on everyone from Russell Crowe to the Mona Lisa to one of the US presidents at Mount Rushmore. Other images that have been rich fodder for such enhancement include the logos for the Beijing Olympics and the Shanghai World Expo. Another example of early *egao* was the Backdorm Boys (Hòushě Nánshēng 后舍男生), whose humorous lip-synching of pop songs by such artists as the Backstreet Boys and Jessica Simpson (easily accessible on YouTube) went viral and quickly turned them into megastars in China in 2005.

Perhaps the most famous *egao* production, and arguably the reason that *egao* has generated as much attention as it has, is *The Bloody Case that Started from a Steamed Bun* (*Yīge Mántou Yǐnfā de Xué'àn* 一个馒头引发的血案) ("Steamed Bun" hereafter), made in 2006 by Hu Ge, a thirty-one-year-old unknown (at the time) sound engineer. Hu's twenty-minute film is a parody of *The Promise*, a 2005 movie by Chen Kaige, perhaps best known outside of China for the film *Farewell My Concubine*. Prior to its release, *The Promise* had received much publicity due to its famous director and its lavish budget. The fanfare surrounding the opening of the film combined with the pricey tickets meant that expectations were high. Critics and audiences, however, were generally not pleased with *The Promise*. Hu Ge has said in interviews that the reason he made his spoof was to express his disappointment as well as to have some fun. *Steamed Bun* imitates a popular China Central Television (CCTV) show, *China Legal Report*, while cutting and splicing parts of *The Promise*, dubbing voices, and inserting Chinese pop songs and mock commercials. It is funny but also includes social critique on issues plaguing contemporary China, including official corruption and the exploitation of migrant workers. As noted in a March 2006 article in the *Shanghai Daily* (an official English publication) titled, "Director Gets His Nose Properly Rubbed in It," Hu's film was

> [not] just a victory of grassroots wisdom over a film guru's mediocrity. It's the hallmark of a new era in China, when small potatoes are free to satire public figures in a way that's short of actual malice.... It has won the hearts of tens of millions of netizens, who share its author's joy in undoing that pompous film.

Steamed Bun was a viral sensation, and it became even more popular after Chen Kaige sued Hu for copyright infringement.

Online forums buzzed with debate about the case, with most commentators siding with Hu. Official newspapers also covered the issue extensively. Eventually Chen Kaige dropped his lawsuit, which further strengthened the notion that Hu and his parody represented the "spirit of the grass-roots [*cǎogēn* 草根] majority" against the out-of-touch elite.

Egao as Social Critique and Political Satire

Since Hu Ge's parody, the Chinese Internet has been awash in *egao*. *Egao* productions can be merely humorous mash-ups of songs and films, leading some to argue that *egao* has no logic or agenda. Like "Steamed Bun," however, much *egao* has an underlying social critique even as it is meant to be entertaining, and because in China there is not always a clear distinction between the state, the society, and the market, *egao* that contains social commentary and/or references political figures or government policies can be read as an implicit critique against the government. One of the earliest examples of *egao* that contained indirect political commentary was a spoof of a 1974 propaganda film called *Sparkling Red Star*. In the parody, the hero of the original film is now a young boy who competes in a CCTV singing contest, where the judges are not above taking bribes. This short film was seen as immoral by some because it allegedly profaned China's revolutionary history. Other Mao-era films have also served as the basis for *egao*, including a segment from the 1965 *The Long March Suite* that has been edited and dubbed with numerous songs, including Jay Chou's "Ninja" and Michael Jackson's "Beat It" (the latter was an Internet sensation in China in 2010).

While spoofs of sacred revolutionary texts can be understood as only indirectly political, *egao* has also been created in direct response to Chinese government policies. For example, in early 2009, the government launched an "Anti-Vulgarity Campaign" to "strike hard" against Internet pornography and indecency in order to promote a "clean" and harmonious Internet environment (in line with the government's stated goal of creating a "harmonious society" or *héxié shèhuì* 和谐社会). As a result, thousands of websites were censored, blocked, or deleted, and certain applications became inaccessible. Many people surmised that the purpose of the campaign was to block not only indecent but also political content that the government deemed undesirable. At the beginning of 2009, in the midst of this crackdown, Baidu's Baike (a Chinese-style Wikipedia) was hacked, and there appeared entries for "Ten Mythical Creatures," nearly all of which had crude names that referred to male and female genitalia or were in other ways rather vulgar. The most famous of these was the Grass-Mud Horse (*Cǎo Ní Mǎ* 草泥马), which in Chinese also sounds like an obscene insult having to do with one's mother. Soon a short video, the *Song of the Grass-Mud Horse*, appeared in Chinese cyberspace. In the narrative of the video, alpaca-like creatures run free in the desert and are courageous and tenacious. They eventually defeat the "River Crabs," an Internet meme that means censorship or the government, since the Chinese word for "river crab" (*héxiè* 河蟹) also sounds like "harmony" (in reference to the government's harmonious society). With its nursery rhyme–like melody—it uses the Chinese version of the *Smurfs'* theme song—the *Song of the Grass-Mud Horse* sounds like an innocent children's song, yet it is laced with homophones for dirty words in Chinese. The point of the video was to mock the government's censorship campaign and to get past the censors by relying on the richness of the Chinese language. The *Song of the Grass-Mud Horse* was seen by millions and spawned other derivative *egao*, as well as merchandise that could be purchased, including stuffed alpacas, T-shirts, and mugs.

Since the Grass-Mud Horse, other *egao* have also been created in response to government censorship efforts. In May 2009, for example, the government announced that by July of the same year all new computers for sale in China had to have Green Dam Youth Escort software preinstalled in order to keep minors from accessing obscene or other "harmful" content. This announcement was met with widespread condemnation, both inside and outside of China, not only because there was concern that such a mandate was a violation of users' rights, but also because the software was found to be extremely unreliable when tested. The creators were also accused of stealing computer code. As part of the protest against the software, the Green Dam Girl (*lǜbàniáng* 绿坝娘), which also sounds like "filter tyrant" in Chinese, appeared online. She is a manga-style character that exists in various forms, but she usually holds a rabbit (the software's mascot), wears a hat with a river crab, and dons a red arm band (like a Red Guard). Her purpose is clearly to ridicule the government and its efforts at creating a "healthy" Internet environment. Eventually, the government did, in fact, back down from its decree, although the software has been installed in computers in schools and libraries.

Significance of *Egao*

For those outside China, the significance of *egao* might not be immediately clear. User-generated content proliferates on the web in a range of countries. In the Chinese context, however, where for decades media have been tightly controlled by a large state bureaucracy, *egao* represents an important sociocultural phenomenon. To understand *egao*, many scholars have drawn upon the Russian literary theorist Mikhail Bahktin and his notion of the carnival. To Bahktin, the carnival allows for the temporary leveling of social hierarchies and creates an environment where laughter, parody, and the grotesque are deployed to deflate the pompous and to subvert authority. *Egao* can be seen as carnivalesque in its irreverent attitude toward officialdom and its mockery of sacred texts and mainstream media, as well as in its use of humor that is at times crude. Yet, such humor has also been critiqued for its often regressive gender politics.

Egao is also seen by some as an important means for those who lack social power to have a mediated voice. In the "Steamed Bun" case, Hu Ge was described as an "ant" who took on an "elephant" (Chen Kaige as well as the larger societal elite) and won. In a nation where people are not able to criticize the mainstream establishment (at least not openly), *egao* is further understood as a mode of grassroots resistance to censorship and official discourse, even when it is not made in direct response to censorship efforts. As the media and communications professor Bingchun Meng (2009, 63) has pointed out, although "*egao* practices are rather dispersed and those who engage in this activity do not have a common agenda or coherent strategy," the political significance of *egao* should not be discounted. *Egao* has been used both implicitly and explicitly to lodge critiques against widespread official corruption. Finally, just as *egao* disrupts conventional notions of authorship and copyright by borrowing and remixing, it also upsets norms of distribution and exhibition, as traditional media gatekeepers are bypassed through the flow of online content.

The Chinese government and cultural elite have not looked kindly upon *egao*, believing it to be at odds with a "harmonious society" (Lu 2007). As such, there have been numerous efforts on the part of the State Administration of Film, Radio, and Television (SARFT) and the Ministry of Industry and Information Technology (MIIT) to control its dissemination. In 2007, new regulations required that all music that had been altered from its original form had to be approved before it could be uploaded online. A 2008 declaration decreed that only state-controlled companies could broadcast online videos. After the popularity of the "Song of the Grass-Mud Horse," in March 2009 SARFT implemented further Internet broadcasting licensing requirements and new prohibitions on certain types of online content. It is likely that new *egao* will continue to spur new regulations.

Implications

Although the Chinese government has sought to control *egao*, it continues to proliferate online in China. On the one hand, *egao* could be viewed as merely a means for netizens to have fun and blow off steam; in other words, it is a mode of resistance that does not lead to political change. On the other hand, *egao* has been deployed within the context of larger public opposition to unfair regulations (such as the Green Dam Youth Escort software), official corruption, and social inequality. It also is a means for dispersed individuals to debate issues, express themselves, and form an "imagined community." In this sense, *egao* is a grassroots expression that is an important indicator of the potentials for social change in China, and the role of the Internet in those developments.

Cara WALLIS
Texas A&M University

See also Blogging; Chinese Language and Computing; Internet Events; User-Generated Content

Further Reading

Barmé, Geremie R. (2007, April 20–21). Eating Chinese—A historical banquet. Paper presented at the Future of US-China Relations conference, Los Angeles, CA.

Coonan, Clifford. (2006, November 16). The new Cultural Revolution: How Little Fatty made it big. *The Independent*. Retrieved September 11, 2013, from http://www.independent.co.uk/news/world/asia/the-new-cultural-revolution-how-little-fatty-made-it-big-424469.html

Director gets his nose properly rubbed in it. (2006, February 20). *Shanghai Daily*. Retrieved September 11, 2013, from http://www.china.org.cn/english/features/film/158551.htm

Esarey, Ashley, & Xiao Qiang. (2008). Political expression in the Chinese blogosphere. *Asian Survey, 48*(5), 752–772.

Gong Haomin, & Yang Xin. (2010). Digitized parody: The politics of *egao* in contemporary China. *China Information, 24*(1), 3–26.

Hu Jiangfeng. (2008). *E'gao yu qingninan yawenhua* [Spoofing and youth subculture]. *China Youth Study, 6*(148), 5–10.

Hu Yong. (2008). Zhongsheng xuanhua: Wangluo shidai de geren biaoda yu gonggong taolun [The rising cacophony: Personal expression and public discussion in the Internet age]. Guilin, China: Guangxi Normal University Press.

Huang Qing. (22 July 2006). Parody can help people ease work pressure. *China Daily*. Retrieved March 3, 2009, from http://www.chinadaily.com.cn/cndy/2006-07/22/content_646887.htm

Jenkins, Henry. (2006). Convergence culture: Where old and new media collide. New York: NYU Press.

Li, Henry Siling. (2009). The turn to the self: From "Big Character Posters" to YouTube videos. *Chinese Journal of Communication, 2*(1), 50–60.

Li, Hongmei. (2011). Parody and resistance on the Chinese Internet. In D. K. Herold & P. Marolt (Eds.), *Online society in China: Creating, celebrating, and instrumentalizing the online carnival* (pp. 71–88). London: Routledge.

Lu Bo. (2007). Hexie shehui jianche yujingzhong de "fenqing" "e'gao" xianxiang pingxi [A critique of the "angry youth" "parody" phenomena in the context of building a harmonious society]. *China Youth Study, 9*(139), 69–70.

Martinsen, Joel. (2009, February 11). Hoax dictionary entries about legendary obscene beasts. Retrieved May 21, 2014, from http://www.danwei.org/humor/baidu_baike_fake_entries.php

Meng, Bingchun. (2009). Regulating *egao*: Futile efforts of recentralization. In X. Zhang & Y. Zheng (Eds.), *China's information and communications technology revolution: Social changes and state responses* (pp. 52–67). New York: Routledge.

Meng, Bingchun. (2011). From Steamed Bun to Grass Mud Horse: Egao as alternative political discourse on the Chinese Internet. *Global Media and Communication*, 7(1), 33–51.

Rosen, Stanley. (2009). Contemporary Chinese youth and the state. *Journal of Asian Studies, 68*(2), 359–369.

Tang, Lijun, and Peidong Yang. (2011). Symbolic power and the Internet: The power of a "horse." *Media, Culture & Society*, 33(5), 675–691.

Tapscott, Don. (1996). The digital economy: Promise and peril in the age of networked intelligence. New York: McGraw-Hill.

Voci, Paola. (2010). *China on video*. New York: Routledge.

Wallis, Cara. (Forthcoming). Gender and China's online censorship protest culture. *Feminist Media Studies*.

Wallis, Cara. (2011). New media practices in China: Youth patterns, processes, and politics. *International Journal of Communication, 5*, 406–426.

Wines, Michael. (2009, March 11). A dirty pun tweaks China's online censors. *New York Times*. Retrieved September 11, 2013, from http://www.nytimes.com/2009/03/12/world/asia/12beast.html

Wu Jiao. (2007, January 22). E'gao: Popular art criticism or just plain evil? *China Daily*. Retrieved January 22, 2007, from http://www.chinadaily.com.cn/cndy/2007-01/22/content_788540.htm

Yang Guobin. (2009). *The power of the Internet in China: Citizen activism online*. New York: Columbia University Press.

Yu Haiqing. (2007). Blogging everyday life in Chinese Internet culture. *Asian Studies Review, 31*, 423–433.

Zhao Jinqiu. (2008). A snapshot of Internet regulation in contemporary China: Censorship, profitability and responsibility. *China Media Research*, 4(3), 37–42.

Text Messaging

Fā duǎnxìn 发短信

Summary: Text messaging (or SMS), or the sending and receiving of short text messages on a wireless handheld device, has experienced a remarkable development and has stayed a daily communication means in the Chinese people's everyday lives since its launch. It is widely used by diverse age groups, social classes, and economic statuses, in both private and public discourses.

Text messaging, referring to the short message service (SMS) available on most digital wireless phones, allows the sending and receiving of short text messages between wireless phones and other handheld devices. The first text messaging service was officially released by China Mobile in the second half of 2000, and text messages have been exchanged across wireless carriers since 1 May 2002.

Text messaging has experienced a remarkable development in China since its launch. It quickly took off as a business and cultural phenomenon and has grown steadily since. Between 2001 and 2012, the annual SMS traffic volume (i.e., messages sent) rose from 18.9 billion to 897.3 billion. (See table 1.) Text messaging is widely used by people from diverse age groups, social classes, and economic statuses. A Nielsen report shows that China had an 80 percent penetration rate of text messaging by the first quarter of 2009, ranking second highest among the fourteen countries surveyed, including the United States, Canada, United Kingdom, Mexico, Russia, Brazil, and South Africa (Stewart and Quick 2009).

Table 1. The Rapid Growth of SMS Traffic Volumes in China

Year	2001	2003	2005	2007	2009	2011	2012
Annual volume in billions	18.9	137	305	592	772.6	878.8	897.3

Sources: MIIT (2008, 2009, 2010); Jiang (2007).

A few factors contributed to the rapid development of text messaging in China. First, compared to personal computers (PCs), mobile phones are cheaper and more accessible to most Chinese consumers. A Morgan Stanley report released in 2004 shows that the penetration rate of mobile phones in China in 2002 was eight times larger than PCs, and more than three times the number of Internet users (Meeker, Choi, and Motoyama 2004). In 2012, nearly 75 percent of all Internet users in China were using their mobile devices to get online. Because of the availability of the technology and its high penetration rate, text messaging has been used for various work and personal activities, as well as on occasions when email would be used instead in other countries such as the United States. Second, as a new means of communication, text messaging supports quick and direct contact with the other party without requesting an immediate response. This asynchronous and implicit feature is particularly appealing to people in a high-context culture such as China. The anthropologist Edward Hall (1989) describes the cultures across the globe with a high-low-context continuum. He suggests a big part of the meaning of a message exchanged in a high-context culture usually comes from its surrounding multilayered contexts (e.g., historical context, social norms, roles, situational and relational contexts), and the rest from the verbal message itself. Many indirect messages, such as love notes, apologies, reminders to supervisors, and check-ins with friends, can be sent via text messaging. Third, the service plans of mobile phones in China encourage the use of text messaging. Unlike the United States, where text messages are charged separately from voice services, a text package is often part of a standard monthly plan in China. Fourth, mobile text messaging has been regarded as a driving force of Internet economy in China. A few of the major Chinese web portals that suffered financial deficits began to turn a profit after they provided text messaging services around 2001. This huge market success makes text messaging an eye-catching cultural phenomenon celebrated by the mass media, wireless carriers, phone manufacturers, and even the government. When text messaging was first introduced to the public, it was promoted as a new cultural practice that no one should miss: *SMS culture.*

Technology

A text message contains alphanumeric characters with a maximum length of 160 characters for Latin alphabets, and 70 characters for non-Latin alphabets such as Chinese. In the Chinese language, a phrase is the smallest unit of meaning, consisting of one or two characters. Due to this linguistic brevity, a 70-character Chinese text message can contain more meaning units than an English text message.

Text entry methods for Chinese text messaging are divided into two input modes: sound-based input (e.g., pinyin mode) and shape-based input (e.g., stroke mode). The sound-based input mode is built on pinyin, the standard notation for the Romanization of the Chinese simplified character set, which is based on the standard Mandarin pronunciation. In the pinyin mode, a user spells the character phonetically using pinyin. In the stroke mode, the technology divides Chinese characters into a few basic strokes, with each key representing one stroke. To type a phrase or word of two characters with predictive typing, it usually takes two or three taps to locate the first character with the pinyin mode, and then takes another one or two taps to choose the second one from a list of recommended characters that are predicted based on phrase relevancy. A stroke-based input method could locate the same character even faster.

Compared to English language systems, Chinese inputting has its own challenges, particularly for sound-based input methods (stroke-based methods are chosen less often because of the learning curve involved). Text entry using the sound-based method can be problematic for older generations because pinyin was not introduced until the 1970s by the Chinese government. Furthermore, there are many dialects in China that pronounce words very differently from Mandarin (the official spoken language of China that is based only on the northern dialect), making sound-based input harder for many people.

Patterns of Use

Text messaging is a daily means of communication for many Chinese people, and it is deeply embedded in their everyday lives. The content of Chinese text messages usually falls into one of these seven categories: greetings (including holiday greetings); chat and socializing; practical coordination; business communication; jokes (including political and sexual jokes); tricks, scams, and unsolicited advertisements; and government messages.

According to a comparative study conducted from 2003 to 2006 involving Chinese and American frequent texters, Chinese users text differently than their American counterparts (Sun 2012). The verbal data analysis of the 2,474 text messages collected from a study of nineteen American participants and twenty-two Chinese participants (813 messages from the Americans and 1,661 from the Chinese) shows that American messages were primarily sent to express feelings and to share current experiences (33.1 percent), while Chinese text messages were sent more often to exchange information (31.6 percent) and initiate actions such as instructing (16.5 percent) and coordinating (8.4 percent). On the American side, participants were interested in *expressing* their feelings, and their chats were usually short. A majority of messages can be regarded as small talk in which participants had quick exchanges about their current activities (e.g., "watching TV") or other minute life details. In contrast, Chinese participants liked to stay in contact with friends via text messaging and sent messages to *inform*. Long chat exchanges between friends were very common in the Chinese message logs, and participants usually had more in-depth conversations about various topics, such as borrowing money, buying a house, sending gifts to the boss, and exchanging job information—in short, every aspect of daily life. In China text messaging is accepted as a formal genre: a bride can even invite friends to her wedding banquet using text messaging.

Text messaging has also entered the public discourse in China: many government officials sent holiday greeting messages to citizens and voters after the mayor of Beijing sent all Beijingers a text message wishing them a happy New Year on the eve of the Spring Festival in 2006. It is also a common practice among journalists to conduct interviews via text messaging, and listeners send text messages instead of calling to join live discussions on radio programs. As described earlier, in China text messaging is often used more as email. One common perception of email versus text messaging among Chinese users is that email is a tool to send files and documents to another party. All other communication can be taken care of by using text messages. Indeed, SMS in Chinese is referred to as *duǎnxìn* 短信, which literally means "short letter." This translation clearly shows the link of SMS to more traditional styles of communication, such as letters and mail.

Culture of Text Messaging

Text messaging is gradually changing many aspects of Chinese communication and cultural practices. One peculiar text-messaging-related phenomenon is paying a New Year's "visit" with a text message. Holiday greetings during the Spring Festival have been an important ritual in China for centuries. With the development of telecommunication technologies, its form changed first from a physical visit to a person's house, to a phone call, and now to a text message. The volume of New Year's greeting messages exchanged during the period of the Spring Festival holiday makes records every year. For example, in 2010 the record reached 23 billion messages, up by 10 percent from 2009; it is estimated that each mobile phone user sent 30.8 greetings messages in that period (Xinhua Net 2010).

As a tool for interpersonal communication, text messaging also makes it easy to circulate jokes. A well-crafted text message is often forwarded and followed by many people. Because of this phenomenon, certain literary formats surrounding text messaging technology appeared in China, and professional SMS writers emerged. These writers are hired by big web portals and telecommunication companies and compose text messages for various occasions. During the high time of SMS (before mobile Internet and 3G service were widely adopted by Chinese users), there were websites devoted to literature generated through SMS (e.g., cell phone novels), national SMS writing competitions, and books collecting fun and smart text messages.

Control and Complaint

With the ability to reach a massive audience through chain letters or group messages, cell phones are mentioned by some communication researchers as "the fifth medium," following print, radio, television, and the Internet, which can spread desired and undesired ideas and information fast, particularly in a country where control over mass communication is usually tight. After the SARS (severe acute respiratory syndrome) crisis in 2003, when political text messages were circulated widely, the Chinese government established an effective infrastructure to monitor and censor text messages. Sensitive words and phrases, such as *June* or the names of China's highest officials, are often filtered out by the wireless carriers. For example, text messages with the name of Liu Xiaobo, the 2010 Nobel Peace Prize winner who is considered a dissident in China, were banned. Smart texters, however, often come up with some shorthand or alternative character to replace those sensitive words to get their message across.

One complaint about text messaging in China is that users get a lot of messages of tricks, scams, and unsolicited advertisements on a daily basis. For example, in the first half of 2010, Chinese messaging users received twelve scam messages a week, accounting for 27.6 percent of all messages received (12321 Anti-Spam Informant Center 2010).

Future Outlook

The development of Chinese mobile communication has entered the age of 4G and mobile Internet access. While text messaging has passed its prime, it continues to be a central means of communication in Chinese culture that influences the everyday lives of Chinese people. Nowadays text messages are usually exchanged through WeChat, a free mobile text and voice messaging communication service released by Tencent in 2011 and a major competitor of WhatsApp worldwide.

Huatong SUN
University of Washington Tacoma

See also Chinese Language and Computing; Email; Telecommunications Industry

Further Reading

12321 Anti-Spam Informant Center. (2010). 2010 survey results of SMS use (first half year) [in Chinese]. Retrieved October 10, 2010, from http://anti-spam.cn/pdf/sms1001.pdf

Hall, Edward. (1989). *Beyond culture.* New York: Anchor Books.

He Zhou. (2008). SMS in China: A major carrier of the nonofficial discourse universe. *The Information Society, 24,* 182–190.

Jiang, Haishen. (2007). Shou ji duan xin / cai xin [Mobile messaging / multimedia messaging]. In Gong Chengbo (Ed.), *Xin meiti gailun* [Intro to new media] (pp. 248–258). Beijing: China Radio & Television Publishing House.

Mallick, Martyn. (2003). *Mobile and wireless design essentials.* New York: John Wiley & Sons.

Meeker, Mary; Choi, Lina; and Motoyama, Yoshiko. 2004. *Chinese Internet Report.* New York: Morgan Stanley.

Ministry of Industry and Information Technology of the People's Republic of China (MIIT). (2008). 2008 年12 月通信业主要指标完成情况 2008 nian 12 ye tongxinye zhuyao zhibiao wancheng qingkuang [Monthly statistical report on the telecommunications industry of December 2007]. Retrieved August 18, 2009, from http://www.miit.gov.cn/n11293472/n11293832/n11294132/n11302706/11766761.html

Ministry of Industry and Information Technology of the People's Republic of China (MIIT). (2009). *Report of major benchmarks accomplished by the telecommunications industry in December 2008* [in Chinese]. Retrieved Mai 16, 2014, from http://www.miit.gov.cn/n11293472/n11293832/n11294132/n12858447/12864623.html

Ministry of Industry and Information Technology of the People's Republic of China (MIIT). (2010). *2009 annual statistical report of the telecommunications industry* [in Chinese]. Retrieved June 29, 2010, from http://www.miit.gov.cn/n11293472/n11293832/n11294132/n12858447/13011909.html

SINA. (2006, January28). Beijing shiwei shizhengfu tongguo duanxin xiong shimin bainian [Beijing city government sent text message greetings to citizen]. Retrieved April 15, 2006, from http://news.sina.com.cn/c/2006-01-28/02088098887s.shtml

Stewart, Jon, & Quick, Chris. (2009, October 6). Global mobile: Strategies for growth. Retrieved June 30, 2010, from http://blog.nielsen.com/nielsenwire/online_mobile/global-mobile-strategies-for-growth/

Sun Huatong. (2012). Cross-cultural technology design: Creating culture-sensitive technology for local users. New York: Oxford University Press.

Xinhua News. (2002). 我国手机短信发展迅猛已有 5500 万人在使用Woguo shouji duanxin fazhan xunmeng yi you 5500 wan ren zai shiyong [55 million users have been using SMS]. Retrieved March 20, 2003, from http://it.sohu.com/03/10/article203961003.shtml

Xinhua Net. (2010). 虎年春节期间中国各类短信发送量达 230 亿条 Hu nian chunjie qijian Zhongguo gelei duanxin fasongliang da 230 yi tiao [The volume of SMS reached 23 billion in the Spring Festival holiday of the Tiger Year]. Retrieved October 10, 2010, from http://news.xinhuanet.com/internet/2010-02/22/content_13027128.htm

Virtual Reality

Xūnǐ xiànshí 虚拟现实

Summary: The emergence of virtual reality (VR) in China since the 1990s opened up a new realm for the development of human-computer interaction, digital entertainment, and social networking. Facilitated by the widespread usage of the Internet, VR technologies have been aiding the overall development of fundamental infrastructure as well.

Since the 1990s, virtual reality (VR) (*xūnǐ xiànshí* 虚拟现实), defined as a computer-generated artificial environment that is experienced by humans through one or multiple sensory stimuli, has drawn much attention in China. In the early days, most of the research on VR was focused on large-scale simulations in areas such as manufacturing and military. With the development of the Internet industry in China, many Chinese researchers turned their interest to online virtual reality, as well as related areas such as social networking, massively multiplayer online role-playing games (MMORPG), online marketing, advertising, and so on. In addition, efforts have been made recently to preserve material and nonmaterial cultural heritage in China using VR technology.

Research and "Traditional" Uses of VR

With the rapid development of the economy in recent years, the Chinese government has put significant effort in supporting the development and application of virtual reality in both academic and industrial realms. In 1995, the Community of the National Science Foundation of China and the National Key Programs of Science and Technology listed virtual reality as one of their main research topics. Since that designation, many universities have established research institutes on computer graphics and virtual reality.

In the realm of manufacturing and industry, the main focus of VR research has been on the concept of "low cost, high efficiency," such as using VR to maximize functionality and robustness of products and minimize the usage of physical resources. Since the 1990s, numerous Chinese researchers have focused on the development of various traditional applications of virtual reality, such as computer graphics, real-time rendering and simulation, and distributed virtual environments.

At Tsinghua University, the Virtual Reality & Human Interface Technology Lab has conducted research using virtual reality technology on the analysis of human machine systems, or systems that integrate the functions of a human operator (or a group of operators) and a machine, in order to enhance both the credibility and efficiency of the analysis. They have also created new multi-input and feedback technologies that allow designers to "touch" and visualize the designed object in a virtual environment (Zhang, Lin, Ma, and Chen 2004).

In contrast, the lab at Beijing University of Aeronautics and Astronautics has focused on the use of VR for military, medical, and cultural purposes such as museum exhibitions. Research areas include modeling methods in VR, enhancing the integration and interaction between virtual and real environments, distributed VR technology, and VR platform tools and systems. They created the simulation platform and presentation environment for the 2008 Olympic Games ceremonies in Beijing, which allowed people to retrieve and review the Olympic competitions and performances via the Internet. It provided a new way to document memorable moments in digital format, and it also allowed people to interact with it using virtual reality.

The Virtual Reality Technology Lab of the Institute of Computing Technology at the Chinese Academy of Sciences is focusing on "virtual human synthesis" and "virtual environment interaction." "Virtual human synthesis" aims to present human geometric properties and behaviors in computer-generated space (i.e., a virtual environment). They focus on 3-D virtual human modeling, including movement access and understanding, motion generation and control technology, and ways to develop these techniques into digital simulations for sports training, crowd-movement analysis, intelligent human-computer interactions, games, entertainment, and other fields. "Virtual environment interaction" researches digital techniques such as virtual environment modeling, rendering, and interaction. This direction focuses on the fast and efficient modeling and rendering of digital environments, multimedia convergence, augmented reality, and other key technologies, together with their applications in public safety and event simulations, media production, and games animation.

At Zhejiang University, the Lab of Computer Aided Design & Computer Graphics (CAD&CG) aims to improve the accuracy and integrity of the representation and reproduction of virtual environments, which they believe limits the authenticity of the generated digital content to a large degree. Their research focuses on real-time rendering of large-scale virtual environments, natural human-computer interactions and interfaces, and consistency of mixed environments in augmented reality. All these areas of research can be applied to cultural entertainment, building a smart city, military purposes, and manufacturing as well.

New Directions for VR

Besides these fundamental uses of virtual reality, personal entertainment also constitutes a significant part of the virtual reality research in China. With the rapid development of the Chinese economy, people in China are becoming more and more interested in social communication and entertainment, for example, connecting to each other through the Internet and mobile phones, playing video games, or watching 3-D movies. This attracted researchers' interest in the application of virtual reality for social networking and immersive visual entertainment. At the same time, as the quality of people's everyday life is improving, they are also becoming more interested in their traditional cultural heritage. As a result, researchers have begun to develop ways to use virtual reality technology to make cultural and national traditions available to a broader audience and simultaneously preserve these cultural heritages.

Social Networks and Virtual Reality

Virtual reality for enhancing social networks is an important aspect of current research. The blurring of the boundaries between our virtual and reality-based activities means that we will increasingly need to access and interact with digital information while participating in the real world.

New technologies, such as 3-D virtual world, combine virtual reality with social networking. They have evolved the Internet into a platform with new digital media technologies for the development of business and educational purposes. In conjunction with web 3-D technology, social networking has already begun to foster an intuitive and immersive system that, compared to the traditional static and text-oriented web, uses visual communication and delivers real-time natural and interactive experiences to enhance user motivation and engagement. *Second Life* is a good example.

Since the success of *Second Life* in Western countries starting from 2006, Chinese companies have also developed similar 3-D virtual world products, such as *Hipihi, NovoKing, UWorld,* and *MWorld.* Great effort has been put into the development and marketing, including collaborations with well-known companies such as Intel, IBM, and HP. These efforts, however, have been slow to pay off. Even the most popular virtual world, *Hipihi,* only had a total of 48,000 registered users in 2008 (China Digital Times 2008), which is very small considering the massive amount of Chinese "netizens" and the growing Internet penetration rate in China. Researchers have been studying the user acceptance problem of 3-D virtual world in a Chinese environment and compared *Second Life* with local Chinese 3-D virtual worlds. They pointed out that the strategies used for 3-D virtual worlds in Western countries don't translate well in the Chinese context, where they are subjected to different challenges such as government policy, law, and cultural barriers (Zhang, Vogel, Chen, and Guo 2009).

As an alternative, some companies are beginning to shift their focus to virtual worlds for younger generations. Children use social networking sites to establish their identity and to find support and comfort as they go through the cognitive, physical, and emotional transitions of early adolescence (Clarke 2009). For example, Mole Manor, a virtual community for six- to fourteen-year-olds founded in 2007, had fifty million registered users by 2010, almost a quarter of the total number of children in China. Similar child-centric social networking sites include Aobi Island, Pica Town, and others. Combining social networks with 3-D virtual worlds, such sites usually have cute user interfaces and provide a range of online role-playing games that appeal to young children. Since these sites are designed for kids, safety naturally becomes an important concern. Most social networking sites for children provide specially designed web browsers as well as parental control systems.

Educational Purposes

Apart from being used as a tool for communication and entertainment, scholars are also exploring the possibility of using social networks as an education aid (Liccardi et al. 2007). Moreover, online virtual learning is gaining popularity in academic institutions as an alternative means for experimental and distance education. Researchers also tried to utilize 3-D virtual worlds for learning. For example, IBM China Business Innovation Center constructed several 3-D tutorial scenarios in *Second Life* based on the business models for operating an online garment store in a 3-D virtual world (Dong, Ma, and Wang 2010).

Cultural Heritage

VR has also been used to preserve and revive China's cultural heritage. Chinese culture includes art, music, dance, literature, and poetry, and many of these traditions can be reconstructed or enhanced with virtual reality. Instead of visiting the museum in person, the digitalization process can be helpful for drawing a wider audience to appreciate and cherish the pieces handed down from generation to generation. There are numerous works like this, from academic research to industry applications, covering a wide variety of both tangible and intangible cultural traditions. One example was the use of an animated scroll of the famous Song dynasty (960–1279) painting *Riverside Scene at Qingming Festival* 清明上河图 featured in the China Pavilion at the Shanghai Expo in 2010.

Besides making ancient masterpieces more accessible to people, researchers have also been trying to apply VR technology to restore lost or extinct cultural items. There are quite a few researchers working on digitization and reproduction of large scale cultural heritage sites such as the Grand Canal, completed during the Sui dynasty (581–618 CE), that connected Beijing with Hangzhou; the Old Summer Palace in Beijing; and mountain-based UNESCO World Heritage Sites, such as Huangshan and Taishan mountains (Zhang and Fang 2009). Relevant research questions range from 3-D data acquisition to the navigation of the 3-D virtual environment.

Digital Puppets

Researchers are working not only on preserving tangible but also intangible cultural heritage. Cultural practices that have been captured using VR include the folk art of origami, shadow play, and Chinese calligraphy. Researchers have developed techniques to simulate traditional Chinese shadow play, turning traditional shows into electronic forms to make them more accessible and preserve the art for future generations (Zhu et al. 2003). Similarly, the online application ShadowStory allows children to freely create digital puppets and perform stories, using virtual tools that are similar to the tools for creating physical puppets. Public performances of stories can be held on a projected screen, and the puppets are controlled by handheld orientation sensors, emulating the atmosphere of traditional shadow puppetry plays (Fei et al. 2011).

Confucius Computer

The Keio-NUS CUTE Center at the National University of Singapore has also made significant efforts to introduce Chinese culture into human-computer interaction for the purpose of entertainment, education, and preserving Chinese cultural heritage. One such project is the Confucius computer. Confucianism is an ethical and philosophical system that has had a great impact, especially in East Asian countries, for more than 2,500 years. Confucian philosophy, however, is extremely complex and is not easily accessible and understandable to all people, especially given the cultural, generational, and language barrier. Traditional media, such as reading a textbook, is very passive and provides only a linear understanding of these teachings, restricting the learning process. But modern digital technologies allow the integration of Confucian teachings, Eastern philosophy, and culture with the media of the new digital generation, including social networks, chat, and interactive games.

The core of the Confucius computer is a virtual Confucian thought engine (a sort of "virtual Confucius") that models Confucius's (551–479 BCE) knowledge from the *Analects*—the central text of Confucianism consisting of sayings and ideas attributed to Confucius—and his teaching method of *yīn cái shī jiào* 因材施教(teaching the student according to his/her aptitude). Based on the question asked by the user, the virtual Confucius identifies the *yu* (subdomain of knowledge) in the *Analects*, then further queries the user to determine his *hui* (aptitude), and then replies to the user. In addition, the system incorporates music and painting to help users better understand the full range and depth of Confucian ethics and moral values.

Future Outlook

In the past decades, research on virtual reality in China has made a significant shift from pure industrial and military simulation to more user-oriented applications, such as education aids, cultural heritage preservation, social networking, and gaming. Virtual reality has become more accessible to the public, and with the increasing level of public awareness about the importance of social communication and cultural heritage in China, these two trends are expected to continue and evolve in the near future. Virtual reality is likely to integrate even more with other technologies to enrich the user experience, such as computing, multimedia, and the Internet.

Adrian David CHEOK
Keio-NUS CUTE Center, National University of Singapore

Jun WEI
Keio Graduate School of Media Design

See also Communities Online; Distance Education; Game Industry Online

Further Reading

Barboza, David. (2007). Internet boom is built on virtual fun. Retrieved August 16, 2007, from http://www.chinadaily.com.cn/china/2007-02/05/content8 01304.htm

Chen Liyan, Wang Beizhan, & Chen Bing. (2009). Research on digital museum for the intangible cultural heritage. *International Symposium on IT in Medicine and Education, 1,* 734 –737.

China Digital Times. (2008). Not much life in China's virtual worlds. Retrieved May 30, 2014, from http://chinadigitaltimes.net/2008/05/hipihi-empty/.

China Internet Network Information Center (CNNIC). (2008). The 25th survey report on the Internet development in China [in Chinese]. Retrieved August 16, 2013, from http://www.cnnic.cn/hlwfzyj/hlwxzbg/hlwtjbg/201206/P020120612484949500779.pdf

Clarke, Barbie. (2009). Friends forever: How young adolescents use social-networking sites. *IEEE Intelligent Systems, 24*(6), 22–26.

Dong Pingjun, Ma Biao, & Wang Fengchun. (2010, May 13–14). Development and evaluation of an experiential learning service in 3D virtual world. In *International Conference on Service Sciences* (pp. 374–378). doi: 10.1109/ICSS.2010.37

Fei Lu, et al. (2011). ShadowStory: Creative and collaborative digital storytelling inspired by cultural heritage. Proceedings of the 2011 Annual Conference on Human Factors in Computing Systems (CHI '11). New York: ACM. Retrieved April 22, 2014, from http://caoxiang.net/papers/chi2011_shadowstory.pdf

Huang Yetao, Jiang Zhiguo, Wang Yongtian, & Liu Yue. (2011). Interactive design of augmented reality device in Yuanming yuan for public use. In *Proceedings of the 10th International Conference on Virtual Reality Continuum and Its Applications in Industry* (VRCAI '11). New York: ACM.

Jin Li; Psarrou, Alexandra; Cao Sanxing; & Chen Yajing. (2009, September 20–22). Trends on interactive platforms for social media through web2.0. In *International Conference on Management and Service Science,* (pp. 1–2).

Liccardi, I, et al. (2007). The role of social networks in students' learning experiences. In *ITiCSE-WGR '07: Working group reports on ITiCSE on Innovation and technology in computer science education* (pp. 224–237). New York: ACM. doi: 10.1145/1345443.1345442

Ruan Jianhai & Deng Xiaozhao. (2009). On the *Second Life*-based education in virtual world. *International Symposium on IT in Medicine and Education* (vol. 1, pp. 1017–1020).

Zhang Wei, Lin Heng, Ma Liang & Chen Delin. (2004). Human-computer interaction in free-form object design and simultaneous manufacturing. *SPIE, 5444,* 265–272. doi: 10.1117/12.561171.

Zhang, X., & Fang, X. (2009). On the digital development of mountain-based world cultural heritage sites in China. In *International Symposium on Information Science and Engineering* (pp. 235–238). doi: /10.1109/ISISE.2009.122

Zhang Xi; Vogel, Doug; Chen Zhenjia; & Guo Chuanjie. (2009). Exploring 3D virtual world strategies in the Chinese environment: An institutional-based view. In *Hawaii International Conference on System Sciences* (pp. 1–10). doi: 10.1109/HICSS.2009.724

Zhu Yibo; Li Chenjia; Shen, I. Fan; Ma Kwan-Liu; & Stompel, Aleksander. (2003). A new form of traditional art: Visual simulation of Chinese shadow play. In *ACM SIGGRAPH 2003 Sketches & Applications* (SIGGRAPH '03). New York: ACM.

Part 4
Society and Social Welfare

Children Online

Értóng jí wǎngluò 儿童及网络

Summary: Children in China use the Internet mainly for entertainment, communication, education, and escape. A large majority use domestic online social sites such as Sina Weibo that offer a large Chinese-speaking community (and because Western sites such as Twitter are heavily censored). The role of the web in children's emotional development is currently unclear.

Chinese children are enthusiastic about the web. In many ways, relationships between Chinese children and the web are similar to this relationships in other parts of the world, probably because the fundamental needs of children (e.g., making friends, identity exploration) and some key qualities of the web (e.g., entertainment, anonymity) are similar regardless of the user's geographic location. Chinese children are unique in their web usage, however, because both the children and the web in China are influenced by Chinese traditions, values, and sea changes in a developing socioeconomic landscape.

A Portrait of Today's Chinese Children

According to the Constitution of Law and Administrative Regulations for Public Security of the People's Republic of China, "children" are defined as citizens under fourteen years who are exempt from legal responsibilities if they violate administrative regulations (Central Government of the People's Republic of China 2004, 2005). In Chinese elementary and junior high schools, children younger than fourteen years old are typically required to participate in the Chinese Young Pioneers, an organization similar to the Boy Scouts and the Girl Scouts in the United States.

Chinese children born after 1996 possess a number of interesting characteristics. First, they are the first "one-child only" generation as a result of the implementation of the One-Child Policy in 1978, a policy designed to control China's burgeoning population, although there are exceptions to the one-child only rule, for instance for non-Han minorities (National Population and Family Planning Commission 2001). Being an only child in a Chinese family means that that child is the recipient of a great deal of attention from six adults: father, mother, and four grandparents. Children without siblings are the recipients of more parental investment in their educational and entertainment needs, including web consumption, than children with siblings in China and "typical" children elsewhere around the world.

Second, Chinese children today grow up with the web. The web was introduced into China in 1996. ChinaNet (the Chinese Public Computing Network) began operating in January 1996. Since that year, China has become the country with the largest Internet population—more than half a billion users by the end of 2012 (CNNIC 2013). To Chinese children born after 1996, the web is a common everyday tool as indispensable to everyday life as water and air.

Third, Chinese children born after 1996 belong to a generation interested in exploring the world outside of China and expressing themselves more so than were previous generations (MOE 2010). Since China joined the World Trade Organization in 2001, the increasing globalization of the economic and social world has allowed Chinese children to explore life beyond China, including popular symbols of the Western world: McDonald's, Hollywood movies, the NBA, Nike, Google, and Twitter. Although Twitter is currently banned in China, Chinese children have learned to visit Twitter by bypassing the official Chinese firewall (the "Great Firewall of China") and web restrictions. Clearly the web has become an important tool for Chinese children to appreciate and participate in a global society (MOE 2010).

The web also amplifies and supports Chinese children's intrinsic interest in expressing their social identity through the use of Sina Weibo, blogs, photos, videos, and games. The web's tolerance for different voices is especially meaningful to children who otherwise have little opportunity to express their honest thoughts and personal identities at home, in school, or in the public domain.

The fourth reason that Chinese children born after 1996 are a notable study group is that one thread of continuity for Chinese children across generations is the extremely high academic pressure placed on them. Although today's Chinese children have almost limitless entertainment, freedom, and information via the web, and are "entitled" to an unprecedented amount of parental care and investment (Zhao 2009), it is still essential that they excel academically. Academic success in China means success on high-stakes tests, many of which require years of preparation. Education in China is much more test score–driven than education in other countries. Children who survive the first twelve years of intensive education then take a college entrance examination that determines their future career and personal success.

Chinese Children on the Web

The *Blue Book of Internet Usage among Chinese Children and Adolescents*, issued in 2010 by the Ministry of Education, the Chinese Social Science Academy, and several universities, provides an in-depth review of current issues and research on web use, including such topics as cyber-bullying, Internet addiction, and critical thinking skills in consuming and creating web content, among others. The following is a summary of some of that research, as well as other existing research.

Population

A large percentage of web users in China are children or adolescents. According to a 2009 survey by the China Internet Network Information Center (CNNIC 2010a), children and adolescents comprised about one half of the Internet population at that time: 195 million of the 384 million total Internet population (a population that has since grown by approximately 140 million, to 520 million), a larger percentage than any other age group (CNNIC 2010b). Approximately 70 million secondary school students (junior high and senior high school students) and 13 million elementary school students were regular web users at the time of the survey, spending an average of 16.5 hours a week on the web (CNNIC 2010b).

Locations for Web Use

Home, schools, and Internet cafés are the main locations where Chinese children use the web. As of 2010, home was the primary place for children to surf the web: roughly three-quarters of Chinese children and adolescents used the web at home (CNNIC 2010b). Surveyed children preferred home over schools and Internet cafés for web use.

Chinese children are eager to obtain help and guidance on how to use the web (MOE 2010). This finding contradicts the common perception among parents and the general public that Chinese children prefer Internet cafés and are sometimes "addicted" to them (MOE 2010). As the *Blue Book* pointed out, many children chose Internet cafés not because they preferred them, but because they had no choice when their parents could not afford home Internet access, or if the children thought their parents overcontrolled or restricted their web activities.

Interestingly, the popularity of Internet cafés among children is decreasing in China, especially in urban areas, dropping below 50 percent for the first time in 2009. Nevertheless, Internet cafés remain a primary location for using the web among rural children (CNNIC 2010b). Schools are also becoming more popular, thanks to the investment of the Chinese government and private sectors in school network infrastructure and child-oriented web content (MOE 2000). In 2010, data showed that 36 percent of elementary school students and 46 percent of secondary school students used the web in school at that time (CNNIC 2010b).

Web Activities

Children's activities related to the web in China are not altogether different from those of children elsewhere. But given the unique circumstances surrounding Chinese children discussed earlier, there are some areas in which we could expect to see more web-using activity from Chinese children: in entertainment, communication, education, and as escape.

Entertainment

The search for entertainment is the most frequent use of the web by Chinese children (MOE 2010). According to a CNNIC survey (2010b), the degree that Chinese children used the web for entertainment, including music, videos, games, and reading novels, was much higher than that of the Chinese population as a whole.

Online games had a particularly high penetration rate among elementary school

Chinese students—82.3 percent at the time of the survey, higher than any other web activities for this age group. Online games were equally popular among secondary school students, 81 percent of whom played online games (CNNIC 2010b). Children are avid players of *World of Warcraft* and other popular massive multiplayer online role play games (MMORPGs). Chinese children are also enthusiastic about social games that are driven by turn-taking actions between two or more players (O'Neill 2008).

Online music and videos are the second most popular web activities among Chinese children: 90 percent of secondary school children and 61 percent of elementary school children listened to, created, or downloaded music from the web at the time of the survey (CNNIC 2010b). Two-thirds (67 percent) of secondary school children and 51 percent of elementary school children created, downloaded, or watched videos online (CNNIC 2010b). Online videos and music can be important ways for children to express themselves creatively. High-quality online videos and music provide a powerful stimulation of children's creativity. But there is an ongoing debate in China, as there is in many places, about what constitutes high-quality videos and music, and what kind of guidance is needed to translate online video and game consumption into creativity.

Communication

Chinese children use the web extensively to cement bonds with friends and to make new friends. Given that this is the one-child generation, the web plays an important role in Chinese children's social life. It is often a way for them to deal with the loneliness of being an only child. Chinese children use online social communication tools extensively, such as instant messaging (IM), blogs, social networking sites (SNS), email, and discussion forums (CNNIC 2010b).

In contrast to Chinese children's preference for daily consumption of Western culture, they actually use domestic social media brands much more frequently than foreign social media brands (Nielsen Company 2009). Chinese adolescents use *weibo*, which means "microblog," rather than Twitter. As of 2009, approximately nine-tenths of Chinese teenagers used QQ, Kaixin001, or Xiaonei as their major social networking sites rather than Facebook or MySpace. (As with all things related to the Internet, especially when it relates to teenagers, it is somewhat of a lost cause to try to keep up with the latest trends.)

Chinese Internet censorship is one reason why Chinese children seldom visit Western cultures' social networking sites such as Facebook, Twitter, or Flickr, sites that are heavily censored in China. Chinese children cannot log on to Facebook or Twitter without first having to bypass Chinese Internet censorship rules and firewalls. A second reason why Chinese children do not frequent Western social networking sites is that domestic sites offer a large community with whom Chinese children can communicate in their native language and in the context of shared cultural values.

Web-based social communication among Chinese children has prompted parental behavior not often seen in Western cultures. In particular, parents whose children use social networking sites use them as well, in an effort to stay in touch with their children. In elementary schools in China, for example, it is common for parents to establish online groups of school parents to swap ideas about child rearing or improving their children's academic performance. Parents are often invited to sign in to "QQ" groups (online groups similar to Facebook groups). Parents engage in mobile-phone short-messaging groups that encourage communication between school administrators, teachers, and parents. Schools are now able to deliver school alerts, announcements, parent-teacher conference notifications, and even student assignments directly to parents.

Education

The pursuit of education is another important reason why Chinese children use the web. In schools, Chinese children, especially children in poverty-stricken rural and mountain areas, have benefited from a distant learning project, the Xiao Xiao Tong project, launched by the Chinese government in 2000 (MOE 2000). The project has been successful in its objective to improve access to educational resources, thereby improving the quality of education throughout the nation by building a network infrastructure to deliver educational resources (MOE 2000). Educational institutions in China have begun to use applications that leverage the convergence between Internet technologies to promote interactive forms of learning. Project MILLEE (Mobile and Immersive Learning for Literacy in Emerging Economies), for example, is a partnership between the Chinese Academy of Sciences, the University of California at Berkeley, and Carnegie Mellon University, where games that run on cell phones and other mobile devices are used to promote basic literacy skills among children in rural China (Carmody 2010).

During their after-school free time, Chinese children use the web as a resource for preparing for exams, learning a foreign language such as English, and obtaining news, especially national news, which is far more available than news from other nations. There remains a concern that web content available to Chinese children is inadequate in terms of meeting their needs for information about the global society (MOE 2010).

Escape

The web has been an important place for Chinese children to escape, whether that be from academic pressure, loneliness, boredom, conflicts in everyday life, or for other reasons. Research has shown that escaping through social networking has the potential to produce either positive or negative outcomes, depending on a variety of factors. On the one hand, the web may serve as a coping strategy to help children deal with academic pressure, disturbing family environments, boredom, isolation, discrimination, and depression (Cabiria 2008; Hwang, Cheong, and Feeley 2009). On the other hand, using the web to escape may lead to dysfunctional and even physically harmful social relationships as well as an unhealthy lifestyle that comes with the inactivity of screen time.

Concerns and Directions for Future Research

Although the web is still a relatively new phenomenon in the lives of Chinese children, it has drawn a considerable amount of attention from scholars, parents, and policy makers. Most concerns are infrequently discussed in the literature but are nevertheless important to the role of the web in Chinese children's cognitive, psychological, and emotional development.

The first of these concerns is that there is a mounting need for empirical research on the influence of web use on Chinese children's cognitive development, as evidenced in such outcomes as reading skills and habits, literacy development, and creativity, to name a few. Existing research indicates that web use has a strong influence on students' reading habits and literacy development, attributable to the use of hyperlinks, multimedia, and multiple ways of organizing web content (National Center for Education Statistics 2005). More research on the influence of web use on cognitive outcomes is essential to developing educational practices that incorporate children's natural affinity for the web.

A related issue is the need to redefine what we mean by such amorphous constructs as "talent" and "creativity" among Chinese children. The current school assessment system in China is not designed to acknowledge the possibility of multiple intelligences or to distinguish intelligences from talents or creativity. Since the web provides multiple channels for expression (e.g., visual, auditory, textual, behavioral, or some combination), it allows for the possibility that different intelligences, talents, and levels of creativity will be able to "shine," which encourages a broader assessment of children's cognitive abilities (Zhao 2009). This will then encourage educators and policy makers in China to rethink curriculum decisions so as to foster the development of cognitive abilities needed in the twenty-first century.

A second concern is one that was raised early in the Internet's history: the unknown social effects of Internet use, particularly use of online social media. Sherry Turkle and other media scholars have raised concerns about the implications for social development of never being alone: solitude is a critically important and time-honored opportunity for an individual to gain maturity and to confront one's inner voice and the outer world independently (Deresiewicz 2009; Turkle 2011). In the wired society of today's Chinese children, there is the sense of constantly being "on stage." Web profiles and blogs require continual updating. Social networking websites exert an almost constant demand to attend to the virtual social world. In addition to the web are cell phones and other handheld devices that put the user constantly "on call." It appears that the web and other information technologies have made solitude a thing of the past, at least in any traditional sense. Chinese children, like other children unschooled in ways of coping with the technology, may be socially disadvantaged by its use and overuse. Research needs to address this possibility.

Third, it is unclear whether web use by Chinese and other children is helpful or harmful to their emotional development. Take, for example, the development of empathy, an area sorely lacking in empirical research. As Turkle (2011) noted, web use often gives children an illusion of companionship without the demands of a friendship. Children have the luxury of being hyper-connected via text messages, Facebook profiles, and endless tweets on Twitter (and their Chinese equivalents). These activities have more to do with "becoming known," however, than in knowing others. A 2010 meta-analysis of studies, whose combined sample size was 14,000 undergraduates over a thirty-year span, indicated that college students in 2010 showed 40 percent less empathy than college students of the 1980s and 1990s (O'Brien, Hsing, and Konrath 2010). Although this decline in empathy cannot be attributed unequivocally or entirely to technology use, it suggests a potential role for technology in children's emotional development that future research should explore.

Wei QIU
Webster University

Alexander GAMES
Microsoft

Yong ZHAO
University of Oregon

Linda A. JACKSON
Michigan State University

See also Digital Divides; Distance Education; Game Industry Online; Internet Cafés

Further Reading

Cabiria, Jonathan. (2008). Virtual world and real world permeability: Transference of positive benefits for marginalized gay and lesbian populations. *Journal of Virtual Worlds Research, 1*(1), 1–13.

Carmody, Tim. (2010, October 19). In rural China, students use phones to learn to read. Retrieved July 25, 2013, from http://www.wired.com/gadgetlab/2010/10/in-rural-china-students-use-phones-to-learn-to-read/

Central Government of the People's Republic of China. (2004). Constitution Law of China [in Chinese]. Retrieved October 23, 2010, from http://www.gov.cn/gongbao/content/2004/content_62714.htm

Central Government of the People's Republic of China. (2005). Administrative penalties for public ecurity [in Chinese]. Retrieved November 1, 2010, from http://www.gov.cn/flfg/2005-08/29/content_27130.htm

China Internet Network Information Center (CNNIC). (2007). Milestones of Internet development in China (1987–2007) [in Chinese]. Retrieved October 23, 2010, from http://www.cnnic.net.cn/html/Dir/2003/10/22/1001.htm

China Internet Network Information Center (CNNIC). (2010a). 2009 statistical survey report on Internet development in China. Retrieved May 14, 2010, from http://www.cnnic.cn/uploadfiles/pdf/2010/3/15/142705.pdf

China Internet Network Information Center (CNNIC). (2010b). Research report on the 2009 online behavior of Chinese adolescents and youth [In Chinese]. Retrieved May 14, 2010, from http://research.cnnic.cn/img/h000/h11/attach201004261314150.doc

China Internet Network Information Center (CNNIC). (2013). 30th statistical report on Internet development in China. Retrieved July 15, 2013, from http://www.google.com/url?sa=t&rct=j&q=&esrc=s&source=web&cd=1&ved=0CC0QFjAA&url=http%3A%2F%2Fwww1.cnnic.cn%2FIDR%2FReport-Downloads%2F201302%2FP020130221391269963814.pdf&ei=MiPkUYy-aBYb_ygHmi4HYBg&usg=AFQjCNFXATtsM7VEg-BOJzYn9eXaC2Xwfg&sig2=0BvxwHBt3J-QNSJXinO0kA&bvm=bv.48705608,d.aWc&cad=rja

Deresiewicz, William. (2009). The end of solitude. *The Chronicle of Higher Education*. Retrieved July 25, 2013, from http://chronicle.com/article/The-End-of-Solitude/3708

Hwang, J. M.; Cheong, P. H.; & Feeley, T. H. (2009). Being young and feeling blue in Taiwan: Examining adolescent depressive mood and online and offline activities. *New Media Society, 11*(7), 1101–1121.

Jackson, Linda A., et al. (2008). Cultural differences in morality in the real and virtual worlds: A comparison of Chinese and US youth. *Cyberpsychology and Behavior, 11*(3), 79–286.

Lukoff, Kai. (2009). Top 10 social games in China.*The Next Web*. Retrieved April 17, 2010, from http://thenextweb.com/asia/2009/12/15/top-10-social-games-china/

Ministry of Education (MOE). (2000). Notification about implementing the "wired schools (*xiaoxiaotong*)" project in secondary and elementary schools [in Chinese]. Retrieved October 23, 2010, from http://www.edu.cn/20030210/3077091.shtml

Ministry of Education (MOE). (2010). *Blue book of Internet usage among Chinese children and adolescents (2009–2010)*. Beijing: Chinese Social Science Academy.

National Center for Education Statistics. (2005). *The condition of education (NCES 2005–094)*. Washington, DC: Government Printing Office.

National Population and Family Planning Commission of the People's Republic of China. (2001). The law of population planning of the People's Republic of China [in Chinese]. Retrieved October 23, 2010, from http://www.chinapop.gov.cn/zcfg/flfg/200403/t20040326_87200.html

Nielsen Company. (2009). Global faces and networked places: A Nielsen report on social networking's new global footprint. Retrieved November 1, 2010, from http://blog.nielsen.com/nielsenwire/wp-content/uploads/2009/03/nielsen_globalfaces_mar09.pdf

O'Brien, Edward; Hsing, Courtney; & Konrath, Sara. (2010). Changes in dispositional empathy over time in American college students. Paper presented at the Association for Psychological Science Annual Convention. Retrieved July 25, 2013, from http://sitemaker.umich.edu/skonrath/files/empathy_decline.pdf

O'Neill, Nick. (2008). What exactly are social games? *Social Times*. Retrieved April 17, 2010, from http://www.socialtimes.com/2008/07/social-games/

Shen, Li-Bi. (2006). Computer technology and college students' reading habits. *Chia-Nan Annual Bulletin, 32*, 559–572. Retrieved November 1, 2010, from http://lib.chna.edu.tw/bulletin/files/v32_559_572.pdf

Turkle, Sherry. (2011). *Alone together: Why we expect more from technology and less from each other*. New York: Basic Books.

Zhao Yong. (2009). *Catching up or keeping the lead: American education in the age of globalization*. Alexandria, VA: ASCD.

Chinese Diaspora Online

Huáyì zàixiàn 华裔在线

Summary: The Chinese-language Internet has extended the borders of the People's Republic of China by connecting users with ethnic, language, and cultural ties in cyberspace. Although some obstacles to communication still exist, a wide variety of transregional and transnational exchanges takes place within this online community. Government websites, sites promoting e-commerce and economic integration across the Taiwan Strait, and (increasingly) exchanges among the various parts of civil society all provide platforms for communication.

The Chinese-language Internet provides connectivity for users within the People's Republic of China (PRC), Taiwan, Hong Kong and Macao, and the large Chinese diaspora in North America and Southeast Asia. These users have access to the most advanced Internet infrastructure in the world, a fact that should not be disregarded. Transnational and transregional conversations take place within this cyberspace despite several obstacles, such as censorship and differences in culture and languages. This raises the question of the extent to which Chinese cyberspace offers a space for intellectual exchange, for trade across the Taiwan Strait, and for Chinese-language users around the world—and which information and communication technologies (ICT) have facilitated these exchanges.

Both English- and Chinese-language research on cross-Strait and other transnational Chinese networks employing this cyberspace has been somewhat limited to date. Most of the existing Internet research focuses on the PRC and on Taiwan and Hong Kong, and case studies have dealt only occasionally with newly established ICT links between the Chinese diaspora and China. This is astonishing, given the fact that cross-Strait integration in economics, politics, society, and culture is developing fast (Schubert 2010).

If Chinese language use or cultural and ethnic bonds are employed as criteria, to some extent the Chinese cyberspace corresponds to what variously has been called Greater China, Cultural China, the Chinese World, and the Sinosphere (Harding 1995;

Tu 1994). In terms of geography, Greater China is composed of four distinct areas: (1) the PRC; (2) Hong Kong and Macao (which have a wide degree of political, social, and cultural autonomy as Special Administrative Regions of the PRC and part of the "one country, two systems" formula); (3) Taiwan (officially the Republic of China); and (4) overseas Chinese communities, or the Chinese diaspora (Damm 2010). This diaspora is spread all over the world, in locations that include Singapore—the only country in Southeast Asia with an ethnic Chinese majority (the population is approximately 77 percent ethnic Chinese); countries such as Malaysia—which have very distinctive groups of ethnic Chinese (24 percent in Malaysia) and a high degree of Chinese-language ability within these groups; other Southeast Asian countries, such as Thailand (14 percent ethnic Chinese), Indonesia, and the Philippines—which have strong minority groups of ethnic Chinese who are almost completely assimilated and have only limited knowledge of (written) Chinese; overseas communities outside Southeast Asia (Pan 1999); and newly emerged communities where the so-called new migrants (Chan 2005; Charney, Chee, and Yeoh 2003; Wang 2002) form a majority who are reported to show great interest in their countries or regions of origin, in particular the PRC (Barabantseva 2004; Sun 2005; Ip 2006). A common written language is essential for communication across borders (notwithstanding some of the new, more interactive applications that use video and audio material, and—to a lesser extent—spoken language). At first glance, it seems this should be Mandarin in its localized variants—such as *pǔtōnghuà* 普通话 (the "common language") in the PRC, Hong Kong, and Macau; and *huáyǔ* 华语 (the "language of the ethnic Chinese") in Singapore, Southeast Asian countries, and in Taiwan (where it is still known to some as *guóyǔ* 国语, the "national language"). In Taiwan and Hong Kong traditional Chinese characters are used, while the PRC and Singapore employ simplified Chinese characters.

Characteristics

Users in mainland China constitute 95 percent of Greater China cyberspace users; as of 2012 there were 564 million in the PRC (CNNIC 2013, 4). Taiwan (17.53 million) (TWNIC 2013) and Singapore (4.02 million) (Internet World Stats 2013) together comprise the second largest group of users. There were also 5.15 million users in Hong Kong and Macao (CNNIC 2010, 4). Until June 1999, the total number of users outside the PRC was higher than the number inside the PRC (there were 4 million in the PRC, 4.02 million in Taiwan, 1.44 million in Hong Kong and Macau, and 1.2 million in Singapore), and as of 2011 the percentage of the population that use the Internet in these areas still exceeds the percentage of users in the PRC: 72.56 percent in Taiwan, 67 percent in Hong Kong and Macao, and 77.8 percent in Singapore; considerably higher than the PRC's 34.3 percent (Internet World Stats 2011).

During the early phase of Internet development in the Chinese-speaking world, the various mechanisms for Chinese encoding led to massive compatibility problems, which hindered use across different user populations. For example, the state-sponsored GB23125 developed by the PRC did not support traditional characters, and Taiwan's de facto official Big5 standard (developed by five of the largest IT firms in Taiwan and Hong Kong) did not support simplified characters (Lunde 2006). Internet users in each territory therefore were unable to read content produced in the other without installing additional software. The underlying encoding systems have declined in importance, however, since the introduction of Unicode. Today all Han Chinese characters—usually known as CJK (Chinese, Japanese, Korean) characters—have been unified, and the Unicode Standard supports more than seventy thousand CJK characters.

Although most encoding problems have been resolved—for example, it is no longer necessary to download specific fonts, to mark Chinese words in mixed texts as specific two-byte encoding, or to guess what sort of encoding has been employed—several issues related to language, and therefore to the mutual understanding among various user communities, are still outstanding. First, different areas still use different characters even when writing the same form of standard Chinese: the PRC and Singapore employ simplified Chinese characters, while Taiwan and Hong Kong use traditional Chinese characters. Even though most of the characters are mutually comprehensible, many people are reluctant to read texts written in an unfamiliar form.

Second, Internet users reside in a distinct social, political, and geographically defined environment. They have been brought up and educated in a particular way with regard to questions of identity and belonging, and are also accustomed to using certain language and writing styles (Braman 1996). Language variations therefore exist that often can hinder smooth communication. These variations reflect political, cultural, and social differences, which can be seen most obviously in the different expressions used for the Internet itself: *hùliánwǎng* 互联网 or *yīntèwǎng* 因特网 in the PRC, and *wǎngjì wǎnglù* 网际网路 in Taiwan. In addition, the Chinese diaspora often uses languages other than Chinese: for example, the use of written English in Singapore is much more widespread than would be expected given the number of Chinese-speaking people (Damm 2010). Chinese language variants are also problematic: although Mandarin essentially has become the lingua franca in Taiwan, some people write in Hoklo (Taiwanese) on Internet websites. The colloquial form of written Cantonese is also found on many websites and Internet forums in Hong Kong, but even Mandarin (the standard written language) often includes Chinese characters unknown in other parts of the Chinese-speaking world (e.g., Big5's Hong Kong Supplementary Character Set, or HKSCS).

Third, there are differences in Internet use and applications among different locations. PRC users in particular have distinct software and applications, partly because of the state control of online content there. In the PRC, for example, QQ is used for instant messaging, Youku or Tudou for videos, and RenRen Network or Kaixin001 for social networking, while Taiwan and Hong Kong users tend to use MSN or Yahoo Messenger, YouTube, and Facebook (respectively) for the same purposes. Another difference is that PRC users do not use email as frequently as Chinese users elsewhere because fewer people have access to the Internet there than in Taiwan and Hong Kong (Internet World Stats 2011). The Internet also arrived relatively late in the PRC, so when it was introduced, communications software tools other than email were already in place.

Fourth, the PRC blocks websites from Taiwan, Hong Kong, and other overseas regions based on political content. National laws on state security, pornography, libel, hate speech, and so on also apply to websites for which official registration is not required, and forums are monitored, either by specific government agencies or by the Internet providers themselves (MacKinnon 2008; Xia 2008; Weber and Lu 2007).

Government Websites

Taiwan and mainland China have had an uneasy relationship since 1949, when the Guomindang (GMD, or Chinese Nationalist Party) retreated to Taiwan after losing the civil war (1945–1949). It was only after the democratization of Taiwan and the introduction of the reform and opening-up policy in the PRC that contact across the Taiwan Strait slowly began to reemerge. After 1991 the two sides began to engage in semiofficial contact, and they both set up websites with the aim of promulgating their policies to the other side. More recently, these websites also have been used to provide information to the increasing number of cross-Strait visitors—although Taiwanese business people and tourists were allowed to travel to the PRC after 1987, Taiwan only opened its doors to a greater number of mainland Chinese after the Cross-Strait Agreement Concerning Mainland Tourists Traveling to Taiwan was signed in June 2008.

The agencies for cross-Strait affairs are the Mainland Affairs Council of the Executive Yuan, Republic of China (Taiwan) and the Taiwan Affairs Office of the State Council (PRC). These two agencies do not contact each other directly, instead communicating through technically private organizations called the Straits Exchange Foundation (Taiwan) and the Association for Relations Across the Taiwan Straits (PRC). The website of the Mainland Affairs Council (MAC; www.mac.gov.tw/) contains news, information on the organization and its areas of responsibility, mainland policy documents, laws and regulations, cross-Strait trade, dialogue and negotiations, and statistics. The website is directed mainly at those Taiwanese who are interested in cross-Strait commerce and need information about doing business in mainland China (as illustrated by the site's slogan, "Defending the Core Interests of Taiwan's People While Advancing Cross-Strait Relations"). The site of the Taiwan Affairs Office (TAO) is located at www.gwytb.gov.cn/ and contains headlines, remarks made by spokespersons, cross-Strait interactions and exchanges, and cross-Strait trade information. The information provided is similar to that offered on the MAC website but focuses more on the PRC's political perspective of cross-Strait relations. Users can view the text of PRC policies and official declarations on the website, such as Jiang Zemin's Eight-Point Proposal, white papers on the Taiwan Issue, the One-China Principle, and the "one country, two systems" formula (see www.gwytb.gov.cn/), all of which are aimed at the unification of Taiwan and mainland China.

A very interesting website directed at the Taiwanese doing business in the PRC is the site of the All-China Federation of Taiwan Compatriots (www.tailian.org.cn). This official organization was established in 1981 in Beijing and describes itself as an "association for Taiwanese compatriots residing in mainland China." Its vision is described on the website as "a patriotic mass organization for promoting the peaceful unification under the 'one country, two systems' formula." The organization also studies relations between the PRC and Taiwan in the fields of economics, science, technology, culture, academia, and sports. Practical services and information also are offered (www.tailian.org.cn/jianjie/tljianjie.asp). The federation's website is oriented specifically toward Taiwanese businessmen living in China and combines political propaganda with practical information. The site obviously is intended to construct a common sense of "Chineseness" between people on both sides of the Taiwan Strait, but without a doubt it also serves as an official propaganda tool for the PRC. Due to the large amount of useful information provided, however, it is likely that Taiwanese read the propaganda sections also.

Civil Society

In addition to the information and discussions posted on these static and semiofficial websites, passionate debates also take place within the transnational Chinese cyberspace on topics such as Chinese nationalism, Taiwanese independence, the historical role of Japan, and the position of ethnic Chinese residing in Southeast Asia. The growing demand of mainland Chinese to participate in the PRC's political system, environmental issues, and social divisions also are discussed (Yang 2005). Academic analysis of these discussions, however, has yielded fundamentally different conclusions. The anthropologist Aihwa Ong (2003, 2005) in particular has described the way in which the Internet has constructed a borderless new identity for Chinese, which still retains a master narrative of irrefutable racial and cultural links to the motherland. She shows the crucial importance of ethnicity and nation for the self-conceptualization of Chinese modernity in both China and in the Chinese diaspora, and in her case studies of the 1990s riots in Indonesia (located at www.huaren.org) she also showed the dangers of uncontrolled borderless nationalism. On the other hand, Yang Guobin (2003), a scholar of sociology and communication, speaks of the "rise of a transnational Chinese cultural sphere" shaped by elements of a public sphere as proposed by the German sociologist and philosopher Jürgen Habermas (b. 1929), consisting of a rational debate between the state and civil society (the state hereby dissolving in the transregional and national constructs). Yang regards the same protests against atrocities in Indonesia as a positive development for Chinese group identity, since they demonstrated a self-clarification of being Chinese in the age of globalization (Yang 2003, 486).

In a more recent study based on the meetings on popular Internet forums between Taiwanese nationalists who are strongly in favor of an independent Taiwanese republic, and mainland Chinese nationalists who are demanding the unification of Taiwan and China under the conditions stated by the PRC, Liu Shih-Diing (2008) highlights the importance of emotions and preformed identities, and shows that rational discussion of highly emotional topics (such as historical relations with Japan) is not possible between Taiwanese and Chinese nationalists. Liu called these discussions "undomesticated hostilities," in which popular subjectivities and identities are reproduced in cyberspace as "us" and "them" to a hitherto-unknown degree (Liu 2008, 437).

Networks of social groups, nongovernmental organizations (NGOs), and self-help groups have also been established. Some facilitate positive social endeavors, such as those for the groups in Hong Kong that have organized HIV-prevention measures in the PRC (one is the Chi Heng Foundation, whose site is located at www.chihengfoundation.com), and the NGOs that are working against child prostitution and arranged marriages. At the same time, however, cyberspace also offers opportunities for the exploitation of females through marriage migration, ranging from voluntary acts to the quasi-sale of women (Liu and Liu 2008).

E-Commerce and Economic Integration

Trade between the PRC and Taiwan increased after 2008, and a Cross-Strait Internet Development Forum 两岸互联网发展论坛 was held in Beijing in 2009 and in Taipei in 2010. These forums included discussions of Internet developments across the Strait, focusing on business development and Internet integration (see www.chinataiwan.org).

The academic world has had far fewer discussions about the role of the Internet in establishing and supporting transregional and transnational business networks at various levels. There are, however, some examples of e-commerce portals directed at increasing cross-Strait integration. For instance, in October 2010 Taiwan's Executive Yuan (the executive branch of government) launched the Chinese Language E-commerce Action Plan 华文电子商务行动计划 to promote the usage of e-commerce. The goal of this project is "to promote Taiwan as a relieved, meticulous, and widely-used global Chinese language e-commerce operation center." This six-year project is focused primarily on the PRC market and seeks to establish an effective e-commerce strategy first for the PRC, and then for the global Chinese language market.

In the context of e-commerce within the PRC, Alibaba.com certainly deserves mention. Founded in Hangzhou, China, in 1999, Alibaba.com allows millions of buyers and suppliers around the world to do business with the PRC through three online marketplaces: a global trade platform for importers and exporters (www.alibaba.com), a Chinese platform for domestic trade in China (www.1688.com), and a Japanese platform that facilitates trade to and from Japan through an affiliated company (www.alibaba.co.jp). These marketplaces form a community of more than 56 million registered users in more than 240 countries and regions, which clearly demonstrates the huge influence of this website in Greater China and beyond.

A study by Chen Wenhong shows how ethnic Chinese—new migrants to Canada in particular—employ the Internet in developing and maintaining business relations with China, including technology transfer and the establishment of networks for ethnic Chinese residing in North America and in China. These kinds of initiatives also have led to enhanced business opportunities within and across the groups of ethnic Chinese (Chen 2006).

Overcoming Borders

At first glance, the existence of a common, widespread written language seems to present the most obvious argument for the existence of a distinct Chinese cyberspace. Problems such as the encoding issues associated with the use of both simplified and traditional characters have become less important with the adoption of Unicode systems, which can show different characters simultaneously, and helper programs (such as Google translation) that easily can convert the characters. This cyberspace has its parallel in Greater China, geographically defined as the PRC, Taiwan, Hong Kong, and Macao, and the Chinese diaspora.

Although Chinese cyberspace is global and reaches (to some extent) beyond national borders, it is characterized by various types of constraints (Lessig 1999). PRC censorship (Damm 2004, 2010; Keane 2001) in particular hinders communication between the two sides of the Taiwan Strait by blocking many official Taiwanese websites, along with Taiwanese pro-independence websites that discuss cross-Strait issues. In areas of civic engagement and e-commerce, however, diasporic Chinese cyberspace has helped to overcome borders and has led to new forms of communications and interaction.

Jens DAMM and Terrence Ying-tai LAI
Chang Jung Christian University, Taiwan

See also Chinese Language and Computing; Communities Online; Internet Governance; Social and Political Impact

Further Reading

Barabantseva, Elena. (2004). Chinese nation-negotiation in the period of modernisation. *SEAS Electronic Working Papers*, 2(5), 1–20. Retrieved May 5, 2007, from http://www.shef.ac.uk/content/1/c6/05/02/57/Barabantseva.pdf

Braman, Sandra. (1996). Interpenetrated globalization: Scaling, power, and the public sphere. In Sandra Braman & Annabelle Sreberny (Eds.), *Globalization, communication, and transnational civil society* (pp. 21–36). Cresskill, NJ: Hampton Press.

Chan, Brenda. (2005). The Internet and the construction of Chinese cultural identity: A case study of new Chinese migrants in Singapore. (Doctoral dissertation). Nanyang Technological University, Singapore.

Charney, Michael W.; Chee Kiong Tong; & Yeoh, Brenda S. A. (Eds.). (2003). *Chinese migrants abroad: Cultural, educational, and social dimensions of the Chinese diaspora*. Singapore: Singapore University Press.

Chen Wenhong. (2006). The impact of Internet use on transnational entrepreneurship: The case of Chinese immigrants to Canada. In Law Pui-Lam, Leopoldina Fortunati & Yang Shanhua (Eds.), *New technologies in global societies* (pp. 197–220). Singapore: World Scientific Publishing.

China Internet Network Information Center (CNNIC). (2010). Statistical report on Internet development in China: July 2010. Retrieved March 10, 2011, from http://www.cnnic.net.cn/uploadfiles/pdf/2010/8/24/93145.pdf

China Internet Network Information Center (CNNIC). (2013). Statistical report on Internet development in China: Janaury 2013. Retrieved August 26, 2013, from http://www1.cnnic.cn/IDR/ReportDownloads/201302/P020130312536825920279.pdf

Damm, Jens. (2004). Internet and the fragmented political society. *IIAS Newsletter*, 33, 10–11.

Damm, Jens. (2010). Chinese cyberspaces: Defining the spatial component of a "borderless" media. *Electronic Journal of Communication*, 20, 3–4.

Foreseeing Innovative New Digiservices (FIND). (2011). Homepage. Retrieved February 25, 2011, from http://www.find.org.tw/eng/home.asp

Harding, Harry. (1995). The concept of "*Greater China": Themes, variations and reservations. In David L. Shambaugh (Ed.), Greater China: The next superpower?* (pp. 8–34). Oxford, UK: Oxford University Press.

Internet World Stats. (2011). Homepage. Retrieved February 25, 2011, from http://www.internetworldstats.com/

Internet World Stats. (2013). Asia Internet use, population data and Facebook statistics. Retrieved May 29, 2014, from http://www.internetworldstats.com/stats3.htm#asia

Ip Manying. (2006). Chinese media in New Zealand: Transnational outpost or unchecked floodtide? In Sun Wanning (Ed.), *Media and the Chinese diaspora: Community, communications, and commerce* (pp. 178–200). London: Routledge.

Keane, Michael. (2001). Redefining Chinese citizenship. *Economy and Society, 30*(1), 1–17.

Lessig, Lawrence. (1999). *Code and other laws of cyberspace.* New York: Basic Books.

Liu Lihui, & Liu Hong. (2008). Boundary-crossing through cyberspace. In Khun Eng Kuah-Pearce (Ed.), *Chinese women and the cyberspace* (pp. 249–270). Amsterdam: Amsterdam University Press.

Liu Shih-Diing. (2008). Undomesticated hostilities: The affective space of Internet chat rooms across the Taiwan Strait. *Positions: East Asia Cultures Critique, 16*(2), 435–455.

Lunde, Ken. (2006). *CJKV information processing: Chinese, Japanese, Korean & Vietnamese computing.* Sebastopol, CA: O'Reilly Media.

MacKinnon, Rebecca. (2008). Cyber zone. *Index on Censorship, 37*(2), 82–89.

Mainland Affairs Council (MAC), Executive Yuan, Republic of China. (2011). Homepage. Retrieved March 10, 2011, from http://www.mac.gov.tw/mp.asp?mp=3

Ong Aihwa. (2003). Cyberpublics and diaspora politics among transnational Chinese. *Interventions: International Journal of Postcolonial Studies, 5*(1), 82–100.

Ong Aihwa. (2005). Chinese diaspora politics and its fallout in a cyber age. In Melvin Ember, Carol R. Ember & Skoggard, Ian A. (Eds.), *Encyclopedia of diasporas: Immigrant and refugee cultures around the world* (pp. 65–76). New York: Springer.

Pan, Lynn. (1999). (Ed.). *The encyclopedia of the overseas Chinese.* Cambridge, MA: Harvard University Press.

Schubert, Gunter. (2010). Cross-Strait integration: A new research focus in the Taiwan studies field. *Journal of Current Chinese Affairs, 39*(1).

Sun Wanning. (2005). Media and the Chinese diaspora: Community, consumption, and transnational imagination. *Journal of Chinese Overseas, 1*(1), 65–86.

Taiwan Affairs Office (TAO) of the State Council PRC. (2011). Homepage. Retrieved March 10, 2011, from http://www.gwytb.gov.cn/en/

Taiwan Network Information Center (TWNIC). (2013). Homepage. Retrieved August 28, 2013, from http://www.twnic.net.tw/index2.php

Tu Wei-ming. (1994). Cultural China: The periphery as the center. In Tu Wei-ming (Ed.), *The living tree: The changing meaning of being Chinese today* (pp. 1–34). Stanford, CA.: Stanford University Press.

Wang Gungwu. (2002). New migrants: How new, why new? In Chang Ts'un-wu & Tang Shi-yeoung (Eds.), *Essays on ethnic Chinese abroad: Vol. 1. Migration, entrepreneurs and commerce.* Taipei, Taiwan: Overseas Chinese Association.

Weber, Ian, & Lu Jia. (2007). Internet and self-regulation in China: The cultural logic of controlled commodification. *Media, Culture & Society, 29*(5), 772–789.

Xia, Bill. (2008). Cat and mouse. *Index on Censorship, 37*(2), 114–119.

Yang Guobin. (2003). The Internet and the rise of a transnational Chinese cultural sphere. *Media, Culture & Society, 25*(4), 469–490.

Yang Guobin. (2005). Environmental NGOs and institutional dynamics in China. *China Quarterly, 181*, 46–66.

Communities Online

Zàixiàn shèqū 在线社区

Summary: Online communities, or cybercommunities, have the potential to influence the broad societal, political, and cultural transformations that in recent decades have shaped China toward becoming a postmodern society. They can provide means of empowerment and communication among civic and nationalist communities, marginalized groups, and the Chinese diaspora, and they could help narrow the socioeconomic and digital divide within China.

In 2011, one-third of China's population was online, and with the ongoing popularity of Bulletin Board Systems (BBSs), cybercommunities have become one of the dominant features of China's Internet. These communities exist in the fields of civic engagement and nationalist endeavors; marginalized groups are present as well as users enjoying leisure and entertainment activities. Links to Chinese-speaking regions worldwide transcend national boundaries.

By the end of 2012 the number of Internet users in China had reached 564 million with an Internet penetration rate of 41.1 percent (CNNIC 2013), and all the major portals, search engines, university websites, and many privately owned websites were offering BBSs and other Internet forums for a virtually endless number of cybercommunities. Users sharing similar interests ranging from the private sphere, such as dating and cars, to nationalist discussions, have been meeting in the virtual world and forming new and sometimes long-lasting relationships, thus defying the physical borders of the "real" world. While other applications of the Internet, such as the social networks, are gaining importance, BBSs and Internet forums remain much more popular in China than elsewhere (CNNIC 2010, 3).

This article explores the potential of cybercommunities in China and beyond, taking into account Western and Chinese sources, and provides an introduction to the particular applications for community building that are popular in China. It offers several examples of cybercommunities that have developed in the areas of civic engagement, commerce and trade, nationalism, and cultural interests, and highlights as well the broad spectrum of interests they represent. Finally, it examines what the boundaries of these communities will be, focusing particularly on transregional and transnational elements involving the People's Republic of China, Hong Kong, Taiwan, and the global Chinese diaspora.

Cybercommunities and China's Transformation

Experts in the field often debate whether cybercommunities embody the potential to change China's political and social structures. Can they narrow the socioeconomic and digital divide between the developed urban areas and the coastal areas to help empower marginalized groups? Or do these cybercommunities reflect only the current situation in China, where the emergence of narrow interest groups precludes active social and political engagement in a postmodern society. Another question, therefore, is whether the sheer variety of different cybercommunities is congruent with the broad societal, political, and cultural transformations that have shaped China toward becoming a postmodern society. The term "postmodern" is being used here as defined by Arif Dirlik and Xudong Zhang (1997, 3): "The coexistence of the precapitalist, the capitalist, and the postsocialist economic, political, and social forms represents a significant departure from the assumptions of a Chinese modernity, embodied above all in the socialist revolutionary project." A further reference is to the overcoming of societal expectations with regard to clear-cut class and gender roles, which has led to the blurring of former distinctions such that individuals are able to make more deliberate choices in what they want to be and how they want to behave. This does not deny that ongoing enormous gaps in income and development have resulted in extremely uneven growth in China; this is mirrored in the so-called digital divide, which ranges from an Internet penetration rate of 15 percent in the southwestern province of Guizhou to 65 percent in the capital, Beijing (CNNIC 2010, 105).

It cannot be disputed that computer-mediated communication (CMC) has enabled new worldwide communities to form in cyberspace, which, at least for the participants, represents real communities (Watson 1997). Cybercommunities can be broadly defined as online virtual networks where social interactions take place between participants who share common ideas, interests, and hobbies so that a sense of community and belonging can develop. These online communities offer opportunities for a wide range of activities, from individual bonding (friendship, romance, dating, hobbies, and professional networking) to civic engagement (environmentalism, calls to political action). Ethnic and nationalist groups have formed virtual communities, as have fantasy and celebrity fan groups (Fernback 1999, 203).

Most authors agree that a certain level of commitment on the part of the cybercommunity participants is necessary. The writer Howard Rheingold (1993, 5) defined cybercommunities as "social aggregations that emerge when enough people carry on those public discussions long enough, with sufficient human feeling, to form webs of personal relation in cyberspace." Traditional communities are linked to certain places, whereas cybercommunities easily cross geographical, territorial, and national boundaries. More important than "cyber" is the term "community," as described by Steve Jones (1998, 3): "Crucial to the rhetoric surrounding of the Internet ... is the promise of a renewed sense of community and, in many instances, new types and formations of community."

In these cybercommunities it is possible, but not necessary, to obtain a particular identity within a community that is close to or identical to one's actual identity in the real world, or to establish a completely new identity with regard to gender, age, ethnicity, and interests. The first online communities emerged in the Usenet (the oldest computer network communications system, which has been in widespread use since 1980) and later in BBSs and various related Internet forums. These are still very popular in China, but new forms of social networks have now come into existence, such as Facebook and its Chinese counterparts, which offer more sophisticated applications for building cybercommunities.

In Chinese, the term used for "community" is usually *shèqū* 社区or *shèqún* 社群 (the latter being used more often in Taiwan); for specific reference to CMC communities, terms in use include *wǎngluò* 网络, meaning "net" or "cyber" (in Taiwan: *wǎnglù* 网络), and *xūnǐ* 虚拟, that is, "virtual," and *zàixiàn* 在线, meaning "online." In the context of the social interactions and the perception of a cybercommunity as a symbolic form of community, the term *wangluo shequ* is probably the most useful and the most often employed. Baike Baidu, the Chinese equivalent of Wikipedia, defines a cybercommunity as an "online communications space, such as BBS/forums, Tieba [also known as "Baidu Paste Bar," a Chinese communication platform provided by form provided by Baidu, the largest search machine in China], personal web space, dating, online chat, including value-added wireless services, focusing on participants with a common interest" (Wangluo shequ 2010).

In the Chinese world, the term *xūnǐ shèqù* 虚拟社区 ("virtual community") places greater emphasis on its opposition to the "real" world and on anonymity, and also on the possibility of creating new virtual worlds, such as MUD (Multi-User Dungeon), computer role-play games set in a fantasy world, and other gaming applications. The Chinese cybercommunities described here exist between the real and virtual worlds; for example, in the cybercommunity of the Chinese diaspora the boundaries between the real world and newly created online spaces are vague, and the cybercommunity is more or less a borderless extension of existing networks.

Building Cybercommunities in China

Applications used to build cybercommunities in China differ from those used in the West in several ways. First, China's Internet policy, often referred to as the "Great Firewall," renders the use of Usenet, Facebook, and MySpace difficult and sometimes impossible inside the country. As a result, the Chinese versions of Facebook, such as the Renren Network (www.renren.com, formerly known as the Xiaonei Network, www.xiaonei.com), which is popular among college students, and Kaixin001 (www.kaixin001.com) are more popular in the People's Republic of China (PRC), than, for example, in Hong Kong and in Taiwan. Second, cultural differences between the West, Japan, South Korea, and

China have made certain applications and search engines more popular in the West than in East Asia; although they are often more censored than international versions, East Asian users prefer the local versions. Third, there might be a nationalist bias against Western products, particularly within the Chinese nationalist groups. Finally, in China as elsewhere, applications are changing rapidly from Web 1.0 to Web 2.0, and different communities employ different applications that have their own characteristics, benefits, and drawbacks with regard to building and maintaining cybercommunities. Despite the fast-changing technology, however, the various cybercommunities and their user loyalty remain the same; cybercommunities, in particular, are less technology-determined than are other Internet features.

In spite of the existence of specific Web 2.0 applications, BBSs remain in vogue on China's Internet and are used especially for creating cybercommunities. Most Chinese web portals offer various forms of BBSs or the specific entity Baidu, called Tieba (www.tieba.baidu.com). These BBSs and forums are more important than social networks, although maintaining anonymity and coping with the sometimes-enforced name registration can pose problems for these kinds of communities, particularly when they are involved with politically sensitive issues. They do, however, offer more security than the new social network applications such as Renren and Kaixin001. While the influence of blogs on the development of China's society and political system is frequently debated, the continuing influence of BBSs should not be underestimated and deserves equal consideration. Internet companies, search engines, universities, city governments, and even individuals have set up BBSs on their websites, and these offer ample space for community building.

The first BBSs were set up at universities; the first was Shui Mu Tsinghua at the prestigious Tsinghua University in Beijing, and others soon followed, such as Tianya and the Strong Nation Forum (Qiángguó lùntán 强国论坛, bbs.people.com.cn), both offered by the *People's Daily Online*. According to Yong Hu (2010), these BBSs differ in various respects: "Tianya, MOP, KDnet, Tiexue and other sites work on a 'forum + editor' model, while the Strong Nation Forum, Sina Forum, Sohu Forum, Phoenix Forum, Baidu Post and other such sites are important components of larger news forums." The major web portals and search engines, such as Baidu (www.baidu.com), QQ (www.qq.com), Sina (www.sina.com.cn), Netease (www.163.com), Taobao (www.taobao.com), and Sohu (www.sohu.com), have set up BBSs on their sites. QQ, an instant messaging tool that is second only to MSN in China, has gradually evolved into a large portal that contains, in addition to many other applications, one of the largest instant message–based BBS forums. The web portal Netease runs an alumnicentric BBS community, and the e-business site Taobao is well known for its commercial and business-oriented BBSs (Jin 2008, 11). MOP (www.mop.com), with its focus on entertainment, and Tianya (www.tianya.cn), with its focus on culture and social matters, are important BBSs with huge user-generated forums that account for about half of the BBS traffic in China. In addition to the all-embracing BBSs of the major portals, many smaller and more topic-oriented BBSs have survived and are frequently visited.

The specific mode of a BBS leads to community-building; the many-to-many communication capability coupled with the fact that users—unlike bloggers—cannot delete other users' comments make BBSs highly interactive (Jin 2008, 30). A greater proportion of the content of China's BBSs is related to leisure activities, such as dating, recreation, and entertainment than to public affairs or political issues. This encourages the creation of specialized cybercommunities that, although they bring together people with the same interests, are unlikely to create a public sphere where the exchange and discussion of different opinions is a precondition. The Chinese BBS sphere has probably not accomplished the critical functions of the Habermasian public sphere. According to Jürgen Habermas, this "public sphere" refers to "a realm of our social life in which something approaching public opinion can be formed. Access is guaranteed to all citizens.... Citizens behave as a public body when they confer in an unrestricted fashion—that is, with the guarantee of freedom of assembly and association and the freedom to express and publish their opinions—about matter of general interest" (Habermas 2001, 102). In the Chinese BBS sphere, however, the "homogenous space of embodied subjects in symmetrical relations" (Poster 2001, 265) is unlikely to occur because BBS moderators exercise their right to regulate the information on BBS sites, and the hierarchical structure that gives preference to "opinion leaders" on BBSs overshadows the voices of the normal BBS participants (Jin 2008, 36).

Variety of Cybercommunities

The literature of cybercommunities classifies the following groups, although many of these overlap and various other communities have recently come into existence. These cybercommunities could be further divided according to whether they are civic communities or are in the public sphere (political action, environmental protection, web-based nongovernmental organizations), or are entertainment, relaxation communities, and private communities (also leisure, games, and dating) (Yang 2003, 2009).

Nationalist Cybercommunities

Benedict Anderson's 1983 concept of "imagined communities" makes cybercommunities suitable for nationalist communications (Fernback 1999, 211). The Internet offers Chinese nationalists, the Han ethnocentrists, the Uygur separatists, the Taiwanese independence activists, and similar groups the opportunity to create ideal forums for pursuing nationalist ideas beyond geographical limitations and boundaries; this activity has also helped to revitalize nationalist feelings in the Chinese diaspora. Recent emigrants from the PRC find each other in cyberspace, thus linking the new diaspora and the homeland in a hitherto unknown intimacy (Chan 2006).

The nationalist cybercommunity includes a large number of Chinese students studying abroad who have gained sufficient confidence to challenge the Western perception of China. The Internet serves as a tool to bring together activists living in China and activists living abroad to attack, in particular, US and Japanese media descriptions of China that they regard as misrepresentations. In 2007, for example, Chinese "netizens" launched a website named Anti-CNN (www.anti-cnn.com) that listed alleged distortions or misrepresentations that appear in the Western media. These new nationalist communities have also employed BBSs, forums, and the newer Web 2.0 social networking sites such as Facebook and MySpace, and they have gravitated toward certain blogs. Xu Wu, in "Chinese Cyber Nationalism: Evolution, Characteristics, and Implications" (2007, 23), showed that Internet technology has enabled the more formalized, advanced, and well-organized activists to build up power communities to carry this nationalism back to China. Furthermore, the Chinese government is in constant negotiation with these online activists, often trying to exert a calming influence when their nationalist policies show signs of endangering the foreign policy objectives of the PRC. Careful monitoring takes place in the community of the *People's Daily*'s Strong Nation Forum. Although it allows many discussions, it is probably one of the most highly controlled forums in China.

The essentialist stance of this nationalist community has been mentioned in connection with the anti-Chinese riots in Indonesia in 1998, which were probably the first of a handful of events that led to a drastic increase in Chinese cybernationalism. The riots against ethnic Chinese in Indonesia during the Asian crisis led to the formation of a vitriolic community of Chinese students in the United States, and this has also spread to the Chinese diaspora in Southeast Asia, where Internet usage has just started to gain strength. Popular websites, such as the newly established World Huaren Federation (www.huaren.org), have employed essentialist approaches that do not acknowledge the various hybrid identities of Indonesians of Chinese descent in the simplistic discussions found online, which could be counterproductive for the rights of Indonesians of Chinese descent (Suryadinata 2007). This case, as the professor of anthropology Aihwa Ong (2003) pointed out, demonstrates the potential shallowness and one-sidedness of cybercommunities. Without taking any personal risks, Chinese nationalists from all over the world were able to criticize the Indonesian government, but the essentialized perception of "Chineseness" and even racist undertones also deepened the rifts within Indonesian society, where many Indonesians of Chinese descent suddenly began to be called Chinese again.

Another example can be drawn from the PRC itself: the protest against Japan's 2004 bid for permanent membership in the United Nations (UN) Security Council, which drew fierce online protests from the Chinese diaspora (for example, in Singapore) and from PRC Chinese, because both groups, with their memories of the atrocities of World War II, were hostile toward Japan. The subsequent political action extended the virtual space and led, in 2005, to huge street gatherings all over China that were tolerated (to some extent) by the Chinese Communist Party (CCP) (Tai 2006, 255–292).

Uygur leaders, often intellectuals and activists residing outside the Xinjiang Uygur Autonomous Region, have used the Internet to shape a borderless national identity for the Uygurs. This has probably also led to increased tension in the region and has hindered the reconsolidation of the various ethnic groups residing there (Petersen 2006). Uygur "cyber-separatism," together with exotic representations of the Uygur by the PRC, has resulted in the simultaneous construction of a homogeneous, monolithic Han majority in conflict with an essentialized group of Uygurs (Gladney 2004). Although the conflict here is certainly not a new phenomenon, the use of the Internet by nationalists on both sides seems to have brought the unbridgeable differences between the Uygurs and the Han, in terms of race, religion, language, and culture, into even sharper relief.

The Taiwanese independence network also employs the Internet, but this is an extension of a much older network existing between activist groups in Japan and the United States that can be traced back to the 1950s. Because the promotion of Taiwanese independence has been more or less legally tolerated in Taiwan since the late 1980s, the Internet has not played such an important role in this regard; nevertheless, various websites and groups are active and promote specific Taiwanese communities (Chung 2003).

Other nationalist groups within China, such as the Muslim groups in Xinjiang fighting for an independent East Turkestan, and the Taiwanese independence activists arguing online against the claims of the CCP and the Chinese nationalists that Taiwan is a part of China, show that cybercommunities tend to be "bonding" groups rather than "bridging" groups—a phenomenon that has been described by Robert Putnam (2002) and researched by Pippa Norris (2004). In this context, the term "bridging groups" refers to groups that bring together members of disparate communities and enable communication (approximating Habermas's public sphere), while "bonding groups" reinforce close-knit networks of people sharing similar backgrounds and beliefs (Norris 2004, 31). More recently, nationalists have shown an increasing tendency to use blogs, media-sharing platforms, and personal communication tools, including social network applications (Nyiri, Zhang, and Varrall 2010).

Cybercommunities of Marginalized Groups

Although nationalist cybercommunities often spontaneously form and expand rapidly in response to certain events, such as the Japanese bid for UN Security Council membership and the bombing of the Chinese embassy in Belgrade in 1999, cybercommunities composed of marginalized groups tend to be longer-lasting and often develop a sense of *Gemeinschaft* (Ferdinand Tönnies's concept of "community"). In such communities the participants are oriented toward the group as least as much as toward their own self-interest, and a "unity of will" can be observed (Tönnies 2001, 22).

With regard to sexual minorities such as lesbians, gays, bisexuals, and transgendered people (collectively, LGBT), the Internet has led to shared communities in many places all over the world (Ho 2010, 13). In China especially, where sexual minorities are still shunned by the official media and society, LGBT cybercommunities are regarded as providing opportunities for empowerment (Martin 2009). Unlike the nationalist cybercommunities, the LGBT online communities are very localized and highly influenced by sociocultural specifics (Ho 2010, 108–109); cross-border communities of sexual minority groups are seldom found. For example, the Taiwanese "same-sex" online spaces are very separate from the those of the Chinese; in Taiwan, universities established sexual-minority cybercommunities with BBSs called MOTTS ("member of the same sex") as early as 1994 (Damm 2001; Martin 2009; Yang 2000).

Research on the use of the Internet by women in China shows that cyberspace serves as a kind of social capital and enables women to forge cybersocial networks and communities to facilitate their activities and needs (Kuah-Pearce 2008, 11). But the sociologist Khun Eng Kuah-Pearce (2008, 15–16) goes on to observe that members of cybercommunities seldom develop offline relationships, with the exception of dating and some support groups that have reported personal contacts at a later stage. Other marginalized groups include Chinese migrants and emigrants who have established networks between their new locations and their places of origin. Through the use of Internet cafés, families are connected with the migrants working in the more prosperous urban and western regions (Law and Chu 2008; Peng 2008).

Rural populations still lag in general economic development and largely lack personal computers, information and communications technology (ICT) skills, and Internet infrastructure. This has created an enormous digital divide that is only slowly being narrowed through various government-sponsored efforts to improve the infrastructure, and the Internet is still only beginning to offer opportunities to build up rural cybercommunities. The result is hierarchical use of ICT in rural regions (Zhao 2008, 137–141); only through state and individual initiatives can an ICT infrastructure be developed to enable the establishment of rural cybercommunities. These rural groups, which the communications and new media scholar Jack Linchuan Qiu (2009) describes as the "information haveless," are heterogeneous in terms of gender, regional origin, and ethnicity, and have developed new methods to access the Internet, but financial restrictions and their often unstable living conditions still obstruct the development of a truly active cybercommunity. Qiu argues that these groups are highly vulnerable to commercial exploitation and state control (Qiu 2009).

Ethnic groups are an interesting subset in the cybercommunity. One well-researched group is the Hakka, a subethnic Chinese group found in southern China (for example, in Guangdong) and also in Southeast Asia and Taiwan. Unlike the nationalist discourses, which tend toward essentialism, the global Hakka community uses more Web 2.0 applications such as blogs, YouTube, and forums, and shows a high degree of hybridization. Online, the Hakka ethnic identity is continuously rearticulated, and the Hakka cultural, linguistic, and historic heritage is experienced via the new technologies (Damm 2008).

An interesting case was researched by Weidong Zhang (2002), who observed the communications on a BBS of a Manchurian website to gain a clearer picture of how the identity of "Manchuness" has been articulated via Internet communication, and to what degree the Internet helped to revoke the identity of an ethnic group that today has largely been assimilated with the dominant Han Chinese. The specific Manchu language is almost extinct, and only small groups of mostly elderly people in very remote and rural areas of northeastern China are able to communicate in Manchu (Zhang 2002).

Leisure and Entertainment

The cybercommunities connected with leisure and entertainment are too numerous to count. Some of those found in the various leisure, hobby, and finance sections of typical BBSs on the larger web portals focus on culture and art, lifestyle (film gossip, pop stars, love and emotion, and night life), health, women, cars, real estate, finance, and the stock market (Damm 2007, 287–288). These communities are topic oriented, but various BBSs also offer localized cybercommunities; Sohu, for example, lists numerous BBS topics specifically for Beijing but lists fewer BBSs for provinces with a lower Internet penetration, such as Guangxi.

A very specific transnational cybercommunity is found in the online fan clubs, which often focus on celebrities from outside the PRC proper, in places such as Hong Kong, Taiwan, Japan, and South Korea. For example, a transnational cybercommunity focused on Kimura Takuya, a highly popular Japanese singer and actor, has spread over fourteen countries, where participants define their gender, cultural, global, and hybrid identities through their mutual interaction; this has led to a complex process of virtual cross-cultural identity formation (Darling-Wolf 2004). In various forums, soap operas and actors are discussed among the fans of this entertainment genre. According to Yuni Koyun Ko (2009), the shared affinity (widespread, at present) of many female participants with Korean stars or TV dramas develops into "a subject of their 'play' in the form of cyber-space communication." Cultural and literary exchanges also take place on blogs and BBSs, and, as shown by Jia Liu (2010), cybercommunities are starting to play an increasingly significant role in the reception of popular novels.

Commerce

E-business and e-commerce-related cybercommunities have expanded exponentially over recent years and both are widely expected to continue their rapid development (for example, bbs.taobao.com). They function primarily as communication channels between enterprises and users in the form of improved customer relationship management, but social networks also enable the enhancement, at many levels, of the relationships of enterprises with their customers and those of the business community in general (Thomas 2006).

Dissident Cybercommunities

The Chinese government has been investing heavily in developing an adequate Internet infrastructure as part of its increasingly successful strategy to overcome the nation's digital divide. At the same time, however, it has introduced one of the most efficient surveillance and control mechanisms in the world (Chase, Mulvenon, and Hachigian 2006; Hughes and Wacker 2003). Although computer experts might be able to override the censorship measures, normal users are denied access to regime-critical voices by the blocking devices set up on the Internet in China. Dissident voices involved in the current "big taboos" in China are thus often based outside of China and Hong Kong, and, while they might form a dissident cybercommunity, it is very difficult for them to reach users within China. The best-known examples of dissident groups are probably the Falun Gong, the

Chinese Democracy Party, and the Tibetan exile groups. All these groups employ or have employed two-way communications to build up communities to coordinate political action and transmit information. The authorities in Beijing regard this information as politically sensitive or even subversive, which makes it difficult for PRC citizens to participate (Chase and Mulvenon 2002, 1–43).

Two-way communications via email and BBSs helped tremendously with the organization and development of the China Democracy Party (CDP), a short-lived party that was established in 1998 and was declared illegal by the CCP in that same year. Here, however, the Internet played a contradictory role (Zheng 2008, 147): without the new communication technologies, the rapid organization and coordination of the CDP within China and beyond would have been not possible but, on the other hand, the uncoordinated discussion on the Internet led to the CDP's apparent radicalization which, in the end, provided the Chinese authorities with the arguments they needed to crack down on the party.

The Internet played a significant role in coordinating the Falun Gong movement, a spiritual movement that was built upon elements of traditional Chinese qigong practices, but with a modern and hierarchical structure. The Chinese authorities launched a crackdown in 1999, declaring the movement an "evil cult" and issuing orders for its members to be prosecuted. Since the crackdown, relevant BBSs and chat rooms have been inaccessible or have been subjected to direct attacks by the Chinese authorities, so that today the Falun Gong community is more concentrated outside of China (Chase and Mulvenon 2002; Zheng 2008, 17).

Empowerment or Entertainment?

In recent years various forms of cybercommunities have come into existence in the PRC and Greater China that are clearly much more than extensions of existing networks. Some of these cybercommunities have helped to develop the Internet itself as a medium of communication, while others possess social characteristics and features that may even challenge the existing structures of the state. From an optimistic perspective, cybercommunities may empower marginalized and scattered groups, may lead to transnational networks, and may also provide a new public sphere. These cybercommunities in China can therefore be seen as presenting something new and innovative—certainly much more than merely extensions of already existing networks. As participation in cybercommunities requires only limited levels of commitment, participants are able to enter and leave without using their real identities. Cybercommunities, by bundling interest groups together, can thus be seen as contributing to the fragmentation of society, as jeopardizing real communication and hindering the development of a Habermasian public sphere.

For the time being, cybercommunities are only able to exert limited influence on emerging political and societal discourses and on the creation of a public sphere. They are part of an increasingly postmodern Chinese society with a very personalized use. Their transregional and transnational character, however, helps to link users in various parts of greater China, and also leads to new ideas and information being disseminated at an unprecedented speed. This is particularly true for the marginalized groups that are able to overcome societal and legal restrictions and to form virtual communities offering opportunities to disseminate news and grant each other mutual support; in this way, regional disparities can also be overcome. The nationalist groups on the Internet, however, can often be seen in quite a different light: these tend to ignore any voices raised in opposition and to form narrow-minded, ethnocentric, and, to some extent, racist groups. Here a true public sphere with the participation of manifold voices would be especially desirable. In this context, the government blocking of certain websites and the censorship within BBSs can be regarded as one of the most crucial issues: women and LGBT members can easily reach their respective groups within greater China, while Chinese nationalists are cut off from the discussions of Tibetan and Uygur nationalists as well as Taiwanese independence activists.

Jens DAMM
Chang Jung Christian University, Taiwan

See also Blogging; Chinese Diaspora Online; Internet Regulation; User-Generated Content

Further Reading

Chan, Brenda. (2006). Virtual communities and Chinese national identity. *Journal of Chinese Overseas*, 2(1), 1–32.

Chase, Michael S. & Mulvenon, James C. (2002). *You've got dissent! Chinese dissident use of the Internet and Beijing's counter-strategies*. Santa Monica, CA: Rand.

Chase, Michael S.; Mulvenon, James; & Hachigian, Nina. (2006). Comrade to comrade networks: The social and political implications of peer-to-peer networks in China. In Jens Damm & Simona Thomas (Eds.), *Chinese cyberspaces: Technological changes and political effects* (pp. 64–101). London: Routledge.

China Internet Network Information Center (CNNIC). (2010, January). 25th statistical survey report on Internet development in China. Retrieved August 1, 2010, from http://www.cnnic.cn/uploadfiles/pdf/2010/3/15/142705.pdf

China Internet Network Information Center (CNNIC). (2011, January). 27th statistical survey report on Internet development in China. Retrieved May 25, 2010, from http://www1.cnnic.cn/uploadfiles/pdf/2011/2/28/153752.pdf

China Internet Network Information Center (CNNIC). (2013, January). Statistical report on Internet development in China. Retrieved on April, 15, 2013, from http://www1.cnnic.cn/IDR/ReportDownloads/201302/P020130312536825920279.pdf

Chung, Peichi. (2003). *Crafting national identity in cyberspace: The formulation of a Taiwan nation and the rise of an alternative media culture*. (Doctoral dissertation). Indiana University, Bloomington.

Damm, Jens. (2001). The World Wide Web in China and Taiwan: The effects of heterogenization and homogenization in a glocal discourse. *Chinese History and Society/Berliner Chinahefte, 20*, 66–78.

Damm, Jens. (2007). The Internet and the fragmentation of Chinese society. *Critical Asian Studies, 39*(2), 273–294.

Damm, Jens. (2008). The Chinese diasporic cyberspace: Cultural essentialism, nationalism and hybrid identities. *Chinese History and Society/Berliner Chinahefte, 34*, 130–148.

Darling-Wolf, Fabienne. (2004). Virtually multicultural: Trans-Asian identity and gender in an international fan community of a Japanese star. *New Media & Society, 6*(4), 507–528.

Dirlik, Arif & Zhang, Xudong. (1997). Introduction: Postmodernism and China. *Boundary 2, 24*(3), 1–18.

Fernback, Jan. (1999). There is a there there: Notes toward a definition of cybercommunity. In Steve Jones (Ed.), *Doing Internet research: Critical issues and methods for examining the net* (pp. 203–220). Thousand Oaks, CA: Sage Publications.

Gladney, Dru C. (2004). *Dislocating China: Reflections on Muslims, minorities, and other subaltern subjects.* Chicago: University of Chicago Press.

Habermas, Jürgen. (2001). The public sphere: An encyclopedic article. In Meenakshi Gigi Durham & Douglas Kellner (Eds.), *Media and cultural studies: Keyworks* (pp. 102–107). Malden, MA: Blackwell.

Ho, Loretta Wing Wah. (2010). *Gay and lesbian subculture in urban China.* London: Routledge.

Hu, Yong. (2010). BBS sites on China's changing web. Retrieved May 25, 2011 from http://yong.hu/57.htm

Hughes, Christopher R., & Wacker, Gudrun. (2003). *China and the Internet: Politics of the digital leap forward.* London: RoutledgeCurzon.

Jin, Liwen. (2008). Chinese online BBS sphere: What BBS has brought to China. (Master's thesis). Massachusetts Institute of Technology, Cambridge, MA. Retrieved July 15, 2010 from http://cms.mit.edu/research/theses/LiwenJin2008.pdf

Jones, Steve. (1998). Information, Internet, and community: Notes toward an understanding of community in the information age. In Steve Jones (Ed.), *Cybersociety 2.0: Revisiting computer-mediated communication and community* (pp. 1–34). Thousand Oaks, CA: Sage Publications.

Ko, Yuni Koyun. (2009, May 26). Riding with the Korean wave: Reflections on trans-Asian cultural flows. Retrieved July 15, 2010, from http://reasonandrespect.rwu.edu/journal/index.php/2009/05/26/riding-with-the-korean-wave-reflections-on-trans-asian-cultural-flows

Kuah-Pearce, Khun Eng. (Ed.). (2008). *Chinese women and the cyberspace.* Amsterdam: Amsterdam University Press.

Law, Pui-lam, & Chu, Wai-chi. (2008). ICTs and migrant workers in contemporary China. *Knowledge, Technology & Policy, 21*(2), 43–45.

Liu, Jia. (2010). *The reception of the works of contemporary Chinese glam-writers in mainland China.* (Doctoral dissertation). University of York, York, UK. Retrieved August 1, 2010, from http://etheses.whiterose.ac.uk/94

Martin, Fran. (2009). That global feeling: Sexual subjectivities and imagined geographies in Chinese-language lesbian cyberspaces. In Gerard Goggin & Mar J. McLelland (Eds.), *Internationalizing Internet studies: Beyond Anglophone paradigms* (pp. 285–301). New York: Routledge.

Norris, Pippa. (2004). The bridging and bonding role of online communities. In P. N. Howard & Steve Jones (Eds.), *Society online: The Internet in context* (pp. 71–83). Thousand Oaks, CA: Sage Publications.

Nyiri, Pal; Zhang, Juan; & Varrall, Merriden. (2010). China's cosmopolitan nationalists: "Heroes" and "traitors" of the 2008 Olympics. *China Journal, 63,* 25–55.

Ong, Aihwa. (2003). Cyberpublics and diaspora politics among transnational Chinese. *Interventions,* 5(1), 82–100.

Peng, Yinni. (2008). Internet use of migrant workers in the Pearl River delta. *Knowledge, Technology & Policy, 21*(2), 47–54.

Petersen, Kristian. (2006). Usurping the nation: Cyber-leadership in the Uighur nationalist movement. *Journal of Muslim Minority Affairs, 26*(1), 63–73.

Poster, Mark. (2001). Cyberdemocracy: The Internet and the public sphere. In David Trend (Ed.), *Reading digital cultures* (pp. 259–271). Malden, MA: Blackwell.

Putnam, Robert D. (2002). Introduction. In Robert D. Putnam (Ed.) *The dynamics of social capital.* Oxford, UK: Oxford University Press.

Qiu, Jack Linchuan. (2009). *Working-class network society: Communication technology and the information have-less in urban China.* Cambridge, MA: MIT Press.

Rheingold, Howard. (1993). *The virtual community: Homesteading on the electronic frontier.* Reading, MA: Addison-Wesley Publishing.

Suryadinata, Leo. (2007). Chinese politics resurgence of ethnic Chinese identity in post-Suharto Indonesia: Some reflections. *Asian Culture, 31,* 11–17.

Tai, Zixue. (2006). *The Internet in China: Cyberspace and civil society.* New York: Routledge.

Thomas, Simona. (2006). Net business: China's potential for a global market change. In Jens Damm & Simona Thomas (Eds.), *Chinese cyberspaces: Technological changes and political effects* (pp. 148–170). New York: Routledge

Tönnies, Ferdinand. (2001). *Community and civil society.* Cambridge, UK: Cambridge University Press.

网络社区 *Wangluo shequ* [Cybercommunity]. (2010). Retrieved May 29, 2014, from http://baike.baidu.com/view/102897.htm

Watson, Nessim. (1997). Why we argue about virtual community: A case study of the phish.net fan community. In Steve Jones (Ed.), *Virtual culture: Identity and communication by cybersociety* (pp. 102–132). London: Sage.

Wu, Xu. (2007). *Chinese cyber-nationalism: Evolution, characteristics, and implications*. Lanham, MD: Lexington Books.

Yang, Chung-Chuan. (2000). The use of the Internet among academic gay communities in Taiwan: An exploratory study. *Information, Communication & Society*, 3(2), 153–172.

Yang, Guobin. (2003). The Internet and the rise of a transnational cultural sphere. *Media, Culture & Society*, 25(4), 469–490.

Yang, Guobin. (2009). *The power of the Internet in China: Citizen activism online*. New York: Columbia University Press.

Zhang, Weidong. (2002). Displaying culture, voicing identity: A study of the Manchurian website "Eight Banners Descendant." *Netcom*, 6(3-4), 175–190.

Zhao, Jinqiu. (2008). *The Internet and rural development in China: The socio-structural paradigm*. Bern, Germany: Peter Lang AG.

Zheng, Yongnian. (2008). *Technological empowerment: The Internet, state, and society in China*. Stanford, CA: Stanford University Press.

Social and Political Impact

Shèhuì yǔ zhèngzhì yǐngxiǎng 社会与政治影响

Summary: Although the Internet has not ushered in a revolution in China as it was widely expected to do, it has resulted in a noticeable impact on Chinese politics by serving as a space for nongovernment discourse, facilitating policy change, expanding political participation, initiating political agendas, and helping to reduce ideological dissonance.

When the Internet was introduced into China in the late 1980s and early 1990s, it was expected to provoke a full-blown revolution and usher in a new era of freedom and democracy (Kluver 2005). That revolution, however, has not (yet) materialized. The Internet has remained heavily regulated and confined to nonsubversive parameters by the government.

Nevertheless, the Internet has exerted a noticeable and potentially profound impact on the country's politics. It has facilitated the formation of a public sphere that is not structured primarily by government discourse and that has served as a relatively free platform for nonofficial expressions, setting political agendas, pressuring the government to change unpopular policies, boosting direct and indirect political participation, and providing an avenue for people to express their dissatisfaction and reduce ideological dissonance.

China's courtship with the Internet started in 1987, when Professor Qian Tianbai of Peking University sent out the first electronic mail from China to Germany. Following this attempt, several institutions experimented with Internet connections. In May 1989, the Chinese Research Network (CRN) successfully hooked up to the Internet through the German Research Network (CNNIC 1999). After the student protests in Beijing in 1989, however, the Chinese government imposed strict control over all communication channels with the outside world in an effort to block incoming and outgoing messages about the crackdown on the student protests. As a result, the development of the Internet in China slowed. Although China registered its country domain (.cn) in September 1990, it was not until 1994 that the Ministry of Post and Telecommunications signed an agreement with Sprint, and China connected to the

Internet in a more systematic way (He and Chen 1998).

Throughout the development of the Internet in China, the Chinese government has held an ambivalent attitude toward this revolutionary innovation. On one hand, the government itself uses the Internet to enhance its scientific, technological, and telecommunications development and to make China a member of the international community. It invested considerable amounts of money and manpower in the development of the Internet. The year 1999 was even designated as that of the "government going online." On the other hand, the government fears that the influx of information through the Internet might undermine the rule of the Communist Party.

Those contradictory interests have led to conflicting policies and regulations on the Internet that in return have shaped the network's impact. Politically and culturally, the policies and regulations have been restrictive, aiming to curtail the spread of "deviant" (i.e., undesired by the central government) ideas. Economically, the regulations have been largely liberal and relaxing, designed and implemented to boost the development of a "new economy." As a result, the impact of the Internet on the country's political system has been curtailed and confined to a scale on which a revolution could not easily break out.

The Internet came to China at a time when Communist countries were collapsing in Eastern Europe and the ideology was challenged in China itself. After years of a painstaking experiment with dogmatic and utopian Communism and the devastating Cultural Revolution from 1966 to 1976, the Chinese people gradually lost faith in a grand ideology that had plunged the country into poverty and depression. Ever since the economic reforms in the late 1970s, the Chinese leadership had gradually departed from the Communist ideology. All the cardinal principles of Communism—class struggle, egalitarianism, proletarian dictatorship, and public ownership of property—had been quietly revised or shelved. Almost all the measures of the economic reforms in China, such as privatization, marketization, the concept of "letting some people get rich first," and special economic zones, had been devised to undo an economic system based on the Communist ideology. What the Chinese Communist Party had embarked on in the reform years was actually a reluctant move toward "state capitalism" or "bureaucratic capitalism" (He 2000).

In light of this dramatic change and the prospect of the "end of ideology," politicians and scholars in the West expected that the Internet would eventually bring freedom and democracy to China. President George W. Bush, for example, asserted that the Internet would bring freedom to China, while Secretary of State Colin Powell stated that "the rise of democracy and the power of the information revolution combine to leverage each other" (Kalthil and Boas 2001).

The Internet, however, has not brought freedom and democracy to China—yet. After a short period of confusion and futile efforts to control the Internet, the Chinese government has managed to devise probably the world's most sophisticated and effective reactive and proactive mechanisms to tame the beast of the Internet, ranging from restrictive and punitive policies and regulations to blocking, filtering, and deleting websites and messages, and deploying a large army of Internet police to monitor and control the content in cyberspace.

Nevertheless, the Internet has inflicted a subtle but noticeable political impact on China, which is most ostensible in the role of the Internet as the primary carrier of an emerging virtual universe not defined by government discourse. As Communism has lost its tenets as a genuinely believed ideology and become a ritualized facet of a political system that strives to justify its mandate, there have emerged two distinct discourse universes in China. One is the "official discourse universe," characterized by vagueness, abstractness, ambiguity, and indoctrination, and the other is the "nongovernment-discourse universe," characterized by nonhegemonic expressions ranging from radical nationalism to liberalism, materialism, and extreme cynicism. While the official universe has occupied all the public space of expression, especially the state-controlled mass media, the nongovernment universe survived primarily in the (private) oral sphere (He 2000).

When the Internet was introduced to China, people found a new medium to express their personal (alternative) opinions that could not be aired through the tightly controlled mass media. As the Internet developed into a massive platform of civil expression, it has been turned into the newest form of mass media.

Setting the Agenda

The most discernible impact of the Internet on Chinese politics is arguably in the area of "agenda setting," a function of the mass media that influences what the audience thinks about and how it ranks the salience of important issues. Despite the relatively tight control, the Internet, as a new mass medium on which horizontal and bottom-up communication are possible, has also carried issues initiated at the grassroots to the top of the country's agenda. A good example is the disclosure and publicizing of the outbreak of the SARS (severe acute respiratory syndrome) epidemic by millions of "netizens." In 2003, in southern China's Guangdong Province, a mysterious disease started to spread quietly and rapidly. Threatened by the spread of this fatal and unknown epidemic, health officials reported the incidents to the national authorities, who started to treat the disease as a national secret. An anonymous email reached a journalist at the *Southern Metro* 南方都市报, a popular tabloid in the province, who published the first story on what later became known as SARS. Several news organizations followed suit, but before long, all reporting by local news organizations was censored, and the only coverage that appeared in the official media was cover-up stories by the official Xinhua News Agency 新华通讯社. A large number of messages, however, were posted on the Internet each day by citizens who updated news on the epidemic across the entire country. These messages included statistics and hearsay about the incurable nature of SARS, the sealing off of Beijing, and the imposition of martial law. The extensive "information campaign" by these netizens, together with the spread of the epidemic that directly affected millions of people, pushed this issue to the top of the agenda, first on the Internet, then in the government-controlled mass media, until finally it became an issue of top priority in the entire country.

Agenda-setting functions like this have manifested themselves in several other issues, ranging from natural disasters and accidents (such as the 2011 Wenzhou train crash), civil unrests, and food poisoning to the corruption of local government officials. Although the issues expressed by people on the Internet primarily have been ones that do not directly threaten the fundamental political system, they have leveraged, to a great extent, the monopolized right to build and set the agenda in the country by the government and the government-controlled mass media.

Political Impacts

The Internet has also managed to pressure the government to change some unpopular policies and decisions. This has been possible because the Chinese government has started to transform its administrative system from a control-orientation one to a service-orientation one, along with its departure from socialism to state capitalism in the wake of the collapse of worldwide Communism. Although the transformation is still in the very early stages and remains largely lip service, the Chinese government has set itself up to be responsive to the needs of the governed or to showcase such responsiveness, which has left a little bit of leeway for public opinion to put pressure on political policies and decisions—at least in areas where the fundamental political system is not threatened.

The following two examples are a case in point. One is the so-called Sun Zhigan Incident 孙志刚事件. In 2003, Sun, a college graduate, was detained by Guangzhou police as a "floater" for not carrying his resident ID card, and he was subsequently beaten to death while in custody. The incident was first disclosed by a college student on the Bulletin Board System (BBS) Xisi Hutong 西祠胡同and then picked up by a journalist at the *Southern Metro*, which published a detailed investigative report. During the following days, thousands of postings and comments appeared on the Internet, condemning the brutality in detention camps and challenging the validity of the country's detention system. Benefiting from the circulation and rating boost of an eye-catching story, the mainstream media also joined the exposé campaign. Pressured by this outpouring of public opinion, the State Council had to respond. In the end the Council decided, within three short months, to change the country's fifty-year-old detention system. Although this policy change was induced by several factors, including the government's willingness to yield on some administrative regulations, it was hailed as the first political victory won by the Internet in concert with other media organizations.

A second example is the Xiaman PX Incident 厦门 PX 事件. Xiamen, a coastal city in Fujian Province, is known for its well-protected environment and ranked as one of the top five best cities to live in China. In 2007, some members of the National Political Consultative Conference uncovered that a major chemical plant was being constructed about 16 kilometers from the city center of Xiamen and that the project's potential damages to human health and the environment had not been adequately assessed and disclosed to the public. They filed a bill with the Conference and initiated talks with the authorities, warning that the project, through its emitted pollutants and potential leakages, might devastate or even completely wipe out the city. As their appeal was ignored, the Internet and text messaging were employed to mobilize the masses in what was later called the "defense of Xiamen." Messages about the potential devastation and the city government's persistence in building the lucrative project soon spread among citizens in the city and across the country. BBS groups were formed, and protests were planned—primarily through Internet communication. Defying police interrogations of online activists and warnings of punishment by the government, more than ten thousand Xiamen citizens held a two-day protest on 1–2 June 2007. The pressure exerted by this unprecedented peace rally and the widespread publicity on the Internet finally compelled the city government to stop the construction of the project and move it to another location. In this event, the Internet played not only the role of a public platform but also the role of an advocate and an organizer—a role the government did not wish to see and endorse.

Facilitating Participation

Taking advantage of the "online government project," Chinese citizens have used the Internet to participate in the country's politics both directly and indirectly. Since the implementation of the government online project in the late 1990s, all municipal governments have set up online operations, including email and telephone hotlines to key government officials such as mayors and Party secretaries. Similar hotlines were later established by deputies to the National People's Congress and members of the National Political Consultative Conference. Although those hotlines have served more as a symbolic gesture rather than a substantial problem-solving channel, they have given Chinese citizens both an opportunity to reach politicians they previously could not approach and a way to voice their concerns. There have been occasional reports that citizens' views and concerns communicated through those hotlines have been taken seriously and were responded to by politicians—even though those examples are rare.

In addition to the direct access provided by the Internet, there have emerged numerous BBS groups, blogs, and online communities that are devoted to discussions of public and political issues in China and worldwide. Two noticeable examples are the Qiangguo Forum 强国论坛 and Tianya 天涯社区. The former is established and operated by the *People's Daily* 人民日报, the Communist Party's flagship newspaper, and the latter is run by a commercial company. Protected by the anonymity of cyberspace, where control is not as tight as that of the traditional mass media, Chinese citizens have been able to voice diverse political opinions despite the fact that some of the most subversive comments are still often censored or deleted. Even on the Qiangguo Forum, a large number of messages and postings do not toe the party line and are critical of the government's domestic and particularly foreign policies.

Another way of indirect political participation is the creation, dissemination, and appreciation of satirical political pieces that target the rampant corruption and the incompetent leadership in the country. Such satirical pieces, commonly known as *duànzi* 段子, appeared when the government reluctantly loosened control over so-called deviant ideas expressed through means of interpersonal communication during the economic reforms. They found a mass audience online and became trendy items that were widely exchanged. Those pieces reflect the full spectrum of nonofficial political and moral views. At the extreme end of the spectrum are messages that are politically subversive, at the other end are humor and jokes, and in between are smart pieces that are either politically or morally antagonistic toward the Communist political and moral norms. Extreme or mild, most of the politically satirical pieces are subversive in the sense that they serve as a vehicle for citizens to convey their political dissent and challenge the political line propagated in the state-controlled mass media. The process of creating, disseminating, and reading those pieces functions as one of political self-empowerment, in which everybody can join by creating new pieces, editing existing ones, and passing those pieces around. Although the government has set up computer mechanisms to block messages containing politically sensitive words, Chinese netizens have found ways to overcome such a censorship. For example, names of political leaders and high officials, such as Hu Jintao and Jiang Zemin, are often replaced in satirical messages by alternative misnomers, such as Xiao Hu or Lao Jiang, respectively.

Reducing Ideological Dissonance

In their daily lives, Chinese citizens have to express politically correct ideas or tolerate those ideas propagated by the official mass media and live with them in public gatherings, study groups, and meetings. As those ideas often conflict with their own beliefs, they suffer what social psychology calls "psychological dissonance." According to the US social psychologist Leon Festinger and his cognitive dissonance theory, when people are in a "negative drive state," a situation that forces them to hold two conflicting thoughts or act in opposition to their beliefs, they suffer a psychological conflict. As a result, they are motivated to reduce this dissonance (Festinger 1957; Festinger and Carlsmith 1959). The Internet appears to be the place where many people turn as an avenue to strike an ideological and psychological balance. By using the Internet to express their own political ideas, make fun of political leaders, counter argue the thoughts advocated by the official mass media, or even appreciate nonofficial political opinions that accord with their own, people seek to gratify the need to reduce the conflict between their own political values and the political reality of their everyday lives.

Related to the reduction of psychological dissonance is another concept about people's psychology in political communication: the "spiral of silence" is a process in which people keep silent when they feel that their ideas do not match the dominant norms, especially those presented in the mass media, out of fear of being socially isolated (Noelle-Neumann 1984). The Internet has functioned as a platform for people to speak out rather than be quiet because they feel protected by anonymity and, more important, find collective support in the selective cybercommunities where people of the same mind usually converged. This has reversed the spiral of silence: the more an idea is presented as politically correct (by state-owned official media, for example) the more people speak out against it. Liu Jianming, a communications scholar at Tsinghua University, has observed that such a reversed spiral of silence often occurs when audience members react to an obvious manipulation of public opinion, such as when there is a conflict between ideologies and the official media represents only one—often the ideology that the audience members thinks is problematic—or when they encounter "fabricated consensus" (Liu 2002).

Political Role of the Internet in the Future

As the Chinese society continues to change in the direction of state capitalism and diverse ideas accumulate and expand, the Internet is likely to play an increasingly important role as the "fourth medium," after print, radio, and television, serving as a de facto watchdog outside the domain of the official and tightly controlled mass media. The recent development of news-oriented microblogs, "human flesh searches" (*rénròu sōusuǒ* 人肉搜索, a phenomenon where Internet media is used to identify, research, and expose individuals and organizations) for corrupt government officials, and video sharing on platforms such as Youku (the Chinese version of YouTube), are indicative of the expanding political and discursive role of the Internet. When the succession of the country's top leaders is widely discussed and speculated about on the Internet, when traditionally taboo international issues such as the crash of a North Korean jet fighter in China are first reported by netizens online, and when corrupt officials are exposed and "flesh-searched" on- and offline, the monopoly of expression and thought by the state-run propaganda machine has evidently begun to crumble.

Zhou HE
City University of Hong Kong

See also Communities Online; E-Government; The Great Firewall; Internet Regulation; Internet Governance; Internet in Everyday Life

Further Reading

China Internet Network Information Center (CNNIC). (1999). Major events in the development of Internet in China. Retrieved March 17, 2011, from http://www.cnnic.net.cn/internet/

Festinger, Leon. (1957). *A theory of cognitive dissonance.* Evanston, IL: Row, Peterson.

Festinger, Leon, & Carlsmith, James M. (1959) Cognitive consequences of forced compliance. *Journal of Abnormal and Social Psychology, 58,* 203–211.

He Zhou, & Chen Huailin. (1998). *Chinese media: A new perspective.* Hong Kong: Pacific Century Publisher.

He Zhou. (2000). Chinese Communist Party press in a tug of war: A political economy analysis of the *Shenzhen Special Zone Daily.* In C. C. Lee (Ed.), *Power, money, and media: Communication patterns and bureaucratic control in cultural China* (pp. 112–151). Evanston, IL: Northwestern University Press.

Kalathil, Shanthi, & Boas, Taylor. (2001). The Internet and state control in authoritarian regimes: China, Cuba, and the counterrevolution. *First Monday, 6*(8). Retrieved March 17, 2011, from http://ojphi.org/htbin/cgiwrap/bin/ojs/index.php/fm/article/view/876/785

Kluver, Randolph. (2005). US and Chinese policy expectations of the Internet. *China Information, 19*(2), 299–324.

Liu Jianming. (2002). The reversed spiral of silence among the audience. *Modern Communication, 2.* Retrieved March 17, 2011, from http://okuc.net/Article/HTML/1122.html

Noelle-Neumann, Elisabeth. (1984). *The spiral of silence: Public opinion—our social skin.* Chicago: University of Chicago Press.

Zhu, Jonathan, & He Zhou. (2002). Perceived characteristics, perceived needs, and perceived popularity: Diffusion and use of the Internet in China. *Communication Research, 29*(4), 466–495.

Internet Cafés

Wăngba 网吧

Summary: An Internet café is a place where people can pay to have access to the Internet. Emerging in China in 1996, two years after the opening of the world's first Internet café in London, China's Internet cafés have played a unique role in the country's social transformation process. While promoting the development of the information industry and bridging the digital divide between those with Internet access and those without, Internet cafés have also generated social problems such as online pornography, Internet addiction, and juvenile delinquency.

The term *Internet café* refers to a business that offers computer and Internet access to customers for a fee. It is a relatively new cultural and economic form that results from a combination of new technology and social development. According to the annual CNNIC statistics report, as of December 2012 the number of China's "netizens" had reached 564 million people, with an Internet penetration rate of 41.1 percent, a 3.8 percent increase over 2011 (CNNIC 2013). The development and popularization of the Internet promotes a variety of Internet applications and services, including the diffusion of Internet cafés. Also as of 2012, Internet cafés were the second most popular Internet access point in China, accounting for roughly one-fifth of total online access. The home remains the most popular place by far to go online: roughly nine-tenths of users, according to the 2013 report (CNNIC 2013).

Internet cafés play a special role in Chinese peoples' social lives. On one hand, these cafés benefit society by providing computer and Internet access to those who do not have access at home, thus bridging the "digital divide" between those with easy Internet access and those without, satisfying people's informational and cultural demands, creating industries related to the Internet, and producing enormous financial gains. On the other hand, Internet cafés can also have negative effects on Chinese society, and they can generate various social problems, including online pornography and violence, Internet addiction, and juvenile delinquency.

History

The Internet café evolved from traditional cafés. Early in their history, some coffee shops provided customers with computer and Internet access to help them enjoy their leisure time. This practice became increasingly popular, such that some specialized Internet cafés began to take shape. In 1994, a London coffee shop called Cyberia offered free Internet access to its patrons and became the world's first Internet café. The history of Internet cafés in China is a history of technological development and government regulation; the café's history can be broken into four distinct phases.

1995–1998: Initial Rise

In November 1996, a company named Sparkice (Shíhuàkāi 实华开) opened China's first for-profit Internet café, adjacent to the Capital Stadium in Beijing. The first wave of Internet cafés generally emerged in major cities in China. The customers were usually college professors, students, and foreigners. Because computers were high priced and Internet access not widely available at the time, Internet cafés were relatively small, and the service price was rather high, approximately 20 yuan per hour (roughly US$3 per hour). Along with the decrease of computer prices, the development of the Chinese version of operating systems, and the diffusion of the Internet in medium-sized and small cities, the Internet café industry grew, and the price dropped by roughly half. In this phase, the network equipment was relatively primitive and Internet speeds were slow. People went to the Internet cafés mainly to surf the web for fun. Applications were limited to basic web surfing, email, and chat rooms, and regulation was correspondingly very loose. Neither national rules nor systematic management systems existed for the control of Internet cafés; the local governments regulated Internet cafés at their own discretion.

1999–2002: Rapid Development

Since 1998, the further reduction of Internet access fees and the enhancement of general computer performance contributed to the growth of China's Internet café industry. The popularity of online games, in particular, sped up the diffusion of Internet cafés. Other industries began to penetrate the lucrative Internet café industry. In response, the government began to enact legislation to regulate Internet cafés. The State Council, for instance, issued the "Measures on the Administration of Business Sites of Internet Access Services" in April 2001, which defined Internet cafés as business sites of Internet access services. This regulation stipulated many rules that set up the standards for Internet café management in China, including the conditions of establishment, the procedures of application, the obligations of the operators, the restrictions of the business, and the relevant sanctions and penalties for various violations. This regulation marked the formation of China's Internet café policy.

2003–2004: Restriction and Adjustment

In June 2002, a fire at an Internet café in Beijing called Blue Express (Lánjísù 蓝急速) killed twenty-five people and injured thirteen. This was followed by an accident in Chongqing, a large city in southwestern China, in which a middle school student was crushed to death by a train while he was sleeping on the track after excessive Internet use at an Internet café had left him exhausted. Such accidents triggered harsh public criticism against the poor management of Internet cafés. A number of social issues, such as social security risks, minors' Internet addiction, and the public health crisis during the SARS (severe acute respiratory syndrome) epidemic, were all directly related to Internet cafés. (The authorities shut down many Internet cafés during the SARS epidemic because they were popular public venues, not necessarily because of online rumor mongering, although that may have played a part.) Consequently, the authorities were forced to strengthen their control systems and to introduce a series of new policies to enhance the scale and efficiency of Internet café regulation. Many illegal Internet cafés were shut down, and many small Internet cafés were eliminated because of outdated hardware facilities that did not survive the ever-changing market. The overall number of Internet cafés reached a stable level as a result of this adjustment process, with new cafés replacing those that had become outmoded.

2005 to the Present: Slow but Orderly

By 2005, there were 130,000 registered Internet cafés, and an average number of 40 million daily Internet café customers. The Internet café industry yielded an annual production value of 25.68 billion yuan (US$4.13 billion) and generated about 1 million jobs. Statistics indicate that the government and the public began to stress the importance and positive impacts of Internet cafés. Under the increasingly stringent government regulations and monitoring in place (such as the "Great Firewall of China," part of the greater Golden Shield project; see the article "The Great Firewall" for more on this topic), the Internet café industry gradually standardized its business practices. The image of Internet cafés, in turn, improved significantly.

The Internet Café Industry

According to data released by the Ministry of Culture in 2010, the production value of the Chinese Internet café industry had reached 88.6 billion yuan (US$14.7 billion) by that time. The Internet café industry promoted the development of the entire information technology industry chain, including telecommunications, personal computers, video games, digital content and information services industries.

After more than a decade of development, the Internet café industry in China had formed a complete industry chain, consisting of (1) telecommunication operators who provide Internet access, (2) system integrators who build the network systems, (3) hardware suppliers who provide hardware facilities including computers, servers, and storage devices, and (4) software suppliers who provide operating systems, user application software, and management as well as maintenance software.

The dominant management model of the industry is the Internet café chain. The primary goal of the café industry is to promote the expansion of chain-store operations (to facilitate the conglomeration of the business) and to establish the leading role of Internet café chains in the industry.

At a meeting on the management of Internet cafés on 11 January 2011, the Deputy Minister of Culture asserted that China will make great efforts to promote Internet café chains and to gradually shut down isolated Internet cafés over the next five years, with the overall number unchanged. Since the government's encouragement of chain-store operations in 2003, Internet café chains developed in terms of size, number, and standardized management. By 2009, there were more than 150 Internet café chains, with more than 4,500 chain stores in the country. The further development of Internet café chains, however, faces two major challenges.

First, the lack of reliable funding is a bottleneck to continuing growth. Because supportive government policies are not always stable, taxes are relatively high, and the industry's profit margin is shrinking, it is difficult for the Internet café industry to attract strong investments. Capital comes mainly from small- and medium-sized private enterprises. The entrepreneurs at this level usually lack long-term planning, strategic innovation, and advanced management systems, which weakens the competitiveness of individual Internet cafés in the market.

Second, Internet café chains are still limited to the traditional business model, based on hourly Internet access fees. The lack of new business models and value-added services significantly hinders the profit of the industry. In addition, the lack of a successful franchise system also makes the chain model just a theoretical possibility rather than a real working model that contributes to the industry's overall revenue.

Bridging the Rural-Urban Digital Divide

There is a great digital divide between the rural and urban areas in China. The term *digital divide* was originally defined as a gap between those who have access to digital technologies, particularly the Internet, and those who do not. As in other societies, geography is one of the significant factors that contribute to the digital divide in China. Due to the lower disposable income, lower educational level, and inferior information infrastructure, rural residents have far lower Internet access rates than do urban dwellers, although that is slowly changing. According to the China Internet Network Information Center (CNNIC), by June of 2012, rural Internet users had reached 156 million (up from 115 million in 2010), accounting for 27 percent of all Chinese Internet users, a percentage that had not changed much since 2010. Internet users in Beijing and Shanghai, in contrast, represented roughly 70 percent of netizens as of 2012 (CNNIC 2011, 2013).

The diffusion of Internet cafés in rural China helped bridge the rural-urban digital divide. An Internet café is an ideal site where those who do not have Internet access at home can connect to the Internet at a reasonable price. Even for those who do have Internet access at home, Internet cafés are often preferable in that usually they are equipped with more advanced hardware and software and often have higher Internet speeds than do rural households. Consequently, over half of rural Internet users access the Internet from Internet cafés, which is roughly 16 percent higher than urban users.

As rural residents' information and entertainment needs increase, the Internet café industry grows at a remarkable speed. It not only generates new markets and lucrative business but also facilitates the dissemination of information across Chinese society. Before the new information and communication technologies (ICTs) become widely diffused in rural China, Internet cafés will serve as an important instrument to narrow the technological gap and to make up the deficiency of public resources through the market.

Despite the overall positive impacts of Internet cafés in rural China, there are a few social problems to be addressed. First, more minors frequent rural Internet cafés than is the case in urban cafés. According to the 2009 China Youth Internet Behavior Survey by CNNIC, nearly 18 million rural minors went to Internet cafés at that time, accounting for over 60 percent of underage rural Internet users. Second, there are more illegal Internet cafés in rural areas. As this industry is still lucrative, particularly in rural China, many investors circumvented the complicated licensing procedures and related regulations to maximize their profit. Such underground Internet cafés, or locally called "black Internet cafés," caused unfair competition with legal Internet cafés and disturbed the order of the industry.

Internet Cafés and Adolescents

Adolescents constitute the number-one age group of Internet users in China. By the end of December 2009, the survey showed that the number of China's adolescent Internet users had reached 195 million, accounting for just over half of the total number of Internet users at that time (CNNIC 2010).

For teenagers, an Internet café is a social space with multiple social functions. It is not only a place of entertainment and social interaction but a sphere where teens can experience emotional and social satisfaction of various kinds. Nevertheless, the negative role Internet cafés play in adolescents' lives has received more attention. The most striking issues include Internet addiction cyber pornography and violence, and social security.

Internet Addiction

Internet addiction refers to excessive Internet use that interferes with daily life. This term was originally (jokingly) proposed as a disorder by psychologist Ivan Goldberg of the United States in 1995. It was then developed by US psychologist Kimberly Young, the director of the Center for Internet Addiction Recovery, in her seminal 1998 book *Caught in the Net: How to Recognize the Signs of Internet Addiction—and a Winning Strategy for Recovery.* In China, Internet cafés have played a significant role in exacerbating teenagers' Internet addiction. According to a CNNIC report, nearly half of the adolescents who are Internet addicts prefer Internet cafés as venues for playing video games. In contrast, those who are not addicts are more likely to play games at home. In addition to video game addiction, another disorder among Chinese adolescent Internet users is social networking addiction, which refers to the overuse of social networking applications, such as chat rooms, instant messaging, microblogs, and social networking sites.

Cyber Pornography and Violence

As cyber pornography is one of the most lucrative businesses on the Internet, it is also widespread in China's cyberspace even under the intensive government policing that exists. Because teenagers' consumption of online pornography is often interfered with at home by their parents, they prefer Internet cafés for such content, under the assumption that many Internet cafés normally do not restrict what people do online as long as the café makes money. And because teenagers are at a special stage in their physiological and psychological development, they feel particularly curious about sexual content (online or otherwise) yet are poorly prepared for resisting the potentially negative effects of online pornography. Moreover, pornography is increasingly integrated with violence in the Chinese online game sphere. More and more violent video games are full of explicit sexual content, which is particularly provocative to teenagers. Heavy exposure to online pornography and violence and the influence from other players in the Internet café may produce significant effects on a teenager's sexual cognition, attitude, and behavior.

Social Security

The diffusion of Internet cafés in China has brought about several social security issues. First, Internet cafés run the risk of becoming hotbeds of juvenile crime. Some of the common crimes that occur at Internet cafés include robbery, theft, intentional injury, fraud, and rape. Second, some Internet cafés may have fire hazards, especially the ones set up more haphazardly that did not hire professionals to install the required safety equipment or undergo the proper fire risk assessment with the fire department. Many factors specific to Internet cafés, such as densely packed computer equipment, tangles of crossed cables, and poorly labeled emergency exits, may lead to a fire disaster. Third, Internet cafés may generate public health problems. As some Internet cafés have poor ventilation, there are risks of causing infections. During the SARS (severe acute respiratory syndrome) epidemic in 2003, the State Council shut down many Internet cafés as a precaution against further contagion.

Future Trends

The booming Internet café industry in China is a product of the social transition from industrialization to so-called informationization, or the diffusion of information technologies across society in order to promote a more knowledge-based economy. As this transition process continues and the diffusion rate of ICT increases, the role of Internet cafés in Chinese peoples' daily lives is expected to become weaker. Although Internet cafés remain the second most important Internet access point in China, the rates of access at home, work, and public facilities increase more rapidly than that of Internet cafés.

The future development of Internet cafés in China will likely reflect the following trends. First, the government will reinforce the existing regulation of Internet cafés to protect minors against negative impacts, to improve social security, and to maintain the order of the industry. Second, chain-store operations will take the lead in the Internet café industry and will dominate the market. Third, video games will become the central business of Internet cafés. Fourth, other value-added services, such as Internet Protocol (IP) phone services, photo and document printing services, and food and beverage services will be integrated into cafés' business models. Fifth, and most importantly, the Internet café is a transitional business that will eventually fade away. When Internet access becomes as widely available as television, and when people have multiple devices, particularly handheld devices, to go online, Internet cafés will either disappear or evolve to other lines of business, much as older, leading technology companies such as IBM have had to evolve in order to keep up with the ever-changing modern world.

Lu WEI and Wen CHEN
Zhejiang University

See also Children Online; Digital Divides; Internet Addiction; Internet in Everyday Life; Telecommunications Industry

Further Reading

China Internet Network Information Center (CNNIC). (2009). Internet development survey in rural China. Retrieved January 10, 2011, from http://www.cnnic.net.cn/uploadfiles/pdf/2009/4/13/172038.pdf

China Internet Network Information Center (CNNIC). (2010). 2009 China youth Internet behavior survey. Retrieved January 10, 2011, from http://research.cnnic.cn/html/1272258870d2105.html

China Internet Network Information Center (CNNIC). (2011). China Internet development statistics report. Retrieved February 5, 2011, from http://research.cnnic.cn/img/h000/h12/attach201101211723380.pdf

China Internet Network Information Center (CNNIC). (2013, January). Statistical report on Internet development in China. Retrieved April, 15, 2013, from http://www1.cnnic.cn/IDR/Report-Downloads/201302/P020130312536825920279.pdf

China Youth Internet Association & Survey and Statistics Institute at Communication University of China. (2010). 2009 Youth Internet addiction survey [in Chinese]. Retrieved January 10, 2011, from http://mat1.gtimg.com/edu/pdf/wangyinbaogao.pdf

Endeshaw, A. (2004). Internet regulation in China: The never-ending cat and mouse game. *Information & Communications Technology Law, 13*(1), 41–57.

Hong Junhao, & Huang Li. (2005). A split and swaying approach to building information society: The case of Internet cafes in China. *Telematics and Informatics, 22*(4), 377–393.

Liang Bin, & Lu Hong. (2010). Internet development, censorship, and cyber crimes in China. *Journal of Contemporary Criminal Justice, 26*(1), 103–120.

Liu, Fengshu. (2009). It is not merely about life on the screen: Urban Chinese youth and the Internet café. *Journal of Youth Studies, 12*(2), 167–184.

Ministry of Culture. (2010). *2009 Annual report of China Internet cafés market* [in Chinese.] Retrieved January 10, 2011, from http://game.people.com.cn/GB/48604/48623/11816909.html

Qiu, Jack Linchuan, & Zhou Liuning. (2005). Through the prism of the Internet cafe: Managing access in an ecology of games. *China Information, 19*(2), 261–297.

Zhang Mingxin, & Wei Lu. (2009). Knowledge, attitude, and home Internet adoption in rural China: A case of Hubei. *China Media Research, 5*(4), 1–12.

Internet Events

Wǎngluò shìjiàn 网络事件

Summary: Large numbers of people in China participate in online efforts to express their sentiments and opinions, address collective needs, or influence public opinion and policy. In an authoritarian country with over 500 million Internet users and over 300 million microbloggers, Internet events occur often and have the potential to rally public opinion, pressure government, and reshape China's public life. The Chinese government also tries to shape public opinion using the same tools.

Internet events are public events where large numbers of "netizens" participate in often unorganized, autonomous online efforts to express their sentiments and opinions, address collective needs, or influence public opinion and policy. The popularity of Internet events, otherwise known as new media events, online public incidents, or online collective incidents in China, has grown considerably over the last decade, a growth that parallels the rise of online public opinion and the surge of Internet users in China.

In an authoritarian country of 564 million Internet users and 331 million microbloggers (CNNIC 2013), Internet events occur often as netizens seek alternative sources of information, channels of expression, and means of mobilization. The case of Sun Zhigang in 2003 symbolizes for many the power of Chinese public opinion, as hundreds of thousands of netizens reacted to the death of the twenty-seven-year-old in police custody, detained for failing to carry proper identification papers. Online fury and sympathy eventually resulted in the abolition of the "custody and repatriation" system.

Although few Internet events have produced victorious institutional changes as did the Sun Zhigang case, they have left indelible marks on public consciousness and remained part of the collective public memory. In fact, Internet events are such an indispensable component of the Chinese Internet that the government and web companies have polled netizens on the most influential events to gauge public opinion. One such poll, conducted jointly by fifteen influential Chinese mainstream Internet companies, attracted more than 90 million netizen votes, publicizing the notorious

"Eluding the Cat" incident. (This was an incident in 2009 in which a twenty-four-year-old named Li Qiaoming died in police custody in Yunnan Province; the local officials' absurd explanation for his death was that Li had died while participating in a game of hide and seek, or "eluding the cat," with fellow inmates.) Eventually, the Yunnan publicity department had to invite media and netizen representatives to participate in the investigation to diffuse public anger (Branigan 2009).

Who: Netizens as New Broadcasters and Agenda Setters

Historically, media events have been conceived of as live broadcasts of momentous events by mass media organizations that have a profound impact on audience experiences and knowledge (Dayan and Katz 1992). With the ever-expanding use of the Internet and mobile devices, however, the means of reporting on and producing new media events and reshaping public life are increasingly in the hands of common people.

Chinese netizens actively participate in the consumption, sharing, and production of Internet events as state-dominated mainstream media often fail to cover certain events for fear of triggering public anger and social unrest. In particular, a small number of citizen journalists have taken upon themselves the task of collecting and distributing news of public interest. Zola (the nickname of prominent Chinese citizen journalist Zhou Shuguang), for instance, became known for his online coverage of the "coolest nail house" story that exposed the plight of two Sichuan homeowners in defiance of wealthy developers. (A "nail house" is a term coined by developers to refer to stubborn homeowners who refuse to let their homes be demolished to make way for development projects.) Besides the growth of citizen journalism that uncovers and amplifies public voices, many Chinese journalists who work for state media now blog, under real or false names, have managed to publish stories otherwise censored by official news outlets (MacKinnon 2008).

Joining these watchdogs and muckrakers are hundreds of millions of Chinese netizens who actively seek information and post commentaries. Many Chinese netizens frequently post comments via such popular online venues as Sina Weibo (popular Chinese microblogging site) and Weixin (popular group messaging platform developed by Chinese Internet giant Tencent), making Chinese Internet a space of growing cacophony where controversial issues can rise to the top and become prominent Internet events (Hu 2008). The State Online Public Opinion Monitor Office reported that in 2008 and 2009, twenty-three out of seventy-seven influential Chinese events emerged from online to garner public attention. Among these, information and discussions about natural disasters, public health, economy, governance, and legal cases were widely shared by netizens through news commentary, online bulletin boards, and personal blogs. The political scientists Tong Yanqi and Lei Shaohua's paper "Creating Public Opinion Pressure in China: Large-scale Internet Protest, (2010) provides a brief overview of twenty-four large-scale events that made the rounds on the Chinese Internet between 2003 and 2009.

What: Types of Issues

Chinese Internet events cover a wide range of issues. The media sociologist Guobin Yang divides such events into seven major categories: (1) popular nationalism, (2) rights defense, (3) corruption and power abuse, (4) environment, (5) cultural contention, (6) muckraking (i.e., publicizing scandalous behavior by people), and (7) online charity (Yang 2009). Further, rights defense issues often involve vulnerable persons, homeowners, and forced relocation. In a similar manner, other researchers have identified four major types of issues: nationalism, rights defense, morals and privacy, and abuse of power (Qiu and Chen 2009). A great deal of overlapping exists between different types. For instance, rights defense cases are often intertwined with power abuse, as in the aforementioned Sun Zhigang case.

Although many Internet events are contentious, others do not have any apparent reference to conflict or power struggle. For example, "Jia Junpeng, your mother wants you to go home to eat" is a post left at Baidu Post Bar, a popular online forum affiliated with China's search giant Baidu, in its *World of Warcraft* online game section in 2009. It became an instant hit, attracting almost 400,000 views and 17,000 comments within six hours. Anonymous and nonsensical, the post channeled gamers' frustrations toward web portal Netease's delay in resuming its gaming service. It also ignited an online carnival for individual gamers, who, from their isolated dwellings, collectively reminisced about their childhood pastimes spent with their playmates on street corners close to their homes. Many other types of Internet events center instead on such issues as pornography, extramarital affairs, and plagiarism that convey netizens' yearnings for morals and values in a fast-changing Chinese society.

Overall, Chinese Internet events reflect an overwhelming public concern over rights defense and power abuse. For instance, among the ten most popular Internet events in 2009, eight directly questioned authority and evoked sympathy for the underprivileged. Rights defense has also moved from a focus on the individual to the collective. Online public opinion, for example, vehemently defended Deng Yujiao, a young waitress who stabbed and killed a local official who had approached her for sexual favors. Intense public pressure kept Deng from a lengthy prison term.

In another case, public pressure helped force Beijing to halt its plan in 2009 to preinstall Green Dam Youth Escort software on all new computers sold in China. The software was touted by the government to filter pornographic websites harmful to minors on individual computers, but was found to also monitor individual users, filter a wide range of content including religious and "sensitive" political materials and threaten the security of individual computers (BBC 2009).

Why: The Causes of Internet Events

Despite the variety of issue types, the causes of Internet events, most believe, can be located in offline public sentiments, concerns, and demands. As an amplifier, not a mere reflection, of the hopes and fears in our society, the Internet mediates the real and the virtual, reinforcing existing relationships and institutions (Agre 2002). If the previous analysis of issue types such as rights defense and clashing moral values is indicative of the specific kinds of reasons that trigger various Internet events, one can uncover deeper societal roots of these events when viewing them collectively.

Chinese Internet events differ from those in other societies partially because the social forces that bring them about are distinctive. The Chinese scholar Yu Jianrong (2010 observes that contemporary Chinese society is characterized by social fracture and a deep resentment of the rich and powerful as it transitions from a socialist economy to one dominated by crony capitalism. This social chasm is intricately related to society-wide structural problems such as a widening income gap, unequal distribution of resources, and rampant corruption, as well as changing morals, values, and ethics. Specific social issues like land seizure (as in the cases of "nail houses"), forced relocation, pollution, legal injustice, and restructuring of state-owned enterprises, when handled inappropriately, may trigger social confrontations that sometimes take on more destructive forms like social venting and riots (Yu 2009). Previously private domains such as family, sexuality, and marriage also start to assume a carnivalesque quality when making their way online.

Public participation in environmental protection, for example, was seen as pivotal in halting and relocating the construction of a controversial petrochemical project worth $1.6 billion near Xiamen, Fujian Province, in 2007. Informed by both traditional and online media, particularly short message service (SMS), over ten thousand residents marched peacefully through the city, or "took a stroll" as locals prefer to call it, to protest the project as being hazardous to public health and the environment. On the other hand, public curiosity and voyeurism made the "Sexy Photo Gate Scandal," involving the online leakage and spread of nude photos of Hong Kong pop star Edison Chen and his girlfriends, the biggest Internet sensation of 2008 (Song 2008).

Where: Internet Events Both Virtual and Real

Although most agree that Internet events are driven by what happens offline, there is little agreement on how to differentiate the deeply intertwined real and virtual aspects of such events in order to determine the role played by the web. Three types of Internet events can be discerned based on how the real and virtual worlds interact: (1) events that take place online only, (2) offline events amplified by the Internet, and (3) a hybrid of the first two.

While some events remain solely in the virtual space (e.g., the Jia Junpeng case), others are amplified by the Internet. For instance, the sudden collapse of a shoddily built condominium building in Shanghai in 2009 attracted the public's scrutiny. As dramatic pictures of the debris were widely circulated and amplified online, netizens started to rigorously debate hot-button issues such as housing markets, building quality, and public safety. The third hybrid event type was previously less common. An incident must be instantly amplified through the Internet as it unfolds. But the arrival of mobile microblogging and photo sharing has made it more likely to occur. Speaking at a public lecture at Peking University in June 2010, the propaganda official Li Baozhu proudly announced that "with a wave of my hand, tens of millions of posts about the Deng Yujiao incident were all deleted" (China Digital Times 2010). The comment, accompanied by live pictures, was quickly circulated via microblogging before being taken down by commercial portals soon afterward. With deeper integration of the mobile web into people's everyday life, Chinese netizens are more likely to document and magnify anything they find provocative, scandalous, and intriguing.

How: The Mobilization of Internet Events

Regardless of where an event occurs first, online or offline, an Internet event gains momentum through various means of mobilization, including resources, discourses, and emotions. Resources utilized in social activism increasingly include cheaper and more ubiquitous information and communication technologies (ICTs). It is well recognized that ICTs such as mobile phones and social networks could help lower the barrier to participation in online activities, facilitate group formation, and increase the speed of collective action (Shirky 2008). Less optimistic observers (e.g., Goldsmith and Wu 2006; Morozov 2009b) think that the more resourceful government and business institutions, which have been strengthened by the same technologies, could produce more bane than boon. Authoritarian states like China, and increasingly nominally more democratic countries, have marshaled technological, legal, and social resources to control, filter, and suppress, if necessary, Internet events or activities deemed harmful by authorities. The well-known Great Firewall of China is the epitome of state resource mobilization.

It would be inaccurate, however, to cast the mobilization of Internet events in direct opposition to the authoritarian state. An examination of Internet events discourse will quickly reveal that some events support the state out of popular nationalism (for example the anti-CNN movement in response to what was seen as the Western media's biased coverage of unrest in Tibet and the Beijing Olympics in 2008). Many others are directed at specific individuals and local governments instead of the state. The Chinese government is taking an increasingly active role in guiding, shaping, and producing online public opinion to increase its legitimacy in a process known as "authoritarian deliberation" (Jiang 2010a). The allowance of limited, yet expanding, spaces of public discourse, contrary to popular belief in the West, can be regime-supporting rather than regime-threatening. Such flexible tactics serve as safety valves to release social tension and to control government excesses, part and parcel of the "resilient authoritarianism" (Nathan 2003) employed by the state to adjust its relationship to society.

Although the swelling of public participation via online authoritarian deliberation may be read as a positive sign, the employment of web commentators to shape public opinion in favor of the state on popular news websites and online bulletin boards—propaganda, to state it baldly—is troubling. Such guided manufacturing of public opinion, unlike the practice of "astroturfing" (i.e., masking the source of sponsorship) often employed by Western politicians, severely undercuts the democratic potential of the Internet. The creation of online spin doctors thus adds a layer of sophistication to the existing repertoire of government offline and online regulation of the web, a repertoire that previously had been limited to physical manipulation of information gateways, filtering, regulation of Internet service providers, Internet policing, and disciplining of Internet cafés (Deibert et al. 2010).

Given the state's active role in shaping public perception of Internet events, "frame analysis," the definition and construction of a public issue or controversy, is key in revealing how the parties involved in an Internet event mobilize through "contentious conversations" to define and frame the issues in question. The Deng Yujiao case acutely demonstrated, for instance, how Deng was not viewed by the public as a murderer, but as a powerless woman confronting an immoral official seeking sexual favors.

Such framing, however, would be ineffective if not for the emotional mobilization of netizens through joy, anger, sadness, sympathy, parody, and humor (Yang 2009). Nor would it be possible without a growing netizen culture of participation often swayed by the ebbs and flows of these emotions. Traditional means of mobilization, through rational discussion and persuasion, may sometimes have limited utility in online events, whereas the employment of human emotions can be more engaging and compelling. Moreover, emotions can be gained and spent monetarily. Emotions matter not only to netizens but also to commercial websites that profit from online traffic and attention. Emotions, as a part of fundamental human expressions, thus should not be dismissed as purely irrational, biased, or even dangerous in order to have public emotions monitored, managed, and contained.

Outlook for Future Events

The popularity of Internet events in China is attributable, at least partially, to the unprecedented growth of Internet use in China that gives netizens the tools and space to engage in information exchange, online discourse, and collective actions. Netizens participate in setting the agenda on a wide range of issues to reshape public life via online and offline channels. The Internet, while amplifying public voices in an age of sociopolitical transformation in China, has also strengthened the state's monitoring, filtering, and regulatory capabilities. More fundamentally, the Chinese state arguably has been successful in gaining popular compliance and cementing its political rule, despite grassroots challenges, by building and promoting state legitimacy through economy, nationalism, ideology, culture, and governance (Jiang 2010b). The complexity of Internet events thus cannot be reduced to a simple zero-sum game between the state and the individual or between the state and an emergent civil society. The mosaic composition and dynamics of Chinese society defy such simple dichotomies.

Instead, the impact of such events on individuals and Chinese society at large is far from clear or straightforward. Of the various topics swarming through the Chinese Internet, very few actually rise to visibility and create powerful social impact, let alone instigate institutional change (Wang and Fang 2009). Online discussions on a given public issue rarely sustain over time, partially because they hardly produce immediate, palpable change in public institutions or decision making. Regular exposure to increasingly dramatic Internet events in the public space may even create emotional fatigue on the part of spectators and participants alike. Public responses to such events are worth exploring in the future.

Despite being sporadic and often inconsequential, Internet events may be exerting an incremental yet profound influence on the individual psyche and social mentality over time. For instance, how do Chinese netizens react to Internet events, particularly the ones demanding social and institutional change? How do their attitudes evolve? Do they choose to participate in public affairs? In what ways? On the other hand, how do Chinese cyber-activists and their communities evolve? How do they mobilize their resources, sustain their activities, negotiate with government institutions, and engage average netizens? The consequences of Internet events and cyber-activism in China need to be studied in greater depth and at greater length.

In addition, government responses to the regular occurrence of Internet events also deserve our attention. Viewed by Chinese authorities as something more than conduits of public sentiments, demands, and opinions, Internet events are increasingly seen by the authorities as unstable, dangerous, and rupture prone, and thus in need of being monitored, contained, and diffused (Zhu 2009). Since 2010, there was not only the mobilization of government resources to minimize the "damaging" effect of Internet events but also a growing bureaucratic consensus that favors tighter Internet control. In the near future, a fundamental challenge facing the Chinese government in adjusting its relationship to various social groups and strata is to find ways to build more effective channels for the public to meaningfully participate in local and national affairs and to address the underlying structural issues of governance.

Min JIANG
University of North Carolina–Charlotte

See also Blogging; Communities Online; Microblogging; Internet Monitoring; Social and Political Impact

Further Reading

Agre, Philip E. (2002). Real-time politics: The Internet and the political process. *The Information Society, 18*(5), 311–331.

BBC. (2009). Anger in China over web censorship. Retrieved June 30, 2009, from http://news.bbc.co.uk/2/hi/technology/8124735.stm

Bandurski, David. (2008). China's guerrilla war for the web. *Far Eastern Economic Review*. Retrieved December 20, 2008, from http://www.feer.com/essays/2008/august/chinas-guerrilla-war-for-the-web

Branigan, Tania. (2009). Chinese internet users asked to help investigate suspicious death in custody. *The Guardian*. Retrieved May 29, 2010 from http://www.guardian.co.uk/world/2009/feb/20/china-internet-death-custody

China Digital Times. (2010). Li Baozhu: Deleting Internet posts with a wave of his hand. Retrieved June 22, 2010, from http://is.gd/d2CsZ

China Internet Network Information Center (CNNIC). (2013, July). The 32nd statistical report on Internet development in China. Retrieved August, 10, 2013, from http://www.cnnic.cn/hlwfzyj/hlwxzbg/hlwtjbg/201307/P020130717505343100851.pdf

Dayan, Daniel, & Katz, Elihu. (1992). *Media events: The live broadcasting of history*. Cambridge, MA: Harvard University Press.

Deibert, Ronald; Palfrey, John; Rohozinski, Rafal; & Zittrain, Jonathan. (2010). *Access controlled*. Cambridge, MA: MIT Press.

Goldsmith, Jack, & Wu, Tim. (2006). *Who controls the Internet? Illusions of a borderless world*. New York: Oxford University Press.

Hu Yong. (2008). Zhongsheng xuanhua: Wangluo shidaide geren biaoda yu gonggong taolun [Rising cacophony: Individual expressions and public discussions in the age of the Internet]. Guiling, China: Guangxi Normal University Press.

Jasper, James. (1998). The emotions of protest: Reactive and affective emotions in and around social movements. *Sociological Forum, 13*, 397–424.

Jiang Min. (2010a). Authoritarian deliberation on Chinese Internet. *Electronic Journal of Communication, 20* (3&4).

Jiang Min. (2010b). Authoritarian informationalism: China's approach to Internet sovereignty. *SAIS Review of International Affairs, 30*(2), 71–89.

MacKinnon, Rebecca. (2008). Blogs and China correspondence: Lessons about global information flow. *Chinese Journal of Communication, 1*(2), 242–257.

Morozov, Evgeny. (2009a, July 15). The Spinternet goes global: The Nigerian chapter. Foreign Policy. Retrieved December 20, 2009, from http://neteffect.foreignpolicy.com/posts/2009/07/15/the_spinternet_goes_global_the_nigerian_chapter

Morozov, Evgeny. (2009b, November 18). How dictators watch us on the web. *Prospect*. Retrieved December 20, 2009, from http://www.prospectmagazine.co.uk/2009/11/how-dictators-watch-us-on-the-web/

Nathan, Andrew J. (2003). Authoritarian resilience. *Journal of Democracy, 14*(1), 6–17.

People's Daily (2010a). 2009 nian shida wangluo shijian pingxuan chulu: Duomaomao jushou [Top 10 Internet incidents of 2009: Eluding the cat tops the chart]. Retrieved January 5, 2010, from http://bbs1.people.com.cn/postDetail.do?boardId=1&treeView=1&view=2&id=96630400

People's Daily (2010b). Renminwang tuichu "08-09 nian tufa gonggong shijian anliku": Huiji liangnian yuqing redian, fenxi zhengfu yingdui deshi [People's Daily Online publishes case studies of 2008–2009 public emergencies: Collect hot button issues in two years, analyze the pros and cons of government responses]. Retrieved June 2, 2010, from http://politics.people.com.cn/GB/1026/11697703.html

Qiu, L. & Chen, W. (2009). Maixiang xinmeiti shijian yanjiu [Toward new media events research]. *Chinese Journal of Communication and Society, 9*, 30–38.

Shirky, Clay. (2008). *Here comes everybody: The power of organizing without organizations*. New York: Penguin Press.

Song, R. (2008). Sexy photo gate. Retrieved September 9, 2009, from http://www.zonaeuropa.com/20080209_1.htm

State Council Information Office of the People's Republic of China (SCIO). (2010). The Internet in China. Retrieved June 9, 2010, from http://china.org.cn/government/whitepaper/node_7093508.htm

Tong Yanqi, & Lei Shaohua. (2010). Creating public opinion pressure in China: Large-scale Internet protest. National University of Singapore, East Asian Institute, EAI Background Brief No. 534. Retrieved June 15, 2011, from http://www.eai.nus.edu.sg/BB534.pdf

Wang, C., & Fang Kecheng. (2009). Buying gaogu wangluo yanlun: Jiyu 122 ge wangluo yiti de shizheng fenxi [Online discourse should not be overestimated: An empirical study of 122 online issues]. *Guoji Xinwenjie [Journal of International Communication], 2009*(5), 98–102.

XinhuaNet. (2010, December 31). 450 million Chinese use Internet. Xinhuanet.com. Retrieved January 8, 2011, from http://news.xinhuanet.com/english2010/china/2010-12/31/c_13671684.htm

Yang Guobin. (2009). *The power of the Internet in China*. New York: Columbia University Press.

Yu Jianrong. (2010). Maintaining a baseline of social stability: Speech before the Beijing Lawyers Association [in Chinese]. Retrieved February 27, 2010, from http://new.21ccom.net/plus/view.php?aid=6390

Zhu, H. (2009). Gei difang zhengfu yingdui wangluo yulun de 10 tiao jianyi [10 recommendations for local governments on handling public opinion]. Retrieved December 18, 2009, from http://yq.people.com.cn/htmlArt/Art335.htm

Internet in Everyday Life

Rìcháng shēnghuó zhōng de hùliánwǎng
日常生活中的互联网

Summary: In the short time of its existence, the Internet has become an integral part of the everyday life of large numbers of people in China. Bloggers, microbloggers, and other users participate in every kind of online activity, serious and frivolous alike, from political activism to multiplayer gaming to music and film downloading to the making of spoof films. The diffusion of this technology has spawned debates on governance, commerce, education, social security, and ethnic relations, among many other topics.

The Internet has become an integral part of the everyday lives of ordinary Chinese people. "Everyday life" means different things to different people in their experiences with the Internet: for information and communication technology (ICT) entrepreneurs, it means an expanding terrain of technological and business innovation and growth; for white-collar office workers, it means compiling, sharing, and spreading information more efficiently and cheaply; for the "information have-less" (including migrant workers, retirees, students, and the unemployed), it means cross-regional, cross-generational, and cross-class connectivity and mobility.

Furthermore, the Internet, together with mobile phones, newspapers, magazines, television, and radio, is a large part of one's everyday experience with media and communication systems. The migration of the Internet from research laboratories to the homes of the average person over the past quarter century or so has had a huge impact on how people live their lives. The process of "mobile privatization"—a term proposed by the Welsh cultural critic Raymond Williams (1974, 26) to describe the privatization or domestication of screen media (television) and mobility afforded by technologies such as the automobile in the United Kingdom of the 1960s and 1970s—has also been experienced by the emerging middle class, clustered in urban China, with the expansion of Chinese television and the automobile industry. This process has been further intensified by the introduction and proliferation of mobile communication technologies since the mid-1990s.

The term "privatized mobility," proposed by the US popular culture scholar Lynn Spigel (2001, 71) in her analysis of ads for portable television sets in the United States, has informed much of the thinking of small-screen technologies and their impacts on one's experience with the Internet in everyday life. Both these terms—mobile privatization and privatized mobility—are informative but seem insufficient to describe the trans-spatial-temporal and hyper-public (yet at the same time private) nature of contemporary experiences with the Internet in our everyday lives.

Transformations, for Better or Worse

There is no doubt that the Internet has transformed everyday life in China. Some people invoke the transformation in an enthusiastic and celebratory tone, focusing on the uptakes in media marketization and globalization and their democratic potentials. The notion of the active consumer or "prosumer" (a combination of "producer" and "consumer") generates discussions of power and empowerment, identity and citizenship, civil society, and digital democracy.

Others invoke the moral and ideological panic of the Chinese Internet by focusing on China's media and Internet censorship, on the ominous implications of Internet addiction and stalking (particularly among young people and children), or legal issues common to the "darknet" era, a term referring to the copyright no-man's-land that is much of the material found on the Internet. Still others voice guided optimism about the Internet's diffusion in China; the drive to make profits from the digital economy goes hand in hand with the demand to be politically responsible (to the state and its agenda), and the drive and demand are contingent on the user's desire for fun, expression, networking, and empowerment. The Internet in China represents, on one hand, state-engineered practices to embrace the market dynamism in order to compete in the global market, and on the other hand the struggles between the governing and the governed (Ong 2006).

According to the China Internet Network Information Center (CNNIC 2013), by the end of June 2012 China's Internet popular had reached over half a billion people. The growth and diffusion of the Internet in China in the last few years—from being a low-penetration country with a mere half million dial-up users in the mid-1990s to becoming an intermediate-penetration country twenty years later—is impressive. The Chinese government has been instrumental in the Internet development and diffusion in China. It has made the diffusion of the Internet a high priority for developing an advanced information industry. As the core component of China's long-term strategy for sustained growth as a global technological, economic, and political powerhouse, the development and diffusion of the Internet (and ICT in general) has been viewed as representing the second stage of China's reform policies. Beginning with its open door and reform policy in 1978, China catapulted itself into the world of capitalism by turning itself into the world's factory. Since the mid-1990s, Chinese reform has entered the second stage, with advanced technologies and services as the driving force to stimulate domestic consumption and to expand overseas market.

Led by the Ministry of Information Industry (established in 1998), the Chinese government has increased investments in infrastructure facilities and has encouraged domestic and foreign entrepreneurs and venture capitalists to compete in the world's biggest market, in both hardware and software, from routers to filtering technologies and cloud computing, from search engines to social network sites and e-commerce applications. Underlining the leapfrogging discourse is the "techno-nationalist" narrative that is currently underpinned by the "created in China" drive, a top-down imperative to boost China's information technology (IT) and telecommunication sectors and to be a world leader in technological innovation, regulation, and governance. The issuing of three 3G licenses in the lead-up to the Beijing Games in 2008, and the launch of these networks (W-CDMA [Wideband Code Division Multiple Access], CDMA2000 [Code division multiple access], and TD-SCDMA [Time Division Synchronous Code Division Multiple Access]) nationally in January 2009, have significantly boosted the growth of Internet users in China, particularly that of mobile users. Accessing Internet by mobile phone via the 3G networks lowered the threshold of Internet access, allowing faster and cheaper access to the web, particularly for those who do not own a computer or cannot afford broadband connection at home. Broadband and mobile Internet is driving a new round of growth in Internet users in China.

From Internet Cafés to Mobile Internet

Internet cafés have played an important role in disseminating the new media to the broader Chinese society (particularly for the working class), for educating average people on how to go online in the early days, and for accelerating China's construction of an information society and its move toward an open society. Internet cafés first emerged in 1996 around China's equivalent to the United States' Ivy League universities. It did not take long before they migrated from being salons for intellectual and social elites to being an everyday experience for students, migrant workers, and other members of the information have-nots working class. They are now everywhere across the country.

Since 2009 mobile (phone) Internet has taken over from Internet cafés to become the newest area for growth in the development of China's Internet. Young people are the most active and dynamic force in the mobile Internet market, having truly embraced the new era for communication, entertainment, information, and commerce.

The diffusion of the Internet from research institutions to Internet cafés, home computers, and mobile phones clearly implies the changing roles of the Internet in everyday life. We have gained some understanding of the use of mobile phone in social networking; information sharing and dissemination via services such as short message services (SMSs); and instant messaging and microblogging through platforms like the popular QQ and Sina Weibo. (The Chinese word *weibo* means "microblogging"; Sina Weibo is one of the most popular of several Chinese microblogging platforms, similar to a combination of Facebook and Twitter.) Enabled by 3G wireless and broadband platforms, high-definition video streaming and photo sharing technologies, blogging, microblogging, and "problogging" (referring to multimedia blogging that incorporates audio, video, image, and text) are made an everyday reality via multiple terminals at an extremely low cost. The seamless and real-time intercommunication between personal computers and mobile phones made instant messaging (IM), social networking, and microblogging big hits in the Chinese market. Tencent's highly successful IM tool QQ occupies a particular space in China's techno-cultural sphere. It was one of the first social network services (SNSs) to be "created in China."

Riding on the success of QQ, Tencent launched its SNS, Qzone, in 2005, and its microblogging service (t.qq.com) in 2010. Qzone is one of the most popular SNSs in China. There are many types of SNSs in China, representing different classes, communities, and lifestyles. Sites such as Qzone, Xaionei/Renren (akin to Facebook and popular among students), Kaixin001 (particularly popular among female office workers), 51.com (akin to Friendster), together with foreign SNSs such as Facebook, MySpace, and Cyworld, are often simultaneously opened and used on people's desktops and mobile phones. There is much room for growth in SNS in China, particularly mobile SNS and its associated services.

Microblogging at Sina.com, along with its competitors like QQ.com, People.com.cn, 139.com, Netease.com, and Digu.com, is one of the most popular services in China. Unlike the text-only Twitter, which is blocked in China in any case, Sina Weibo provides a richer user experience by integrating audio, video, and texts into the microblogging experience. It also offers threaded discussions, and voting and polling functions. Many bloggers have their (micro)blogs with more than one blog service providers. The number of bloggers will continue to grow; so will the total number of Chinese Internet users. Blogging appeared in China in 2002, took off in 2003, and exploded in 2005–2006. It introduced new terrains for expression, networking, entertainment, and knowledge production and circulation (Yu 2007a). Since Sina.com introduced Chinese-style microblogging in 2009, the Chinese Internet has entered a "micro-era" that is characterized by the integration of *weibo* in social media marketing strategies of businesses, propaganda and publicity campaigns of governmental and nongovernmental organizations, and social mobilization for common causes by concerned citizens. A series of microblogging-mediated Internet events, debates, and campaigns—ranging from rescuing child beggars to various government cover-ups—are illustrative of the role of the Internet (microblogging in particular) in transforming social relations on the interpersonal as well as interclass and interregional levels.

Hardware such as mobile phone handsets has also seen growth in recent years. The unique phenomenon of *shānzhái* 山寨 ("copycat" or "bandit") culture derives from the economic activities of bandit phone production and sales in southern China. "Bandit phones" are cheap replicas of famous brands, but loaded with functions. They fall into a gray zone in that they are not fully legal or completely illegal in the Chinese context. They are popular among trendy youths who upgrade their handsets regularly, as well as low-income migrant workers, who use the cheap but powerful gadgets to maintain and expand their social networks with family and friends all over China. Bandit phones are an expanding business in China, and from China they have spread to South and Southeast Asia and Africa.

How Chinese innovations and initiatives in ICT software (such as Internet filtering) and hardware (such as routers and smartphone handsets) will influence the ways that the global Internet is governed, regulated, and used in everyday life needs more study. What is also needed is a study of nontraditional and nonmainstream venues and sites of new media practices, including places of transit, such as airports, subways, and tourist zones. There is a great need for spatial attention to be paid to the varied patterns of Internet development, diffusion, and uses in less-developed areas and among ethnic minorities, both in their hometowns and in migrant clusters in areas dominated by the majority Han. Discussion of the Internet in everyday life thus leads to a vast array of issues. It concerns not only everyday and popular culture, but also debates on Internet governance, commerce, education, social security, public relations, and ethnic relations—to name just a few. The everyday is embedded in the interstices of all these contingent issues and dimensions.

Entertaining the Youth to Death?

Most Internet users in China are youths under thirty-five years old, with more than half under twenty-five years old. With the introduction of mobile Internet in 2008, an increasing number of young "netizens" have turned to mobile phones as their first and only port to access the web.

For young Chinese netizens, the Internet provides aggregated sources of a rich variety of entertainment: music, games, video streaming, online literature, and social networking. Apart from microblogging, online music is a high-growth area, even amid legal disputes over copyright issues between the music industry and Chinese Internet content providers (ICPs). China's Ministry of Culture has stepped up measures to regulate the transmission of cultural information (including music and film) and to curb rampant piracy and intellectual property rights violations. In reality, it is difficult to implement, and tens of thousands of websites and peer-to-peer file-sharing networks in China continue to provide music- and video-sharing services. College students routinely use university-hosted servers to download, store, and share their audiovisual collections. Some of the newly released singles or albums and films from foreign markets quickly find their way into these amateur collections, even before they make their official entry into the Chinese market. As students are the most active segment of mobile Internet users, they are targeted as the main consumers of "mobile music": phone makers, record companies, mobile operators, and ICPs are united in their mission of cross-promotion through music marketing and SNS marketing platforms, targeting China's young netizens (Wang 2005).

Online gaming is another popular pastime among Chinese young Internet users. Apart from numerous casual games provided by almost all Chinese websites, SNSs, and blog and microblog services, MMORPGs (massively multiplayer online role-playing game) such as *World of Warcraft* and the Chinese-developed *Fantasy Westward Journey* are extremely popular, particularly among youths and Internet café players. China's gaming industry is a multi-billion-dollar business.

The Chinese government is the major proponent of the digital economy and the major regulator of online gaming. A "techno-nationalist" discourse has underlined the state policy toward China's digital economy, that is, to nurture the domestic market, support joint ventures with foreign companies and venture capital, and to promote Chinese companies' international competitiveness. At the same time, the Chinese government is keen on regulating online gaming in the name of promoting a healthy Internet culture (Ernkvist and Ström 2008). The state media regularly run stories on the perils of Internet addiction, which is supported by research findings that decry the negative impact of online gaming on the youths from the sociopsychological perspective. (The issue of Internet addiction is discussed in this book's article of that name.)

Gaming companies are a key component of China's creative industry. Favorite policies from the central and local governments have nurtured a growing domestic gaming industry. Compared with Western, Japanese, South Korean, and Taiwanese companies, mainland Chinese gaming companies have the local knowledge, connections, and talent to develop and market games that target the massive market of gamers in China. Like hundreds of other online gaming companies, Shanda Interactive Entertainment, a leading interactive entertainment media company in China, has grown from a distributor of foreign games to a game developer and distributor that meets local and national demands while targeting the international market (Chung and Yuan 2009).

"Networked Authoritarianism"

Government policies, ICT entrepreneurship, and foreign venture capital have played crucial roles in the diffusion of the Internet in everyday life in China. Apart from strategic concerns for China's long-term competitiveness in the global market, the Chinese government has promoted ICT, including the Internet, as part of its efforts to reshape its image, both domestically and internationally, as being responsible, democratic, and competent. The Internet is an integral part of the Chinese government's efforts to extend its control over information management, enhance its legitimacy, and to promote its soft power on the international stage (Wu 2009; Zhang 2009). China Central Television (CCTV), *People's Daily*, Xinhua News Agency, China Radio International, and other major press and broadcast groups all have active online presences. Backed by the government, they have extended their brands into blogging and social media platforms and continue to dominate news production and circulation, both online and offline.

Private ICT companies, which normally have absorbed foreign venture capital and/or are listed on US stock markets, have enjoyed a cozy relationship with the state-owned telecommunications company and media organizations. They have been pioneering Internet applications and services from Bulletin Board Services (BBSs) and emails to IM, blogging, and SNS, from online games, digital music, and video streaming to e-commerce and cloud downloading. They have also developed censorship software for the Chinese government. Consumer business has taken a strong hold in Chinese cyberspace, immediately after entertainment (such as online music and gaming) and information searching. Chinese e-commerce sites like Taobo, Alibaba, Dangdang, Eachnet, and Paipai have continued to attract customers both inside and outside China by offering customers deals that traditional retailers cannot compete with.

For the Chinese government and businesses, pragmatism and engagement prevail over ideology and rhetoric, as the drama with Google's threat to withdraw from the Chinese market and its license renewal in 2010 demonstrated (MacKinnon 2010b). New media and communication technologies are increasing the chances for cross-promotion and concentration of the Chinese Communist Party–market complex. The scale and resources of CCTV, Lenovo, China Mobile, Sohu, Sina, Netease, Tencent and other new media portals allow them to compete as well as cross-promote one another. Their domination of Chinese television, mobile communication, and the new media markets allows them to maximize profit, as well as to shape and guide public opinion.

China is an economic system in which the marketplace is shaped by a cozy relationship between government and big business. All major players in Chinese cyberspace are either directly or indirectly part of the state-dominated "socialist market economy." During the 2008 Beijing Olympic Games, for example, CCTV and its business partners—most are state-owned enterprises, while others hold state-issued licenses for audio-video contents—were able to consolidate their cross-media business models by adopting user-generated content through blogging, problogging, and SNS. They were able to moderate what was posted online, set media agendas, and shape public opinion by selectively promoting certain posts while deleting others. While encouraging and transforming prosumers' creativity and productivity into added value, big businesses can also harness such creativity and productivity in line with what the Chinese state wants its citizens to do online. It is interesting to note that the Chinese government claimed in its white paper on Internet policy in 2010 that it protected and upheld citizens' freedom of speech on the Internet, while the country was ranked 181 out of 195 countries in the global press freedom ranking, with an index of 78 out of 100 in Internet freedom in 2009 (the higher the index, the less freedom; see www.freedomhouse.org).

One scholar has used the term "networked authoritarianism" to describe the give-and-take dynamic between government and citizens on the Internet (MacKinnon 2010a). On one hand, China's media control regime is getting more sophisticated, normalized, synergized, and dispersed (or outsourced and decentralized) to local and private sectors (Zhao 2009, 19–74); on the other hand, people in China have a greater sense of freedom to express themselves and call attention to social problems or injustices, and they even manage to have an impact on government policies through online networking. The networked authoritarianism permits freedom within limits, engagement with principles, and resilience in the give-and-take relationship between the citizenry and the state. Under this networked authoritarianism, the Internet in China is both a global network without borders and a gigantic intranet that has clearly defined boundaries; it is both an information highway and an entertainment highway.

The Importance of Play

"Play" is a prominent and ubiquitous feature of the Internet in everyday life in China. Entertainment ranks number one in Internet usage in China. Information is the second largest category, but much of the news and information that people in China search and read on the Internet is "infotainment" (about celebrities, for example). People do use the Internet to pursue social causes. Zheng Yongnian, in his 2008 book on the role of the Internet in mediating relations between the state and society in China, shows that Internet discussions can get contentious and that average Internet users can be better informed on politics and participate in collective actions through three interaction strategies with the state: loyalty, exit, and voice. Most of the everyday use of the Internet in China falls into the voice category. As it does not pose any direct challenge to the state but promotes gradual political change in specific issues or policies, the voice option has been the most widely accepted form of online activism in China. What Zheng fails to identify are the diversified forms and styles of "voice." The playful element in "voicing" is a defining feature of the everyday online activism. In the name of entertainment, or entertainment for entertainment's sake, online citizen activism becomes "activistainment," that is, activism through entertainment.

Despite the increasingly sophisticated efforts by the Chinese government to control the Internet (see the article elsewhere in this book titled "The Great Firewall" for more on this topic), the new media can become a new venue for individuals to exercise citizenship, not through overt resistance, but through a playful production and circulation of SMS messages, BBS or blog posts, or spoof videos (Yu 2007a; 2007b). The prevalence of the mobile phone as the immediate platform for accessing the Internet has brought means of communication, information, and education within one's grasp. In the spring of 2008, during the Tibetan riots and the Sichuan earthquake, for example, ordinary Chinese people used their mobile phone and video recorders to record and transmit onsite real-time reportage of the happenings, which were uploaded to major bulletin boards, video-sharing websites, and blogs. These citizen journalists—many of whom were China's *fénqīng* 愤青, or "angry youth"—provided timely reports as an alternative to mainstream media frameworks. These youth are sometimes guided by cyber-nationalism to voice outrage at Western media reportage of China (as in the case of www.Anti-CNN.com), and sometimes prompted by their anger and disappointment with the Chinese government to seek control over public opinion and to reset media agendas (Reese and Dai 2009; Nip 2009). The playful, exhibitionist, evocative, humorous, and portable small-screen realities intersect and infiltrate, rather than resist or oppose, any existing structure or culture. They offer a different way to view online activism as light and playful expressions of individuality and collectivity, and vice versa.

The playful element in activistainment is also diagnosed in Guobin Yang's excellent 2009 book on citizen activism online, *The Power of the Internet in China*. In the book, Yang identifies new forms of online activism. There are two broad categories of online activism, the confessional/autobiographical genre and the parodic/satirical genre. Of the former, the confessional blog of Muzimei about her sexual adventures catapulted blogging into popular consciousness in 2003, and has been followed by many imitators. Audio tracks (podcasting) and visual images (photographs, videos, and flash animations) are an important part of the confessional/autobiographical genre. They are posted on BBS forums, blogs, Flickr, Fotolog, Youtube, Tudou, or Youku.

The confessional / autobiographical genre overlaps with the parodic/satirical genre. The latter includes jokes, doggerel, satire (in both prose and verse), and parody. The most well-known form of this genre is *ègǎo* 恶搞, or spoof, which is a multimedia expression using digital alterations of Chinese and non-Chinese elements to poke fun at an original work, concept, or person (mostly celebrities).

Shanzhai, as discussed earlier, derives from the economic drive for profit through bandit phone production, retail, and usage. Since 2008 it has migrated to the Internet to become a cultural phenomenon, with playful mimicry of celebrities, films, TV programs and pop songs. *Shanzhai* has become an extension of *egao* in the Chinese cyberspace. While *egao*—a bit like cultural jamming—utilizes found footage, digital remixing, and creative use of copyrighted audio-visual images, *shanzhai* gains it name from "original" production of media contents that copy, mimic, and mock the existing originals from the mainstream culture.

Play, one of the most prominent features of the Internet in the everyday life, can become a new way of expressing citizen activism that breaks into, and also out of, entertainment discourses and mainstream cultures. The Internet also has opened up more opportunities for cultural and political expressions under the networked authoritarianism than ever before. Entertainment is fused with information, education, and even citizen activism. Everyday online practices like posting a dispute on a bus shot with one's mobile phone, spoofing a blockbuster film, or poking fun at the establishment through *egao* or *shanzhai* video making constitute a liminal situation that allows ideas, visions, and emotions to be tested and contested.

The playfulness and lightness of the everyday Internet practices—whether playing online games, downloading music, or posting an *egao* piece in one's blogs, SNS sites, and video-sharing sites—indicate how creative cultural practices can survive and thrive, with positive but also negative and unequal impacts on individuals and communities. Further research needs to be done on this fascinating, and ever-changing, subject.

Haiqing YU
University of New South Wales

See also Children Online; Consumers Online; The Great Firewall; Internet Addictions; Internet Cafés; Parody; Social and Political Impact

Further Reading

China Internet Network Information Center (CNNIC). (2013, January). Statistical report on Internet development in China. Retrieved April, 15, 2013, from http://www1.cnnic.cn/IDR/Report-Downloads/201302/P020130312536825920279.pdf

Chung, Peichi, & Yuan, Jiangping. (2009). Dynamics in the online game industry of China: A political economic analysis of its competitiveness. *Revista d Economia Politica de las Tecnologias de la Informacion y Communicacion, XI*(2). Retrieved July

22, 2010, from http://www.eptic.com.br/arquivos/Revistas/vol.XI,n2,2009/11-PeichiChungJiangPingYuan.pdf

Dibbell, Julian. (2007, June 17). The life of a Chinese gold farmer. *New York Times*. Retrieved July 28, 2010, from http://www.nytimes.com/2007/06/17/magazine/17lootfarmers-t.html

Ernkvist, Mirko, & Ström, Patrik. (2008). Enmeshed in games with the government: Governmental policies and the development of the Chinese online game industry. *Games and Culture*, 3(1), 98-126.

Golub, Alex, & Lingley, Kate. (2008). "Just like the Qing empire": Internet addiction, MMOGs, and moral crisis in contemporary China. *Games and Culture*, 3(1), 59-75.

Guo Liang. (2007). Surveying Internet usage and its impact on seven Chinese cities. Retrieved July 22, 2010, from http://www.markle.org/downloadable_assets/china_internet_survey_11.2007.pdf

Koch, Pamela T.; Koch, Bradley J.; Huang, Kun; & Chen, Wei. (2009). Beauty is in the eye of the QQ user: Instant messaging in China. In Gerard Goggin and Mark McLelland (Eds.). *Internationalizing Internet studies: Beyond anglophone paradigms* (pp. 265–284). London: Routledge.

Lin Jun. (2009). *Feiteng 15 nian: Zhongguo hulianwang 1995-2009* [Bubbling 15 years: Chinese Internet 1995-2009]. Beijing: China CITIC Press.

Lindtner, Silvia, et al. (2008). A hybrid cultural ecology: *World of Warcraft* in China. In *Proceedings of the 2008 ACM conference on Computer supported cooperative work*. New York: Association for Computing Machinery. Retrieved July 15, 2010, from http://darrouzet-nardi.net/bonnie/fp559-Lindtner.pdf

MacKinnon, Rebecca. (2010a, June 15). China's Internet white paper: Networked authoritarianism in action. Retrieved July 20 2010, from http://rconversation.blogs.com/rconversation/2010/06/chinas-internet-white-paper-networked-authoritarianism.html

MacKinnon, Rebecca. (2010b, July 9). On Google's license renewal and principled engagement. Retrieved July 20, 2010, from http://rconversation.blogs.com/rconversation/2010/07/on-googles-license-renewal-and-principled-engagement.html

Morley, David. (2003). What's "home" got to do with it? Contradictory dynamics in the domestication of technology and the dislocation of domesticity. *European Journal of Cultural Studies*, 6(4), 435-458.

Nip, Joyce Y. M. (2009). Citizen journalism in China: The case of the Wenchuan earthquake. In Stuart Allan and Einar Thorsen (Eds.), *Citizen journalism: Global perspective* (pp. 95-106). New York: Peter Lang.

Ong, Aihwa. (2006). *Neoliberalism as exception: Mutations in citizenship and sovereignty*. Durham, NC: Duke University Press.

Priest, Eric. (2006). The future of music and film piracy in China. *Berkeley Technology Law Journal*, *21*, 795-871.

Qiu, Jack Linchuan. (2009). *Working-class network society: Communication technology and the information have-less in urban China*. Cambridge, MA: The MIT Press.

Reese, Stephen D., & Dai, Jia. (2009). Citizen journalism in the global news arena: China's new media critics. In Stuart Allan and Einar Thorsen (Eds.), *Citizen journalism: Global perspective* (pp. 221-232). New York: Peter Lang.

Spigel, Lynn. (2001). *Welcome to the dreamhouse*. Durham, NC: Duke University Press

Sun Wanning. (2009). *Maid in China: Media, morality, and the cultural politics of boundaries*. New York: Routledge.

Sun Wanning. (2010). Scaling Chinese media: A geographic turn to future research. *International Journal of Communication*, 4(Feature), 537–543.

Voci, Paola. (2010). *China on video: Smaller-screen realities*. London: Routledge.

Wang, Jing. (2005). Youth culture, music, and cell phone branding in China. *Global Media and Communication*, *1*(2), 185-201.

Williams, Raymond. (1974). *Television: Technology and cultural form*. London: Fontana.

Wu Guoguang. (2009). In the name of good governance: E-government, Internet pornography and political censorship in China. In Xiaoling Zhang and Yongnian Zheng (Eds.), *China's information and communications technology revolution* (pp. 68-85). London: Routledge.

Yang, Guobin. (2009). *The power of the Internet in China: Citizen activism online*. New York: Columbia University Press.

Yu Haiqing. (2007a). Blogging the everyday life in Chinese Internet culture. *Asian Studies Review, 31*, 423-433.

Yu Haiqing. (2007b). Talking, linking, clicking: The politics of AIDS and SARS. *Positions: East Asia Cultures Critique, 15*(1), 35-63.

Zhang Xiaoling. (2009). From "foreign propaganda" to "international communication": China's promotion of soft power in the age of information and communication technologies. In Zhang Xiaoling and Zheng Yongnian (Eds.), *China's information and communications technology revolution* (pp. 103-120). London: Routledge.

Zhao Yuezhi. (2009) *Communication in China: Political economy, power, and conflict*. Lanham, MD: Rowman & Littlefield.

Zhao Yuezhi. (2007). After mobile phones, what? Re-embedding the social in China's "digital revolution." *International Journal of Communication, 1*, 92–120.

Zheng Yongnian. (2008). *Technological empowerment: The Internet, state, and society in China*. Stanford, CA: Stanford University Press.

Internet Addiction

Wǎngyǐn 网瘾

Summary: Internet addiction has become a serious social problem in China, especially among young people. China now has the world's largest population of netizens, and the influence of Internet addiction continues through the proliferation and development of the Internet and online entertainment. Facing increasing public concern, China is attempting to cope with Internet addiction through government regulations, clinical treatments, and studies.

In June 2008, the "netizen" population in China surpassed that of the United States—ranking first in the world for the first time, with the Internet penetration rate (i.e., the percentage of people using the Internet) exceeding the world average of 21.9 percent (CNNIC 2009). According to statistics from the China Internet Network Information Center (CNNIC), the number of Internet users in China had climbed to 618 million by December 2013, with an Internet penetration rate of 45.8 percent (CNNIC 2014).

Behind the boom, however, the Internet is still regarded ambivalently in China, as both an economic opportunity and a social threat. With more and more public concern, academic research, and professional treatments, Internet addiction has become a widely debated issue. China is now struggling with a new plight: millions of Chinese Internet users are suffering from Internet dependence, particularly among adolescents. Internet addiction has become a significant disorder that negatively impacts peoples' jobs, finances, and personal relations.

Public Concern

With the rapid development of the Internet, public attention in China has also been drawn to certain downsides of this new medium. Past research in both China and in the West shows that excessive Internet use may lead to declines in social involvement, since many online relationships represent "relatively weak ties with strangers, acquaintances, or non-intimate kin" (Subrahmanyam et al. 2001, 94). These types of social contacts online have been found to provide less social support than more intimate ties do. With a preponderance of evidence, researchers argue that uncontrolled or compulsive Internet use negatively affects the state of psychosocial well-being. For example, excessive Internet use may contribute to overly reclusive behavior by young people. Individuals with problematic levels of Internet use have been reported to have high rates of social withdrawal, loneliness, and depression (even when previous depression scores were controlled for). To examine how excessive Internet use influenced people's psychological health in China, psychological symptoms were investigated in previous studies; some Chinese scholars reported that Chinese adolescents who use the Internet excessively subsequently exhibited significantly more psychiatric symptoms than those who used the Internet less frequently.

Violent and sexually explicit content on the Internet is another major concern among parents, educators, and policy makers. A majority of online games involve aggression, competition, and, quite often, violence. Online games are more intensive, more complex, more graphic, more violent, and more bloodthirsty than earlier computerized games, and with a larger and more thriving social network (Chuang 2006). Studies have found that many players appear to display the core components of addiction, such as modified moods, tolerance for large amounts of gaming, and withdrawal symptoms. Unsurprisingly, researchers, parents, educators, counselors, psychologists, and policy makers have been concerned about the effects on those who play these games.

With the Internet's rapid development in China, many social problems related to Internet activities and online entertainments have been heavily reported in the Chinese media. Teenagers and young adults, especially college students, are particularly susceptible to the lure of the Internet, and they are often described as being obsessed. It is easy to come across a variety of tragic stories in the news related to the effects of the Internet, and the theme is overwhelmingly about academic failure, reduced work performance, juvenile delinquency, social alienation, and other social and psychological disorders. The Chinese media has metaphorically framed online games and other online activities as "Internet opium" or "electronic heroin." In recent years, a large number of stories of maladaptive behavior related to excessive Internet use have been reported in China. Two examples among many were a boy who battered his parents for forbidding him from going to an Internet café—especially shocking in China, where obedience to one's parents is considered a vital part of the social fabric—and a man who killed another online game player for theft of his virtual items.

In light of these stories, public concerns continue to mount regarding the risks of Internet use. People suffering from Internet addiction may seek the same pleasure other escapists seek from drugs, gambling, or alcohol. Just as some people struggle to keep from taking a drink or popping a pill, some now struggle to turn their computer off.

Internet Addiction as a Health Risk

The definition and diagnostic criteria in academic research on Internet addiction in mainland China is mainly based on previous studies in the West. The term "Internet addiction" was coined in the United States in 1995, when Dr. Ivan Goldberg used the term as a satirical hoax. He took pathological gambling, as diagnosed by the *Diagnostic and Statistical Manual of Mental Disorders, Fourth Edition* (*DSM-IV*), as his model for the spoofed description.

Despite Dr. Goldberg's intended satire, Internet addiction was promoted as a real condition by some researchers. The first empirical study on Internet addiction was conducted in 1996 by the US psychologist Dr. Kimberly Young, a pioneer in the field and the leading proponent of regarding the issue as serious; she wrote the groundbreaking book on Internet addiction titled *Caught on the Net: How to Recognize the Signs of Internet Addiction—and a Winning Strategy for Recovery*. Since then, Internet addiction has received much attention in various disciplines, ranging from public health, social psychology, education, social work, and communication. Researchers have explored the features of addicts, symptoms, consequences, and corresponding measurement items. Internet addiction, however, has commonly been viewed as a broad topic with few common definitions and little guidance (Byun et al. 2009). Current studies on Internet addiction have focused on proving its existence, while the inconsistent criteria and the lack of consensus have motivated researchers to develop new measures.

Although many societies have increasingly witnessed treatments and clinics coping with this new plight, there is still a heated controversy questioning the existence of Internet addiction disorder. Born nearly two decades ago, Internet addiction has still not received the official validation in the United States, its birthplace, but Internet gaming disorder is now listed in the fifth version of the *Diagnostic and Statistical Manual of Mental Disorders* (*DSM-V*) (2014). The release of the Chinese diagnostic criteria in 2008 put China at the forefront of this growing field. China even planned to lead the world by registering Internet addiction with the World Health Organization.

The Chinese diagnostic criteria include four domains—symptoms, severity, course, and exclusion (Tao et al. 2010). The criteria echo Young's (1998b) eight-item diagnostic questionnaire, based on the criteria for pathological gambling in *DSM-IV*. As for symptoms, there are eight items—preoccupation, withdrawal from social ties, tolerance (for excessive levels of time spent online), difficulty controlling the addiction, ignoring harmful consequences, loss of social communication and interests, alleviation of negative emotions, and hiding from friends and relatives (Tao et al. 2010). To adopt a cut-off point differentiating normal use from addictive Internet use, the researcher Dr. Ran Tao and his colleagues employed a "2 + 1 rule," in which the respondents had only to identify with the first two items (preoccupation and withdrawal symptoms) and one or more of the other six items to be considered an addict (Tao et al. 2010). Attempts have also been made to define Internet addicts by the amount of time they spend online. As for the course criteria in clinical treatment, the duration of the Internet addiction must have lasted for three straight months, with at least six hours of consecutively nonessential Internet use per day (Tao et al. 2009).

Some researchers have argued, however, that Internet addiction disorder is neither a true addiction nor a specific disorder (Suratt 2006). Past research has attempted to differentiate Internet addiction from obsession, self-medication for depression or other disorders, and compulsion. Although the classification of Internet addiction has aroused widespread skepticism in Chinese cyberspace, research projects, therapeutic clinics, psychiatric counseling centers, and self-help groups have mushroomed in urban areas all over the country.

Internet Addiction among Chinese Adolescents

According to the CNNIC (2014) report, Internet users under thirty years of age now account for 57.2 percent of the total netizen population, making young people the main body of Chinese Internet users. The latest report on Internet addiction conducted by the China Youth Internet Association (CYIA) showed that young people are more vulnerable to Internet addiction (CYIA 2012).

Based on Young's (1998a) eight-item definition of Internet addiction—which was based on a typical list modified from *DSM-IV* criteria for pathological gambling and focused on whether respondents used the Internet to escape their problems and felt anxiety when they could not go online—nationwide investigations were conducted by the CYIA to examine Internet addiction among Chinese adolescents; it found that 26 percent of adolescent Internet users in China were addicted to the Internet. At the time of the investigations, there were also about 12 percent of adolescent Internet users in China who showed a tendency toward Internet addiction (CYIA 2012). A slightly higher percentage of males were addicted than females, but the incidence of female addicts has been rising. At the time of the study, there was also an increase in the proportion of Internet addicts aged six to twenty-three, among which the two largest groups were those aged thirteen to seventeen (30.5 percent) and those aged eighteen to twenty-three (26.6 percent) (CYIA 2012). Internet addiction therefore became an important public concern not only among adolescents, but also among young adults.

According to the scores based on Young's eight-item scale with the cutoff point of five, during the time of this study, 35.1 percent of addicts were classed as suffering from a mild degree of addiction, followed by moderate (34.6 percent) and severe (30.3 percent) addiction (CYIA 2012). On average, adolescent Internet users in urban China spent about 80 minutes online every day, while those with severe Internet addiction stayed online an average of 135 minutes, almost double the time spent by those without Internet addiction tendencies (around 73 minutes) (CYIA 2012).

Internet addiction can also be divided into different types according to different Internet usage purposes. Addicted adolescent Internet users tend to use the Internet for recreation, while non-addicts tend to go online for practical purposes. Slightly less than half of adolescent Internet addicts suffered from online game addiction at the time of the study, followed by 13 percent who suffered from excessive time being immersed within the virtual worlds of the Internet (CYIA 2012).

As the Internet is a borderless medium, the content online is difficult to control. Parents and educators therefore tend to worry that violent and sexually explicit content online may harm adolescents. Adolescent Internet addicts show more tolerance to misconduct, such as truancy, smoking, drinking, and engaging in violent behaviors (CYIA 2012; Huang et al. 2010; Tao et al. 2009). In addition, the study also showed that adolescent Internet addicts usually felt more reluctant to associate themselves with others offline. This was especially true for the 38 percent of adolescent addicts who experienced moderate Internet addiction and the 42 percent who suffered from severe Internet addiction (CYIA 2012).

Coping with Internet Addiction

The increasing public concern over Internet addiction has been accompanied by questions of how to address the problem. The release of the diagnostic criteria of Internet addiction as a mental illness by Dr. Tao and his research team (Tao et al. 2010) was regarded as a breakthrough in clinical practice in China, even though they are still pending official endorsement by the Ministry of Health (MOH) due to the ongoing debate (MOH 2009). Although the diagnostic criteria have caused substantial controversy, related media reports, academic research, therapeutic clinics, psychiatric counseling centers, and self-help groups have mushroomed in urban areas all over the country. With the released diagnostic criteria, Internet users can also conduct self-tests and adjust their Internet activities.

In response to the increasing concern about Internet addiction, the Chinese government addressed the social concerns by making relevant changes in related regulations and laws, such as the nationwide anti-addiction software, real-name registration, the regulation of online game industry and Internet cafés, and the amendment to the Law of the People's Republic of China on the Protection of Minors (Tao 2007). For example, Internet cafés and game labs are not allowed to be within 200 meters of schools, their business hours are controlled, and restrictions in minors' entry into Internet cafés have been imposed (Tao 2007). The Ministry of Information Industry (MII) is the primary body responsible for telecommunications and high-tech industry in China, playing a major role in legislation and regulation of the Internet. Companies engaged in Internet business, however, face the daunting task of compliance with the network of agencies and regulatory regimes at different levels, many with conflicting interests. Ministries and administrative offices often jointly issue the regulations, laying a foundation for strengthening the administration of the Internet. Anti-addiction software was proposed and promoted by eight governmental ministries, for instance.

China was also among the earliest to set up Internet addiction clinics. There are hundreds of institutions offering treatment for Internet addiction, including clinics, special schools, and so on, but not all of them are well developed or well managed. The Internet addicts in these institutions are generally middle school and high school students, as well as some college students. Many of them are deceived into entering or forced by their parents to enter these institutions—only a few of them go there voluntarily. The institutions are distinguished from one another by different higher authorities, and regulation has not been standardized, with a series of controversial circumstances. These institutions do help to prevent and treat Internet addiction, but there have also been many problems reported, such as the application of different diagnostic criteria and electroconvulsive therapies, as well as the death of an adolescent Internet addict beaten by staff in an institution—to name a few.

There is a lack of commonly acknowledged or accepted diagnostic criteria among the institutions treating Internet addiction in China. The diagnosis of Internet addiction is based on observations, counseling interviews, or criteria proposed by different researchers, but the time spent using the Internet is the most important indicator. Some institutions are operated as clinics, where Internet addiction is treated as a new mental illness, while others cope with Internet addiction as a kind of deviant behavior among adolescents or a form of escapism.

As for therapeutic measures, a combined treatment of psychological counseling, affective communication, study coaching (i.e., coaching on how best to get studying done amid so many online distractions), pedagogical activities, physical exercise, military training, walking trips, and medication are used. In-patient treatment and closed management are adopted in almost all institutions, and usually the clients cannot go outside freely. Although these institutions use different therapeutic techniques, they are all dedicated to fostering self-control and good behavioral habits.

The General Hospital of Beijing Military Region's Addiction Medicine Center (AMC) was one of China's first Internet addiction disorder (IAD) clinics. Based on findings from US scholars and his own research, the AMC director (the aforementioned Dr. Ran Tao) proposed the IAD diagnostic criteria in 2008. Tao proposed an interdisciplinary "Five-in-One" integrated model to treat patients with Internet addiction. The treatment includes the aid of medicine, psychology, pedagogy, social conditioning theory, and social experiences together with military-style training. Tao and the center have been interviewed by many media organizations, including CCTV (China Central Television), *People's Daily*, and foreign media such as CBS, NHK (Japan's public broadcaster), and the *Washington Post*. This media exposure has drawn much public attention and also stirred heated controversy about whether Internet addiction should be treated as a new mental illness.

Outlook for the Future

In China, Internet-related entertainment is becoming more and more popular. While most young Internet users are veteran participants in gaming sessions, Internet cafés both in large cities and in remote villages are crowded with mostly young men glued to the screen as they engage in virtual battles and social chat. Further studies on Internet addiction may provide guidance for policy makers to formulate programs in the areas of regulation, prevention, and intervention in the future development of online entertainments and Internet-related health care services.

Such programs may be transformed into opportunities for future expansions of Internet addiction clinics. In China, since Internet addiction–related social problems are quite serious, even before the release of the diagnostic criteria, there were already hospitals and clinics providing treatment or counseling on Internet addiction, similar to Tao's center at the Military General Hospital in Beijing. When Internet addiction can be officially classified as a clinical disorder, there will be more educational institutions, mental health clinics, and corporations dealing with Internet misuse in a more serious and organized manner.

Concerns about possible health risks associated with the Internet and other new information communication technologies (ICTs) are prevalent in more and more countries. Internet addiction is becoming a prominent issue both in China and in many other societies. As a country with an authoritarian government and the highest absolute number of Internet users in the world, China provides an interesting context to study the case of Internet addiction as a new mental illness.

China is in a transitional period, and the development of the Internet is integrated into the long-term strategies for China's advancement toward an industrialized, information-based, urbanized, market-oriented, and internationalized country. Thus, China continues to strengthen its efforts to develop and manage Internet culture and to foster a good online environment. Further studies on Internet addiction in China can bring fresh perspectives to the understanding of health risk issues related to Internet use in a non-Western social background.

Qiaolei JIANG
Dalian University of Technology

Louis LEUNG
The Chinese University of Hong Kong

See also Game Industry Online; Internet in Everyday Life; Internet Governance

Further Reading

Byun, S., et al. (2009). Internet addiction: Metasynthesis of 1996–2006 quantitative research. *CyberPsychology & Behavior, 12*(2), 203–207.

China Internet Network Information Center (CNNIC). (2009). *The Internet timeline of China (2008)*. Retrieved April 11, 2010, from http://www.cnnic.cn/html/Dir/2009/05/18/5600.htm

China Internet Network Information Center (CNNIC). (2014, January). Statistical report on Internet development in China. Retrieved April, 19, 2014, from http://www.cnnic.net.cn/hlwfzyj/hlwxzbg/hlwtjbg/201403/P020140305346585959798.pdf

China Youth Internet Association (CYIA). (2012, August 7). Research report on Internet addiction among Chinese adolescents [in Chinese]. Retrieved April 19, 2014, from http://d.youth.cn/shrgch/201208/t20120807_2337374.htm

Chuang, Y. (2006). Massively multiplayer online role-playing game-induced seizures: A neglected health problem in Internet addiction. *CyberPsychology & Behavior, 9*(4), 451–456.

Goldberg, I. (1995, March 16). Internet addiction disorder. Retrieved March 8, 2010, from www.urz.uni-heidelberg.de/Netzdienste/anleitung/wwwtips/8/addict.html

Holden, C. (2010). Behavioral addictions debut in proposed *DSM-V*. *Science, 327*(5968), 935.

Huang, X.; Zhang, H.; Li, M.; Wang, J.; Zhang, Y.; & Tao, R. (2010). Mental health, personality, and parental rearing styles of adolescents with Internet addiction disorder. *CyberPsychology & Behavior, 13*(4), 401–406.

Miller, G., & Holden, C. (2010). Proposed revisions to psychiatry's canon unveiled. *Science, 327*(5967), 770–771.

Ministry of Health (MOH). (2009, November 4). The letter for opinion collection of "Guidelines for minors' healthy Internet use (draft for opinion collection)" from the Bureau for Disease Control and Prevention of Ministry of Health [in Chinese]. Retrieved April 29, 2010, from http://www.moh.gov.cn/publicfiles/business/htmlfiles/mohjbyfkzj/s10606/200911/44359.htm

Morahan-Martin, J. (2005). Internet abuse—Addiction? Disorder? Symptom? Alternative explanations? *Social Science Computer Review, 23*, 39–48.

Morahan-Martin, J., & Schumacher, P. (2000). Incidence and correlates of pathological Internet use among college students. *Computers in Human Behaviour, 16,* 13–29.

Ni, X., Yan, H., Chen, S., & Liu, Z. (2009). Factors influencing Internet addiction in a sample of freshmen university students in China. *CyberPsychology & Behavior, 12*(3), 327-330.

Sohmen, P. (2001). Taming the dragon: China's efforts in regulating the internet. *Stanford Journal of East Asian Affairs, 1,* 17–26.

Subrahmanyam, K., Kraut, R. E., Greenfield, P. M., & Gross, E. F. (2001). New forms of electronic media: The impact of interactive games and the Internet on cognition, socialization, and behavior. In D. G. Singer & J. L. Singer (Eds.), *Handbook of Children and the Media* (pp. 73–99). Thousand Oaks, CA: Sage.

Suratt, C. G. (2006). *The psychology of netaholics.* New York: Novinka Books.

Tao, R. (2007). *Internet addiction: Analysis and intervention* [in Chinese]. Shanghai: Shanghai People's Press.

Tao, R.; Huang, X.; Wang, J.; Zhang, H.; & Zhang, Y. (2009). SCL-90-R, EPQ-R, and EMBU profiles of adolescents with Internet addiction disorder. *Chinese Journal of Drug Dependence, 18*(4), 294–301.

Tao, R.; Huang, X.; Wang, J.; Zhang, H.; Zhang, Y.; & Li, M. (2010). Proposed diagnostic criteria for Internet addiction. *Addiction, 105,* 556–564.

Young, Kimberly S. (1998a). Internet addiction: The emergence of a new clinical disorder. *CyberPsychology and Behavior, 1*(3), 237–244.

Young, Kimberly S. (1998b). *Caught in the net: How to recognize the signs of Internet addiction and a winning strategy for recovery.* New York: J. Wiley.

Dating Online

Wǎngshàng yuēhuì 网上约会

Summary: Online dating emerged in China in the 1990s with the rising popularity and increasing accessibility of the Internet. It is especially popular among the younger generations that often struggle with finding partners offline, due to busy personal and professional lives and other factors. China's One-Child Policy, which has led to many millions more men than women, also is a contributing factor in the popularity of online dating.

Online dating (*wǎngshàng yuēhuì* 网上约会) refers to the activity of finding a romantic relationship using online tools and services. In China, cyber love (romantic love that is found online), cybersex, and the online dating industry are all related to online dating. Due to technical limitations of the Internet during the early days of its use in China, users could only read articles and send simple messages online. In addition, there were very few female users—in 1997, only 12 percent of all Internet users were women, a number that quickly rose to nearly 45 percent of China's 538 million Internet users in 2012 (CNNIC 1998; 2012).

Online dating emerged in the late 1990s, made possible by technological developments and increased accessibility to the Internet in China. Since then, Chinese "netizens" have become accustomed to looking for relationships online. Most guests on the popular TV dating show *If You Are the One* 非诚勿扰 are registered users at some of the biggest online dating sites in China, such as Shijijiayuan.com 世纪佳缘网 and Baihe.com 百合网.

Origins of Cyber Love

Bulletin Board Systems (BBSs) were the earliest social networking sites (SNSs) in China, introduced in 1994 as teaching and learning platforms used only in universities (CNNIC 2003). Most users of these BBSs were university students and predominantly male. In the early period, BBS users could read texts, send simple messages, and exchange information on this platform. While the main topics were politics, economy, and computer and Internet technologies, some love stories and erotic articles were shared among the male users as a kind of entertainment (Ren 2007).

In 1998, a romantic cyber-novel telling the sad story of a doomed cyber-romance rapidly spread on China's BBSs. *The First Intimate Touch* (*Di yige qinmi jiechu* 第一次亲密接触), written by the Taiwanese cyber-novelist Chai Zhiheng, was first posted in Taiwan, and then passed on to BBSs in mainland China. In this novel, a young boy falls in love on the Internet with a beautiful girl who suffers from a fatal illness, until the girl finally passes away. This was the first time that the first generation of Chinese Internet users got to know cyber love. The hero of the novel, Pi Zhicai 痞子蔡, was representative of many Chinese male Internet users, who often are shy and modest when speaking offline but speak freely online. Most importantly, some of them were now dreaming to meet a beautiful girlfriend on the Internet themselves. The story of Pi Zhicai and his cyber-girlfriend presented a possibility to Chinese netizens that their dreams could come true. To them, cyber love was the purest love, a wonderful process of curiosity, mysterious feelings, and romantic passion, mostly with a sad ending. Some cyber-terms introduced in the novel, such as "MM" (*měiméi* 美眉, "beauty"), "Dinosaur" (*kǒnglóng* 恐龙, "ugly girl") and *jiàn guāng sǐ* 见光死 ("to break up at the first offline date"), became prevalent at that time. All of these factors prompted more and more young people to eagerly look for their true loves on the Internet.

Around the same time, Tencent.com, now the biggest Internet company in China, issued an instant messaging (IM) software, OICQ, which is similar to ICQ, and has since changed its the name to QQ. OICQ was the most popular IM software in 1999, and users could search for and chat with (cyber) friends and strangers from all over China on the Internet with it. Making more friends online and chatting with cyber-friends started to become easier with OICQ than with previous IM programs, such as Microsoft Net Meeting. With their new-found passion for looking for pure cyber love, young Internet users made Tencent.com one of the first companies to benefit from a large wave of Internet marketing development.

Online Dating for Marriage

The main reason Chinese Internet users look for a partner online is that they do not have enough time and opportunities to get to know other men and women offline. Research posted on Hongniang.com (2008) on love and marriage among Chinese netizens showed that busy schedules left young people no time to socialize. The main relationships they had were with colleagues and clients, and they were not willing to ruin their careers by getting involved in a relationship with somebody from their office.

As Gong Haiyan, CEO of Jiayuan.com said, "Due to urbanization, many young Chinese people have moved from the countryside or small towns and cities to work in big cities, and the traditional way of finding one's spouse through relatives' matchmaking is disappearing" (*People's Daily Online* 2012).

For these young netizens, online dating makes it convenient to get in touch with others. The results of the 2008 Hongniang.com study showed that 45.5 percent of the participants used online dating services, and 32.6 percent of the 154,386 netizens surveyed said they had met their partner through online dating. China Computer World (CCW) research said that online dating has three advantages for young people looking for a partner: it saves time, it is easier to communicate, and it introduces them to a wider social range (CCW 2007).

During the early years of online dating, safety was a big problem. Newspapers often reported tragic stories about young girls who were kidnapped, raped, or killed when they went to meet their cyber-boyfriends alone and outside the safety of their hometowns. Research showed that there were four types of safety risks in online dating that netizens were most concerned about: roughly half of netizens were concerned about the real motives of their cyber-partner; a third worried about a false profile given by their cyber-partner, 12 percent were concerned about their personal information being released, and only 4 percent of netizens were afraid of not getting support from their family and friends for their online romance (CCW 2007).

Online Dating and Sex

Cyberspace is thought to be a public place. With the development of IM software, Tencent, 163.com, and other Internet companies issued chat room services. All QQ users can get into hundreds of chatting rooms with their QQ accounts. There are a number of online chat rooms with erotic names, such as "Appointment within the City" 同城约会 and "Midnight Passion" 午夜激情, where QQ users can talk about sex and look for sexual partners. On 9 January 2009, however, Tencent shut down all QQ chat rooms in an attempt to clear the Internet of such content.

Chinese netizens got to know cybersex as "chatting naked" (*luǒliáo* 裸聊) in 2004, when a news article reported that seven women were hired to chat naked with their overseas clients before the webcam (Ren 2007). In an ethnographic research conducted by Ren Jue, sixteen informants, mainly male Internet users, were interviewed about their experiences with cybersex. The three main types of cybersex they engaged in were cybersex by texting ("sexting"), by voice through QQ, and with the use of a webcam (Ren 2007).

These cybersex participants come from different socioeconomic backgrounds, and they used their social capital and resources to support their virtual sexual behaviors. For example, a manager had his own office and always used it to have cybersex after work. The participants also didn't present their real world identity during cybersex, whatever kind of cybersex they preferred. In front of the webcam and computer monitor, the cybersex participants presented a different side of their personality and desires, or, in the words of the Canadian sociologist Erving Goffman, they use the cybersex experience as the backstage performance of their daily life (Goffman 1973). All of them had a public QQ account, visible to their colleagues, classmates, and family members, but they created another QQ account, which they called their "little account" (*xiǎohào* 小号), to engage in cybersex. This alternative account provided them with a cover to keep their real social identities safe and to avoid any moral and legal risks. It prevented their everyday lives from being influenced by their cybersex activities, but it also confirms the anxiety of being exposed that exists. Most of them called it "cyber passion" (*wǎngluò jīqíng* 网络激情), a popular term that replaced "chatting naked." Some of them admitted to having had sex with their online sex partners in the real world (Ren 2007).

Why do people need cybersex? Based on the study there are four types of motives directing to cybersex in China (Ren 2007):

- Cybersex is a replacement for a sex life in the real world.
- Cybersex is supplemental to real-life sex.
- Cybersex enriches the sex life in the real world.
- Cybersex is a way to display an identity that would not be accepted in the real world.

A similar study with more female participants provided some additional insights: female participants indicated that they have their own agency through cybersex, and that they tried to use their sexual capital in cybersex to gain economic and social capital offline (Pei 2007).

Online Dating Industry in China

Due to the safety concerns and more professional demands from users for online dating, more and more young netizens would prefer online dating sites and services to look for love and marriage, friends and partners. The major Chinese online dating websites are Shijijiayuan (www.jiayuan.com), Zhenai, Baihe, Marry5, Zhiji, and Juedui100 (Chow 2009). Huatian (www.love.163.com), founded by 163.com, started in November 2012 as a new participant in the Chinese online dating market. The *Wall Street Journal* reporter Tom Orlik (2011) points to jiayuan.com as the market leader, claiming 44 percent of the sector's revenue and being the only company that operates on a fee-for-results model. Zhenai.com and Baihe.com are in second and third place.

The first website focusing on online dating services was Shijijiayuan, built in 2003 by Gong Haiyan 龚海燕, followed by Baihe.com, Zhenai.com, and other professional online dating sites. Based on a research by iResearch (2007), the marketing scale for China's online dating industry has been rising steadily since 2004, and large amounts of money are invested in the Chinese online dating industry. The total revenue from China's online dating market is expected to expand from an estimated US$74 million in 2010 to US$290 million in 2015 (Orlik 2011).

In 2010 there were 19 million visitors to Chinese online-dating websites, only a fraction of the estimated 156 million single adult Internet users at the time. That number is expected to increase to 60 million by 2015 (Orlik 2011).

With the rapid development of mobile Internet, technology companies such as MoMo and Weixin (the Chinese version of WeChat) are taking the lead in online dating applications for iOS and Android smartphones. Using location-based services (LBS) technology, MoMo and Weixin help users locate strangers in their area, send a message to them, and add them to their contact list. MoMo was launched in 2011, and within just one year, it had 10 million registered users (Wang 2012).

The online dating market focused on a gay audience is also substantial, and new mobile applications for gay communities, such as Zank, has emerged in mainland China. Zank's operations team wants the application to be primarily focused on friendship, not on sexual relationships. Only twenty days after its online launch, Zank got its first venture capital, indicating the application's expected popularity and growth (New Business Weekly 2013).

Conclusion

Although it has its inherent dangers, online dating provides more opportunities for younger generations, with fast-paced professional and personal lives, looking for love, sex, and marriage. It has accelerated the development of relationships. Adding to the attractiveness of finding a mate on the Internet is the fact that China's One-Child Policy, implemented in 1978 for most people in China, means that the gender ratio in China is remarkably skewed, with millions more men than there are women. There are many possible reasons for this, but the end result is that, as the single child in a family, the younger generation lacks the social networks of their parents who grew up in larger families. Young netizens, with a new-found individualism not seen in previous generations, also have different notions of love and marriage; online dating empowers them to choose a partner on their own, instead of having their love and marriage decided by their parents.

Jue REN
The Chinese University of Hong Kong

See also Cybersex; Internet in Everyday Life; Internet Regulation

Further Reading

Chai Zhiheng. (1999). *Di yige qinmi jiechu* [The first intimate touch]. Beijing: Knowledge Press.

China Computer World (CCW). (2007). 2006 Zhongguo wangluo hunlian jiaoyou shichang yanjiu baogao [The China online dating market report in 2006]. Retrieved November 7, 2012, from http://www.ccwresearch.com.cn/store/downloads/20061030151212%D6%D0%B9%FA%CD%F8%C2%E7%BB%E9%C1%B5%BD%BB%D3%D1%CA%D0%B3%A1%D1%D0%BE%BF%B1%A8%B8%E6%BC%F2%B0%E6.pdf

China Internet Network Information Center (CNNIC). (1997). The first statistical report of China Internet development. Retrieved April 4, 2011, from http://www.cnnic.net.cn

China Internet Network Information Center (CNNIC). (1998). The 2nd statistical report of China Internet development. Retrieved April 4, 2011, from http://www.cnnic.net.cn

China Internet Network Information Center (CNNIC). (2003). The memorabilia of China Internet, 1987–2007. Retrieved April 10, 2011, from http://www.cnnic.net.cn/html/Dir/2003/10/22/1001.htm

China Internet Network Information Center (CNNIC). (2011).The 27th statistical report of China Internet development. Retrieved April 4. 2011, from http://www.cnnic.net.cn

China Internet Network Information Center (CNNIC). (2012). Statistical report of China Internet development. Retrieved November 6, 2012, from http://www1.cnnic.cn/IDR/ReportDownloads/201302/P020130221391269963814.pdf

Chow, Steven. (2009). China online dating market report. Retrieved April 10, 2011, from http://www.china-online-marketing.com

Constable, Nicole. (2003). *Romance on a global stage: pen pals, virtual ethnography, and "mail order" marriages.* Berkeley: University of California Press.

Duhamel, Damieu, & Chu, Calvin. (2006). Online dating in China: White paper. Retrieved April 4, 2011, from http://www.synovate.com

Goffman, Erving. (1973). *The presentation of self in everyday life*. New York: Overlook Press.

Hongniang.com. (2008). The report of love and marriage of Chinese Internet users [in Chinese]. Retrieved April 5, 2011, from http://www.hongniang.com/news/9/965/1.html

iResearch. (2007). China making-friends online research report: 2006. Retrieved April 2, 2011, from http://www.ireseach.com.cn

New Business Weekly. (2013). Guonei tongzhi shenqi Zank: Yuehui bu yaobao. Shangxian 20 tian naxia jingwei touzi [National gay dating app Zank: dating for appointment not for sex;

20 days after launch Zank receives JingWei Venture investment]. Retrieved August 15, 2013, from http://www.iheima.com/archives/45703.html

Ni Xiaofeng. (2012). Online dating rape: New trend in acquaintance rape. *Public Security Science Journal*, *2*, 80–83.

Orlik, Tom. (2011). Turning love into money in China's online dating. Retrieved August 15, 2013, from http://online.wsj.com/article/SB10001424052702303763404576420001947330580.html

Pei Yuxin. (2007). Born in the 70's: Sexuality of young women in contemproary Shanghai. (Doctoral dissertation). Hong Kong University, Hong Kong.

Pei Yuxin. (Under review). Gender, cyberspace and sexual capital: Young women's experience of cybersex in contemporary Shanghai. *Gender, Place & Culture: A Journal of Feminist Geography*.

People's Daily Online. (2012). Online dating, a rising trend in China. Retrieved August 15, 2013, from http://english.peopledaily.com.cn/90882/8001871.html

Ren Jue. (2007). Cyber passion: the research on cybersex phenomena in mainland China. (MPhil dissertation). The Chinese University of Hong Kong, Hong Kong.

VC for social networking sites in China: Online dating prevails. (2007). Retrieved August 21, 2013, from http://www.my-life-in-china.com/business/vc-for-social-networking-sites-in-china-online-dating-prevails

Wang Genwang. (2012). Momo keji tang Yan: Women bu chou mei qianzhuan tan yingli hai tai zao. [MoMo technology's Tang Yan: We don't worry about earning money, it's too early to talk about profit]. Retrieved August 15, 2013, from http://www.iheima.com/archives/6777.html

Zan Yulin. (2010). Development of cyber love and marriage. *China Youth Study*, *2*, 87–89.

Cybersex

Wǎngluò xìng'ài 网络性爱

Summary: Cybersex refers to online sexual behaviors and activities. China is the world's largest nation of Internet users, which has led to widespread concern over the possibilities of Internet addiction, including addiction to cybersex. Researchers have identified several criteria to help determine if someone's behavior has caused them to cross the line from being a "recreational" user of cybersex to being a "problematic" user.

The term *cybersex* is a catchall word used to describe various sexual behaviors and activities performed while on the Internet. Examples of behaviors or activities that may be considered cybersex include sexual conversations in Internet chat rooms, retrieving sexual media (for example, photographs, stories, or videos) via the Internet, visiting sex-related websites, masturbating to sexual media from the Internet, engaging in sexualized videoconferencing activities, creating sexual materials for use or distribution on the Internet, and using the Internet to obtain or enhance offline sexual behaviors.

As sexual mores in China have changed rapidly during the period of economic growth and the concurrent growth of Internet use in China, the continually evolving subject of cybersex calls for academic attention. Since its debut in China around 1995, use of the Internet has soared. In 2008, China became the largest nation of Internet users in the world, exceeding the number of users in the United States. By the end of 2012, the number of China's Internet users had risen to over half a billion people (CNNIC 2013).

Cyberspace venues in China are similar to those elsewhere, although the specific websites and programs used differ. There are adult sites, cartoon sites, anime, and a whole host of search engines that lead surfers to "hot" sites. People with bilingual skills can also access other countries' search engines, entering into more varieties of cybersex. With such a large audience, commercial producers of cybersex activities see the potential to profit from the high growth market in China. As a result of the increased number of people online, together with the availability of sex online, professionals from many countries have reported a significant rise in the number of individuals seeking help to deal with their compulsive cybersex behavior.

The Chinese government has tightened its policies around Internet access, including attempts to control access to sexualized content on the Internet for fear of the negative impact cybersex may have on its "netizens." A 2007 study by Guo Liang of the Center for Social Development at the Chinese Academy of Social Sciences on the impact of the Internet in seven of China's major cities revealed that around one-third of the interviewed Internet users at that time visited sites with sexual content; 3 percent of these users visited these sites daily, 7 percent weekly, and 2 percent more than once a day. Some have argued that a scarcity of Internet-based sex education programs in China is one of the reasons that students visit sexually oriented websites and online sex venues (e.g., sex educational sites and sex stores). Academic journal articles also provide information on problematic online behavior, such as Internet addiction (which is covered elsewhere in this volume in the article of that name).

Healthy versus Problematic Cybersex

It is important to remember that not all online sexual activity is necessarily problematic. Worldwide, many of those who engage in online sexual activity may be considered "recreational users" and do not report significant problems related to their online behavior. Both youth and adults report using the Internet to research sexual information on issues such as preventing the spread of sexually transmitted infections, purchasing and reviewing options for contraception, exploring healthy sexuality, and more. For those individuals who struggle with problematic online sexual behavior, however, the consequences can be devastating and long lasting. Some individuals become compulsive about collecting and viewing pornography, others cross legal boundaries, while still others find themselves spending hours each day online in search of intimacy or romance, often at inappropriate times and in inappropriate places.

One of the difficulties in defining cybersex as either healthy or problematic is the fact that there are few agreed-upon definitions about what constitutes sexually healthy behavior. Most societies have clearly delineated some behaviors as being unhealthy; for example, sex with children or other nonconsenting partners. People disagree, however, about whether masturbation, multiple affairs, bondage, and fetishes are healthy or unhealthy. In the world of cybersex, a similar gray area exists between "healthy" and "unhealthy" that is often even more difficult to define, since the behavior does not include actual sexual contact.

It is also important not to assume that frequency is the key factor in determining whether or not an individual is engaged in unhealthy cybersex. Some individuals engaging in cybersex at a high frequency have few problems, while others who engage in it only a few hours a week experience significant negative consequences.

The physician and researcher Jennifer Schneider proposed three criteria to help determine if someone's behavior has become compulsive—that is, whether the person has crossed the line from a recreational to a problematic user of cybersex: (1) loss of freedom to choose whether to stop the behavior; (2) negative consequences as a result of the behavior; and (3) obsessive thinking about engaging in the behavior. The Internet Sex Screening Test (ISST) described by counseling professor David Delmonico and professor of school psychology Jeffery Miller can be used to conduct an initial screening of whether an individual has a problem with cybersex.

The Appeal of the Internet

In 2001, Delmonico, Moriarity, and marriage and family therapist Elizabeth Griffin proposed a model called "the CyberHex" to help understand why the Internet is so attractive to its users. ("Hex" has a double meaning here: the model has six components, like a hexagon, and the Internet can put users into a hex-like trance if they are deeply engrossed in their online activities.) Their model lists the following six characteristics.

Integral: The Internet is nearly impossible to avoid. Even if a cybersex user decided to never use the Internet again, the integral nature of the Internet would make that boundary nearly impossible, since many users need the Internet for work or to access bank information, for example. In addition, public availability, the use of email, and other activities like shopping and research make the Internet a way of life that is integrated into our daily routines.

Imposing: The Internet provides an endless supply of sexual material seven days a week, 365 days a year. The amount of information and the imposing nature of marketing sexual information on the Internet contribute to the seductiveness of the world of cybersex.

Inexpensive: For a relatively small fee—or even no money at all—a user can access an intoxicating amount of sexual material on the Internet. In the offline world such excursions can be cost-prohibitive to many.

Isolating: Cybersex is an isolating activity. Even though interpersonal contact may be made during the course of cybersex, these relationships do not require the same level of social skills or interactions that offline behaviors require. The Internet becomes a world in itself, where it is easy to lose track of time, consequences, and real-life relationships. The isolation of cybersex often provides an escape from the real world, and while everyone takes short escapes, cybersex often becomes the drug of choice to anesthetize any negative feelings associated with real-life relationships.

Interactive: While isolating in nature, the Internet also hooks individuals into pseudo relationships. These pseudo relationships often approximate reality without running the risks of real relationships—like emotional and physical vulnerability and intimacy. This close approximation to reality can be fuel for the fantasy life of those who experience problems with their cybersex behaviors.

Intoxicating: This is the result of adding the preceding five elements together. This combination makes for an incredibly intoxicating experience that is difficult for many to resist. The intoxication of the Internet is multiplied when cybersex is involved, since behaviors are reinforced with one of the most powerful rewards—sex.

Any single aspect of the Internet can be powerful enough to entice a cybersex user. It is typically a combination of these six factors, however, that draws problematic cybersex users into their rituals and leads to a loss of control over their cybersex use.

The CyberHex for Internet Users in China

The CyberHex model can be used to facilitate understanding of the reasons that people in China may be drawn to the Internet. In China today the trend that pervades urban living is surfing the Internet for information, entertainment, and communication. Cyberspace allows Internet users to fill gaps in their social lives that may exist from living far from home, working unusual hours or working from home, and more. This phenomenon holds true for many working-class people, as well as college and graduate students who relocate to another city, living by themselves and away from their families. It also applies to single adults who are still living with their parents. It is still a tradition in China that children, no matter how old they are, reside with their parents as long as they are single. Most parents of this generation do not delve into the subject of sex and sexuality, and often, their values and interests are quite different from their children's. Many of the parents do not use the Internet—although that, like many things in Chinese society, is changing—and they often have little interest in what their children are doing online. All of these phenomena echo the characteristics as listed in the CyberHex model.

While there are ways that the CyberHex certainly is a valid model in China, other factors seem to negate the model as being directly applicable to Chinese culture. For example, both users and nonusers of the Internet prefer retail shopping to online venues since cash—not credit cards—remains the preferred method of payment. (This preference, too, is changing as Internet usage becomes more and more widespread.) This cultural influence negates much of the power of the integral aspects of the CyberHex. In addition, the Chinese government's restrictions and curbing of violent and sexual websites affect the ability of the CyberHex's "imposing" component—more than might be present in noncensored areas of the world. These measures do seem to create an impact on the applicability of the CyberHex model to Chinese culture. In consideration of these factors, the CyberHex model appears more culturally bound, and not directly applicable to Chinese or other foreign cultures. This phenomenon serves to demonstrate that ongoing studies are needed to document the continual rise in Internet use in China and in the rest of the world.

Cultural Considerations in China

Sex education began in China many centuries ago: books on sexuality were published as early as 200 BCE. Despite this long history, Chinese people in contemporary society have mixed perceptions and attitudes toward sex and sexual behavior. These perceptions and attitudes are changing along with changes in the political, socioeconomic, and demographic spheres. It is not uncommon to hear Chinese parents respond in a shy way when approached by their children about the subject of sex. Many parents feel embarrassed and overwhelmed by the issues of sexuality. Chinese people's conservative values and attitudes may affect responses made to surveys on sex-related topics—including cybersex.

A phenomenon known as "Internet hunting" serves to demonstrate this conservative bent in Chinese society. In numerous cases, throngs of people have gathered online to castigate people for adultery and other transgressions, both real and imagined, often crossing the line into the "real" world with harassment and, occasionally, violence (French 2006).

The Chinese government has tightened policy and censorship on all forms of communication, including the Internet. The government regularly prohibits overseas websites with objectionable content. The Ministry of Health ordered that only government-approved medical institutions can offer websites with sex-related content. Xiao Qiang, a scholar of the Chinese Internet at the University of California at Berkeley, has viewed censorship of sexual content as political action that is cloaked as an antipornography measure campaign. According to BBC News in 2010, during the first month of these new government restrictions, over sixty-two thousand pornographic websites were identified and blocked. In addition, twenty-four network operators were "named and shamed" for offering websites with lewd or pornographic contents. With the widespread amount of cybersex available online, the implications for the Chinese government and its people remain uncertain. As the culture shifts, so will the use and implications of cybersex behavior in China.

Implications

Cybersex is changing sexuality in both Western and Eastern cultures. China's media reports on government campaigns against websites with lewd content suggest that culture in China is being affected by cybersex. After all, is it possible for cybersex to be controlled? Regardless of the cultural context, cybersex behavior can develop into an obsessive-and-compulsive behavior. As mentioned earlier in this article, cybersex does not imply good or bad. Yet, when people have online sexual activities that become part of their daily living pattern, their well-being and health are jeopardized, and prompt action is warranted. Specifically, medical professionals, educators, and researchers in China and in other countries should explore the cross-cultural impact of cybersex and define common, universal thresholds of excessive engagement. They can discuss noticeable traits of people who engage excessively in cybersex, what causes such levels of engagement, and what sources are available for people to restore their well-being and health. In effect, professionals with a better grasp of China's prevailing socioeconomic climate and other crucial factors can further refine and reshape existing concepts and models of cybersex that are more sensitive and relevant to Chinese culture.

Helena K. Y. NG and David L. DELMONICO
Duquesne University

See also Dating Online; Internet Addiction; Internet Content Filtering; Internet Regulation

Further Reading

BBC News. (2010). China rewards online porn surfer. Retrieved June 12, 2010, from http://news.bbc.co.uk/2/hi/asia-pacific/8451946.stm

Carnes, Patrick; Delmonico, David. L.; Griffin, Elizabeth.; & Moriarty, Joseph. (2001). *In the shadows of the net: Breaking free of compulsive online behavior*. Center City, MN: Hazelden Educational Materials.

Carnes, Patrick J. (1983). *Out of the shadows*. Minneapolis, MN: CompCare.

Chan, Jeremy. (2009, June 26). China tightens restrictions for web sites on sexual health. *Wall Street Journal*, p. A9.

Chao, Loretta. (2009, December 17). China porn measures raise fear of censors. *Wall Street Journal*, p. A10.

China Central Television. (2009). Porn crackdown includes mobile sites. CCTV.com. Retrieved May 6, 2010, from http://english.cctv.com/program/chinatoday/20091126/101263.shtml

China Daily. China shuts down another 16,000 websites in porn crackdown. (2010). Retrieved May 29, 2014, from http://www.chinadaily.com.cn/china/2010-02/11/content_9465127.htm

China Internet Network Information Center (CNNIC). (2013, January). Statistical report on Internet development in China. Retrieved April, 15, 2013, from http://www1.cnnic.cn/IDR/ReportDownloads/201302/P020130312536825920279.pdf

Cooper, Al. (Ed.). (2002). *Sex and the Internet: A guidebook for clinicians*. New York: Brunner-Routledge.

Cooper, Al; Delmonico, David; & Burg, Ron. (2000). Cybersex users, abusers, and compulsives: New findings and implications. *Sexual Addiction and Compulsivity: Journal of Treatment and Prevention*, 7(1–2), 5–30.

Cooper, Al; Scherer, Coralie; Boies, S. C.; & Gordon, B. (1999). Sexuality on the Internet: From sexual exploration to pathological expression. *Professional Psychology: Research and Practice*, *30*(2), 154–164.

Delmonico, David L., & Miller, Jeffrey A. (2003). The Internet sex screening test: A comparison of sexual compulsives versus non-sexual compulsives. *Sexual and Relationship Therapy*, *18*(3), 261–276.

Delmonico, David L.; Griffin, Elizabeth J.; & Moriarity, Joseph. (2001). *Cybersex unhooked: A workbook for breaking free of compulsive online behavior*. Wickenburg, AZ: Gentle Path Press.

Delmonico, David L. (1997). SAST: Sex Addiction Screening Test. Retrieved May 29, 2014, from http://www.sexhelp.com/isst.cfm

French, Howard W. (2006, May 31). Mob rule on China's Internet: The keyboard as weapon. *New York Times*. Retrieved August 20, 2013, from http://www.nytimes.com/2006/05/31/technology/31iht-chinet.1861775.html?pagewanted=all&_r=1&

Guo Liang. (2007). Surveying Internet usage and its impact in seven Chinese cities. Center for Social Development. Retrieved March 16, 2011, from http://www.policyarchive.org/handle/10207/bitstreams/16013.pdf

Hong Yan; Li Xiaoming; Mao Rong; & Stanton, Bonita. (2007). Internet use among Chinese college students: Implications for sex education and HIV prevention. *CyberPsychology & Behavior*, *10*(2), 161–169.

Jeffreys, Elaine. (2006). *Sex and sexuality in China: Routledge studies on China in transition*. New York: Routledge.

Lam, Lawrence T.; Peng, Zi-wen; Mai, Jin-cheng; & Jing, Jin. (2009). Factors associated with Internet addiction among adolescents. *CyberPsychology & Behavior*, *12*(5), 551–555.

Li Ying; Cottrell, Randall R.; Wagner, Donald I.; & Ban, Maosheng. (2004). Needs and preferences regarding sex education among Chinese college students: A preliminary study. *International Family Planning Perspectives*, *30*(3), 128–133.

Miniwatts Marketing Group. (2010). Asia Internet usage stats and population statistics. Retrieved May 19, 2010, from www.Internetworldstats.com/stats3.htm

Ni Xiaoli; Yan Hong; Chen Silu; & Liu Zhengwen. (2009). Factors influencing Internet addiction in a sample of freshmen university students in China. *CyberPsychology & Behavior*, *12*(3), 327–330.

Pang Xizhe & Guo Zhigang. (2000). *The changing population of China: Family, sexuality & social relations in past times*. Malden, MA: Blackwell.

Roper Starch Worldwide. (1999). The America Online / Roper Starch youth cyberstudy. Retrieved March 18, 2011, from http://www.nozy.org/nojimaweb-old/nojima-old-WWW/Archive/AOL-199911-youthstudy.pdf/

Ruan Fang-fu, & Lau, M. P. (2001). China. In Robert T. Francoeur (Ed.), *The international encyclopedia of sexuality*. Retrieved June 12, 2010, from http://www2.hu-berlin.de/sexology/IES/china.html

Schneider, Jennifer, & Weiss, R. (2001). *Cybersex exposed: Recognizing the obsession*. Center City, MN: Hazelden Educational Materials.

Schneider, Jennifer P. (1994). Sex addiction: Controversy within mainstream addiction medicine, diagnosis based on the DSM-III-R and physician case histories. *Sexual Addiction & Compulsivity: The Journal of Treatment and Prevention, 1*(1), 19–44.

So, Ho-wai, & Cheung, Fanny M. (2005). Review of Chinese sexual attitudes & applicability of sex therapy for Chinese couples with sexual dysfunction. *The Journal of Sex Research*, 42(2) 93–101.

Vascellaro, Jessica E., & Fowler, Geoffrey A. (2009, March 22). China blocks local access to YouTube, once again. *Wall Street Journal*, p. B1.

Young, Kimberly S. (2001). *Tangled in the web: Understanding cybersex from fantasy to addiction*. Bloomington, IN: 1st Books Library.

Young, Kimberly S. (1998). *Caught in the net*. New York: John Wiley & Sons.

Conclusion

The Internet in China: Cultural, Political, and Social Dimensions

A comprehensive account of the Internet's effects on Chinese society, including the myriad ways in which it has transformed economics, politics, and social life, has yet to be written. It is our hope that this book has helped somewhat to fill this lacuna, not by providing an all-encompassing narrative, but by illuminating numerous areas in which the Internet has powerfully affected how Chinese people learn, shop, hang out, and even participate in politics. Two decades ago it was still possible to imagine China without the Internet or to envision a "Chinternet," an intranet accessible only to a limited number of approved users. Such a reality is now inconceivable for the hundreds of millions of Chinese "netizens" who utilize Internet applications every day for communication, international trade, or entertainment.

The digital revolution that took place in the developed world in the mid-1990s entered the mainstream of Chinese society in the early 2000s. Subsequently, the Internet has amplified the influence of social organizations. New media technologies have liberated and empowered individual citizens for a variety of purposes—both public and private. Netizens have taken to the web to start online businesses and assert their legal rights. They blog about literature, popular culture, politics, and race-car driving, or all of the above in the case of China's most popular blogger, Han Han.

One of the most salient features of the Internet's development has been the ruling Chinese Communist Party's confidence during the period of "reform and opening" (*gǎigé kāifàng* 改革开放) that it could handle new political challenges resulting from the proliferation of information and communications technologies. After the 1989 demonstrations and the Tiananmen Square crackdown, the Communist leadership grew wary of communications technologies, including fax machines and cellular phones, as tools for the organization of political opposition. Regime changes that took place in the wake of the Central European "color revolutions" in the early 2000s and the Arab Spring in the Middle East that began in 2010 underscored the power of the Internet, in particular, to serve as an enabler of opposition to authoritarian rule. Yet rather than limiting access to the latest technologies, the Chinese state has sought to manage Internet use by developing strategies to de-emphasize, censor, and propagate certain political information.

China's decision to embrace the net, albeit while imposing restrictions on users, differs from the more isolationist policies of Cuba and North Korea and requires the Chinese regime to negotiate a delicate line between openness and control (Greitens 2013). Websites, instant messaging, Bulletin Board System (BBS) forums, and Twitter-like microblogs (*wēibó* 微博) are bound by restrictions similar to those governing the country's official media. The quantity and diversity of online content and platforms have, however, challenged the party-state's efforts to control public expression. In response, the state has adapted its technique for Internet censorship and strived for synergy with the corporations serving users (Earp 2013). The number of Chinese Communist Party and governmental organizations active in managing public opinion online has also increased dramatically, introducing difficulties for coordination among the party and state institutions seeking to control web spaces.

While contributors to this volume have addressed in detail the state's influence over the Internet in entries on the telecommunications industry, Internet regulation, monitoring, filtering, and the Great Firewall, the book has also explored the ways in which Chinese society has responded to the simultaneous popularization of Internet applications and the expansion of government control. Chinese Internet users cloak political and social criticism in satire, track down alleged wrongdoers in "human flesh" searches (*rénròu sōusuǒ* 人肉搜索), and mobilize in autonomous and spontaneous collective action known as "Internet Incidents" (or Internet events, *wǎngluò shìjiàn* 网络事件).

The Internet's political ramifications inside China tend to receive the most attention from scholars outside China (Kluver and Yang 2005; Yang 2012a). Researchers within China, however, place less emphasis on the Internet's political effects. Studies on Internet censorship, for example, represent just a tiny fraction of all studies (Qiu and Bu 2013). Instead, Chinese writers have preferred to take up such topics as technological development, the rise of new online services in e-government, and the utility of the net for the dissemination of product information. A major survey of trends in Chinese Internet research found that "ICT [information communications and technology] business operation is the most studied topic (54.2 percent) in domestic publications" (Qiu and Bu 2013, 16). Contributions to this volume bridge the gap between the emphases of scholars in China and elsewhere through attention to a range of political and nonpolitical topics, with the latter type of contributions emphasizing "practice," or the ways in which individual Chinese users experience the net.

Many of the Internet's most dramatic effects concern the facilitation of new patterns of social interaction in China. Cybercommunities of enthusiasts of hobbies as different as Chinese literature and motorcycle riding have proliferated, creating new networks for information sharing and the organization of offline events. Online dating has become prevalent among busy young Chinese. One large-scale survey of Internet users suggests that one-third of netizens found their romantic partner online. For many of the reasons that cybersex is common around the world—it permits a sense of anonymity, freedom from prevailing social norms, and the prospect of low-consequence thrills—cybersex has also appeared in China, although not without extensive efforts by the central government to crack down on sites that promote pornography, prostitution, or hookups.

While Internet deployment and use in China has many elements in common with usage outside of China, one of our goals in this volume has been to highlight areas in which the development and use of the Internet in China is distinctive. Concern over the rising rate of "Internet addiction," while not unheard of in South Korea or Japan, differs greatly from the relatively benign view of high levels of Internet use in Europe or North America. The Chinese government's extraordinary efforts to guide the public online set it apart: local officials are encouraged to become active microbloggers, and anonymous public affairs workers, known as "50 Cent Party members" (*wǔmáo dǎng* 五毛党), post pro-regime sentiment online.

Distinctive patterns in Chinese Internet use have emerged through the localization or Sinicization of globally available technologies, such as Youku, as well as the indigenous development of technology. In the notable case of China's Twitter-like microblogs (*weibo*), Chinese sites such as Sina (*Xīnláng* 新郎) and Tencent (*Téngxùn* 腾讯) have bettered their global counterpart by allowing users to directly post photos and personalized "retweets," or responses to the comments of other users (Yang 2012b). Yet the interconnections between Chinese netizens and Internet users around the world (despite state-sponsored blocking of such sites as YouTube, Twitter, Facebook, and the *New York Times*) are so extensive that it remains more appropriate to view the Internet as a global medium affecting China rather than as a "Chinese Internet," or a distinctly Chinese and even separate medium.

While scholarship on the Internet in China employs a range of methodologies and has toeholds in a number of academic disciplines, this growing area of scholarship remains in its infancy. A survey of research on the Internet in China by the social anthropologist David Kurt Herold found steady growth in related studies and observed that one-third of research on the Internet in China has been published since 2009 (Herold 2013). Many conclusions concerning the effects of Internet use in China are thus necessarily tentative. That the Internet technologies popular in China and the manner of their use will inevitably change further complicates the task of analyzing the effects of the medium in the world's most populous country. In such a context, this volume helps to illuminate the medium's horizons, outline major developments, and provide reference points for the future.

Ashley ESAREY
University of Alberta

Further Reading

Earp, Madeline. (2013, July). Throttling dissent: China's new leaders refine Internet control. Washington, DC: Freedom House. Retrieved April 23, 2014, from http://www.freedomhouse.org/sites/default/files/resources/Throttling%20Dissent_FOTN%202013_China_0.pdf

Greitens, Sheena Chestnut. (2013). Authoritarianism online: What can we learn from Internet data in nondemocracies? *PS: Political Science & Politics, 26*, 262–270.

Han, Rongbin. (2013). Adaptive persuasion in cyberspace: The "fifty cents army" in China (paper, American Political Science Association 2013 Annual Meeting). Retrieved September 17, 2013, from http://ssrn.com/abstract=2299744

Herold, David Kurt. (2013, June 15). Through the looking glass: Twenty years of research into the Chinese Internet (draft paper, Chinese Internet Research Conference). Oxford, UK.

Kluver, Randolph, & Yang, Chen. (2005). The Internet in China: A meta-review of research. *The Information Society, 21*(4), 301–308.

Li, Hongmei. (2010). Chinese diaspora, the Internet, and the image of China: A case study of the Beijing Olympic torch relay. In Wang Jian (Ed.), *Chinese soft power in China public diplomacy through communication* (pp. 135–155). New York: Palgrave Macmillan.

Qiu, Jack Linchuan, & Bu, Wei. (2013, June 15). China ICT studies: A review of the field, 1989–2012 (draft paper, Chinese Internet Research Conference). Oxford, UK.

Yang Guobin. (2012a). Lightness, wildness, and ambivalence: China and new media studies. *New Media & Society, 14*, 170–179.

Yang Guobin. (2012b). A Chinese Internet? History, practice, and globalization. *Chinese Journal of Communication, 5*, 49–54.

List of Contributors

All contributors are listed alphabetically, followed by their affiliations. Last names are indicated by capital letters to avoid confusion due to differences in the order of names in Chinese and Western naming conventions. The names of articles are in italics.

ANG, Peng Hwa, Nanyang Technological University
Internet Governance (co-author: CHEN Xiaoyan)

CHEN Wen, Zhejiang University
Internet Cafés (co-author: Lu WEI)

CHEN Xiaoyan, Xiamen University
Internet Governance (co-author: Peng Hwa ANG)

CHEOK, Adrian David, National University of Singapore
Virtual Reality (co-author: WEI Jun)

CHEUNG, Anne S. Y., The University of Hong Kong
Internet Regulation (co-author: ZHAO Yun)

CHUNG Peichi, The Chinese University of Hong Kong
Game Industry Online

DAI Jia, Tsinghua University
Blogging

DAMM, Jens, Chang Jung Christian University
Chinese Diaspora Online (co-author: Terrence Ying-tai LAI)
Community Online

DEIBERT, Ronald, The Canada Centre for Global Security Studies
Internet Content Filtering

DELMONICO, David L., Duquesne University
Cybersex (co-author: Helena K. Y. NG)

ESAREY, Ashley, University of Alberta
Volume Conclusion

GAMES, Alexander, Microsoft
Children Online (co-authors: QIU Wei, ZHAO Yong & Linda A. JACKSON)
Digital Divides (co-authors: Linda A. JACKSON, QIU Wei, & ZHAO Yong)

GOODWIN, Andrew D., Independent scholar
Microblogging

HARWIT, Eric, University of Hawaii at Manoa
Telecommunications Industry

HE Zhou, City University of Hong Kong
Social and Political Impact

HONG Yu, University of Southern California
Internet and Economic Development

HU, Henry L., Shanghai University of Finance and Economics
Internet Service Providers (ISPs)

JACKSON, Linda A., Michigan State University
Children Online (co-authors: QIU Wei, Alexander GAMES & ZHAO Yong)
Digital Divides (co-authors: QIU Wei, Alexander GAMES & ZHAO Yong)

JIANG Min, University of North Carolina, Charlotte
Internet Events

JIANG Qiaolei, Dalian University of Technology
Internet Addiction (co-author: Louis LEUNG)

KLUVER, Randolph, Texas A&M University
E-Government
Volume Introduction

LAI, Terrence Ying-tai, Chang Jung Christian University
Chinese Diaspora Online (co-author: Jens DAMM)

LEUNG, Louis, The Chinese University of Hong Kong
Internet Addiction (co-author: JIANG Qiaolei)

LIAO, Han-Teng, University of Oxford
User-Generated Content

LIN Lin, University of Southern Maine
Chinese Language and Computing (co-author: Marilyn SHEA)

MARTINSONS, Maris Gunars, City University of Hong Kong
Shopping Online

NG, Helena K. Y., Duquesne University
Cybersex (co-author: David L. DELMONICO)

QIU Wei, Webster University
Children Online (co-authors: Alexander GAMES, ZHAO Yong, & Linda A. JACKSON)
Digital Divides (co-authors: Linda A. JACKSON, Alexander GAMES, & ZHAO Yong)

REN Jue, The Chinese University of Hong Kong
Dating Online

SHEA, Marilyn, University of Maine at Farmington
Chinese Language and Computing (co-author: LIN Lin)

SHI Song, McGill University
Email

SUN Huatong, University of Washington Tacoma
Text Messaging

SUN Shaojing, Fudan University
Consumers Online (co-author: WANG Ying)

TAI Zixue, University of Kentucky
The Great Firewall

TIAN, David, Global Internet Freedom Consortium
Internet Monitoring

WALLIS, Cara, Texas A&M University
Parody

WANG Minjuan, San Diego State University
Distance Education (co-author: ZHANG Hai)

WANG Ying, Youngstown State University
Consumers Online (co-author: SUN Shaojing)

WEI Jun, Keio Graduate School of Media Design
Virutal Reality (co-author: Adrian David CHEOK)

WEI Lu, Zhejiang University
Internet Cafés (co-author: Wen CHEN)

YANG Hongwei, Appalachian State University
Advertising Online (co-author: ZHOU Liuning)

YU Haiqing, University of New South Wales
Internet in Everyday Life

ZHANG Hai, Northeast Normal University
Distance Education (co-author: WANG Minjuan)

ZHAO Yong, University of Oregon
Children Online (co-author: QIU Wei, Alexander GAMES & Linda A. JACKSON)
Digital Divides (co-authors: Linda A. JACKSON, QIU Wei, & Alexander GAMES)

ZHAO Yun, The University of Hong Kong
Internet Regulation (co-author: Anne S. Y. CHEUNG)

ZHOU Liuning, University of Southern California
Advertising Online (co-author: YANG Hongwei)

Editors and Staff

Editors
Ashley Esarey, University of Alberta
Randolph Kluver, Texas A&M University

Publisher
Karen Christensen

Project Coordinator
Marjolijn Kaiser

Copyeditors
Bill Siever
Kathy Brock

Design
Anna Myers

Information Management
Trevor Young

Glossary

English	Chinese	Pinyin
(Baike) Baidu	百度	Bǎidù
(Internet) censorship	(互联网) 审查	*(hùliánwǎng) shěnchá*
administrator	管理员	*guǎnlǐyuán*
advertising, online	网络广告	*wǎngluò guǎnggào*
Alibaba	阿里巴巴	Ālǐbābā
application (app)	应用程序	*yìngyòng chéngxù*
avatar	头像 / 化身 / 阿凡达	*tóuxiàng / huàshēn/ āfándá*
backbone network	骨干网络	*gǔgàn wǎngluò*
banking, online	电子银行 / 在线银行	*diànzi yínháng / zàixiàn yíháng*
blog	博客	*bókè*
blogger	博主	*bózhǔ*
broadband	宽带 or 宽频	*kuāndài* or *kuānpín*
browser	浏览器	*liúlǎn qì*
Bulletin Board System	论坛	*lùntán*
chatroom	聊天室	*liáotiān shì*
China Internet Network Information Center (CNNIC)	中国互联网络信息中心	Zhōngguó hūliánwǎngluò xìnxī zhōngxīn
comment	评论	*pínglùn*
community, online	网络社区	*wǎngluò shèqū*
computer (desktop)	台式机	*táishì jī*
computer game	电脑游戏	*diànnǎo yóuxì*
consumers, online	网上消费者	*wǎngshàng xiāofèizhě*

content filtering	内容过滤	*nèiróng guòlǜ*
copycat	山寨	*shānzhài*
cybersex	网络性行为 / 网络性爱 / 网淫	*wǎngluòxìngxíngwéi wǎngluò xìng'ài / wǎngyín*
cyberspace	网络空间	*wǎngluò kōngjian*
dating, online	网上约会 / 网恋	*wǎngshàng yuēhuì / wǎngliàn*
digital divide	数字鸿沟	*shùzì hónggōu*
distance education	远程教育	*yuǎnchéng jiàoyù*
domain name (system)	域名 (系统)	*yùmíng (xìtǒng)*
e-commerce	电子商务	*diànzǐ shāngwù*
e-government	电子政务	*diànzǐ zhèngwù*
email (to send an email)	电子邮件 (发邮件)	*diànzǐ yóujiàn (fā yóujiàn)*
fifty cent party (member) (also known as "50 cent army", referring to people who post comments on online forums to direct public opinion)	五毛党	*wǔmáo dǎng*
firewall	防火墙	*fánghuǒqiáng*
gaming, online	网游 / 网络游戏	*wǎngyóu / wǎngluò yóuxì*
geek (somebody who stays home and online all the time)	Female: 宅女 Male: 宅男	*Zhái nǚ* (F) / *hái nán* (M)
Google	谷歌	Gǔgē
grass-mud horse (famous internet meme. The name is homophone to a profanity in Chinese)	草泥马	*Cǎo-ní-má*
Green Dam Youth Escort software	绿坝 · 花季护航	Lǜbà Huājì Hùháng
hacker	黑客	*hēikè*
hardware	硬件	*yìngjiàn*
human flesh search engine	人肉搜索	*rénròu sōusuǒ*
instant messaging (IM)	实时通信/即时通讯	*shíshí tǒngxìn/ jíshí tōngxùn*
Internet	互联网	*hùliánwǎng*

Internet addiction	网瘾	*wǎngyǐn*
Internet cafe	网吧	*wǎng bā*
Internet Service Provider (IPS)	互联网服务提供商	*hùliánwǎng fúwù gòngyìngshāng*
IP address	IP 地址	IP *dìzhǐ*
Kaixinwang (social networking site, mainly for professionals. Also referred to as Kaixin001)	开心网	Kāixīnwǎng
keyword	关键字	*guānjiànzì*
laptop	笔记本	*bǐjìběn*
link	链接	*liànjiē*
login	登录	*dēnglù*
microblogging (often described as the Chinese Twitter)	微博	*wēibó*
The Ministry of Industry and Information Technology (MIIT)	工业和信息化部 (also known as 工信部)	Gōngyè hé Xìnxīhuàbù (Gōngxìnbù)
mobile device	移动设备	*yídòng shèbèi*
modem	(调制) 解调器	*(tiáozhì) jiětiáo qì*
moderator (e.g., of a forum/blog)	版主	*bǎnzhǔ*
multimedia	多媒体	*duōméitǐ*
netizen	网络公民	*wǎngluò gōngmín*
network	网络	*wǎngluò*
offline	离线	*líxiàn*
online	上线	*shàngxiàn*
parody	恶搞	*ègǎo*
podcast	播客	*bōkè*
post (on a blog)	帖子	*tiězi*
QQ (Instant messaging program)	QQ	QQ
register	注册	*zhùcè*
Renrenwang (social networking site, mainly for	人人网	Rénrénwǎng

students		
search engine	搜索引擎	*sōusuǒ yǐnqíng*
shopping, online	网购 (网上购物)	*wǎnggòu (wǎngshàng gòuwù)*
Sina (Chinese Yahoo)	新浪网	Xīnlàng wǎng
smartphone	智能手机	*zhìnéng shǒujī*
social network (or Social Networking Sites SNS)	社交网络	*shèjiāo wǎngluò*
software	软件	*ruǎnjiàn*
Spam	垃圾邮件	*lājī yóujiàn*
Taobao (Chinese eBay-like site for online shopping)	淘宝	Táobǎo
telecommunications (industry)	电信(工业)	*diànxìn (gōngyè)*
text message (to send a text message)	短信 (发短信)	*duǎnxìn (fā duǎnxìn)*
touchscreen	触摸屏	*chù mōpíng*
tweet (on Sina Weibo, China's Twitter)	发微博	*fā wēibó*
Unicode	统一编码	*tǒngyī biānmǎ*
user	用户	*yònghù*
user-generated content	用戶生成內容	*yònghùshēng chéng nèiróng*
virus	病毒	*bìngdú*
VPN (Virtual Private Network)	虚拟专用网络	*xūnǐ zhuānyòng wǎngluò*
webpage	网页	*wǎngyè*
Wikipedia	维基百科	Wéijī bǎikē
wireless / wifi	无线 / 无线局域网	*wúxiàn / wúxiàn júyùwǎng*
Youku (Chinese YouTube)	优酷	Yōukù

The following online resources provide substantial and valuable repositories of terms related to the Internet in China, and vocabulary used by Chinese netizens:

- The Grass-Mud Horse Lexicon. China Digital Times. http://chinadigitaltimes.net/space/Main_Page
- A glossary of Chinese Internet slang on ChinaSmack: http://www.chinasmack.com/glossary
- Marilyn Shea's Chinese English Dictionary and Study Center, hosted at the University of Maine, has a section devoted to Internet Terminology: http://hua.umf.maine.edu/Chinese/topics/computer4/douying.html
- The somewhat outdated but still functional Intelligent Database for Standard Chinese Computer Terminology (hosted at the City University of Hong Kong): http://ccts.cs.cuhk.edu.hk/.

Index

Bold entries and page numbers denote articles in this book. Book titles are in italics, as are pinyin transliterations. Chinese terms are generally indexed under their English translation.

H

I

J

K

L

M

N

O

Printed by Libri Plureos GmbH in Hamburg,
Germany

9 781614 729358